Vietnam's American War

The Vietnam War was more than the sum of its battles. The ground war in South Vietnam and the air war in the North were certainly important in shaping its course, but they alone fail to explain why Hanoi bested Washington in the end. After all, communist forces lost most battles and suffered disproportionally higher casualties than the United States and its allies throughout the conflict. To make sense of the Vietnam War, we must look beyond the war itself. Above all, we must understand the formative experiences and worldview of the men who devised communist strategies and tactics during the conflict, and the rationale for – as well as impact of – those strategies and tactics. And that is the story this book relates: how the Vietnamese David defeated the American Goliath.

Pierre Asselin is Professor of History and Dwight E. Stanford Chair in the History of US Foreign Relations at San Diego State University. His books include *A Bitter Peace: Washington, Hanoi, and the Making of the Paris Agreement* (2002), and *Hanoi's Road to the Vietnam War, 1954–1965* (2013).

Cambridge Studies in US Foreign Relations

Edited by

Paul Thomas Chamberlin, *Columbia University*
Lien-Hang T. Nguyen, *Columbia University*

This series showcases cutting-edge scholarship in US foreign relations that employs dynamic new methodological approaches and archives from the colonial era to the present. The series will be guided by the ethos of transnationalism, focusing on the history of American foreign relations in a global context rather than privileging the US as the dominant actor on the world stage.

Also in the Series

Vietnam's American War

A History

PIERRE ASSELIN
San Diego State University

CAMBRIDGE
UNIVERSITY PRESS

CAMBRIDGE
UNIVERSITY PRESS

University Printing House, Cambridge CB2 8BS, United Kingdom

One Liberty Plaza, 20th Floor, New York, NY 10006, USA

477 Williamstown Road, Port Melbourne, VIC 3207, Australia

4843/24, 2nd Floor, Ansari Road, Daryaganj, Delhi – 110002, India

79 Anson Road, #06-04/06, Singapore 079906

Cambridge University Press is part of the University of Cambridge.

It furthers the University's mission by disseminating knowledge in the pursuit of education, learning, and research at the highest international levels of excellence.

www.cambridge.org
Information on this title: www.cambridge.org/9781107510500
DOI: 10.1017/9781316222591

© Pierre Asselin 2018

First published 2018

Printed in the United States of America by Sheridan Books, Inc.

A catalogue record for this publication is available from the British Library.

Library of Congress Cataloging-in-Publication Data
Names: Asselin, Pierre, author.
Title: Vietnam's American war : a history / Pierre Asselin, San Diego State University.
Description: Cambridge: Cambridge University Press, 2018. | Series: Cambridge studies in US foreign relations | Includes bibliographical references and index.
Identifiers: LCCN 2017040153 | ISBN 9781107104792 (hardback) | ISBN 9781107510500 (paperback)
Subjects: LCSH: Vietnam War, 1961–1975. | Vietnam (Democratic Republic) – History, Military.
Classification: LCC DS557.7.A86 2017 | DDC 959.704/3–dc23
LC record available at https://lccn.loc.gov/2017040153

ISBN 978-1-107-10479-2 Hardback
ISBN 978-1-107-51050-0 Paperback

*For those teachers who have taught and inspired me the most,
and to whom I owe all of my professional successes and much of
my personal happiness:
the exigent Tom Tynan,
the admirable Huynh Kim Khanh,
the exemplary Yves Frenette,
the indefatigable Tim Naftali,
the fatherly Steve O'Harrow,
and the incomparable Idus Newby.*

Contents

Figures and Maps

FIGURES

MAPS

Acknowledgements

I first became interested in the Vietnam War after watching *Rambo: First Blood Part II* on television. I was a high school student in Quebec City, Canada, at the time. Growing up in a highly homogenous white, French-Canadian, Catholic environment, I had no idea who or what the Vietnamese were, or even that the United States had lost a war in their country a little over a decade earlier. Watching the movie, only parts of which I understood because it was in its original English version, I thought Sylvester Stallone's character was going after mean Chinese soldiers detaining Americans for no other reason than that they were Chinese, and mean. (I had only ever personally interacted with one Asian person at the time, a nice kid in my high school whom I assumed was Chinese on account those were the only Asians I knew of [turns out he was, by way of Madagascar, no less!]) My ignorance became apparent the next day when I asked my History teacher about the movie and he pointed out that it was actually set against the backdrop of the Vietnam War, and the United States had never gone to war against China, as far as he knew. I ended up writing a paper for his class naively entitled "The Vietnam War" relating the various types of booby-traps used by Vietnamese communist forces against US troops, and based on a single book with lots of pictures in it. Rambo and that paper were all it took to pique my curiosity in the conflict and set me on the path to becoming a History professor specializing in the Vietnam War.

This book represents a culmination of my efforts to make sense of the people who were mean to Rambo and his buddies, of the "other side" in the Vietnam War. It is a summation of what I have come to understand about the leaders of that side and how they won that war. It is also a labor of love, a testament to my deep respect and appreciation for a country, a people, and a history that have fascinated me since I began studying them.

Several individuals and organizations contributed in various ways to this project. Lewis Bateman of Cambridge University Press expressed interest in it before its first page was written. Had it not been for Lew, this book may never have been produced. My gratitude extends to Debbie Gershenowitz, who assumed charge of the project following Lew's retirement, Kristina Deusch, her assistant, Josh Penney, my content manager, and John Bowdler, my copyeditor. It was a privilege to work with such a diligent and competent editorial team.

My comrades in Vietnam War and Cold War studies have made learning about those topics fulfilling to the extreme. Pierre Journoud, Pierre I as our peer group has labeled him on account of his superior looks (and intellect too, I am sure), has done more for me professionally than I could ever repay him. "Mon Journoud" has organized several of my visits to France and provided invaluable feedback on my writings. I will never regret choosing Vietnam as my field of expertise if only because it allowed us to become friends. I can say the same about Lien-Hang Nguyen, whose scholarship and generosity sharing source material have been of tremendous benefit. Larry Berman has never turned me down when I needed his assistance, and meaningfully impacted my professional development. Antoine Coppolani has been most supportive and a joy to be around, along with "La Dominique." Ed Miller is an ebullient colleague and collaborator. Fred Logevall and Chris Goscha remain exemplars: Fred on account of his assiduousness and prolificacy, Chris for his meticulousness and unparalleled knowledge of modern Vietnamese history. I also appreciate the support and friendship of David Anderson, Jessica Chapman, Sean Fear, Marc Gilbert, Pierre Grosser, Martin Grossheim, Ang Cheng Guan, George Herring, Jim Hershberg, Alec Holcombe, Liam Kelley, Ben Kerkvliet, Mark Lawrence, Lorenz Lüthi, Shawn McHale, Mark Moyar, Jason Picard, John Prados, Andrew Preston, Balazs Szalontai, Hue-Tam Tai, Carl Thayer, Nu-Anh Tran, Tuong Vu, Alex Vuving, Qiang Zhai, and Peter Zinoman. Bob Brigham, William Duiker, David Elliott, Sophie Quinn-Judge, Bill Turley, and Odd Arne Westad and continue to inspire me. Marilyn Young always made time for me; I miss her terribly.

Certain organizations have been indispensable for my research. Special thanks to the Cold War International History Project and its director, Christian Ostermann, and program leader, Chuck Kraus; to The

Vietnam Center and Archive at Texas Tech University and its director, Steve Maxner; to the Vietnam Studies Group and its contributors; to the Institut Pierre Mendès France in Paris, its president Eric Roussell, and his assistants Murielle Blondeau and Vincent Laniol; and to the staff at the French Diplomatic Archives at La Courneuve, the National Archives of the United Kingdom in Kew, and Library and Archives Canada in Ottawa. Thanks, too, to the wonderful people at the National Archives of Algeria, and Mesdames Mehareb, Ratiba, and Gater in particular. For their financial support, I am indebted to the National Endowment for the Humanities and Hawaii Pacific University, where I taught for nine years before finding a new home in the History Department at San Diego State University.

A good part of the information and insights I present in the pages that follow derives from time spent in Vietnam mining archives and "talking story" with colleagues and students there. Professors Hoang Anh Tuan, Pham Quang Minh, Nguyen Van Kim, Vu Duong Ninh, and Le Mau Han share an unmatched passion for their country's history and have taught me much. Professor Tuan has also been instrumental in helping me secure access to Vietnamese document repositories. My frequent interactions with graduate students in the History Department at the University of Social Sciences and Humanities in Hanoi have proven equally edifying, as have my exchanges with journalists Bao Trung and Chi Trung. Special thanks to Professor Phan Huy Le for sponsoring my first visits to Vietnam and remaining a good friend through the years. My utmost gratitude extends to the people at National Archives Center 3 in Hanoi, which remarkable collection I have been mining for more than two decades. I am especially appreciative of the assistance rendered by *Chu* Dinh, *Em* Thanh, *Em* Ly, and, more recently, Director Tran Viet Hoa, Deputy Director Nguyen Minh Son, and staff members *Em* Nhung and *Anh* Tien. All have been incredibly accommodating and indulgent with me. And I am truly sorry for making their lives so miserable at times!

This book in particular owes much to extraordinary input from certain individuals. Jay Veith volunteered essential feedback, as did Brian Price of Hawaii Pacific University. Ed Moïse read parts of the manuscript and offered precious input. Ho Thanh Tam of the University of Social Sciences and Humanities in Hanoi provided indispensable assistance, facilitating my access to archives and helping me obtain the photos that appear in this book as well as the permissions to reproduce them. The family of Nguyen Ba Khoan, his daughter Hoa in particular, allowed me to use the famous photographer's work. Patrice Côté and my former graduate student Paulina Kostrzewski read several permutations of the manuscript and suggested revisions that significantly enhanced its readability. My colleagues and students at Hawaii Pacific University motivated me to tell this story.

I owe my career and achievements as an academic to those who taught me. John Keyes and Tom Tynan formed me in my younger years at St. Lawrence College. Yves Frenette at Glendon College made me want to become a History professor. The late Huynh Kim Khanh at Glendon, Ron Pruessen and Hy Van Luong at the University of Toronto, and Gary Hess as well as Tim Naftali during their passage at the University of Hawaii at Manoa opened my eyes to important realities of Vietnamese and Cold War history. Stephen O'Harrow of the University of Hawaii has nurtured my passion for Vietnam since 1988. Last but not least, Idus Newby, formerly of the University of Hawaii, meticulously combed over my book and article manuscripts. He was generous with his time and trenchant with his words. He was a scholar's scholar, a man of infinite wisdom and intellect. He passed away shortly before this book went to press. Even though old age precluded him from going over this manuscript, it owes its best aspects to his mentorship, to the judiciousness he imparted to me.

My mother and sister in Quebec City remain an exceptional support system despite the distance that separates us. Our phone conversations and the time we spend together when I visit provide much relief from the stresses of life. I do owe my mother an apology: I should call more often, just not as frequently as I do when the Habs are in the playoffs and I need to vent after each period of play. Pierre-Marie, thanks for still keeping an eye on me.

Grace, my scintillating wife, is still the best thing that has happened to me. I hate growing old as much as she does, but I love getting old with her. She is the reason I have enjoyed, and I mean really enjoyed, the last twenty-plus years of my life. I thank her for putting up with my inadequacies, and for all the love she has given me during our time together. This book, like the others, owes much to her forbearance. As for you, Ursula, you may have come from the streets of Honolulu, are missing a pretty noticeable part of one ear, are wheezy all the time, have disproportionately long toes, and look weird for all your uniqueness, you are still my favorite companion. Thanks for constantly reminding me to take life in stride, for making it impossible for me to be stressed when I am around you, and for making me feel like I can be an indispensable source of support, literally, to another living being. You were far from my first choice that day at the Humane Society but, luckily for us, I have a wife who has much better judgment than I do, especially when it comes to adopting cats.

My father passed away a couple of years ago. If academics are allowed to have fans, he was my most devoted and loyal one. I realize now that one of the reasons I enjoyed publishing to the extent that I did was because it made him so damn happy to see his son's name in print. Pride is just not strong enough a word to convey what he exuded whenever I achieved an important milestone. There has been this deep void in my heart since he passed. I cry as I write these words because they remind me of just how much I enjoyed having him around. Life is not as beautiful without him in it. He was a good, honorable man who made me want to be as decent, respectable, and just. I am still working on that.

All contributions aside, I alone accept responsibility for any shortcomings in this work.

Glossary of Terms and Acronyms

Annam: French colonial administrative region consisting of the central third of Vietnam. Known to the Vietnamese as Trung Bo or Trung Ky.

ARVN: Army of the Republic of Vietnam. Formerly the VNA. Armed forces of the RVN, or South Vietnam.

ASEAN: Association of Southeast Asian Nations.

Bac Bo/Ky: Tonkin.

***Binh van*:** Communist clandestine "proselytizing" among enemy armed forces.

BTA: Bilateral Trade Agreement (US-SRVN, 2001).

Cao Dai: Eclectic Vietnamese religion founded in 1926 in Tay Ninh Province. Largely limited to that region, the Cao Dai proved fiercely independent and staunchly anti-communist during the Indochina and Vietnam Wars.

CCP: Chinese Communist Party.

CEFEO: *Corps expéditionnaire français en Extrême-Orient*, or French Far East Expeditionary Corps. Term used in reference to the French army combatting the Vietminh in the Indochina War and consisting of troops from France, the French Foreign Legion, and various French colonial holdings.

CIA: Central Intelligence Agency (US).

CMAG: Chinese Military Advisory Group. Created in 1950 by the PRC to train and equip Vietminh fighters in the Indochina War.

Cochinchina: French colonial administrative region consisting of the southern third of Vietnam. Known to the Vietnamese as Nam Bo or Nam Ky.

Comintern: Abbreviated from Communist International (1919–43). Outfit created by Moscow to export communism globally.

CORDS: Civil Operations and Revolutionary Development Support. Joint US-RVN "pacification" program created in 1967 to win civilian "hearts and minds," neutralize communist political agents, and encourage defection of enemy combatants in South Vietnam.

COSVN: Central Office (Directorate) for Southern Vietnam. Organ in charge of coordinating communist activity in the southern third of Vietnam (Cochinchina), 1951–4 (including all of Cambodia) and 1961–75. "Upgraded" incarnation of the Nam Bo Executive Committee.

CPI: Communist Party of Indochina (1929–30). Predecessor to the ICP.

CPSU: Communist Party of the Soviet Union.

CPV: Communist Party of Vietnam. The SRVN's current ruling party known as the VWP during the Vietnam War.

Dai Nam: Name of Vietnam, 1839–45.

Dai Viet: Name of Vietnam for much of the period 1009–1804.

***Dan cong*:** "Patriotic workers." Individuals recruited or conscripted by communist authorities during the Indochina War to move supplies to the front. Known derogatorily as "coolies" in the West.

DMZ: Demilitarized Zone. The 17th parallel separating North and South Vietnam between 1954 and 1976.

DRVN: Democratic Republic of Vietnam, or North Vietnam during the Vietnam War. Proclaimed by Ho Chi Minh on 2 September 1945. Its government fled to the mountains of Pac Bo during the Indochina War. Controlled by the VWP and based in Hanoi from October 1954, it claimed sole jurisdiction over all of Vietnam. It formally merged with the South in 1976 and became the SRVN under the CPV.

EDC: European Defense Community.

FLN: *Front de libération nationale (Algérie)*, or Algerian National Liberation Front. Popular national resistance front not unlike the Vietminh created in 1954 to pursue the cause of independence by armed, political, and diplomatic struggle in Algeria.

FPJMC: Four-Party Joint Military Commission. Organ created by the 1973 Paris agreement with representation by the United States, the DRVN, the RVN, and the NLF/PRG to determine the specifics of troop withdrawals and ensure joint action in implementing other core provisions of the agreement.

French Union: Commonwealth of nominally independent states under partial control of France, 1946–58.

Giao Chi: See Jiaozhi.

GMD: *Guomindang*, or Chinese Nationalist Party. Political party founded by Sun Yat-sen in 1911, eventually under Chiang Kai-shek and the archrival of the CCP.

GPD: General Political Department. Organ in charge of ideological conformity within the PAVN.

GTD: General Technical Department. Outfit coordinating the collection, repair, and distribution of weapons for Vietnamese communist forces. It also inventoried, refurbished, and distributed military hardware captured from the ARVN for use by PAVN and LAF troops.

Hoa Hao: Pseudo-Buddhist Vietnamese religion founded in 1939 and practiced mostly in the Mekong River Delta's An Giang Province. The movement was stalwartly anti-communist during the Vietnam War in part because the Vietminh assassinated its founder and leader, Huynh Phu So.

ICCS: International Commission of Control and Supervision. Reconstituted ICSC created by the 1973 Paris agreement consisting originally of members from Poland, Hungary, Indonesia, and Canada. Its mandate included monitoring implementation, documenting violations, and adjudicating disputes between signatories of the agreement.

ICP: Indochinese Communist Party. Previous incarnation of the VWP founded in October 1930.

ICSC: International Commission for Supervision and Control in Vietnam. Organ consisting of representatives from India, Canada, and Poland set up after July 1954 to supervise implementation of the Geneva accords.

Indochina: Geographical area consisting of Vietnam, Cambodia, and Laos.

Indochinese Federation: See Indochinese Union.

Indochinese Union: French colonial territory formally established in 1887 consisting of the Vietnamese regions of Tonkin, Annam, and Cochinchina, plus Cambodia and, after 1899, Laos. Renamed the Indochinese Federation in 1941 and abolished in 1954.

Interzone IV: Vietnamese communist administrative region consisting of northern Central Vietnam, including a portion below the 17th parallel.

Interzone V: Vietnamese communist administrative region consisting of southern Central Vietnam, including the Central Highlands.

Jiaozhi: Chinese province incorporating the Vietnamese heartland during the millennium of Chinese rule, 111 BCE–938 CE.

Kampuchea: Name used in reference to Cambodia during the 1980s.

Khmer Rouge: Radical communist faction led by Pol Pot and responsible for the death of hundreds of thousands of people after it assumed power in Cambodia in April 1975.

LAF: Liberation Armed Forces of Southern Vietnam. Armed wing of the NLF/Viet Cong.

Lao Dong Party: See VWP.

Lien Viet: Communist-led popular front established in 1946. The official name of the Vietminh after 1951.

MAAG: Military Assistance Advisory Group, Indochina (1950–5), Vietnam (1955–62). Created to promote military partnership between the United States and France and the SOVN/RVN. Incorporated into MACV and renamed Field Advisory Element, Vietnam in 1962.

MACV: Military Assistance Command, Vietnam. US military command in South Vietnam, 1962–73.

MIA: Missing-in-action.

Nam Bo/Ky: Cochinchina.

Nam Bo Executive Committee: Organ coordinating communist activity in the southern third of Vietnam (former Cochinchina), 1954–61. "Downgraded" incarnation of COSVN.

NATO: North Atlantic Treaty Organization. US-led organization for collective defense in Europe and North America established in 1949.

NLF: National Front for the Liberation of Southern Vietnam. Broad-based Southern Vietnamese umbrella organization created in 1960 and controlled by Hanoi to oppose the RVN. Also known as the Viet Cong.

OSS: Office of Strategic Services (1942–7). Precursor to the CIA.

PAVN: People's Army of Vietnam. Armed forces of the DRVN controlled by the VWP during the Vietnam War, and of the SRVN under the CPV since 1976.

PCF: *Parti communiste français*, or French Communist Party.

PLA: People's Liberation Army. Armed forces of the PRC under CCP control.

POW: Prisoner-of-war.

PRC: People's Republic of China. Communist-controlled state since 1949.

PRG: Provisional Revolutionary Government of the Republic of Southern Vietnam. Coalition of mostly NLF and PRP members formed in 1969 and operating under VWP guidance. Became the Provisional

Government of Southern Vietnam after 30 April 1975. Merged with the DRVN in 1976 to form the SRVN.

PRP: People's Revolutionary Party, formerly the Party Committee of Southern Vietnam. Ostensibly independent Southern Vietnamese communist party established in 1962, in actuality part of the VWP.

RVN: Republic of Vietnam, or South Vietnam during the Vietnam War. Formerly the SOVN. Proclaimed in October 1955 by President Ngo Dinh Diem from its capital at Saigon. Claimed sole jurisdiction over all of Vietnam.

SDS: Students for a Democratic Society. American antiwar group.

SOE: State-owned enterprise.

SOVN: State of Vietnam. Purportedly independent Vietnamese government organized by France in 1949 under Emperor Bao Dai as Head of State. Became the RVN in 1955.

SRVN: Socialist Republic of Vietnam. Vietnam's official name today. Established in July 1976 following the merger of the PRG/Provisional Government of Southern Vietnam and the DRVN, of South and North Vietnam.

Tirailleur: Colonial/indigenous infantryman in the service of France.

Tonkin: French colonial administrative region consisting of the northern third of Vietnam. Known to the Vietnamese as Bac Bo or Bac Ky.

TPJMC: Two-Party Joint Military Commission. Organ created by the 1973 Paris agreement with representation by the RVN and the NLF/PRG to delineate the areas controlled by the military forces of each party in the South after the ceasefire and ensure the implementation of other core provisions of the agreement.

TPP: Trans-Pacific Partnership.

Trung Bo/Ky: Annam.

UN: United Nations.

VCP: Vietnamese Communist Party. Coalition of Vietnamese communist organizations formed in February 1930. Rebranded the ICP later that same year.

VFF: Vietnam Fatherland Front (1955–present). Mass organization promoting national unity, loyalty to the Party and state, and resistance to foreign aggression and internal subversion in the DRVN during the Vietnam War. Merged with the southern-based Alliance of National, Democratic, and Peace Forces of Vietnam in 1977, kept the same name, and now promotes national solidarity in the SRVN.

Viet Cong/VC: Term used in reference to Southern communists and their sympathizers, including, after 1960, members of the NLF and LAF, by their enemies. Abbreviated form of either *Viet nam Cong san* (Vietnamese Communist) or *Viet minh Cong san* (Vietminh Communist).

Vietminh: Contraction of *Viet nam Doc lap Dong minh Hoi,* or Vietnam Independence League. United front organized in 1941 by Ho Chi Minh and the ICP to fight the Japanese/French occupation of Indochina. Served as the main nationalist/patriotic front in the war against the French between 1946 and 1951, when it was officially dissolved and became part of the Lien Viet front. Blanket term used in reference to those who fought against the French during the Indochina War (1946–54).

VNA: Vietnamese National Army. Armed forces of the SOVN. Previous incarnation of the ARVN.

VNQDD: *Viet nam Quoc dan Dang,* or Vietnamese Nationalist Party. Pro-independence and moderately socialist revolutionary party founded in 1927 and modeled after the Chinese GMD.

VRL: Vietnamese Restoration League. Militant nationalist republican organization formed in 1912 under Phan Boi Chau.

VWP: Vietnamese Workers' Party, also known as Lao Dong Party. Replaced the ICP in 1951 and controlled the DRVN government after 1954. Became the CPV in 1976.

WTO: World Trade Organization.

Cast of Main Characters

Bao Dai (1913–97): Last emperor of the Nguyen Dynasty. Head of the pro-French surrogate State of Vietnam (SOVN), 1949–55.

Chiang Kai-shek (1887–1975): Chinese Nationalist (*Guomindang*) and anti-communist leader. Fought the armies of Mao Zedong during the Chinese Civil War (1946–9). He and his regime fled to Taiwan in 1949 where they reconstituted the pro-American Republic of China.

De Gaulle, Charles (1890–1970): Leader of France, 1944–6 and 1958–69.

Deng Xiaoping (1904–97): Chinese communist leader who succeeded Mao after a long and bitter succession dispute. Paramount leader of the People's Republic of China (PRC) between 1978 and 1989.

Duong Van Minh (1916–2001): South Vietnamese General who briefly served as President twice, in 1963 immediately following Ngo Dinh Diem's assassination and in April 1975 shortly after Nguyen Van Thieu's flight from the country. He was in office when Saigon fell to communist forces.

Ho Chi Minh (1890–1969): Prominent Vietnamese independence leader. Drawn to Marxism-Leninism at a relatively early age, he led the communist movement in Vietnam starting in 1941 until his sidelining by more radical, hawkish peers in 1964.

Khrushchev, Nikita (1894–1971): Leader of the Soviet Union shortly after Stalin's death until his ouster in October 1964. He was a proponent of East-West "peaceful coexistence" and opposed escalation of hostilities in Vietnam.

Kissinger, Henry (b. 1923): National Security Adviser to President Richard Nixon and Secretary of State under President Gerald Ford.

Kissinger represented the United States in the secret Paris talks to end the war in Vietnam.

Le Duan (1907–86): Hardline Vietnamese revolutionary originally from Central Vietnam largely responsible for Ho Chi Minh's political marginalization after 1964. He was paramount leader of the Democratic Republic of Vietnam (DRVN, or North Vietnam) during the American War, and the primary communist decision-maker throughout that period. He oversaw Vietnam's reunification and rechristening as the Socialist Republic of Vietnam (SRVN) in 1976. He ruled until his death in 1986.

Le Duc Tho (1911–90): Le Duan's "war buddy" from their days fighting the French in Southern Vietnam, and also his most trusted colleague in the Party. As head of the Party's powerful Organization Committee, Tho facilitated the promotion of hardliners and the marginalization of dovish moderates in the 1960s. He was instrumental in allowing Le Duan to centralize power into his own hands and dictate the course of the war in the South. Tho was also Henry Kissinger's counterpart in the secret Paris talks.

Mao Zedong (1893–1976): Chinese Communist Party (CCP) leader and architect of the Chinese Revolution of 1949. He presided over the PRC until his death in 1976. Mao was a staunch supporter of armed struggle in Vietnam. He also played a seminal role in precipitating the Sino-Soviet dispute in the early 1960s.

Ngo Dinh Diem (1901–63): Prime Minister of the SOVN in 1954–5. Ardently anti-communist, single-minded, and capable President and Head of State of the Republic of Vietnam (RVN) from 1955 until his murder in a coup in November 1963.

Nguyen Ai Quoc: Alias of Ho Chi Minh.

Nguyen Chi Thanh (1914–67): Five-Star General of the People's Army of Vietnam (PAVN). Hardliner loyal to Le Duan in charge of the Central Office for Southern Vietnam (COSVN) until his death under mysterious circumstances in 1967. Possibly, Thanh was murdered by allies of Vo Nguyen Giap, his arch-nemesis in the PAVN.

Nguyen Huu Tho (1910–96): Chairman of the Central Committee of the National Front for the Liberation of Southern Vietnam (NLF, or Viet Cong) and President of the Provisional Revolutionary Government of the Republic of Southern Vietnam (PRG).

Nguyen Thi Binh (b. 1927): NLF Central Committee member and PRG Foreign Minister who represented the PRG in the semi-public Paris peace talks, 1969–73.

Nguyen Van Linh (1915–98): Succeeded Le Duan as head of COSVN in 1957 until 1964. Reform-minded Secretary of the Communist Party of Vietnam between 1986 and 1991.

Nguyen Van Thieu (1923–2001): Leader of South Vietnam between 1965 and 1975, as Head of State (1965–7) and then President (1967–75). Abdicated and fled the country just days before the fall of Saigon to communist armies.

Pham Hung (1912–88): Close hardline ally and confidant of Le Duan, whom he served with in the South during the Indochina War. Pham Hung was DRVN Deputy Prime Minister and Secretary of the Party Reunification Committee during the American War. He replaced Nguyen Chi Thanh as head of COSVN in 1967 until the final victory of communist armies in 1975.

Pham Van Dong (1906–2000): Affable and widely-respected Prime Minister and, until 1961, Foreign Minister of the DRVN.

Phan Boi Chau (1867–1940): Radical Vietnamese patriot who called for the violent overthrow of French colonial rule and the creation of a republican system in Vietnam.

Phan Chu Trinh (1872–1926): Vietnamese patriot who called for reform of the French colonial system leading to eventual independence by non-violent means.

Stalin, Joseph (1878–1953): Totalitarian leader of the Soviet Union, 1924–53. A role model for Le Duan.

Tran Quoc Hoan (1916–86): Minister of Public Security, the dreaded organ tasked with maintaining public order and silencing dissent in the DRVN and then the SRVN, 1952–81.

Truong Chinh (1907–88): Leading Vietnamese communist theoretician. Served as Party Secretary from 1941 until his demotion owing to a botched land reform campaign in 1956. Rehabilitated in 1963, he became a faithful supporter of Le Duan's hawkish regime.

Westmoreland, William (1914–2005): US General and Commander of the Military Assistance Command, Vietnam (MACV), 1964–8.

Vo Nguyen Giap (1911–2013): First Five-Star General in the PAVN. Longtime friend and ally of Ho Chi Minh famous for leading Vietminh armies during the Indochina War and directing the Dien Bien Phu campaign of 1954. A moderate-at-heart like Ho, he was sidelined by Le Duan in 1964 along with Ho.

Zhou Enlai (1898–1976): Worldly, capable, and accomplished Premier of the PRC until his death in 1976. He also served as Foreign Minister between 1949 and 1958. A consummate diplomat, he represented Mao and the PRC in international negotiations and in meetings with allies and enemies.

US Presidential Administrations, 1945–1975

Harry Truman: 1945–53
Dwight Eisenhower: 1953–61
John F. Kennedy: 1961–3
Lyndon Johnson: 1963–9
Richard Nixon: 1969–74
Gerald Ford: 1974–7

Timeline

111 BCE–938 CE: Subjugation of Vietnamese by China.

939–1009: First Vietnamese Civil War.

1009–1225: Ly Dynasty rules Dai Viet.

1225–1400: Tran Dynasty.

1407–28: China occupies Dai Viet.

1428–1788: Le Dynasty.

1613–1788: Second Vietnamese Civil War.

1788–1802: Tay Son Dynasty.

1789: Emperor Quang Trung defeats Chinese invading forces during Tet.

1802–1945: Nguyen Dynasty. Dai Viet becomes Vietnam (1804) and then Dai Nam (1839).

1858: French punitive expedition arrives to end the persecution of Catholic missionaries and converts by Nguyen monarchs. Gradual conquest of Dai Nam (Vietnam) ensues.

1885–96: *Can Vuong* royalist resistance movement against France.

1887: France completes its conquest of Vietnam, which it partitions into Tonkin, Annam, and Cochinchina. Creation of the Indochinese Union including Cambodia and, after 1899, Laos.

1890: Birth of Ho Chi Minh.

1904–5: Russo-Japanese War.

1911: Nationalist Revolution in China. End of dynastic rule and creation of the Republic of China under the *Guomindang* (GMD). Ho Chi Minh leaves Vietnam.

1912: Creation of the Vietnamese Restoration League under Phan Boi Chau.

1914–8: World War I.

1917: Bolshevik Revolution in Russia leads to formation of the Soviet Union as a communist state.

1919: Formation of the Comintern. Ho Chi Minh creates the Association of Vietnamese Patriots in Paris to petition for the independence of Vietnam during the Versailles Peace Conference.

1920: Creation of the French Communist Party.

1925: Ho Chi Minh establishes the Vietnamese Revolutionary Youth League (*Thanh nien*) in Guangzhou, China.

1927: Creation of the Vietnamese Nationalist Party (VNQDD).

1929: Formation of the Communist Party of Indochina (CPI).

1929–35: Great Depression.

1930: CPI merges with two other communist organizations to form the Vietnamese Communist Party (VCP, February). VCP is renamed the Indochinese Communist Party (ICP, October).

1930–1: Yen Bai mutiny and Nghe-Tinh uprising.

1936–8: Popular Front liberal government in France.

1937: Japan invades China.

1939–45: World War II in Europe.

1940–1: Japanese forces move into Indochina. Collaborationist Vichy regime in France enters into *modus vivendi* with Tokyo allowing continued French colonial control in Vietnam.

1941: Ho Chi Minh returns to Vietnam, assumes leadership of the ICP, and forms the Vietminh as a united front to combat Japanese and French forces in Indochina.

1943: Dissolution of the Comintern.

1944: Creation of the People's Army of Vietnam (PAVN) under Vo Nguyen Giap.

1945: Famine hits Tonkin. Japan turns on France in Indochina (March). Proclamation of the Empire of Vietnam under Bao Dai (May). Surrender of Japan (August). August Revolution culminates in the proclamation of Vietnamese independence by Ho Chi Minh and the founding of the Democratic Republic of Vietnam (DRVN, September).

1945–6: Occupation of Northern Vietnam by Chinese Nationalist (GMD) forces and of the South by British troops to disarm and repatriate Japanese soldiers. French troops return to Indochina as colonial control gradually resumes.

1946: Outbreak of the Indochina, or Franco–Vietminh, War (December). The subsequent recruitment of large numbers of Vietnamese to fight for France, the "yellowing" (*jaunissement*) of the French war effort, marks the onset of Vietnam's Third Civil War.

1949: Proclamation of the State of Vietnam (SOVN) under Bao Dai (July). Victory of Mao Zedong and his Chinese Communist Party (CCP) in the Chinese Civil War results in the establishment of the People's Republic of China (PRC, October).

1950: Recognition of the DRVN by the PRC, the Soviet Union, and the rest of the communist bloc. Creation of the US Military Assistance Advisory Group, Indochina (MAAG). Outbreak of the Korean War (June).

1951: Second Congress of the ICP, renamed the Vietnamese Workers' Party (VWP).

1953: Death of Stalin (March). End of the Korean War (July).

1954: Fall of Dien Bien Phu one day before the opening of the Geneva Conference on Indochina (May). Bao Dai appoints Ngo Dinh Diem Prime Minister of the SOVN (June). Signing of the Geneva accords on Vietnam providing for a ceasefire, creation of two military regroupment zones separated at the 17th parallel, and national reunification elections within two years (July).

1955: "War of the Sects" in South Vietnam. Launching of the "Denounce the Communists" campaign by Diem (July). Creation of the Republic of Vietnam (RVN) under President Diem (October).

1956: Policy of "peaceful coexistence" promulgated by Moscow (February). Deadline for holding elections on Vietnamese national reunification mandated by the Geneva accords passes (July). Le Duan calls for a more "forward" communist strategy in the South.

1957: Appointment of Le Duan as VWP Acting Secretary.

1958: Onset of the Great Leap Forward in China and of the Sino-Soviet dispute.

1959: Endorsement of Resolution 15 by the VWP Central Committee (January). Opening of the Ho Chi Minh Trail and beginning of insurgent activity in South Vietnam and of the infiltration of men (Southern "regroupees") and supplies from the North into the South, marking the onset of Vietnam's Fourth Civil War. Saigon launches the Agroville program of forced relocations of peasants to fortified villages.

1960: Third Congress of the VWP. Le Duan becomes Party Secretary. Creation of the National Front for the Liberation of Southern Vietnam (NLF, or Viet Cong, December).

1961: Deployment of the first helicopter units plus a large contingent of military advisers from the United States to South Vietnam. Saigon abandons the Agroville program.

1962: Beginning of the Strategic Hamlet program in South Vietnam.

1963: Battle of Ap Bac (January). Overthrow of the Diem regime and assassination of US President John F. Kennedy (November). Ninth Plenum of the VWP Central Committee culminates in the endorsement of Resolution 9 calling for annihilations of the RVN armed forces (December).

1964: Le Duan orders the onset of "major combat operations" in South Vietnam. Tonkin Gulf incident and Gulf of Tonkin Resolution (August). Hanoi orders the deployment of the first PAVN combat units to South Vietnam (September).

1964–5: Communist "Winter–Spring Campaign" to win the war before mass deployments of US ground forces to South Vietnam.

1965: Washington initiates sustained bombings of North Vietnam and deploys the first US combat forces to South Vietnam (March). Battle of Ia Drang Valley, the first major encounter between US and PAVN troops (November).

1966: Beginning of the Cultural Revolution in China.

1967: Mysterious death of Nguyen Chi Thanh, a protégé of Le Duan, and onset of the "Anti-Party Affair" in Hanoi.

1968: Tet Offensive (January). Hue massacre (February). US President Lyndon Johnson announces he will not run for a second term as President and suspends the bombing of North Vietnam above the 20th parallel (March). Peace talks open in Paris (April). Washington suspends all bombing of North Vietnam and Richard Nixon is elected President (November).

1969: Sino-Soviet Border War (March). Beginning of the "Vietnamization" of the allied war effort and of phased withdrawals of US troops. Creation of the Provisional Revolutionary Government of the Republic of Southern Vietnam (PRG). Opening of secret US-DRVN talks in Paris (August). Death of Ho Chi Minh (September). Disclosure of the My Lai massacre (November).

1970: Invasion of Cambodia by US and South Vietnamese forces, preceded by the overthrow of the neutralist leader Norodom Sihanouk by the "reactionary" Lon Nol (March). Student protesters killed at Kent State University and Jackson State College in the United States.

1971: Invasion of Laos by South Vietnamese forces (February). Kissinger secretly travels to Beijing to discuss the end of the war in Vietnam and related issues (July).

1972: Nixon visits China (February). Spring or Easter Offensive (March). Washington resumes the bombing of North Vietnam in operation *Linebacker*. Nixon visits Moscow (May). Hanoi calls off the

Spring Offensive and shifts to a "strategy of peace" (June). Le Duc Tho presents Henry Kissinger with the first complete draft of a ceasefire agreement (October). Following the breakdown of peace talks, Nixon orders the "Christmas bombing" of Hanoi and Haiphong in operation *Linebacker II* (December).

1973: Signing of the Paris peace agreement ending the American War in Vietnam (January). Last US troops withdraw (March). Civil war in the South continues. Congress votes to prohibit the resumption of US combat activities in Indochina as Hanoi adopts Resolution 21 calling for renewal of "mass combat operations" in the South (July).

1974: Chinese forces clash with ARVN troops and seize islets claimed by the Vietnamese in the South China Sea (January). Nixon resigns; Gerald Ford succeeds him (August).

1975: Hanoi launches the *Ho Chi Minh* campaign to take Saigon (March). The Khmer Rouge seize power in Cambodia and Saigon falls to communist armies (April). Laos becomes communist (December).

1976: Vietnam is reunified as the Socialist Republic of Vietnam (SRVN) under the Communist Party of Vietnam (CPV).

1978: Vietnam and the Soviet Union enter into the Treaty of Friendship and Cooperation (November).

1979: Vietnam invades Cambodia and overthrows the Khmer Rouge regime under Pol Pot (January). Sino-Vietnamese Border War (February).

1986: Death of Le Duan (July). CPV adopts the policy of *Doi moi* (renovation) during its Sixth Congress.

1988: Chinese forces assault and occupy another Vietnamese position in the South China Sea (March).

1989: Communism collapses in East Europe.

1991: Comprehensive Cambodian Peace Agreement (October). The SRVN normalizes relations with the PRC (November). Dissolution of the Soviet Union (December).

1995: The SRVN normalizes relations with the United States and joins the Association of Southeast Asian Nations (ASEAN).

2001: Hanoi enters into the Bilateral Trade Agreement with Washington.

2007: The SRVN joins the World Trade Organization (WTO).

2016: US President Barack Obama visits Vietnam (May).

2017: US President Donald Trump abandons the Trans-Pacific Partnership (TPP) trade pact.

MAP I Colonial Indochina, 1899–1954

MAP 2 Indochinese Peninsula, 1954–75

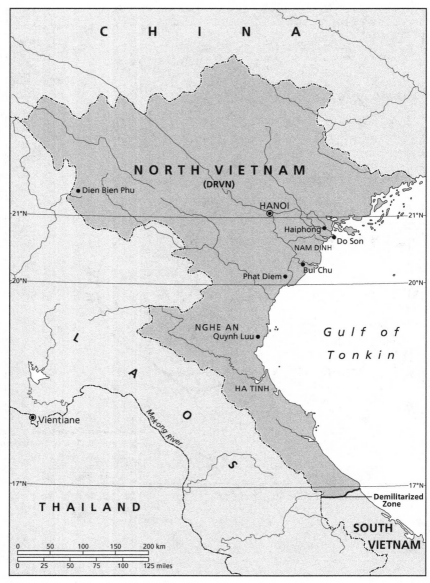

MAP 3 North Vietnam, 1954–75

MAP 4 South Vietnam, 1954–75

Introduction: Why Vietnam Matters

This book relates the story of the Vietnam War from the "other side." Specifically, it explains what Vietnamese communist leaders in Hanoi had to – and did – do to defeat the mighty United States, and its South Vietnamese and foreign allies, and reunify the country under their own authority. The Vietnam War, the narrative that follows demonstrates, was much more than the sum of its battles; an assortment of circumstances shaped its course and decided its outcome. The ground war in South Vietnam and the air war in the North were certainly important in those respects, but they alone fail to explain why Hanoi prevailed and Washington lost in the end. After all, Vietnamese communist forces came up short in most battles, including two major offensives, against American and allied troops in the South, and suffered disproportionally higher casualties throughout the conflict. Above the 17th parallel, North Vietnamese air defense units resisted valiantly, but American air forces still managed to bomb and destroy most targets at will. To make sense of the Vietnam War, to recognize and appreciate the reasons it turned out the way it did, we must look beyond the war itself. Above all, we must understand the personalities, motivations, thought process, and strategies of Vietnamese communist decision-makers. That is, we must see the conflict – and the world – through their eyes. And it is that story this book relates. This is the story of how the Vietnamese David defeated the American Goliath.

VIETNAM AS GLOBAL WAR

Today, Vietnam is much more than a country. It is an evocation, a cause, a slogan. It is a defining chapter in the history of the United States, the label of a global era, an inspiration for the small, the weak, and the oppressed, a model of national liberation. It is, too, a syndrome that cannot be cured, a curse that cannot be exorcised. So much more than a geographical and political entity, it is a veritable incantation for some, a specter for others. Vietnam is a virtual brand name.

Why is this all the case? Why do we keep evoking Vietnam? How did a small, impoverished country the size of a postage stamp on a large map of the world become the object of the second longest war in US history? And how did that war come to mean so much to Americans? After all, if Korea is the "forgotten war," how did Vietnam, similar in so many ways, become the "war that never ends?" What accounts for the enduring preoccupation with it in US political, military, and academic circles? Why can we not discuss American foreign policy since then, including the recent campaigns in Iraq and Afghanistan, without conjuring it, without framing the discussion within a "post-Vietnam" context? Why, after more than four decades, does Vietnam still matter?

American military intervention in the small Southeast Asian country began in earnest in spring 1965. The ensuing Vietnam War, as we call it – the American War to today's Vietnamese – lasted precisely eight years, until spring 1973; though its final outcome was not decided until two years later, in April 1975. It pitted puny North Vietnam, and its ostensibly ragtag Viet Cong supporters in the South, against the United States, the government of South Vietnam (which possessed the fifth largest army in the world at one point), and other allies, in a David-versus-Goliath-esque contest. As each side widely publicized the merits of its cause, and the wicked intentions of its enemies, to garner supporters near and far, their war turned into a global media sensation – the most potent symbol of the political realities of the times. The Vietnam War was the world's first "television war," regularly brought into people's living rooms during nightly news broadcasts. Audiences in the United States, and around the world, closely followed its progression, as one would the storyline of a riveting melodrama or a daytime soap opera. People identified with it, were emboldened by it, and mobilized for it. The war produced more than its fair share of shocking and stupefying moments, immortalized in iconic footage and still images. Its brutalities, reported by ubiquitous correspondents and photographers on-site, eventually prompted governments and ordinary citizens everywhere to demand its end. The war elicited protests and counter-protests of tens, and sometimes hundreds, of thousands of people on six continents.

The Vietnam War was the most consequential conflagration of the Cold War, a symbolic crucible for testing the staying power of the "Free [i.e., capitalist] World" against that of the "Progressive [i.e., communist] World." It has been the most far-reaching armed conflict since World War II, impacting the world in several profound and meaningful ways. It escalated Cold War tensions, which had been abating since the Cuban missile crisis of late 1962, and, just like that crisis, raised the specter of a superpower "hot" war. It marked the ascent of the People's Republic of China as a major player in world politics, a role it has not relinquished since. Elsewhere in Asia, the war impelled closer, and for the most part enduring, US political, military, and economic ties with Thailand, Indonesia, the Philippines, Japan, South Korea, and Pakistan. It also bore directly on the formation of the Association of Southeast Asian Nations (ASEAN) in 1967, and the adoption by the international community of the "One-China" policy that has chipped away at Taiwan's sovereign status ever since.

The war hastened decolonization by rousing independence movements across the Afro-Asian world. It also energized the Non-Aligned Movement of would-be neutral governments against superpower entanglements and bloc politics, and fostered unity and collaboration among newly-independent Third World states at the United Nations and elsewhere. Che Guevara – the Argentine-born revolutionary who helped Fidel Castro seize power in Cuba before traveling to sub-Saharan Africa and returning to Latin America to foment popular upheavals – spoke of creating "two, three, many Vietnams" the world over. In demonstrating the possibilities of national liberation, predicated on a militant Marxist–Leninist template, Vietnamese revolutionaries galvanized insurgent groups, from Mozambique and Angola to Nicaragua and El Salvador. The Palestine Liberation Organization (PLO) drew both lessons and strength from the experiences of the Vietnamese; in fact, it came to see itself as closely intertwined with them in a common struggle against Western imperialism. The Lebanese Civil War, instigated by the PLO, broke out the year America's enemies won the Vietnam War.

The American war in Vietnam was a harbinger for other kinds of transnational causes. In the West, it fueled a counter-cultural movement that electrified and radicalized young people, moving many to become political and social activists in an assortment of causes. A few of them went on to form far-left militant organizations, such as the Red Army Faction (the Baader-Meinhof Group) in West Germany, and the Red Brigade in Italy, responsible for spectacular acts of domestic terrorism. Left-wing political activism prompted massive general strikes and brought down a government in France, as it engendered lasting socio-political changes there and elsewhere. In Canada, it encouraged radical elements in the Quebec Liberation Front to press for that province's secession by violent struggle. Meanwhile, in East Europe, the Vietnam War boosted solidarity and cooperation among members of the communist bloc, even as it aggravated the Sino–Soviet dispute over leadership of that bloc. The dispute eventually precipitated Sino-American rapprochement and Soviet-American détente, which effectively ended the Cold War between Beijing and Washington and, for a period, calmed that between Moscow and Washington. Ironically, the war that exacerbated superpower tensions at its onset impelled their diffusion at its end.

The Vietnam War had equally dramatic consequences in the United States. No Cold War episode captured the domestic imagination to the extent, and for as long, as that conflict did. It left few thinking adults indifferent. In fact, it galvanized them, occasioning an acute national identity crisis that tore at the fabric of American society by exposing and exacerbating old cleavages and creating new ones. Not since the Civil War had Americans been more divided. The Vietnam War incited mass demonstrations in the nation's capital, violent riots across the country, deadly protests on university campuses – and even acts of domestic terrorism. Vietnam remains the only major American war whose outcome was conditioned more by the domestic and international response to it than realities on the field of battle.

The conflict bore directly on the decisions to lower the voting age from twenty-one to eighteen, to end conscription, "the draft," and move to an all-volunteer military service. It exhorted Congress to reassert its role as balancer of executive power, to curtail the "imperial presidency" through the War Powers Act limiting unilateral presidential authority to deploy US troops overseas. The reluctance to raise taxes to pay for the war produced inflation that obliged the United States to abandon the gold standard and "float" the value of its dollar. And, in the wake of it all, an influx of refugees from Vietnam and the neighboring states of Laos and Cambodia, the three formerly constituent parts of French Indochina, redefined the demographic and cultural landscape of localities from St. Paul to San Jose.

In an entirely different vein, the Vietnam era witnessed a new high tide of innovation in popular American art forms, especially music, as social and political commentary. The war and related developments at home inspired a generation of singers and songwriters to produce a body of politically charged, electrifying compositions. Taylor Swift's solipsistic repertory of recent years would have been a hard sell to 1960s college-aged concert-goers, who expected socially significant lyrics from their favorite recording artists. They wanted to be emotionally roused, politically provoked, and intellectually enlightened by them. The success and enduring notoriety of the 1969 Woodstock Music and Art Fair are testaments to the artistic riches, political predilections, and general spiritedness of that generation. Marketed as "An Aquarian [i.e., New Age] Exposition: 3 Days of Peace & Music," with posters featuring a dove perched on a guitar, the festival drew an audience of 400,000, who enjoyed performances by thirty-two of the most uninhibited and innovative artists at the time. This celebration of "peace, love, and rock & roll" signaled a youthful repudiation of the values that underlay American policy in Southeast Asia.

As Woodstock exemplified, the conduct and consequences of the Vietnam War also eroded popular faith in traditional sources of political and cultural authority in the United States, including the presidency. The Watergate affair that led to the resignation of President Richard Nixon was both symptom and consequence of the domestic political malaise caused by the war. Owing to that and other scandals, many Americans openly questioned the virtues of their own socio-political order. "Don't Trust Anyone Over Thirty" became a popular mantra among young demonstrators and activists. Their and others' criticism of American policy and actions in Southeast Asia, and of those responsible for them, boosted the appeal and legitimacy of progressive action groups challenging the status quo, including the civil rights, feminist, Chicano/Hispanic, and anti-poverty movements. By the time the war ended, many Americans had lost faith in their political leaders and the system that kept them in power. That loss still resonates in national politics today.

Finally, defeat in Vietnam shattered the notion of American exceptionalism. It collapsed the nation's self-confidence for a generation and caused the United States to tread more cautiously in the international arena. As Che Guevara had hoped for "many Vietnams," disgraced former President Nixon called for "no more Vietnams." Obsessed with minimizing casualties, his successors became loath to involve US ground forces in combat overseas. The hasty withdrawal from Somalia following the "Black Hawk Down" incident in 1993, and the more recent debacles in Iraq and Afghanistan, attest at least in part to this continued hesitancy. "Vietnam syndrome" still echoes in high American political and military circles. No war since 1945 has had such a cathartic, transformative effect on American society. It provoked a reckoning, a reappraisal of core values and public policies that led to irrevocable political, social, and economic change. Many of the ideals, including a redefined individualism, now evinced among young Americans are direct legacies of the Vietnam era. That war changed the United States in important ways – as much as it changed Vietnam, albeit in quite different ways.

The Vietnam War defined a global period: the 1960s, the "cultural decade," and 1970s, the "pivot decade," would have been very different, in the United States and around the world, without the war and its effects. "The most powerful states dominate international politics," historian Jeremy Suri writes, "but the small places in between define the fate of the world."[1] The American military intervention in Vietnam, and the Vietnamese response to it, certainly left their mark on our world.

VIETNAM AS HISTORY

Washington's decision to become militarily involved in Vietnam was part of a larger effort to contain the spread of communism in Asia and around the world. It was consistent with the Truman Doctrine of 1947, an article of faith for every American president during the Cold War. To prevent South Vietnam from succumbing to aggression from the communist North, US policymakers spent a staggering $200 billion – more than one trillion in today's money, or five percent of the current annual gross domestic product. At the height of the commitment, in 1968–9, more than half a million American military personnel were stationed in Vietnam. A combined total of 2.7 million American men and women – nearly five percent of the relevant age group of that generation – served at one time or another in the war, a quarter of them college-age draftees. During its eight-year involvement in the conflict, the United States dropped in excess of seven million tons of bombs and other ordnance on Vietnam and the rest of Indochina. That represented nearly three times the total expended in all of World War II. In South Vietnam, US planes also sprayed some twenty million gallons of carcinogenic "Agent Orange" and other herbicides, in an effort to deprive enemy forces of food crops and jungle cover. More than 58,000 Americans lost their lives in the war, and another 305,000 were seriously wounded. Vietnamese casualties were in the millions.

In the end, it was all for nothing for the Americans. Though it won most battles, and inflicted far more casualties on its enemies than its own forces suffered, the United States met none of its core goals in Vietnam.

Washington indisputably lost its war against Hanoi. It had to stand by idly as its enemies not only took over the South and reunified the two halves of Vietnam under their own authority, but also seized power in Cambodia and Laos. By protracting the war for so long, Washington may have prevented other "dominoes" in the region from falling to communism, though that remains uncertain. What is undeniable is that the world's most powerful country by conventional reckoning was unable to defeat its foes in Vietnam and the rest of Indochina. It was even, by some accounts, humiliated by them, suffering a loss of credibility so great as to mark the beginning of the end of the *pax Americana*. How was that all possible?

Thousands of works on the Vietnam War have been published in the United States, dating back to the onset of the war itself. A search for titles on the subject on Amazon.com yields over 83,000 results! In recounting the story of the origins, evolution, and outcome of the war, American historians have focused almost exclusively on their own country's experience, retelling the way policymakers managed the conflict, the armed forces waged it, the domestic antiwar movement opposed it, and the national media reported it. Only a handful of them have addressed the Vietnamese side of the story, and fewer still have related that of America's enemies.[2] Most surprising, no one has attempted to explain in any systematic or comprehensive fashion what the "other side" had to do – and did do – to manage its own war effort and win the war. In fact, even the precise nature of its purposes and objectives, and who defined and pursued them, remains unclear, if not completely unknown. To comprehend how astonishing this is, imagine historians of World War II writing about the origins, course, and issues at stake in that conflict without delving into – indeed, making any serious effort to relate – the goals, strategies, and motivations of Adolf Hitler and the Nazi regime in Germany. Could we make any sense of that conflagration generally, and what was truly on the line in it specifically, without exploring these issues?

The story of how Hanoi beat the United States in the Vietnam War matters because it helps us appreciate the limits of American power, the complexities of the Cold War international system, the important role assumed by small states therein, and the dramatic implications of the Sino–Soviet split. It teaches us how a seemingly trivial international actor used public opinion to offset its irrelevance and inherent weakness to prevail over arguably the world's most powerful country at the time in a major war. The Vietnam War demonstrated that brute force alone does not always decide the outcome of an armed conflict;

sound political and diplomatic strategies are also essential. The recent American experiences in Afghanistan and Iraq, and the ongoing fight against the Islamic State of Iraq and the Levant (ISIL), are testaments to these realities. Surely, US policymakers would have been better prepared to take on their enemies in the so-called Global War on Terror had they paid closer heed to the conduct of their rivals, to their strategies and tactics, in the Vietnam War. In this sense, Hanoi's story also matters because it underscores the pitfalls of combatting an enemy without really understanding its capabilities, resourcefulness, organization, and leadership. To be sure, had American leaders known at the time what we now know about that other side in the Vietnam War, that conflict would have followed a different course. It might even never have happened in the first place.

* * *

The narrative that follows is organized chronologically. While its scope is comprehensive, it is far from exhaustive. No single-volume history could ever capture the war in all of its complexities, as suggested above. The purpose here is to underscore the formative experiences and worldview of the men who devised communist strategies and tactics during the war against the United States and its allies, on the one hand, and to explain those strategies and tactics, on the other. In sum, this book aims to help readers come to a better grasp of the outcome of the Vietnam War by shifting the analytical focus, traditionally on Washington, onto Hanoi.

Coming to terms with Vietnam's American War requires awareness of its causes: of how Hanoi and Washington ended up colliding so violently in 1965, with such brutal and far-reaching consequences. Chapter 1 explores the background to the conflict, deeply rooted in Vietnam's own past. The historical experience of the Vietnamese with outside invasion produced over time a national myth of indomitability even as it fractured regional identities. China's millennium-long occupation and frequent intrusions thereafter, the southward expansion of the Vietnamese from the Hanoi-centered heartland and the ferocious conflicts it engendered, repeated triumphs over Mongol armies invading from China – all of these experiences informed Vietnamese reactions to the American involvement in their country that began in the 1940s. So too did instances of internal North–South conflict, and differences of outlook that the United States would exploit.

French colonial rule in the nineteenth and twentieth centuries was equally significant in influencing the distinct self-images of Northern and Southern Vietnamese. The suffering and humiliation, personal as well as national, endured under French domination inspired many nationalist and patriotic Vietnamese to see in Marxism–Leninism an ideology that explained their plight, and could serve as a platform for liberating their nation and reclaiming their dignity as a people. Staunchly anti-colonialist, as well as anti-capitalist, the ideology first informed their understanding of the French presence in their country during the 1920s. It subsequently performed the same function, though with distinctive fluctuations, during the Japanese occupation of Indochina in World War II and the return of French control after the Japanese defeat and withdrawal. It was obvious to Vietnamese nationalists and patriots, from the moment the war ended, that the fate of the world, at least in the short run, and thus the fate of Vietnam, rested on the course of the looming struggle for world domination between the capitalist and the communist superpowers, the United States and the Soviet Union (and, after 1949, the People's Republic of China).

The resulting tensions between these two camps emerged in Vietnam shortly after the Indochina War between France and its Vietnamese opponents began in 1946, covered in Chapter 2. As a result of French manipulation during the course of that war, a consequent misreading in Washington of Vietnamese political realities, and the intensifying state of the Cold War, in 1950 the United States decided to intrude heavily into the communist-led struggle for independence. By the time of the climactic Battle of Dien Bien Phu, in spring 1954, the United States was footing nearly eighty percent of the French war bill, and Washington policymakers had become obsessed with the evolving situation across the Indochinese Peninsula. The Geneva accords of July 1954 concluded the Indochina War by creating two Vietnams separated at the 17th parallel, but did nothing to assuage American concerns about the creeping presence of communism in the region.

Chapter 3 opens with a discussion of the decision by Ho Chi Minh's communist regime in the North to abide by the terms of the Geneva formula, and concentrate thereafter on social recoupment, economic recovery, and development in areas under its jurisdiction. Ho insisted on respecting the basic terms of the Geneva accords and foregoing armed struggle even as it became obvious that the rival regime headquartered in Saigon – headed by Ngo Dinh Diem and underwritten by American political, military, and economic support – was sneering at the peace and reconciliation process and had no intention of participating in elections to reunify Vietnam under a single government. Ho's passivity shocked and dismayed some of his own followers, especially in the South. It was not until 1959 that Hanoi sanctioned insurgent activity below the 17th parallel, but even then under restricting guidelines and with minimal support from the North. Ho feared provoking US intervention, which he thought his side would not be able to overcome given the limited resources then at its disposal. While sensible, his tentativeness alienated growing segments of his communist and nationalist supporters, including a Southerner recently recalled to Hanoi for consultations on the most important matters of strategic policy. The Southerner was Le Duan, a rising star in communist ranks, despite – but also because of – his strong objections to the line of struggle espoused by Ho and his regime in the South after 1954.

By 1963, the tension between Ho and other "doves," on the one hand, and Le Duan and other "hawks" who favored all-out war to "liberate" the South, on the other, had split the Communist Party into two competing, rival wings. Following Diem's overthrow in a coup abetted by the United States in early November 1963, Le Duan and his chief lieutenants staged a coup of their own in Hanoi. They took over decision-making and purged from Party ranks or otherwise demoted and marginalized influential doves, including Ho. In the aftermath of this quiet palace coup, the new regime under Le Duan dramatically escalated hostilities in the South, setting North Vietnam on an irreversible collision course with the United States.

The war with the United States is covered in Chapters 4 and 5. As the Vietnam War became, for American policymakers, an episode in their efforts to contain communism and block Soviet and Chinese expansion in Southeast Asia, for Le Duan and other Vietnamese who coordinated the resistance against them, it was a struggle to achieve, at all cost, national independence and reunification under a Marxist–Leninist, communist regime. Despite public claims to the contrary, Hanoi at that time had no desire to negotiate an end to the war; the leadership there, firmly under Le Duan, was committed to "complete victory" and to the reunification of the country under its own aegis. Nothing short of the surrender of its enemies was going to satisfy it. To meet that end, Le Duan's regime relied heavily on political and material support from the Soviet Union and China, which was not always easy to obtain in light of the growing ideological dispute between the two. Mounting frustration with the course of the war eventually prompted Le Duan to order a major military campaign to break the stalemate and expedite victory: the Tet Offensive of early 1968. Although it dealt the United States a major psychological blow, the offensive fell far short of meeting Le Duan's own expectations, prompting his regime to agree to peace talks with Washington later that same year. As it consented to semi-public, private, and then secret talks with the enemy, it sustained combat operations in the South, albeit on a more limited scale than in the past.

As it turned out, Hanoi had no intention at that point to negotiate seriously; it used the talks merely to probe the Americans, to get a better sense of where they stood on the war's continuation. But then unsettling circumstances intervened. They included: the Sino–Soviet Border War of early 1969; the death a few months later of Ho Chi Minh who, despite his lack of influence over communist decision-making, remained the venerable face of the Vietnamese struggle for reunification and independence and thus an important public relations tool; and, finally, Nixon's decisions to "Vietnamize" the anti-communist war effort in the South and then to authorize incursions into Cambodia and Laos. The period 1969–71 was marked by uncertainty and indecisiveness as communist decision-makers reassessed their strategic priorities and placed greater emphasis on alternative modes of struggle.

Concerned about potential diplomatic isolation and loss of Soviet and Chinese support, Le Duan decided to go for broke once more. In 1972, his regime made preparations for and eventually launched another major campaign against the South intended, like the Tet Offensive, to deliver total victory expeditiously. The campaign got off to a good start, but buckled under the weight of stiff Southern resistance and, most crucially, savage US bombings of communist supply lines into the South and renewed attacks against the North itself. Once again, Le Duan's hopes for victory were dashed. Hanoi then tried its luck at the bargaining table. That culminated in the December 1972 "Christmas bombing" of Hanoi and Haiphong, which dealt a crippling physical and psychological blow to the North Vietnamese and their leaders. In January 1973, the latter swallowed their pride and entered into the Paris agreement with the United States, effectively giving up on total victory, for now. The year 1972 had been difficult for communist forces in the South and civilians in the North. By 1973, they desperately needed a respite from the hostilities.

Shortly after the signing of the Paris agreement – which called for a ceasefire in-place, an exchange of prisoners-of-war, and withdrawal of the last US troops from the South, among other provisions – Hanoi resumed combat operations. The regime in Saigon, communist decision-makers publicly claimed, had failed to honor its side of the bargain, leaving them no choice. In 1974–5, Le Duan's regime mounted yet another major campaign to bring about the collapse of its counterpart in the South. This

time it calculated correctly, and its armies triumphed. Chapter 6 relates
the rationale for Hanoi's decision to proceed with the campaign, despite
the possible resumption of US attacks against the North, and the reasons
for its ultimate – and final – triumph on 30 April 1975.

After the capture of Saigon and formal reunification of the nation in
July 1976, the other goal of the so-called Vietnamese Revolution, building communism nationwide, stalled. This was due, not only to the economic and diplomatic isolation of Vietnam, but also to the unimaginative
conservatism of Le Duan and other Communist Party leaders. The epi-
logue demonstrates that the resilience, conservatism, and stubbornness
of these men before 1975, so critical to procurement of national independence and reunification, hindered the country's reconstruction and
development thereafter. In the decade of life and leadership left for Le
Duan, few positive changes took place in Vietnam. The 1978–9 incursion
into Cambodia eliminated the Khmer Rouge threat, but the decade-long
occupation of that country by Vietnamese forces that followed brought
worldwide condemnation. Vietnam contained the Chinese incursion
into its own territory in 1979, but anti-Chinese campaigns domestically
prompted an exodus of tens of thousands of productive members of society, who were badly needed in a period of reconstruction. Through all
this, Le Duan's unwavering adherence to Stalinist principles of economic
transformation hampered economic growth. Heavy industry developed
with some success, but neglect of light industry and handicraft production, plus the forced collectivization of agriculture in the South, crippled
non-metropolitan and rural areas. All things considered, Le Duan's leadership after the war proved stunningly counterproductive. His death in
1986 paved the way for *Doi moi*, the "renovation" policy that introduced
market reforms. In time, it also ended Vietnam's isolation, opened the
country to foreign investment and tourism, and set the stage for normalization of diplomatic relations with the United States – and of life itself
for average Vietnamese.

NOTE ON VIETNAMESE COMMUNIST PARTY
STRUCTURE

The Communist Party of Vietnam (CPV) – formerly the Indochinese
Communist Party (1930–45) and Vietnamese Workers' Party (1951–
76) – has been the primary decision-making body of Hanoi-based governments since 1954. It is a highly secretive, utterly opaque organization
that leads the state and society. Secrecy itself has been a main source

of its power. The head of the Party is the Secretary, who presides over the Secretariat, the organ responsible for managing day-to-day business, disseminating important information and instructions to the rank-and-file, and ensuring proper implementation of key policies. The Secretary also chairs the Central Military Commission, which controls the armed forces, known as the People's Army of Vietnam, or PAVN. In Vietnam, as in other communist states, the armed forces answer directly to the Party, not to the government. The Secretary is thus acting Commander-in-Chief. The Politburo – the "inner sanctum," comprising about a dozen top-ranking political and military leaders, including the Secretary, who runs its meetings – charts the State's domestic and foreign policy. The Central Executive Committee, or Central Committee, has in recent decades consisted of anywhere between fifty and 200 elite Party members, including all those in the Politburo. Its functions include debating issues, making recommendations to the Politburo, and, on occasion, sanctioning policies.

In a communist country, hand-picked delegates representing the entire Party membership typically convene every five years in a so-called Congress. These conventions are symbolically important occasions for delivering the equivalent to an American state-of-the-union address (usually by the Secretary), outlining plans for the next half-decade, formalizing policies, and investing a new Politburo, Central Committee, and, possibly, Secretary, all selected in advance during secretive meetings among the Party elite. Due to circumstances, the various incarnations of the CPV held only three congresses before 1976: in 1935, 1951, and 1960. After each Congress the numbering of Central Committee meetings, or "plenums," reverts back to one. Thus, the famous Fifteenth Plenum of the Central Committee in 1959 was the fifteenth meeting of that organ since the 1951 Congress; the seminal Ninth Plenum of 1963 was the ninth meeting of the Central Committee confirmed at the Third Party Congress of 1960.

NOTE ON VIETNAMESE NAMES, TERMINOLOGY, CITATIONS, & TITLE

I omitted Vietnamese diacritical marks in the text, notes, and bibliography owing to publishing constraints. As is standard in Vietnam, I use Vietnamese personal names where the entire name is not. In Vietnamese, the personal name is last. For example, Le Duc Tho (surname "Le") is "Tho." Exceptions to the rule include Ho Chi Minh, commonly called "Ho," as well as Le Duan, Truong Chinh, and Pham Hung, who are typically referred to by their full names. Vietnamese place names are written monosyllabically, as in Vietnamese (e.g., Dien Bien Phu, Da Nang, My Lai), with the notable exceptions of Vietnam, Hanoi, Haiphong, Kontum, Pleiku, and Saigon.

I use "Viet Cong" in reference to Southerners affiliated with the National Front for the Liberation of Southern Vietnam, including the Liberation Armed Forces of Southern Vietnam, its armed wing, and the Provisional Revolutionary Government of the Republic of Southern Vietnam, its political wing after 1969. Combined forces from the Viet Cong and the North's standing army, the PAVN, are identified as "communist." Admittedly, the first appellation is unflattering, perhaps even scornful, and the second reductionist. Though neither does justice to the people it denotes, their use enhances the lucidity of the narrative. Besides, each is consistent with American parlance. Certain authors have used "revolutionary" to label combined Southern and Northern anti-American forces. While the term is suitable for the former, it is not for the latter. The North's standing army during the Vietnam War was as professional, disciplined, and well-trained and -equipped as practically any at the time. That army could hardly have been called "revolutionary" in the traditional sense of the word. Communist authorities in Hanoi introduced and remained partial to that designation because it supported their characterization of the war against the United States as a David-versus-Goliath-type struggle.

To further improve the fluidity of the narrative, I have kept the number of citations to a minimum. I mostly reference statements attributed to other scholars and authors, to give them their due credit. Readers interested in the primary sources, including materials from the Vietnamese side, that constitute the foundation of this study, are encouraged to consult my other, more exhaustively referenced works.

Lastly, I recognize that the title of this book is misleading. There were two Vietnams at the time, and the following narrative relates the story of only one. Also, the American War had vastly different meanings to the Vietnamese; their experiences were variegated. But as we label the enterprise sanctioned and coordinated by policymakers in Washington the "Vietnam War," then correspondingly the effort prosecuted by their counterparts in Hanoi may be considered the "American War." Besides, *Vietnam's American War* makes for a much better title than *The North Vietnamese Communist Leadership's War Against the American and South Vietnamese Presidential Leaderships Over Vietnam*!

Notes

1 Jeremi Suri, *Liberty's Surest Guardian: American Nation-Building from the Founders to Obama* (New York: Free Press, 2011), 211.

2 The most insightful works addressing the Vietnamese communist perspective on the war are William J. Duiker, *The Communist Road to Power in Vietnam* [2nd ed.] (Boulder, Col.: Westview Press, 1996); Carlyle A. Thayer, *War by Other Means: National Liberation and Revolution in Viet-Nam, 1954–60* (Cambridge, Mass.: Unwin Hyman Publishers, 1989); William S. Turley, *The Second Indochina War: A Concise Political and Military History* [2nd ed.] (Lanham: Rowman & Littlefield, 2009); Ang Cheng Guan, *The Vietnam War from the Other Side: The Vietnamese Communists' Perspective* (New York: RoutledgeCurzon, 2002); Pierre Asselin, *Hanoi's Road to the Vietnam War, 1954–1965* (Berkeley: University of California Press, 2013); and Lien-Hang T. Nguyen, *Hanoi's War: An International History of the War for Peace in Vietnam* (Chapel Hill: University of North Carolina Press, 2012).

I

From Dai Viet to the August Revolution

"INDOMITABLE" VIETNAMESE IN HISTORY

For more than a thousand years, starting in 111 BCE, the Vietnamese were vassals of China, part of its frontier province of Jiaozhi (Giao Chi to the Vietnamese). At that time, they resided mostly in and around the Red River Delta. The rest of what is now Vietnam, including its Central and Southern regions, belonged to other ethnic groups. The Vietnamese staged several rebellions during the millennium of Chinese rule; all failed. Only in 939 CE, following the spectacular triumph by Ngo Quyen (898–944) over a Chinese fleet on the Bach Dang River near Ha Long Bay the year before, did they finally regain their independence. Over the next seven decades, rival clans vied to rule the now-sovereign nation. This First Vietnamese Civil War ended in 1009, with the founding of the Ly Dynasty, which branded its kingdom "Dai Viet" in 1054 and made Thang Long, now Hanoi, its capital. For the first time, Vietnamese lived under a government of their own in an ostensibly independent country.

Independence remained precarious, however. The Chinese continued to harbor designs over Dai Viet, and invaded again in 1075. They were ousted four years later by forces under the command of General Ly Thuong Kiet (1019–1105), who famously used a poem entitled "Mountains and Rivers of the Southern Country" (*Nam quoc son ha*) to motivate his troops before battle. The poem reads:

The Southern country's mountains and rivers the Southern Emperor inhabits.
   The separation is natural and allotted in Heaven's Book.
   If the bandits come to trespass it,
   You shall, in doing that, see yourselves to be handed with failure and shame!

Regarded by the Vietnamese as their first Declaration of Independence, the poem has since served as a hymn to their courage and desire to live freely, as well as a rallying cry against China and other external threats to Vietnamese sovereignty and territorial integrity.

Then the Mongols came. On three occasions during the thirteenth century (1258, 1285, and 1287–8) the hordes of Kublai Khan, grandson of Genghis, attacked Dai Viet from China, which they had previously conquered. Each time the Vietnamese were equal to the task. Conscious of their relative military inferiority, they fought the invaders with guerrilla tactics, conducting lightning raids and attacking supply lines instead of engaging in large battles. Their final victory in a naval engagement, on the aforementioned Bach Dang River in 1288, was credited to the military genius of one of their commanders, Tran Hung Dao (1228–1300). No sooner had they reclaimed their own country from the Mongols than the Chinese attacked again and successfully subjugated Dai Viet in 1407. Le Loi (1384–1433) and his armies drove them out twenty-one years later.

Ngo Quyen, Ly Thuong Kiet, Tran Hung Dao, Le Loi, and others who led campaigns against the Chinese and Mongols dominate the pantheon of Vietnamese folk heroes. They personify what is arguably the most defining aspect of the Vietnamese national character according to the Vietnamese themselves: their strength, courage, and indomitability in the face of foreign aggression. This ethos, defined in terms of an unshakable will to be masters of their own collective destiny, is a tremendous source of pride among Vietnamese. It is also, in their own eyes, a testament to their keen sense of ethnic identity and solidarity from early times, to their long and glorious tradition of embracing, variously, nationalism (love of nation) and patriotism (love of country).

But as historian William Turley points out, "the image of heroic resistance to foreign rule" and the "myth of indomitability in the face of superior force" are just that: myth.[1] The uprisings that took place during the millennium of Chinese domination – and produced their fair share of national heroes – were typically localized, confined to small areas; they were not nationwide resistance efforts fueled by nationalist or patriotic sentiment. Also, there was nothing distinctively anti-Chinese about them. Rebellions happened just as frequently under sovereign Vietnamese rule, and for the same reason: peasants detested pronounced government intrusion upon their lives.[2] Lastly, the underlying claim that Vietnamese developed through these resistance efforts and other endeavors an acute sense of nationalism and patriotism early in their history is simply untrue. Average Vietnamese at the time were unable to even fathom the meaning of "nation," as their world rarely extended beyond their native villages. Loyalty was to their own families and local communities, not to the nation or state, however defined in premodern and early modern times. When Vietnamese banded together to fight foreign aggressors, it was because the central government conscripted them to do so, or their families and communities were directly threatened; it was not a voluntary, instinctive gesture to serve the greater national good, as historians in Vietnam and elsewhere have long maintained. Not until the twentieth century, after colonization by France, a totally alien country, did Vietnamese acquire a sense of what it meant to be a distinct nation, and the willingness to sacrifice in its name. But even then, national political organizations and their leaders had to mold popular thinking and behavior.

EARLY EXPANSION & CIVIL WAR

As Dai Viet monarchs endeavored to create a functional state and keep foreign aggressors at bay, they launched a series of vicious campaigns against their own neighbors to the South and West. These campaigns were products of both necessity – to squash external threats and acquire land and resources for a growing population – and sheer imperial ambition. The Vietnamese "march to the South," as historians call the nation's southward expansion, came largely at the expense of the Chams, a seafaring people closely related to the Malays of Malaysia and Indonesia who used to occupy present-day Central and parts of Southern Vietnam. It culminated in the seizure of large swaths of territory, including the Mekong River Delta, Vietnam's most fecund "rice basket," from the Cambodian kingdom of Angkor (802–1431). As this demonstrates, the Vietnamese were as capable of victimizing others as they were victimized themselves; they dished out as much as they absorbed. "Aggression against the southern neighbors of Champa and Cambodia rivaled the struggle against foreign invasion" for the Vietnamese, historian Mark Moyar has rightfully noted.[3]

Owing to its late incorporation into the realm controlled by the Vietnamese, the southern half of their country remained until recently an eclectic borderland far less homogenous ethnically and culturally than its northern part. That and other differences between the Northern and Southern populations, plus the polarizing role of provincialism, muddled the Vietnamese identity, which became acutely manifest when the Second Civil War broke out in 1613. That war resulted from a conflict between rival clans, the Trinh and Nguyen, based in Northern and Southern Dai

Viet, respectively. Each clan claimed to defend the honor of the hapless Le Dynasty, but in fact sought to fulfill its own self-serving political and financial agenda. The ensuing savage internecine struggle lasted nearly two centuries and congealed the separate, distinct identities of Northern and Southern Vietnamese. That civil war, the "worst infighting in Vietnamese history" according to one source, ended after armies of disaffected peasants led by three brothers vanquished the Nguyen (1777), and then the Trinh (1786), before overthrowing the Le Dynasty (1788) in the Tay Son Rebellion.

Seeking to capitalize upon the prevailing turmoil and restore their dominion over Dai Viet, the Chinese invaded again. Their armies retreated promptly, however, following a surprise Vietnamese attack on the eve of the lunar New Year – *Tet* in Vietnamese – in 1789. The architect of this first "Tet Offensive" was Nguyen Hue (1753–92), one of the Tay Son brothers, who had declared himself Dai Viet's new ruler the year before. As Emperor Quang Trung (reigned 1788–92), he became the first Vietnamese sovereign to exercise effective control over all that is now Vietnam. National unity still remained precarious, however, as domestic disputes and conflict kept plaguing the country, leaving it deeply fractured. Historian Edward Miller has sensibly argued that Vietnamese politics and identities were, in retrospect, conditioned "less by any external rivalry with China" and other foreign aggressors than by "the fierce internal competition" among Vietnamese themselves.[4]

Unsurprisingly, the peace imposed by Quang Trung and his so-called Tay Son Dynasty (1788–1802) did not last. Intent on restoring the power and wealth of his family, a surviving member of the just-vanquished Nguyen clan, Nguyen Phuc Anh (1762–1820), began plotting against the Tay Son. Anh enlisted the help of a French priest, Pigneau de Behaine (1741–99), and other Western missionaries to procure men, arms, and munitions (Jesuits, the largest missionary order, had been debarking in the region since the early seventeenth century). In 1787, Anh sent his own son, escorted by de Behaine, to France to plead for aid directly from King Louis XVI (reigned 1774–92). The King responded favorably, but because of miscommunication Anh received only a fraction of the aid pledged to him. Still, that aid was enough to meet his needs. Flanked by a motley crew of soldiers and mercenaries from France and elsewhere who also trained his own soldiers in modern warfare and helped him build a naval fleet, Anh overthrew the Tay Son and founded the Nguyen Dynasty (1802–1945). As Emperor Gia Long (reigned 1802–41), he made Hue, in the center, his capital. Following consultations with the Chinese court, which he sought to appease and win over, he adopted "Viet Nam" as the name of his country in 1804. Despite its unification under a single, imperial government, the country remained internally divided and fragile.

ENTER FRANCE

In soliciting assistance from France to claim the mantle of imperial power, Gia Long sowed the seeds of his own nation's demise. For the help they rendered, the French demanded special rights and privileges as concerned trade and Catholic missionary activity in Vietnam. Beholden to them, the Emperor had little choice but to meet their demands. His son and successor, Minh Mang (reigned 1820–41), was of a different mind, however. He felt he owed the French nothing, and committed himself instead to building a modern, centralized, bureaucratically-controlled, Confucian-oriented, and fiercely independent state. As part of his travails, he renamed the country "Dai Nam" and created three administrative zones: Bac Ky in the north, Trung Ky in the center, and Nam Ky in the south. As he expanded his realm, largely at the expense of Cambodia and Laos, he also sought to homogenize it. Concerned about the creeping, socially divisive influence of France in his domain, he prohibited the practice of Catholicism, including missionary work, and went as far as destroying churches and forcing Vietnamese converts to recant. His successors Thieu Tri (reigned 1841–7) and Tu Duc (reigned 1847–83) went even further, executing foreign missionaries and indigenous priests and imposing tight restrictions on foreign trade that effectively closed off their country to the outside world.

The apparent ingratitude of Gia Long's successors and, specifically, their persecution of Catholics, who numbered five percent of the Vietnamese population by then, incensed decision-makers back in Paris. In 1858, following the execution of two Western missionaries by Tu Duc, a punitive expedition under Francis Garnier (1839–1873) arrived in Dai Nam. Its deployment was equally motivated by the aspiration of the French monarch, Napoleon III, to enhance French global prestige and satisfy the desires of banking and business leaders in France who wanted to exploit Dai Nam's human and material potential while establishing a springboard for accessing Chinese markets and resources. This was, after all, the age of High Imperialism, when European and other industrializing countries "scrambled" for colonies in Asia, Africa, and the Pacific.

The Nguyen Dynasty and its armies did their best to resist the invaders, to no avail. Their efforts were too poorly coordinated, and enemy firepower too overwhelming. The French slowly but gradually consolidated their control over Southern Dai Nam before moving against the North and, finally, going after the seat of Nguyen power in Hue. After the French stormed his palace in 1885, the ruling emperor, a boy named Ham Nghi (reigned 1884–5), fled the capital and became nominal leader of a resistance movement, *Can Vuong* ("Help the King"), aiming to drive out the French and return Ham Nghi to power. This was a royalist, not a nationalist, movement. Lacking popular appeal and competent leadership and organization, it fizzled out after a few years. Following Ham Nghi's flight from Hue, the French appointed his brother, the compliant Dong Khanh (reigned 1885–9), emperor. Tempted as they were to abolish the Nguyen Dynasty, the French opted instead to preserve and rule through it, giving a veneer of legitimacy to their actions in Vietnam. Nguyen monarchs counted among France's most willing accomplices thereafter.

By the turn of the century, France had become master of not just Vietnam but of the neighboring kingdoms of Laos and Cambodia as well, portions of which the Vietnamese had previously incorporated into Dai Nam. This collection of territories eventually became known as French Indochina. Vietnam offered the most promise for economic gain and the pursuit of France's "civilizing mission," but also posed the greatest challenge. Its population was substantially larger than that of either Laos or Cambodia, and more prone to rebel. Seeking to nip in the bud future pretensions of nationalist resistance, the French split Dai Nam into three separate entities, more or less along the same regional administrative lines previously decreed by Minh Mang: Bac Ky in the north became "Tonkin," Trung Ky in the center became "Annam," and Nam Ky in the south became "Cochinchina." The French also banned use of the names "Dai Nam" and "Viet Nam." The "Indochinese Union" thus consisted of five "countries" (*pays*) built upon the foundation created by the Nguyen Dynasty and Minh Mang in particular. Owing to the political fracture of Vietnam by France, the different regimes imposed on each region, and the management style of the French, the Vietnamese lived vastly different experiences under European colonialism. Those experiences amplified existing social and ethnic cleavages that tore at the fragile fabric of Vietnamese society even as failed resistance efforts nurtured the myth of national indomitability.

COLONIAL ERA

Exploitation, suffering, and misery characterized French rule in Vietnam. In Cochinchina, a colony under France's direct control (unlike the other four Indochinese territories, known as "protectorates," ruled indirectly through local agents including the Nguyen Dynasty), the French organized and managed the production for export of rice, mostly to Hong Kong and China. In Tonkin and Annam, it was tea and coffee destined for European markets. To optimize yields, colonial authorities concentrated land in the hands of a few wealthy landlords and entrepreneurs able to afford the latest industrial farming tools. The practice dispossessed poor peasants and small farmers, who became marginalized sharecroppers, tenant farmers, and wage laborers. It also widened the income gap between rich and poor. By the 1930s, the majority of peasants in Tonkin and Annam were landless, and among those who owned land, holdings were so small that some ninety percent could barely feed themselves and their families. In Cochinchina, where French imperialism was most aggressive, seventy-five percent of peasants were landless. Never before had Vietnamese lives been so extensively and widely disrupted, and the authority of the presiding government more ubiquitous.

Starting in the 1920s, the French set up large rubber plantations to meet rising demand in the United States, where Henry Ford had recently begun mass-producing automobiles thanks to his perfection of the assembly line. The Michelin brothers, owners of a caoutchouc factory in France, became significant stakeholders in the Indochinese rubber industry. Conditions for workers on plantations, and on the Michelin-owned one at Phu Rieng north of Saigon in particular, were appalling. The labor was unforgiving, claiming the lives of one in every four workers by some accounts. In Tonkin, the extraction of coal destined for Chinese and Japanese markets, another lucrative enterprise for the French, required miners to spend most of their days underground, breathing filthy air. Miners endured even more privation and hardship than plantation workers. Mining sites in fact became known as "death valleys." At the height of the colonial era, more than 100,000 Indochinese labored on plantations, 52,000 in mines, and 86,500 in industrial and commercial enterprises. The French also exported thousands of Vietnamese laborers to their colonies in Polynesia, New Hebrides, New Caledonia, and on Reunion Island.

Wage laborers and poor peasants alike escaped the drudgery and misery of everyday life by consuming copious amounts of opium and rice alcohol. Well aware of that, French authorities monopolized the production and sale of both commodities, in addition to salt, ensuring steady revenue streams and the docility of consumers. Approximately twenty percent of the wealth France generated in Indochina came from the three monopolies. To move goods and labor within Vietnam and between

Vietnam and China, the French built miles of railway tracks. In 1910, they completed a rail line connecting the port city of Haiphong to Kunming in Southern China. In 1936, they opened the Hanoi–Saigon line. The development and modernization of the country's transport infrastructure and the upgrade of irrigation systems were among the positive legacies of the colonial era in Vietnam, as was the creation of an industrial sector to satisfy local demands for concrete, textiles, cigarettes, and beer (the famous 33, because it came in cans of thirty-three centiliters, renamed 333 after 1975) and other beverages. But none of these projects grew out of altruistic concerns; they either profited Europeans financially, facilitated their colonial domination, or both.

For a handful of Vietnamese, French colonial rule was a boon. Families that collaborated with the colonizers and became complicit in the exploitation and dispossession of their own compatriots reaped significant dividends. Those included access to French schools in Vietnam and universities in France for their children, positions in the colonial administration, even rights to full French citizenship. Vietnamese enthralled by French culture renounced "backward" local traditions and adopted Western lifestyles. They converted to Catholicism, gave themselves and their children French names, wore the latest Parisian fashions, drank wine, vacationed on the French Riviera, and befriended and even married Europeans. The most notable collaborators were the members of the Nguyen Dynasty, as previously noted. After Dong Khanh's investiture, it reached an agreement with colonial authorities permitting it to retain its titles and wealth in exchange for tacit endorsement of the French colonial project. Nguyen rule thus continued uninterruptedly, although emperors were reduced to figureheads with little authority.

Across Vietnam, as in the rest of Indochina during the high tide of colonialism, executive power rested with the Governor General in Hanoi, an omnipotent consul of sorts who answered to the Ministry of Colonies back in Paris. A colonial bureaucracy managed day-to-day affairs. Most lower-level bureaucrats were indigenous collaborators: ethnic Vietnamese for the most part, since the French considered the Khmer (Cambodians) and Lao to be lesser, more indolent "breeds." Over time, the colonial regime employed 27,000 Vietnamese as administrators, postal workers, customs agents, and secretaries, and an additional 16,000 as teachers. A good number of those collaborators and members of their families, Catholics in particular, doggedly supported the anti-communist regime in Saigon and its American patrons during the Vietnam War. France also relied on ethnic Chinese and brought in Indians, mostly Christians from its enclave at Pondicherry, to help manage Indochina. The fewer white faces local subjects encountered, the French reasoned, the less likely they would be to revolt against European domination. This reasoning reflected the "conquer-and-divide" approach Western powers typically employed to meet their goals in overseas dependencies. It also enabled France to keep the cost of running Indochina reasonable. Indeed, at no point during the colonial era were there more than 34,000 metropolitan French citizens working and living there. Considering that the Indochinese population surpassed 22 million in 1940, that attested to both the ingenuity of colonial authorities in developing effective control mechanisms, and the important role played by local collaborators and Chinese and Indian contract workers. Other expatriate communities in Indochina included Americans, businessmen and missionaries for the most part, and Japanese.

Whatever the extent of their support for France, and regardless of the degree of their assimilation into French culture, non-whites were never treated as equals by Europeans. As in all colonies they owned, whites dominated the social hierarchy and enjoyed exclusive rights and privileges. Race was always the ultimate determinant of social status. Thus, poor, uneducated French nationals (*petits blancs*, or "small whites") ranked above wealthy, erudite Vietnamese. Over time, discriminatory practices and attitudes frustrated even collaborators. For no matter how much Vietnamese individuals "bought" into the colonial system and became "civilized" by European standards, whites always judged them by the color of their skin and not their merits and contributions.

Discrimination, intimidation, coercion, and violence were the primary instruments of colonial domination. Starting in 1917 a colonial police force, the *Sûreté générale*, monitored the activities of actual and potential dissidents, relying on a vast network of informants. A colonial army consisting of a small French *Gendarmerie*, a larger Native Guard (*Garde indigène*) of indigenous soldiers known as *tirailleurs* under French officers, and, after 1930, an infantry regiment of the French Foreign Legion formed the main safeguards against rebellion. Those Indochinese found guilty of threatening the stability and security of the colony and otherwise acting in ways detrimental to the French colonial project were either executed – usually by the guillotine – or sentenced to lengthy prison terms and hard labor. Political dissidents, if spared execution, often ended up in "tiger cages" on Con Dao Island, off the southern tip of the Ca Mau Peninsula in the South, or at the infamous *Maison Centrale* in downtown Hanoi (Hoa Lo penitentiary to the Vietnamese, which became the

"Hanoi Hilton," a prison for American prisoners-of-war [POWs], during the Vietnam War).

Prisoners regularly endured beatings, torture, food and sleep deprivation, and other forms of abuse. Many did not survive incarceration. Those who did came out more radicalized than reformed, fanatically committed to ending French colonial control and restoring Vietnam's independence. In the 1930s, Vietnamese communist leaders actually tasked Party members behind bars to recruit and indoctrinate fellow inmates. Colonial prisons held in excess of 10,000 political prisoners in the period 1930–6. They became virtual "revolutionary universities," breeding and training grounds, for the Vietnamese communist and nationalist movement. Portraits of communist luminaries, including Karl Marx (1818–83) and Vladimir Lenin (1870–1924), actually hung on the walls of some prison halls. French authorities themselves acknowledged that convicts who did not come out of their prisons dead came out "red," the color of communism. Hard time done in prison became a badge of honor, courage, and merit for communists, and even served as criteria for promotion through Party ranks. The common experience of incarceration also bonded Party members to each other. Top communist leaders during the Vietnam War had all endured and been hardened by long stints in colonial jails, which largely explained their unanimity of purpose, steely resolve, refusal to compromise, and determination to win at any cost.

WORLD WAR I & RUSSIAN REVOLUTION

The outbreak of World War I (1914–8) in Europe had major implications for the Vietnamese. France, like other belligerents, drew extensive human and material resources from its colonies to support its war effort. It enlisted some 90,000 Vietnamese as combatants and support personnel, logistical supply hands and factory workers for the most part. Some combatants came from *tirailleurs* regiments; others volunteered for military service in Europe, lured by signing bonuses, salaries, and promises of pensions for their families. Hoping to receive French citizenship and other benefits after hostilities ended, Vietnamese gave a good account of themselves wherever and in whatever capacity they served.

After the war ended, most Vietnamese servicemen had to return home and resume their lives as second-class citizens in their own country. Only a handful remained in France, becoming the nucleus of the Vietnamese community there, along with students who never returned. Anger at French authorities, compounded by the carnage they had witnessed during the war, prompted many returning veterans to openly question France's supposed civilizational superiority and denounce its rule in Vietnam. Admittedly, nothing had been "civilized" about the way European governments had fought the war, sending young men to their deaths by the hundreds of thousands in human wave attacks showing callous disregard for human life. In exposing the myth of white racial superiority, the "war to end all wars" encouraged Vietnamese, and veterans of World War I among them in particular, to actively challenge French dominion over their nation. That challenge inspired a new generation of anti-colonial, patriotic activists.

Equally stirring for young Vietnamese patriots was the Russian Revolution of 1917. In the midst of World War I, Vladimir Lenin and the Bolsheviks claimed the mantle of power in Russia and, after a bloody civil war (1917–22), founded the Soviet Union. The Bolshevik Party, renamed the Communist Party of the Soviet Union (CPSU) after the Revolution, was a "vanguard" organization of committed revolutionaries inspired by the writings of Karl Marx to reinvent Russian society on behalf of workers, the "proletariat," oppressed by greedy industrialists, the "bourgeoisie." Its penultimate goal was to create a dictatorship of the people leading to the establishment of communism, a radical socio-economic and political order characterized by common ownership of land and commercial enterprises, the absence of social classes, the elimination of government controls and then of the government itself, and, at last, universal equality and harmony. Just months before the 1917 Revolution, Lenin had penned *Imperialism: The Highest Stage of Capitalism*. Based on Marxist theories, the essay unabashedly denounced colonialism as the supreme stage of capitalist development to secure maximal profits for the avaricious bourgeoisie. The triumph of "Marxism-Leninism" – the fusion of Marx's ideas about social revolution with Lenin's methods to bring it about – in Russia and the advent of the Soviet Union resonated across the colonial world, including Vietnam. After all, rarely had Westerners themselves so overtly condemned colonialism, by now a pillar of their own societies' economic and foreign policy and virtual hallmark of their civilization, much less brazenly called for its abolishment.

RISE OF VIETNAMESE PATRIOTISM

The rigors of life under colonial rule produced widespread disenchantment, frustration, and anger among Vietnamese long before World War

I exposed the limits of French civilizational greatness and the Russian Revolution roused young patriots. This shared experience to no insignificant degree contributed to the emergence of patriotism as a popular, mass phenomenon in Vietnam, as did increased literacy rates resulting from the colonial school curriculum and the adoption of *quoc ngu*, a system of writing based on the Latin script and easier to learn than the traditional system based on Chinese characters, as the Vietnamese vernacular language (although some ninety percent of the people remained illiterate under French rule). From the inception of the colonial system in the late nineteenth century, various individuals and groups had attempted to abolish and otherwise restrain it. All had failed, proving no match for the *Sûreté* and colonial armed forces. Even simple calls for reform fell on deaf ears, as French authorities believed that compromise signaled weakness and would only embolden indigenous activists. Intransigence was the best deterrent against subversion, the authorities thought. Poor organization and coordination compounded by uncharismatic leadership largely accounted for the inability of Vietnamese patriots to rally more supporters and rattle colonial authorities early on.

The first individual to distinguish himself as a bona fide patriotic leader because he was able to tap the budding patriotic fervor of his compatriots was Phan Chu Trinh (1872–1926). Trinh served in the imperial bureaucracy until he could no longer stomach the Nguyen Dynasty's collaboration with France. The year of Japan's victory in the Russo-Japanese War (1904–5), he quit the mandarinate and traveled to Tokyo, as many young Eastern Asian nationalists were doing at the time as part of the "Go East" movement. There, he studied Japan's remarkable transformation from victim of Western imperial aggression to victor in a war against a European power. Following his return to Vietnam, Trinh called for abolishing the Vietnamese monarchy and replacing it with a republican system, albeit under French tutelage because he did not think his compatriots were ready for total independence. He was not a revolutionary in the literal sense, but a reformist seeking incremental changes to French rule. Trinh abjured violence as a political tool. He believed Vietnamese patriots should educate themselves instead of fighting, learn about France's democratic and liberal traditions so they could replicate them in their own country later on. He admired France, its republican values in particular, and even appealed directly to Paris for help in preparing the Vietnamese for independence. Under the careful watch of the *Sûreté* he opened the Tonkin Free School in 1907 to teach young Vietnamese modern values, including nationalism and patriotism. Colonial authorities shut it down within a year, and sentenced Trinh to three years on Con Dao Island before deporting him to France, where he met and worked with a man named Nguyen Ai Quoc. Trinh returned to Vietnam in 1925, and died the following year.

Though unsuccessful in realizing his aspirations, Trinh had a marked impact on the Vietnamese political landscape of the early twentieth century, inspiring as he did a generation of younger Vietnamese to advocate for change. Equally important in that respect was his contemporary and acquaintance, but not relation, Phan Boi Chau (1867–1940). Chau was the "Vietnamese icon of the anti-colonial struggle," according to political scientist Céline Marangé.[5] His father had been active in earlier resistance efforts against France, which inspired the young Chau to dabble in anti-colonialism. In 1904, the latter founded the Vietnam Modernization Association, an anti-colonial organization modeled after the *Can Vuong* movement, with the dissident Nguyen Prince Cuong De (1882–1951) as nominal head. Struggling financially, the association turned to Japan for assistance. Chau moved to Tokyo in 1905, meeting Phan Chu Trinh there shortly thereafter. He then went to China, where he fell under the spell of Sun Yat-sen (1866–1925), the architect of Republican China, and developed close ties to other Chinese nationalist leaders. Upon his return to Vietnam around the time of the 1911 Revolution in China, he became a republican and founded the Vietnamese Restoration League (VRL), a political party modeled after Sun's Chinese United League that became the Chinese Nationalist Party (*Guomindang*, GMD) after the 1911 Revolution. The VRL's chief goals were ending French colonial control, reunifying Vietnam, abolishing the monarchy, and establishing a democratic republican system.

Unlike Trinh, Chau sought the complete and immediate overthrow of the colonial order, not its reform, by force if necessary. After returning to China, where he met Soviet representatives for the first time, and being briefly detained by French agents there, Chau traveled to the Soviet Union to study its political ideology and solicit assistance from its leaders to liberate Indochina. Moscow, its political system, the 1917 Bolshevik Revolution, and the Russian people generally impressed Chau, who subsequently urged his compatriots to establish contacts with Soviet decision-makers and the organ they had recently established to export communism, the Comintern (Communist International, 1919–43). Chau returned to China in 1925, and was arrested again by French agents. Possibly, he was betrayed by the aforementioned Nguyen Ai Quoc, a fellow nationalist presumably jealous of his stature and disapproving of his political agenda. Following his transfer to Vietnam, Chau was placed under house arrest. His political activities remained limited until his death in 1940.

Together, the two Phans made seminal contributions to the awakening and growth of the Vietnamese national and patriotic consciousness. They stand out for their ability to arouse the anticolonial passions of their compatriots, for attuning them to the bond they shared as victims of French colonialism, and also, interestingly, for their admiration of American revolutionary ideals (i.e., freedom from foreign tyranny and quest for justice) and republican values (i.e., liberty and unalienable individual rights). They are considered the founding fathers of contemporary Vietnamese patriotism, and role models for the next generation of more radical activists. The two Phans also set up connections with Chinese nationalists, on the one hand, and Soviet communists, on the other, both of whom made invaluable contributions to the struggle for independence and self-government in Vietnam. Chau's ideas were particularly important in inspiring formation of the Vietnamese Nationalist Party (known by its Vietnamese acronym, VNQDD), a mildly socialist revolutionary party calling for the colonizers' violent overthrow, which became the first dissident political organization to develop a mass following in Vietnam. The VNQDD gained notoriety in 1929 for assassinating Alfred François Bazin, the much-reviled Director of the Office of Indochinese Labor tasked with recruiting workers for plantations in Cochinchina and the French territories of New Caledonia and New Hebrides, whom many Vietnamese held personally responsible for the abuses they or their relatives suffered. The VNQDD's growth and popularity were stunted, however, by its inability to appeal to and coopt peasants.

Circumstances galvanized the Vietnamese masses and made them receptive to radicalized patriotic callings in the 1920s, and to Marxism-Leninism specifically. Heavy taxation, mounting personal debt, the inability to own land or ownership of only small parcels of it, and growing economic inequality exasperated peasants. Some had to cede as much as seventy percent of their crop as levy to landlords and/or colonial authorities. Workers on plantations, in mines, and in the budding industrial sector endured interminable workdays, backbreaking labor, and low wages. Beatings and other forms of corporal punishment were common for those failing to meet employers' expectations. As most workers had signed long-term contracts and vast distances separated them from their native villages – those employed on rubber plantations in Cochinchina, to illustrate, were typically recruited in Tonkin – quitting or simply walking away was not an option. Besides, punishment for "runaways" was harsh, and included public execution by hanging, stabbing, or some other cruel method to deter others from doing the same. Contract laborers were not slaves in the traditional sense, but their workplace conditions certainly made them feel like they were. The Great Depression that began in late 1929 aggravated the condition of peasants and workers as France attempted to mitigate the impact of the financial crisis at home by extracting more wealth from its colonies. By the turn of the new decade, Vietnam was ripe for revolution.

HO CHI MINH

Only one Vietnamese individual stands above Phan Chu Trinh and Phan Boi Chau for his ability to inspire and rally his compatriots in support of national independence. That person is Nguyen Ai Quoc, known later in life as Ho Chi Minh (1890–1969). Ho was born Nguyen Sinh Cung in an impoverished part of Nghe An Province, in Northern Annam. His father was a Confucian scholar, teacher, and low-level administrator (District Chief) in the imperial bureaucracy. Ho studied under him before attending the prestigious National College, a high school for the sons of the elite, in Hue. Other illustrious graduates from this school include Vo Nguyen Giap (1911–2013) and Pham Van Dong (1906–2000), who later became Ho's closest allies in the communist movement, and Ngo Dinh Diem (1901–63), the future President of South Vietnam and Ho's arch-nemesis in the 1950s and early 60s. In Hue Ho studied French history and language, and became struck by the dissonance between the liberal values France championed at home and its exploitative practices abroad. Against the wishes and intentions of French authorities, the study of French and the colonial school system in general favored the development of a patriotic consciousness among Vietnamese. In fact, they "opened up a whole new world for Vietnamese youth who came of age in the 1920s and afterwards," as Ho's own experience demonstrates.[6]

Frustrated by his lack of prospects after graduation, and embarrassed by his father's recent demotion for fatally beating a man while intoxicated, Ho got a job as a kitchen helper on a French steamer and left the country in 1911, at age twenty-one. He would not return to Vietnam for thirty years. He first went to Marseille, in France, and applied to the French Colonial Administrative School there. He was rejected. Finding employment on ships, he traveled the world. He visited several African countries and spent time in the United States, in Harlem and Brooklyn, before settling temporarily in the United Kingdom. During his travels, Ho developed a keen interest in the human condition and the suffering endured by men because of the greed of other men, including American blacks at the hands of whites. He also developed a knack for relating to people from different socio-economic and racial backgrounds, facilitated over time by his knowledge of French, Chinese, Russian, Thai, and English. The educated and the rich respected his worldliness; the poor and the oppressed were struck by his capacity to empathize with them. The ability to bridge the gap between those with means and those without served his revolutionary purposes well later. "It was Ho Chi Minh's ability to move between these different realms which finally secured his place as the most successful leader of the independence struggle" in Vietnam, biographer Sophie Quinn-Judge surmises.[7]

In 1917 Ho settled in Paris as Nguyen Tat Thanh and connected with Phan Chu Trinh. With Trinh's encouragement, he penned newspaper articles calling for the independence of Vietnam under the pseudonym Nguyen Ai Quoc (Nguyen the Patriot). He met and developed personal bonds with other Asian nationalists in France, including Zhou Enlai (1898–1976), a future leader of the communist movement in China. Ho founded the Association of Annamese Patriots in the summer of 1919 to rally patriotic Vietnamese exiles in France. During the Versailles Peace Conference that year, Ho and his exiled compatriots petitioned the allied victors of World War I for Vietnamese independence on the basis of US President Woodrow Wilson's Fourteen Points of January 1918. The petition cited the American Declaration of Independence for good measure. The allies completely ignored it.

INDOCHINESE COMMUNIST PARTY

Concluding that appealing to Western sensibilities to secure Vietnam's independence was a waste of time, Ho searched for alternatives. Extremism and militancy, he reasoned, might be necessary to meet his purposes. Marxism-Leninism, the radical political philosophy embraced by the Soviet Union and increasing numbers of nationalists from the colonial world, particularly intrigued him. By many accounts, Ho was drawn to Marxism-Leninism after reading Lenin's *Theses on the National and Colonial Questions*, which pugnaciously denounced imperialism, like his *Imperialism* essay.

Marxism-Leninism, it turned out, not only explained the suffering of Ho's compatriots under the French, but also provided a blueprint for ending that suffering, for bringing down the colonial apparatus and replacing it with a representative regime to ensure that no man or woman ever again suffered because of another. That blueprint included forming a vanguard, a party of professional, committed operatives to spearhead the struggle for national liberation; establishing one-party rule, a "dictatorship of the proletariat," after independence; centralizing economic planning and abolishing capitalist practices, including private ownership of land and commercial enterprises; redistributing wealth; and practicing internationalism by actively supporting revolutionary movements in other countries. The ultimate objective of Marxism-Leninism was to bring about communism, namely, classlessness and governance by the concept of "each according to his ability, to each according to his need." The appeal of that blueprint was enhanced by the fact that the Soviet Union had created a special outfit in 1919, the aforementioned Comintern, to guide vanguard parties and assist them logistically, materially, and financially in meeting their goals. According to historian Odd Arne Westad, Marxism-Leninism was "valuable" in the eyes of nationalists from the colonial world because it was "structured, defined, and first and foremost scientific."[8]

In 1920, while still in France, Ho became a founding member of the French Communist Party (PCF, its French acronym) and a staunch advocate of revolution in the colonial world. He traveled to Moscow in 1923 to study Marxism-Leninism and communism at the renowned University of Toilers of the East. There, he met other aspiring revolutionaries, including Josip Tito (1892–1980), the future leader of Yugoslavia. He also became a Comintern agent, specializing in propaganda and political mobilization. His first mission, in 1924, was to make contact with expatriate Vietnamese intellectuals in Guangzhou (Canton), in Southern China, and "convert" them to Marxism-Leninism. Guangzhou was by then the main base of operation and planning for Vietnamese revolutionaries in exile, a veritable breeding ground for radical nationalists and patriots. Ho established the Vietnamese Revolutionary Youth League, or *Thanh nien*, shortly after his arrival there. The League, whose members included Vo Nguyen Giap and Pham Van Dong, supported anticolonial and class struggle to bring about national liberation. It morphed into the Communist Party of Indochina (CPI) in 1929. With assistance from his old friend Zhou Enlai, Ho was able to offer his followers training in various Chinese communist and nationalist political and military schools. He also married his first wife, a native of Guangzhou, during his time there.

In Hong Kong in February of the following year, the CPI merged with two other Vietnamese communist organizations to form the Vietnamese Communist Party (VCP). Consistent with Ho's wishes, the VCP made national independence, to be pursued jointly with other nationalist organizations, communist or not, its priority. Ho effectively aspired to create a united front that took no account of the socio-economic background of its members to achieve Vietnamese independence. Communism would come later. Ho's emphasis on national independence, his lack of enthusiasm for class struggle, and his relatively cautious attitude toward revolutionary violence did not sit well with radicals within the VCP. Trained and indoctrinated in Comintern schools in Moscow, the radicals espoused the Stalinist, ultra-leftist position endorsed by the Comintern in 1928 that fighting domestic class enemies, "class warfare," was as important as fighting foreign imperialists. In their reckoning, Ho was not doctrinaire enough; he was too pragmatic, too moderate. He was too much of a nationalist, and not enough of a communist. In their eyes, Ho lacked "ideological rigidity," as Sophie Quinn-Judge put it.[9]

During a second meeting of VCP leaders in Hong Kong in October 1930, the radicals slammed Ho and the Party's "moderate" line. After deliberation, the leaders adopted a new strategy calling for a two-stage revolutionary process. In the first stage, the Party would harness patriotism and nationalism to mobilize members of all social classes to defeat colonial authorities, secure national independence, and reunify the three Vietnamese entities of Tonkin, Annam, and Cochinchina. Upon completion of this "bourgeois nationalist revolution," the Party would instigate the second stage, the "communist revolution," characterized by formation of a new government, a so-called dictatorship of the proletariat; class struggle, that is, chastisement and neutralization of "reactionary," "bourgeois," and other domestic class enemies; confiscation of land and property belonging to landlords and redistribution among poor peasants; collectivization of agriculture; nationalization of businesses and other commercial enterprises; introduction of an eight-hour workday; abolition of unfair taxes and other harmful financial practices; democratic freedoms, including free education and health care; and equality between men and women. Communal bliss would ostensibly ensue.

At the behest of the Comintern, and to underscore the shift away from Ho's nationalist agenda, the leaders rechristened their organization the Indochinese Communist Party (ICP). Since Laotian and Cambodian communists were few, the Vietnamese themselves would assume responsibility for leading the revolution in those countries. Besides, ICP leaders thought, Vietnam would never enjoy the fruits of its independence unless French authority was abolished across the entire Indochinese Peninsula; Cambodia and Laos must form a "security belt" along Vietnam's western border. Tran Phu (1904–31), a radical detractor of Ho Chi Minh newly-returned from Moscow, was selected to become the new Party chief.

At once, the ICP set out to consolidate and grow itself, train operatives to become skillful propagandists, and achieve a higher degree of organizational unity and discipline. Tran Phu considered organization and rank-and-file members' respect for rules and procedures key to mobilizing and preparing the masses for meaningful political and economic action, including strikes and boycotts, and, in due course, armed insurrection. Only a mass movement, he and other communist leaders thought, could bring about the demise of the colonial system and its replacement with a new political and socio-economic order under an enlightened revolutionary government. The fixation of these leaders with organization, discipline, and mass mobilization, their no-nonsense approach and unwavering commitment to the liberation, reunification, and reinvention of Vietnam, became in time defining characteristics of the communist movement in that country. Those same characteristics also constituted the most important reason the Party ultimately met most of its goals, including defeating the United States in the Vietnam War, in the "Vietnamese Revolution," as they called their undertaking.

Though he would soon become the face of Vietnam's struggle for independence and his popularity at home and abroad only increased over time, Ho was never able to shed his reputation as a moderate, a "softie," among his more doctrinaire comrades within the Party. The latter would in fact do their best to limit Ho's influence within the Vietnamese communist movement, and even marginalize him. It took nearly three decades, but in the end they were able to accomplish just that. By then the war against the United States was about to get underway, and had it not been for the sideling of Ho by his own, radical peers at that critical juncture, that war's course and outcome could have been vastly different.

ARMED ANTI-COLONIALISM

In 1930–1, against the backdrop of economic hardships resulting from the Great Depression and natural calamities, the ICP, VNQDD, and other political parties fomented popular unrest. In the Yen Bai mutiny of February 1930, Vietnamese *tirailleurs* radicalized and supported by the VNQDD murdered five and seriously wounded three of their white officers. Their own peers loyal to France neutralized them before they could cause more mayhem. About a month later, a popular uprising broke out in the Northern Annam provinces of Nghe An and Ha Tinh. This so-called Nghe-Tinh uprising consisted of 125 separate incidents, namely, strikes, demonstrations, and revolts – some spontaneous, others incited by communist agents – directed against the French colonial administration and the Nguyen Dynasty and its mandarinate, seen as corrupt and responsible for the humiliation and suffering endured by the Vietnamese. The uprising brought peasants and workers together in sizeable numbers for the first time. Spurred by ICP and other radicals, the rebels murdered mandarins, landlords, and civil servants. They also set fire to government buildings, police stations, churches, and other symbols of foreign domination and oppression.

The response of colonial authorities to these treacherous acts was swift, and deadly. More than a thousand rebels and possibly twice that number of innocent civilians were killed in "pacification" and subsequent "mopping up" operations that included aerial bombings raids. Scores more died of malnutrition during incarceration in makeshift detention or "concentration" camps. Two hundred colonial troops died suppressing the Nghe-Tinh uprising, only one of whom was a French national. The superior firepower of colonial troops sealed the fate of insurgents, as did the latter's own lack of organization. In the aftermath of these troubles, colonial authorities aggressively hunted down members of dissident political organizations to prevent and deter future protests. Many were found and executed, and hundreds of their supporters were sent to prison, forced labor camps, or into exile. In 1930–2 colonial authorities sentenced nearly 7,000 Vietnamese for political crimes, executing eighty-eight. Most ICP leaders and operatives involved in the events of 1930–1 were killed or captured, including Tran Phu, the Party head. Ho himself was briefly detained by the British police in Hong Kong.

Miraculously, the ICP survived, but its remnants had to seek refuge in Guangzhou, and reconstitute their organization there under the guise of the Overseas Bureau of the ICP. The VNQDD, the most popular and best organized party at the time, was not so lucky; French retaliation eviscerated it. That proved a boon for the ICP, which thereafter dominated the nationalist movement in Vietnam, and for its ideology, Marxism-Leninism, which became the driving force behind Vietnamese anti-colonialism and the default creed of patriots hoping to make a difference. The failed revolts of 1930–1 impressed upon ICP leaders the imperative need to closely coordinate the activities of its members, to develop superior organizational skills and discipline, to muster popular support, and to prepare its members for combat. They would also need to unite peasants, workers, and other suitable classes in common struggle against the colonial oppressor. To these ends, Ho went back to Moscow in 1934 to undergo further training at the International Leninist School for cadres.

The brutal crackdown on Vietnamese rebels generated public outcry in France. In conjunction with the Great Depression, which underscored the perils of capitalism, and other challenges, misrule in the colonies emboldened French progressives and other liberals. In 1936, a left-wing coalition including communists swept to power in Paris. At once, the new government of Prime Minister Leon Blum (in office 1936–7, 1938), the so-called Popular Front, loosened colonial controls, most notably over the indigenous press, and pardoned political prisoners. More than 1,500 prisoners were reprieved in Indochina alone. The impact of these measures on the Vietnamese anti-colonial movement was electric. The lifting of restrictions on free speech and the release of hardened and unrepentant members breathed new life into the ICP, and may well have saved the communist movement in Vietnam. In 1936–7, communists and other leftists formed a united front and organized strikes, boycotts, and other such actions against the colonial establishment. Never to be outdone, the *Sûreté* clamped down harshly on the ICP, decimating its leadership ranks, again.

Although it lasted less than two years, the Popular Front's tenure in France markedly impacted the struggle for independence and reunification in Vietnam. The same was also true of the rapid industrialization and socialist transformation of the Soviet Union under Josef Stalin (1878–1953), the Spanish Civil War (1936–9), and the rise of Adolf Hitler (1889–1945) in Germany. Troubled and distracted by these alarming developments, policymakers in Paris paid less attention to the situation in Indochina. Admittedly, Japanese aggression in Asia concerned them, but not enough to beef up the French military and security presence in Indochina. Vietnamese communists took advantage of these distractions to reconstitute and grow their organization, train cadres, and spread their message among peasants and workers. By 1938, the ICP comprised 202 members in Tonkin, 483 in Annam, and 655 in Cochinchina, and enjoyed patronage from nearly 30,000 workers and peasants countrywide. Still, its presence and influence nationwide remained negligible, especially in cities.

WORLD WAR II

The onset of war in Europe in September 1939 marked a turning point for Indochina. France conscripted more than 1.5 million Indochinese, mostly Vietnamese, to serve as soldiers and workers in its fight against Nazi Germany. Confronted by the rigors of war and desperate to improve its financial situation, it increased taxes as well as rents across Indochina, and introduced new tariffs on imports. It also reduced Indochinese workers' wages even as it extended their working hours to seventy-two per week. But that did nothing to save France. By the summer of 1940, German troops were marching in the streets of Paris. By order of an agreement signed in September that same year between Germany's allies in Tokyo and the collaborationist Vichy government in France, which remained in charge of overseas territories, the Imperial Japanese Army earned the right to station some 6,000 troops and use three airfields in Indochina. Less than a year later, Vichy and Tokyo signed another, more comprehensive agreement allowing the Imperial Japanese Army to use Indochina as a base of operation in exchange for French autonomy in managing Indochinese affairs.

French colonial authorities served the Japanese in Indochina as the Vichy regime served the Germans in France. Abetted by the Japanese, they brutally cracked down on Vietnamese patriotic and other dissident political organizations. The state of war, the authorities claimed, mandated that they act without mercy. French security forces even went after their own white compatriots loyal to the Free France movement of General Charles de Gaulle (1890–1970), who condemned collaboration with fascism. Collusion with Japan saved the colonial apparatus in the short term, but irreversibly damaged French credibility among Indochinese. The latter were flabbergasted to see Europeans prostrate themselves before fellow Asians just to keep their privileged status. Japanese efforts to coopt the Indochinese with calls of "Asia for Asians," even as they worked alongside the French, fueled Vietnamese patriotic and anti-colonial passions.

Prompted by the Comintern, in late 1940 the ICP attempted to capitalize on the new situation and the apparent vulnerability of the French by instigating armed insurrections as well as mutinies among colonial troops where conditions permitted. The hasty, ill-conceived move proved disastrous. The French crushed the insurgents, killing or capturing most ICP leaders, yet again, including all so-called radicals who had previously studied in Moscow and dutifully observed Comintern revolutionary prescriptions. Yet again, however, the Party would find a way to survive, and reemerge even stronger under a new leader.

VIETMINH

In early 1941, as the French were hunting down his comrades, Ho Chi Minh returned to Vietnam for the first time in three decades. He set up camp at Pac Bo, in the northwestern province of Cao Bang, by the border with China. His detractors within the ICP either dead, in jail, or on the run, Ho could finally take command of the Party and steer it in the direction he wanted. Following the end of his studies in Moscow in 1938, Ho had spent time with Chinese communists at their base in Yan'an Province, the endpoint of the Long March (1934–5) that served as the main base of operation of the Chinese Communist Party (CCP) until 1949. Since then he had become an avid student of the thoughts of Mao Zedong (1893–1976), who became CCP leader during the Long March, on Marxism-Leninism and revolution. As China's circumstances resembled Vietnam's own, Vietnamese communists could learn much from the struggle of their Chinese counterparts, Ho felt. Besides, Ho was never fond of the Stalinist/Comintern revolutionary line. He had tussled with other ICP leaders over it, and been marginalized because of it. "Maoist formulations of internationalism," historian Mark Philip Bradley has written, provided Ho with "an alternative to Soviet models for the national liberation struggle that fit indigenous realities and prompted an ideological affinity with China that would persist and deepen after 1940."[10] For the past ten years the ICP had followed Moscow's counsel; where had that gotten it? In April 1941, the Soviet Union signed a pact of non-aggression with the ultra-nationalist, fascist government of Japan. That shocked Ho and other Vietnamese revolutionaries, encouraging them to pursue closer collaboration with Mao.

Inspired by and per prior agreement with Mao and the CCP, on 19 May 1941, the day of his fifty-first birthday, Ho announced the creation of an indigenous united front to fight French and Japanese imperialism in Indochina. The Vietnam Independence League, commonly known in the West as Vietminh (abbreviated from the Vietnamese *Viet nam Doc lap Dong minh Hoi*), was a broad-based political and military resistance front that rallied fighters and partisans from all segments of Vietnamese society to liberate the nation and secure its independence. With help from Vo Nguyen Giap, a young lawyer and high-school History teacher turned revolutionary whom he had recently met in China, Ho organized month-long military and political training sessions for groups of fifty to sixty rebels in Cao Bang. Recruits learned how to fight, as well as how to engage civilians to win their hearts and minds. Ho was completely sold on the Maoist premise that winning over the people – political struggle – was as crucial if not more fundamental than physically eliminating enemies – military struggle. As Mao's own adage went, rebels must be able to "move amongst the people as a fish swims in the sea." Purportedly patriotic, the Vietminh actually answered to the ICP and to Ho in particular, who downplayed his own ties to communism to broaden the appeal of his organization and encourage more people to join it.

The united front approach marked an important shift in the ICP's revolutionary strategy. Starting in 1941, as Ho's influence in the Party became more pronounced, the ICP ceased toeing the Soviet line and moved toward closer, fuller ideological alignment with Mao and the CCP. As a result of that alignment, the line of struggle espoused by Ho and the ICP became consonant with the "people's war" strategy developed and applied by Mao in China. That strategy called for concerted efforts to drum up support among civilians through propaganda and other political activities, on the one hand, and wage guerrilla warfare (hit-and-run attacks) against the enemy's most isolated and vulnerable military assets to frustrate and demoralize him until he surrendered, on the other. Consistent with the thinking of Russian Bolshevik revolutionary Nikolai Bukharin (1888–1938), endorsed and applied by Mao in his own country, the ICP looked to peasants, the overwhelming majority of the population, to provide fighters and otherwise support its activities. Mao in particular rejected the orthodox premise that communism could only take root in industrialized societies, that industrialization was a prerequisite for communism. Unlike European Marxist-Leninists who held that workers must form the revolutionary backbone, Mao believed peasants could just as easily assume that role in predominantly agrarian societies like China and Vietnam. The latter could even bypass the stage of capitalist (industrial) development and jump straight to communism, he thought.

At the onset, the Vietminh could do little more than harass French and Japanese forces due to its very limited human and material resources. Still, the valiance of its fighters did not go unnoticed by their compatriots, who applauded their efforts as the "cowardly" French kowtowed to and collaborated with the Japanese. While in China in 1942 to meet CCP leaders, Ho was arrested by Chinese Nationalist (GMD) authorities, Mao's archrivals, and spent the next two years in jail. Despite his absence, the Vietminh persevered, gaining more supporters and acquiring better weapons by raiding French and Japanese armories. Shortly after Ho's return to Vietnam, in December 1944, a group of elite Vietminh fighters comprising thirty-one men and three women came together to form the Armed Propaganda Unit for National Liberation under Giap's command. The elite unit's mission was both military and political, and included winning over civilians through "education" sessions, that is, propaganda; recruiting and training new combatants; and acting as vanguard in the armed struggle for independence. Creating this "mobile main force" unit, as ICP leaders called it, fell within the parameters of people's war. Today, the formation of the unit is celebrated in Vietnam as marking the founding of the People's Army of Vietnam (PAVN), the country's standing armed forces.

In early 1945, a famine resulting from a combination of wartime dislocations and natural disasters struck Tonkin and Northern Annam. Vietminh efforts to alleviate the ensuing suffering of peasants in hardest-hit rural areas by raiding government granaries and rice transportation systems and handing over their loot to the starving masses raised the organization's profile, and Ho's and the ICP's by extension. The famine still claimed between 500,000 and one million lives, nearly a tenth of Tonkin's population of seven million at the time. But as historian Huynh Kim Khanh has argued, Vietminh attempts to mitigate its effects – futile as they were – in the end played a seminal role in the rise of the ICP in Vietnam and of Ho as savior and redeemer of the Vietnamese.[11]

The French in Vietnam suffered a devastating blow in spring 1945, when Japan unilaterally abrogated its 1941 pact with the Vichy government. In the so-called coup of 9 March, Japanese troops attacked French military garrisons and raided administrative offices, killing some 800 Frenchmen, mostly members of the armed forces. They jailed surviving ranking members of the French armed forces and colonial government, and confined to urban neighborhoods and makeshift camps nearly 30,000 other French nationals, military and civilian. Desperate to win Vietnamese support as the tide of the war was turning against them, the Japanese restored on 10 May 1945 the "Empire of Vietnam" under the Nguyen sovereign, Bao Dai (1913–97), who at once proclaimed the independence of his country from France. Days later, Bao Dai, supported by Japan, announced the formation of a nominally autonomous government under Prime Minister Tran Trong Kim (1883–1953) which officiated over the formal reunification of the nation. The inability of the French to even protest the Japanese betrayal of their "alliance" attuned Ho and other patriots to the precariousness of France's position in Indochina.

World War II was also a turning point for American policy in Southeast Asia. Prior to the war, the United States had expressed little interest in Indochina, recognizing it as a French sphere of influence. Admittedly, France's mercantilist policy and its monopolies had deterred both the American government and private firms and citizens from seeking economic and other opportunities there. Only a handful of Americans had been to Indochina, to do business, proselytize, or play tourist, as previously noted. Relatives of President Theodore Roosevelt (in office 1901–9) owned a hunting lodge in Ban Me Thuot, in the Central Highlands, used during expeditions to hunt tigers and other exotic wildlife (that lodge became a US military regional headquarters during the Vietnam War). Other than being the source of certain raw materials, the region meant little to Americans.

Japan's invasion changed all of that. Tokyo's pursuit of a Greater East Asia Co-Prosperity Sphere and, specifically, push into Southeast Asia following the invasion of China, alarmed the administration of President Franklin D. Roosevelt (in office 1933–45). The latter feared not only an impending move by Japan against the American colony in the Philippines, but also the loss of access to Indochinese rubber and tin upon which the United States depended rather heavily. Following the first Vichy-Tokyo agreement and the movement of Japanese troops into Indochina, Washington had slapped sanctions on Japan. Those sanctions prompted Tokyo to plan and eventually carry out an attack on the US naval base at Pearl Harbor in Hawaii. The collusion of Vichy authorities with Japan, a strong personal dislike of Free France leader Charles de Gaulle, the conviction that French colonialism had brought nothing but misery to the peoples of Indochina, and a firm desire to end colonial monopolies and open the region to American commerce prompted Roosevelt to insist as early as 1940–1 that France not be allowed to retain Indochina after the war ended, and that the region become an international trusteeship, much as Middle Eastern countries had become after World War I, instead.

Despite Ho's known ties to communism, the Roosevelt administration considered the Vietminh an ally in the war against Japan after 1941. Stalin's mid-1943 decision to dissolve the Comintern, to which the ICP had belonged, made working with Ho more palatable to the Americans.

The Vietminh aided the allies by not only fighting – harassing, really – the Japanese, but also rescuing US pilots downed over Indochina. In July 1945, a team from the American Office of Strategic Services (OSS), the precursor to the Central Intelligence Agency (CIA), parachuted into the Vietminh's main base to train and equip some of its fighters. Ho, who had been battling dysentery and malaria for months, allegedly was on the brink of death when the OSS team arrived. An American corpsman saved his life. In the brief time they were there, OSS members developed a very favorable impression of their hosts. They were particularly impressed with Ho, and moved by his ideals and commitment to their realization.

AUGUST REVOLUTION

By the time World War II ended in Asia in August 1945, Ho was a friend of the United States. He was also the face of Vietnam's struggle for freedom and independence to his compatriots. Indeed, the war allowed his communist party to gain wider acceptance as a legitimate patriotic political organization, despite counting less than 5,000 registered members when hostilities ended. Japan's savage exploitation of human and material resources in Indochina and the rest of Southeast Asia had also validated ICP claims that World War II was a product of capitalist greed, a devastating contest between imperialist powers seeking self-aggrandizement through acquisition of new colonies and markets. That, in conjunction with the Vietminh's valiant efforts during the war, made Vietnamese of all social standings more receptive to ICP propaganda. Ho and the rest of the Party leadership learned a valuable lesson from their wartime experience, namely, that downplaying their Marxist-Leninist credentials facilitated popular mobilization domestically and abroad. That same experience, grueling for most Party leaders, also solidified their own personal devotion to communism.

World War II, like World War I before it, disgraced the French in the eyes of the Vietnamese. In fact, it sealed their fate in Indochina. The Japanese had effectively abolished French colonial rule through their coup of March 1945. If the postwar government of Charles de Gaulle in Paris decided to reinstate French rule, as it would soon attempt to do, at least the Vietnamese now knew that the French were far from invincible. Ho Chi Minh understood this better than anyone. No sooner had the war in Asia ended than he and the ICP instigated the "August Revolution," a general uprising of the population spearheaded by the Vietminh to fill the political vacuum after Tokyo capitulated, before the French had a chance to reclaim control. The Vietminh improved its capabilities by commandeering weapons from the Japanese, who saw no reason to resist. It also bolstered its ranks and popularity by abolishing the despised government monopolies over alcohol, opium, and salt, and adopting other policies that pandered to people's basic needs and wants. On 19 August, Vietminh units marched into Hanoi accompanied by the OSS team for added legitimacy. By orders of the ICP, those units occupied government buildings and took charge of or otherwise provided security for such facilities as power plants, hospitals, and prisons. Opposition was non-existent. In fact, most people enthusiastically welcomed the Vietminh power grab. The regime only recently created by the Japanese under Bao Dai, the Nguyen Emperor, remained silent. The French, for their part, were in too much disarray, with too many of their leaders and soldiers still in jail, to respond. Across the countryside, peaceful popular upheavals, celebrations of the end of the war for the most part, culminated in the formation of "people's committees" under ICP loyalists who assumed local administrative responsibilities thereafter.

After seizing power in Tonkin, the Vietminh and the ICP set their sight on Annam and its most important city, Hue, the imperial capital. On 25 August, under pressure from the ICP, Bao Dai abdicated the throne, ending the thousand-year old dynastic system in Vietnam. This was arguably the most revolutionary aspect of the August Revolution. A provisional government was formed two days later, with Ho as chairman. By that time Cochinchina was under the control of the Vietminh, though the latter's position there was more precarious. Neither the Vietminh nor the ICP enjoyed widespread support in the deep South. What is more, religious sects and other factions there did not trust or had no interest in collaborating with the Vietminh and Ho's new regime. The creation of a regional administrative committee in Saigon dominated by the ICP infuriated them, validating as it did their concerns that the August Revolution was in fact nothing more than a communist power grab.

Over ensuing days, the newly minted Provisional Government consolidated its authority as Vietminh units sought to preempt a counter-revolution by the French and other groups opposed to them. To these ends, they neutralized actual and potential opponents by offering them positions in the new administration, or detaining or killing them. Before the end of the month Ho and the Vietminh had assumed de facto control of most of the country. In retrospect, the ICP termed this series of developments the "August Revolution" less to capture its essence than to dramatize and legitimize an otherwise prosaic, banal, even fortuitous seizure of power.

DECLARATION OF INDEPENDENCE

The August Revolution culminated on 2 September 1945, at Place Puginier (later renamed Ba Dinh Square) in Hanoi, when Ho Chi Minh declared the country's independence and reunification, and proclaimed the advent of the Democratic Republic of Vietnam (DRVN) as a fully sovereign state. Ho's proclamation opened with the following lines:

All men are created equal; they are endowed by their Creator with certain inalienable Rights; among these are Life, Liberty, and the pursuit of Happiness. This immortal statement was made in the Declaration of Independence of the United States of America in 1776. In a broader sense, this means: All the peoples on the earth are equal from birth, all the peoples have a right to live, to be happy and free. The Declaration of the Rights of Man and Citizen of the French Revolution made in 1791 also states: All men are born free and with equal rights, and must always remain free and have equal rights. Those are undeniable truths.

The references to the American Declaration of Independence and the French Declaration of the Rights of Man and Citizen were deliberate. Ho insisted on them to suggest that Vietnam intended to maintain close ties with the West even after independence, and thus pander to public opinion in France and the United States in particular with a view to preempting the resumption of French colonial rule.

Archimedes Patti (1913–98), an OSS agent working with the Vietminh in Hanoi at the time, was stunned when he read the draft text of the Proclamation handed to him by Ho himself. In its tone and substance, the Proclamation exulted freedom and self-determination, and made no allusion to social revolution and class struggle, tell-tale signs of allegiance to communism. The effort to conceal the ideological leanings of the country's new leaders also included appointing the former Emperor, Bao Dai, Supreme Adviser to the new DRVN government. Patti and other OSS staff on-site applauded Ho's proclamation and his new regime. Given the Vietminh's wartime support for the allied cause, they mistakenly concluded that Ho was first and foremost a patriot whose attachment to communism was only skin-deep and self-serving at best.

Unfortunately for Ho, Paris paid no heed to and in fact outrightly rejected the Proclamation. The newly-installed provisional government of Charles de Gaulle, it turned out, had no desire whatsoever to hand Indochina over to the Indochinese. Colonies attested to France's big power status; in light of the national humiliation suffered in World War II, de Gaulle felt France could not afford to lose its empire. Washington privately objected to de Gaulle's decision, but made no effort to dissuade him. Before his death in April 1945, Roosevelt had made an about-face on Indochina, and dropped the trusteeship idea largely because the British vehemently opposed it. His successor, Harry Truman (in office 1945–53), preferred appeasing de Gaulle in hopes of securing his cooperation in restructuring postwar Europe and, perhaps more importantly, checking Soviet ambitions there and elsewhere. The nascent Cold War and, specifically, concerns about the Soviet occupation of East Europe, future of Germany, and spread of communism in the West soon consumed the Truman administration, and conditioned its policy vis-à-vis France and Indochina.

Seeking to convince the United States to reconsider its stance, in fall 1945 DRVN authorities founded the Vietnamese–American Friendship Association in Hanoi. The Association sponsored English-language courses, translations of American books into Vietnamese, and showings of American films. It even hosted representatives and agents from major US firms such as Texaco, General Motors, and Harley-Davidson interested in doing business in Indochina. The prospect of enhanced cultural and, more significantly, economic exchanges might, Ho's new government reasoned, prompt Washington to reexamine its relationship with the DRVN. After all, the French had never been particularly receptive to American economic activity in Indochina. American policymakers were unmoved.

The indifference of the United States plus de Gaulle's intractable stance unnerved Ho and other ICP leaders. Equally unsettling, no government recognized the sovereignty and legitimacy of the DRVN in the weeks and months after 2 September, not even the Soviet Union. Domestically, at least, Ho's declaration of independence electrified the population. Mass celebrations broke out throughout the country. Roused peasants seized land belonging to their landlords and wealthier peers. The Vietminh's popularity soared, as did membership in the Communist Party. Tragically, anti-French pogroms ensued in certain cities, resulting in the killing of dozens of innocents, including a French priest who was stabbed to death. Paris would not soon forget this and other injustices perpetrated against its nationals.

Notes

1   William S. Turley, *The Second Indochina War: A Concise Political and Military History* [2nd ed.] (Lanham: Rowman & Littlefield, 2009), 9, 10.

2   To illustrate, peasants revolted on more than 400 occasions during the first sixty years of rule by the Nguyen Dynasty (1802–1945), Vietnam's last.

3   Mark Moyar, *Triumph Forsaken: The Vietnam War, 1954–1965* (New York: Cambridge University Press, 2006), 2.

4   Edward Miller (ed.) *The Vietnam War: A Documentary Reader* (Malden, MA: Wiley Blackwell, 2016), xiv.

5   Céline Marangé, *Le communisme vietnamien, 1919–1991* [Vietnamese Communism, 1919–1991] (Paris: Presses de Science Po, 2012), 46.

6   Tuong Vu, *Vietnam's Communist Revolution: The Power and Limits of Ideology* (New York: Cambridge University Press, 2017), 33.

7   Sophie Quinn-Judge, *Ho Chi Minh: The Missing Years, 1919–1941* (Berkeley: University of California Press, 2003), 257.

8   Odd Arne Westad, *The Global Cold War: Third World Interventions and the Making of Our Times* (New York: Cambridge University Press, 2005), 108.

9   Quinn-Judge, *Ho Chi Minh*, 42. In a recent study, Tuong Vu takes exception to Quinn-Judge's and others' interpretation. See Tuong Vu, *Vietnam's Communist Revolution*, 46–51.

10 Mark Philip Bradley, *Imagining Vietnam and America: The Making of Postcolonial Vietnam, 1919–1950* (Chapel Hill: University of North Carolina Press, 2002), 41.

11 Huynh Kim Khanh, *Vietnamese Communism, 1925–1945* (Ithaca: Cornell University Press, 1982), 312–15.

2

French War, 1945–1954

FRANCE RETURNS

As agreed by the allies during the Potsdam Conference (17 July–2 August 1945), Chinese Nationalist (GMD) troops entered Vietnam in early September 1945 to oversee the disarmament and repatriation of Japanese forces above the 16th parallel, as British troops fulfilled the same mandate below that line. Pressed by Paris, and unwilling to disappoint leaders there, the British re-armed French forces previously detained by the Japanese and permitted new contingents of troops to arrive from France. On 22–3 September, French forces set out to reclaim control of Saigon. Vietminh units there were no match for them, and retreated. Unaffiliated bands of disgruntled Vietnamese took to the streets with weapons, murdering French civilians, setting up barricades, and sabotaging public facilities, including an electrical power plant and water purification facility. They were swiftly and savagely dispatched by French troops.

Undercover ICP operatives took advantage of the prevailing chaos in the South to get rid of political rivals and weaken their organizations. Communist death squads summarily executed dozens, possibly hundreds of Vietnamese "traitors" and "reactionaries" in fall 1945 and spring 1946, including leaders of what was left of the VNQDD, as well as Trotskyites calling for immediate social revolution. One of their victims was Ngo Dinh Khoi (1885–1945), the elder brother of future South Vietnamese President Ngo Dinh Diem. Diem himself would have been killed, but Ho interceded to spare his life. Khoi's execution by the Vietminh would make Diem's struggle against Ho's regime in the late 1950s and early 60s not just political and military but also personal. The ICP's elimination of political rivals, domination of the new government, and increasingly evident control of the Vietminh unsettled non-communist Vietnamese nationalists, who felt they had been duped by Ho and other communist leaders posing as patriots. Indeed, the latter's now manifest ties to Marxism–Leninism called into question their commitment to Vietnamese *national* interests.

Concerned that the ICP's domination of the government and the ICP itself had become liabilities for the DRVN domestically as well as internationally, Ho dissolved the organization in November 1945. He did so without consulting Moscow, which took great offense. The ICP, it turned out, did not actually disband; it simply went underground, ceasing to exist in name only. A front organization, the Indochinese Marxism Study Association, carried its message and continued its work in the public sphere thereafter. On 1 January 1946, the DRVN's Provisional Government was reconstituted as the more inclusive, politically-diverse Provisional Unity Government. Five days later, the DRVN elected its first National Assembly through universal suffrage. During its opening session in March, the Assembly confirmed Ho Chi Minh as President and appointed a committee of representatives from a broad spectrum of political parties and social classes to draft a constitution. That, Ho felt, would help maintain the pretense of the DRVN's political neutrality, and enhance its legitimacy at home and abroad. To those same ends, Ho picked a new cabinet of members representing all major political persuasions. The state's first constitution, enacted later that same year, said nothing about the communist leanings of the new regime. It stipulated instead that Vietnam was "a democratic republic," and that "all powers in the country belong to the entire Vietnamese people, regardless of their races, sexes, economic conditions, social classes, religions."

Those initiatives, including formation of an inclusive "permanent" government, did little to help Ho and his regime. By early 1946, the French had reasserted their jurisdiction over large chunks of Southern Vietnam, and prepared to reclaim the North. Chinese Nationalist armies occupying that part of the country were less accommodating to the French than the British, however. That bought Ho's regime precious time to organize and consolidate state institutions, including the armed forces. But as Ho's ties to communism became more obvious, despite his best efforts to conceal them, Chinese attitudes changed. After all, GMD-controlled armies had been combatting communists in their own country since the late 1920s, and were about to do that again shortly. Soon, GMD leaders were amenable to the resumption of French colonial control in Northern

Vietnam. In February, the government of Chiang Kai-shek (1887–1975) in China agreed to withdraw its 200,000 troops from Vietnam and allow French forces to return. In exchange, Paris promised special rights and privileges to Chiang's government once it reestablished colonial control.

As their forces began to withdraw, Chinese Nationalist commanders on-site called upon French and DRVN leaders to negotiate a *modus vivendi* to preclude a sudden onset of war. The resulting talks between Ho and Jean Sainteny (1907–78), the French Commissioner for Tonkin and Northern Annam and liaison to Chinese Nationalist forces, were highly contentious. Paris was prepared to grant the Vietnamese nominal independence, but only as part of the French Union, the commonwealth of ostensibly sovereign states created by France in 1946. That meant the Vietnamese would hold sway over domestic policy, but not over foreign and national security affairs. Ho rejected the proposal, insisting on French recognition of Vietnamese independence and national reunification. He did his best to make Sainteny amend his position, to no avail. By the terms of the 6 March 1946 agreement negotiated by the two men, Ho consented to the temporary stationing of 15,000 French troops on Northern soil for a period of no more than five years. In exchange, Paris agreed to recognize the "Republic of Vietnam" as a free state "part of the Indochinese Federation and of the French Union." This was a far cry from what Ho had hoped to get from a diplomatic settlement, but he felt he had no choice but to accept the deal to avoid immediate war with France.

Vietminh and other supporters of the Revolution were outraged by the so-called Ho-Sainteny Accord. Some went as far as accusing Ho of selling out their struggle for reunification and independence. Hardline, radical members of the "underground ICP" concluded from the agreement that Ho remained, after all these years, a moderate at heart – unable to make bold, hard choices to advance the Vietnamese Revolution. During a government rally to discuss the settlement the next day, someone in the crowd threw a grenade at the DRVN President, but missed his target. Ho's government found itself increasingly isolated and unpopular thereafter. Meanwhile, the Chinese presence was diminishing, and the French were comfortably reasserting their control and influence in the North. As a precautionary measure, in April Vietminh forces in Hanoi and elsewhere started regrouping to remote regions of Northeastern Tonkin. In May, communist leaders formed another national united front, the Lien Viet, to rally individuals and organizations loath to pledge allegiance to the DRVN government but opposed to France. As the last Chinese Nationalist troops withdrew from Hanoi in June 1946, communist hit squads went after the remnants of anti- and non-communist political parties, for good measure.

The French were quick to move in as the Chinese left. By late June, their reoccupation of Vietnam and the rest of Indochina was nearly complete. That same month, the new French High Commissioner for Indochina (formerly, Governor General), Thierry d'Argenlieu (1889–1964), announced the creation of the Autonomous Republic of Cochinchina under a puppet president. The move shocked and alarmed Ho, who considered it a flagrant violation of the 6 March agreement. As the situation across Indochina grew tenser and the likelihood of armed conflict increased, Ho called for another round of talks with France. In a last-ditch effort to avert war, he traveled to France to meet with representatives from the Paris government. Their talks opened on 6 July at Fontainebleau, outside the capital. They ended in impasse in mid-September. The two sides could not agree on the degree of Vietnam's autonomy within the French Union, and on the modalities for the reunification of Tonkin, Annam, and Cochinchina. The French maintained that Cochinchina was its own polity, and thus could not be reincorporated into Vietnam (i.e., Tonkin and Annam). Ho, for his part, insisted on the reunification of all of Vietnam and its complete independence from France. Concluding the French were negotiating in bad faith, Ho returned to Vietnam, but not before agreeing to another *modus vivendi* extending certain rights and protections to French citizens in Vietnam in exchange for a pledge from Paris to resume negotiations in early 1947. That agreement did nothing to defuse tensions; in fact, they kept escalating.

In late fall, the French seized control of customs offices at all major ports in Tonkin. Scuffles between French and Vietminh troops ensued in Haiphong, Tonkin's most important port city. Intent on sending DRVN leaders a strong and clear message, the French bombarded and strafed the city's Vietnamese quarters in late November, killing somewhere between 3,000 and 6,000 civilians. Members of the Vietminh and other organizations immediately retaliated against Europeans, going on a killing spree that made no distinction between civilians and military personnel. On 19 December, following issuance of an ultimatum by French authorities calling for the dissolution of Vietminh paramilitary and police units, remobilized Vietminh forces launched coordinated attacks against French military outposts throughout Tonkin, including in Hanoi. The next day Ho Chi Minh and the DRVN government issued a nationwide call to arms. Thus began the Indochina, or Franco–Vietminh, War – the First Indochina War in contemporary American parlance.

WAR

Following the onset of hostilities, Ho and his government retreated to the mountains of Pac Bo in Northwestern Tonkin. From there they coordinated the "Resistance against French Colonial Aggression," which consisted of three separate but interdependent struggles. That approach was largely informed by Mao's "people's war" doctrine and the recent experiences of Vietnam's own communist leaders and armies. Military action, the first struggle, aimed to wear down French forces through strategies of attrition and demoralization. Political action, the second front, amounted to propaganda activity among the Vietnamese masses to recruit fighters and partisans and otherwise turn the civilian population against France and those Vietnamese who collaborated with it. The last mode of struggle, diplomatic action, sought at the onset to muster foreign support for Vietnamese independence through, on the one hand, globalization of the political struggle and exploitation of "contradictions" between France and its allies, and, on the other, between the French government and its own people. Carrying out each of these struggles was no easy feat in light of the Vietminh's shortages of human and material resources, limited logistical capabilities, and inexperienced leaders at all levels. In order to prevail, DRVN leaders had to be cautious, and calculating. They also had to be patient, and avoid large-scale battles as well as fighting in cities, where exposure made their forces too vulnerable to superior French firepower. Owing to that philosophy, major cities and their inhabitants were for the most part spared the horrors of war.

When the war began, the Vietminh counted between 80,000 and 100,000 members, most with little or no training and combat experience, who shared 30,000 guns for which they had little ammunition. Japanese and French deserters, as well as ex-*tirailleurs*, provided what advice and training they could. The Vietminh's main base of operation, its "stronghold," was Viet Bac, an area north of Hanoi extending to the Chinese border. Its military strategy before 1949 consisted of conducting hit-and-run raids against small, isolated French outposts from secret staging areas. Meanwhile, specialized units disrupted the colonial economy by targeting power plants, water purification facilities, rubber plantations, and the transportation infrastructure. On the political front, cadres conducted "patriotic emulation" campaigns to win over the people. This was quintessential guerrilla or "revolutionary" warfare, as Party theoretician Truong Chinh (1907–88) described it. To forestall actual and potential dissent and ensure consensus within his own government, Ho sacked non-communist ministers and replaced them with loyal comrades through a series of cabinet reshuffles after the war began.

The Vietminh's best efforts did little to undermine French militarily strength in the short term, but allowed it to stay in the fight long enough to develop broader appeal among the masses, setting the stage for success later. Ho, ever the conscientious moderate, made further appeals to France for negotiations in April and again in August 1947, over strong protests from some of his own supporters. But it was all in vain. Meanwhile, though Vietminh forces did their best to avoid the trappings of major combat, French military aggressiveness made that difficult. Hostilities were especially brutal in rural Tonkin and Northern Annam, where France's armies mounted several big operations against suspected Vietminh strongholds in 1947–8. Vietminh troops resisted valiantly, but suffered heavy casualties.

During this early phase of the war, DRVN diplomacy focused on securing foreign military assistance to improve Vietminh capabilities. Burmese and Indian nationalist organizations supplied military aid, but it was only a fraction of what DRVN leaders needed. To the latter's chagrin, their closest ally, which also happened to have the greatest means, tended no help. Stalin had not gotten over Ho's unilateral decision to dissolve the ICP in 1945, and still questioned his commitment to Marxism–Leninism. The Soviet leader also feared that assisting the DRVN would alienate French policymakers, encouraging them to formally align with the United States in the budding Cold War. At the time, developments in Europe and collapsing Soviet-American relations consumed Stalin, just as they did his American counterpart. Relative to these concerns, the Vietminh's struggle for national liberation was largely inconsequential. In 1948, the Soviet Union opened a diplomatic mission in Bangkok through which it maintained regular contacts with Ho's government and kept itself apprised of the situation in Indochina. But even that did nothing to change Stalin's stance on helping the Vietminh.

Mao and the CCP were far more sympathetic, but in the throes of a nasty civil war (1946–9) against Chiang Kai-shek's GMD armies. They had no resources to spare. In fact, it was the other way around: the Vietminh supported the CCP, offering sanctuary to its troops and providing them with food and medicine. Ho even loaned Mao's army 1,000 Vietminh combatants during the latter stages of the Chinese Civil War. That decision was partly self-serving, however. On the one hand, the token force gained valuable experience fighting alongside seasoned Chinese troops. On the other, its deployment affirmed the DRVN's commitment to communist internationalism and solidarity, creating a major incentive for Mao and the CCP to reciprocate later. Following China's intervention in the Korean War in November 1950, the DRVN would also send a small detachment of troops to fight alongside North Korean and Chinese forces, to the same ends.

FROM COLONIAL WAR TO CIVIL WAR

The Indochina War exacerbated existing divisions within Vietnamese society and created fresh cleavages that polarized the masses. To minimize their casualties, and meet other pressing needs, the French enlisted ever-increasing numbers of young Indochinese to fight for them. Using local men to fight its own war fit the policy of "conquer-and-divide" traditionally employed by France to alleviate the burden on its nationals and undermine the social unity of its colonial subjects. Non-communist nationalists, Catholics, and members of other religious sects, including the Cao Dai and Hoa Hao in the deep South, were often keen to support France. Many others did so for financial reasons. Before long, the war became a civil war as much as it was a Franco-Vietnamese confrontation. This "yellowing" (*jaunissement*) of the French war effort was the starting point of Vietnam's Third Civil War. It would also serve as precursor to and inspiration for Washington's "Vietnamization" policy of 1969 intended to ease the burden on American forces and offset the consequences of their gradual withdrawal.

Paris also relied on *tirailleurs* from other parts of its empire, particularly Northern Africa, as well as the Foreign Legion, to fight the Vietminh. Owing to these initiatives, only a minority of troops in the so-called French Far East Expeditionary Corps (CEFEO, its French acronym) were actual French nationals. White casualties thus remained low, important for Paris to appease domestic opinion unsupportive of the conflict. To the people of France at the time, the country's reconstruction and mundane daily concerns such as the price of bread mattered far more than the war in Indochina. From the start, a segment of the population actively opposed investing substantial human and material resources there, while France and its people had pressing needs of their own. The "*sale guerre*" (dirty war), as it became known in France, was also a forgotten war even as it took place. The constraints facing Paris policymakers, which included having to put down another colonial insurrection in Madagascar in 1947–8, meant that they had to fight the war on-the-cheap, that they could not send sufficient forces to Indochina. To be sure, throughout the war French troops were spread too thin to maintain an effective offensive posture across the entire territory. That proved a major advantage for the Vietminh.

American decision-makers felt a lot like the people of France about the Indochina War. That is, they only cared about it to the extent that it impacted their other, more pressing and immediate concerns. In March 1947, President Truman had formalized the United States' commitment to the containment of Soviet-style communism in the so-called Truman Doctrine. The Marshall Plan promulgated that same year specifically intended to help West European states, including France, get back on their feet while keeping communism at bay. To the latter end, the Truman administration also pushed for the creation of a European Defense Community (EDC), a joint army to include troops from France, West Germany, Italy, and Benelux countries (Belgium, the Netherlands, and Luxembourg).

In all these pursuits, the United States needed support and collaboration from France. Accordingly, it could not risk offending authorities in Paris by acting in Indochina in ways contrary to French interests. Besides, Truman and his advisers were starting to believe French propaganda to the effect that Ho was an agent of Stalin seeking the communization of Indochina. They figured that, at a minimum, they could not support Ho because he was too susceptible of embracing communism if and when his armies triumphed. Thus, when Ho reached out to Washington via its embassy in Thailand soliciting political and economic support in exchange for concessions to US businesses, Truman's administration snubbed him. According to historian George Herring, the American position on Indochina during the war's early stages amounted to "pro-French 'neutrality'." The United States refused to publicly endorse French military action against the Vietminh for fear of being seen as supportive of colonialism. It did, however, tacitly consent, and otherwise turn a blind eye, to the diversion of Marshall Plan and other aid to Indochina, expressly prohibited by the State Department in January 1948. The Truman administration even approved the sale to France of weapons, including such items as ships and planes, knowing full well they would be used to fight the Vietminh.

That was all well and good for Paris, but still failed to meet its needs. In order to defeat their enemies within a reasonable period, French decision-makers needed the unconditional backing of the United States. Rebuilding efforts at home left them insufficient funds to purchase more military hardware from Washington, and thus insufficient means to crush the Vietminh. According to historian Mark Lawrence, French authorities "embraced a range of strategies to convince, cajole, and if necessary, coerce the United States into backing French aims in Indochina."[1] Following promulgation of the Truman Doctrine, Paris did its best to manipulate American anxieties about creeping communism in hopes of getting direct assistance from Washington, as just mentioned. It did this by connecting its travails in Indochina to the Truman administration's ideological and geopolitical priorities. Stressing the DRVN's and thus the Vietminh's ties to communism and to Moscow in official and public statements, the French recast their war as a struggle to protect Vietnamese nationalist aspirations by defeating communist rebels threatening Indochinese freedoms. They redoubled their effort to demonize Ho, asserting he was nothing but a stooge of the Soviet Union, employed by Stalin to bring about in Southeast Asia the same types of despotic regime being implanted in East Europe. The freedom Ho promised was no freedom at all, the French charged; it was dystopia. Paralleling all this, Paris stressed the positive legacies of its colonization of Indochina and the Indochinese: namely, improvements in education, health, transportation, agriculture, and commerce. Such puffery aimed, not only to enhance the legitimacy of its war effort and win over American decision-makers, but also to plant doubt in the minds of rank-and-file Vietminh combatants and sympathizers, while emboldening the indigenous resistance to them.

If the Truman administration had maintained US ties to Ho's regime or else enjoyed better intelligence, it would have understood that none of this was true, that Ho may have been a communist but was no tool of Stalin, and that Paris was in fact playing the United States. Most importantly, it would have known that Stalin did not even support the Vietminh, politically or militarily, owing to his personal antipathy toward Ho and fear of alienating French decision-makers. Unfortunately, this would not be the last time ignorance of Vietnamese realities prejudiced the judgment of American policymakers and resulted in adoption of deeply flawed, counterproductive policies.

BAO DAI SOLUTION

French efforts to curry favor with American policymakers culminated in the March 1949 signing of the Élysée Agreement between Paris and the former Nguyen Emperor, Bao Dai. Under the terms of the agreement (which the French National Assembly did not ratify until January 1950), France renounced all claims to Vietnam, including Cochinchina, and consented to the creation of the State of Vietnam (SOVN), an ostensibly independent country. This new country, invested on 2 July that same year, was legally subordinated to France and "associated" with – not an integral part of – the French Union. Its government under Bao Dai himself was based in Saigon, had no constitution and, it turned out, very limited authority. It did, however, have an army of its own, the Vietnamese National Army (VNA), trained and commanded by French officers. In making this concession, Paris satisfied the aspiration of non-communist Vietnamese nationalists and republicans, who for years had been urging it to create an autonomous Vietnamese state to rival the one set up by the communists in Hanoi. Claiming sovereignty and jurisdiction over all of Vietnam, the SOVN did challenge the DRVN's own legitimacy, and stole some of the thunder of Ho's regime.

Adoption of this "Bao Dai solution" for Vietnam, and implementation of similar arrangements for Laos and Cambodia shortly thereafter, did the trick for France. Seen as evidence of its willingness to grant independence to the Indochinese once the Vietminh was defeated, the initiatives delighted US decision-makers, who for months had been pressing their French counterparts to devolve political power in Indochina to satisfy local nationalist aspirations, rally world opinion, and make American economic assistance and arms sales to France more palatable to Congress. By late 1949, the Indochina War was no longer a colonial and civil war; it was morphing into a contest between two competing systems, two political visions, a quintessential Cold War proxy conflict.

CHINESE INVOLVEMENT

In October 1949, the Chinese Civil War ended with the triumph of Mao Zedong's armies and the founding of the People's Republic of China (PRC) under the CCP. Chiang Kai-shek's anti-communist government and the remnants of his forces fled to Taiwan, which became the new home base for the Republic of China and the GMD. The advent of the PRC was a turning point in the history of the Vietnamese struggle for reunification and independence. No sooner had Mao had a chance to consolidate his authority in Beijing, and establish a functional government, than he turned his attention to Indochina. In January 1950, the PRC became the first country to recognize the DRVN as Vietnam's sole representative government. Most crucially, it started funneling generous and desperately-needed military assistance to the Vietminh. Within weeks, the Soviet Union and the rest of the communist camp had also extended diplomatic recognition to Ho's government. They were not as keen to proffer weapons, however.

Enthused by these auspicious developments, Ho Chi Minh traveled to Moscow in February 1950 seeking a formal treaty of alliance with the Soviet Union, as Mao had secured for his country just days before. Stalin turned him down. The Soviet Union had no interest in promoting revolution in Asia beyond China. Above all, Stalin feared the implications in Europe and in France in particular of a formal military commitment to the DRVN. Besides, during his recent meeting with Mao, the two men had consented to a "division of labor" in advancing global communism. By the terms of that agreement, China would take the lead in Asia as the Soviet Union took charge in Europe and elsewhere. According to one source, Stalin actually laughed upon hearing Ho's request for a treaty with Moscow. By other accounts, Stalin said "no" because he was getting word from Ho's own Vietnamese comrades that the DRVN President could not be trusted. Recycling many of the charges levied against Ho by ICP radicals in the early 1930s, these hardliners claimed that Ho remained an opportunist, whose political convictions and commitment to the Vietnamese Revolution were not genuine. He was not a true communist; he showed too little actual interest in class struggle and proletarian internationalism. Ho was a bourgeois nationalist at heart who posed as a devout Marxist–Leninist to satisfy narrow personal ambitions. He lacked "faith in the revolutionary forces of the proletariat," and his personality was "divisive."[2] These serious allegations against the DRVN President by his own peers, prompted as they were by Ho's personal history, endorsement of the ICP's dissolution in 1945, and diplomatic compromises with the French, attest to the contentious nature of Vietnamese communist politics, even in wartime. They also demonstrate that Ho, the purportedly universally admired founder of the modern Vietnamese state, always had disparagers, even within his own party.

As part of its aid package to the Vietminh, Beijing dispatched two of its generals plus hundreds of political and military advisers of the Chinese Military Advisory Group (CMAG) for Indochina, created in April 1950. The Chinese also established various training facilities, including a military school, for Vietminh cadres and soldiers on their side of the border. Thousands of members of the Vietminh received training there, markedly improving their efficiency on and off the battlefield, turning them into professional soldiers. Thanks to Chinese intercession on their behalf, Stalin eventually changed his mind and started extending military aid to the Vietminh, but in limited quantities and for use only in Laos and Cambodia to lessen the likelihood of affronting France.

AMERICAN INVOLVEMENT

The "loss" of China to communism, the assistance provided by Mao to the Vietminh, and diplomatic recognition of the DRVN by the communist camp and the Soviet Union in particular resonated in the United States. Most consequentially, these developments alerted the Truman administration to the dangers of leaving communist expansion in Asia unchecked. Their impact was amplified by a string of contemporaneous, disturbing events attributed to communist agitation and provocation. Among those were the advent and consolidation of Stalinist regimes across East Europe; the Berlin Blockade and attendant airlift, lasting from June 1948 until May 1949; the Soviet Union's detonation of an atomic bomb in August 1949; and, the onset of anti-Western and/or communist insurgencies in Malaya (1948), Burma (1948), and Indonesia (1949), which fueled American concerns about Asian countries falling victim to communist subversion, one after another, like a row of tipping dominoes.

Before long, the international situation was causing fear bordering on hysteria among the American public and in Washington. Wisconsin Republican Senator Joseph McCarthy (1908–57) was both a product of and spark plug for that hysteria. During a February 1950 speech in Wheeling, West Virginia, McCarthy claimed to possess a classified document, handed to him by Secretary of State Dean Acheson (1893–1971), containing the names of 205 State Department employees belonging to the Communist Party of the United States. This came a month after Alger Hiss (1904–96), a ranking State Department official, was found guilty of spying for the Soviet Union (though perjury was the official charge) and sentenced to two concurrent five-year terms. But McCarthy was not done. Over ensuing weeks and months, he alleged Soviet spy rings had also infiltrated schools, labor unions, the Hollywood film industry, even the armed forces. Witch-hunts by the House Committee on Un-American Activities and other congressional committees followed. While it turned out that all of McCarthy's claims were either grossly exaggerated or just plain false, they were credible enough at the time to cause a "Second Red Scare" in the United States.[3]

This perfect storm of unsettling international and domestic developments dramatically increased the pressure on Truman to answer real or perceived threats to American interests abroad and, above all, to take a tough stance against communism. Thus press-ganged, and afraid of looking weak in the eyes of Congress and the public, his administration undertook a series of bold initiatives affirming its commitment to halting the spread of communism. The most dramatic and far-reaching of these was adoption in April 1950 of National Security Council document 68. "NSC-68" effectively globalized the Cold War by expanding the focus on containing communism from Europe to the rest of the world, and decolonizing and newly-decolonized "Third World" states in particular. Most significant, it called for militarizing the struggle against communism, until then fought largely by economic means.

The sum of these circumstances prompted the Truman administration to tag the Vietminh as a communist movement, and thus a danger to American geopolitical, economic, and ideological interests. Following that verdict, it extended formal diplomatic recognition to the SOVN in February 1950. Then, on 8 May, Secretary of State Acheson fatefully pledged the first direct US military and economic aid package, worth $15 million, to France's war in Indochina. The package included military advisers of the newly minted Military Assistance and Advisory Group, Indochina (MAAG), Washington's answer to the Chinese CMAG, to train and advise Bao Dai's armed forces. North Korea's invasion of the South in June 1950 validated Americans' worst fears about communism, and convinced Washington to increase and indefinitely extend its assistance to France and the SOVN.

By the middle of 1950, the United States had firmly committed to containing the DRVN: Vietnam. According to Mark Lawrence, the "period of possibility" – that is, the period for avoiding direct entanglement in Indochinese affairs – ended at this juncture. Thereafter, "patterns of thought" laid in place in 1949–50 "drove American policy uninterruptedly to 1965 and beyond."[4] Indeed, for the next quarter century, the "Vietnam problem" would concern, if not outrightly consume, Washington decision-makers.

SECOND PARTY CONGRESS

Buoyed by Chinese support, Ho and the DRVN leadership shifted to a different strategy in 1950. The year before they had begun conscripting men aged eighteen to forty-five in areas they controlled. Now that their

armed forces were larger and better equipped, they moved to system-
atically drive the French out of Tonkin, starting from the Chinese border, in part to facilitate further procurements of military and other aid
from the PRC. Relying upon mass-combat methods for the first time,
they scored a dramatic victory over the French in the border province
of Cao Bang in October 1950. The Vietminh could fight conventional
battles after all, even defeat France's armies in them. Despite a major
setback at Vinh Yen in January the following year, Vietminh troops persevered. Still, the war proved costly as the sustained influx of American aid
substantially increased the lethality of French forces. The Indochina War
was fast becoming a violent expression of the Cold War. While its internationalization made the conflict itself deadlier, it did nothing to change
the balance of forces as Chinese assistance to the Vietminh was offset by
American aid to France.

In February 1951, in the wake of the Vinh Yen defeat, Vietnamese
communists held their Second Congress, the first such meeting in over
two decades. Their numbers had grown exponentially by then, to nearly
half a million members, but their overall quality was poor. Party leaders
called the meeting hoping to redress that and other pressing problems
their movement faced. Before an assembly of more than 200 delegates,
Ho admitted that disbanding the ICP in 1945 had been a mistake, and
strained relations with Moscow while causing dissent and weakness
within the Vietnamese communist movement itself. After largely for-
mulaic deliberations, the delegates rubber-stamped a proposal to formally resuscitate the Party as a Vietnamese, not Indochinese, one, which
Ho had wanted all along. The Vietnamese Workers' Party (VWP), as it
became known, would henceforth decide DRVN domestic and foreign
policy while asserting authority over the Vietminh.

The political platform adopted at the Congress stressed the imperative need to sustain the war against France until complete victory. To
meet that end, it called for improving organizational leadership and discipline by streamlining the Party, among other initiatives. It also mandated better mass organization and mobilization efforts at home, and a
resort to "people's diplomacy" – namely, exploitation and manipulation
of antiwar sentiment – abroad. Since liberating all of Indochina remained
crucial, the delegates also agreed to sponsor the creation of separate communist parties in Laos and Cambodia to spearhead revolutions there.
Ostensibly national organizations, the Pathet Lao and Khmer Issarak in
Laos and Cambodia, respectively, would in fact answer largely to and
remain under the influence of Vietnamese decision-makers.

The outcome of the Congress attenuated to some degree suspicions about Ho's commitment to Marxism–Leninism and proletarian internationalism among his peers and in Moscow. It also affirmed the place of the Vietnamese communist movement in the communist camp, which in turn cemented the DRVN's ties to China and the Soviet Union. Publicly, however, Ho and the DRVN leadership would continue to downplay their links to Beijing and Moscow while maintaining their commitment to nationalism and patriotism to curry favor with public opinion in the West and non-communist nationalists at home. To that same end, in March, DRVN authorities merged the Vietminh with the Lien Viet, the other purportedly non-communist united front created in 1946 to rally patriots hesitant to fight for the DRVN, and christened the new, joint movement the Lien Viet Front (though most people in and outside of Vietnam continued to refer to the organization as Vietminh).

IMPASSE

By late 1952, the Vietminh counted nearly 150,000 troops and more than five million sympathizers. The enemy boasted some 200,000 troops in the SOVN armed forces, the VNA, plus 190,000 men in the French Expeditionary Army. The balance of forces – the barometer by which DRVN leaders measured progress in the war – thus remained unfavorable. It actually worsened because of the introduction of the draft by SOVN authorities in mid-1951 and the consequent swelling of VNA ranks. France's ever-mounting reliance on indigenous soldiers alarmed DRVN leaders, who feared the long-term implications of Vietnamese-on-Vietnamese violence. Civil wars always left deep, sometimes incurable scars.

Despite meaningful gains in Tonkin and Annam in 1952–3, Vietminh efforts to unseat the French in Southern Vietnam and in Laos and Cambodia were largely unsuccessful. As the war stalemated, destruction and casualties mounted, boding ill for the DRVN's long-term prospects. To make up for these and other difficulties on the military front, Ho and the DRVN leadership escalated their political and diplomatic activities. With advice and training from their Chinese allies, they devised propaganda campaigns targeting both domestic and foreign publics. Winning over public opinion at home and abroad, they surmised, would serve to diplomatically "isolate" Saigon and Paris, ratcheting the pressure on them to desist. Central to the purposes of DRVN leaders was convincing people that the Vietminh's struggle against France was first and foremost an anti-colonial resistance to restore Vietnamese independence, territorial unity, and dignity. Almost invariably, official and public statements to that end evoked the myth of Vietnamese indomitability in the face of external aggression by a big power, which resonated deeply in Vietnam and, in time, in the West as well.

To rally peasants and show Moscow their commitment to class struggle and thus obtain more Soviet aid, in 1953 DRVN authorities instituted a land confiscation and redistribution program, and slashed rents in areas they controlled. (In all "liberated" areas, residents were expected to pay reasonable rents and taxes to the local Vietminh administration, which used the revenue to purchase goods and services from these same residents. It was against policy to take from the people without proper compensation. That practice remained in place during the American War, and became one of the reasons Southern peasants tolerated, if not outrightly supported, the communist side.) They had carried out a similar program in 1948, with inconsequential results due to botched implementation. Ho had been hesitant to aggressively pursue the program back then for fear of alienating Vietminh troops and sympathizers from "bourgeois" backgrounds and pushing landlords into the arms of the French. Now, however, he and other DRVN leaders felt that the advantages of land reform outweighed its disadvantages, especially with poor peasants playing such an important role in the Revolution. Besides, during a visit to Moscow in October 1952, Ho had promised Stalin, who insisted on class struggle and thus on land reform, that he would do his best to meet his expectation.

In order to ensure success in the new campaign, Ho asked for, and received from Mao, experts who had previously supervised a similar program in China. For the first time, Ho's party simultaneously pursued political and social revolution. It even established a Ministry of Public Security under Tran Quoc Hoan (1916–86) to ensure compliance with its directives and supervise "people's tribunals" to deal with those accused of standing in the way of the reform process. Hoan was a tough and uncompromising man who became known as the "Beria of Vietnam," after Stalin's own ruthless, infamous public security chief.

Internationalization of the war and radicalization of the Vietnamese Revolution unnerved Ho, as did increased reliance on China. By mid-1953 he was questioning his side's ability to prevail without leading the country to total ruin or dependence on a foreign power. After seven years, the war still had no end in sight. Committed as ever to complete victory, Ho concluded that for the foreseeable future at least that outcome was unlikely. For all their valiance and sacrifices, his forces could not dislodge the French from strategic parts of Vietnam and the rest of Indochina. They had admittedly scored important victories since the war's onset, but not enough to win it. The enemy's troop strength – counting metropolitan French, *tirailleurs*, Foreign Legion, and VNA forces – remained nearly twice that of the Vietminh.

As the war had become by this time inextricably linked to the Cold War interests of the great powers, Ho was also deeply concerned about possible American intervention in it. The death of Stalin in March 1953, plus the end of the war in Korea that July, might well encourage the United States to commit even more resources to Indochina, Ho thought. Judging by the volume of American assistance to France in 1953, the administration of President Dwight Eisenhower (in office 1953–61) seemed determined to preclude a Vietminh victory at all cost. Eisenhower's threat to rain atomic bombs on China unless Beijing concluded the negotiations on Korea that summer attested, in Ho's eyes, to the American President's visceral hatred of communism, and willingness to use any means necessary to meet the goals of his administration in Asia.

NEGOTIATIONS

Ho eventually concluded he had two options: continue hostilities on current terms, or push for a negotiated solution. The first option was consistent with the Party's political platform, but required the nation as a whole to endure more sacrifice, distress, deprivation, and other hardships for an indeterminate period. Most problematic, it risked provoking American intervention. The second option, negotiation, would potentially deliver peace sooner rather than later, but defer national reunification and sovereignty. It also risked emboldening the enemy by signaling weakness on the DRVN's part.

Ho had no easy choices. Luckily for him, Paris blinked first. In October 1953, Prime Minister Joseph Laniel (in office 1953–4) declared his government was seeking an "honorable exit" from Indochina, and to that end would accept a negotiated settlement of the war. Days later, a DRVN representative informed a meeting of the World Peace Council – an intergovernmental organization sponsored by Moscow to counter-balance the adjudged Western-dominated United Nations (UN) – that ending the war with France through negotiations was an "effort" his government could fulfill. In late November, Ho himself openly signaled his willingness to talk, telling a Swedish newspaper that his government was prepared to resolve its differences with France by negotiations. If Paris wanted to "solve the Vietnam problem by peaceful means," Ho affirmed, his side was "ready to meet this desire." But he added an important caveat: the negotiations must be bilateral, between the French and DRVN governments, and involve no other parties, especially the United States.

Not everyone in Ho's camp was pleased with his decision. Some military commanders believed continuing the war until final victory was the only way to achieve the country's liberation, reunification, and independence. Fighting, they argued, was "an essential form of struggle;" only violence could "solve revolutionary problems" and "liberate the people" while guaranteeing the progress of communism.[5] Party hardliners agreed that the war should be fought to the bitter end. Ho, they thought, had reverted to his old, bourgeois habits of seeking accommodation and compromise with the enemy to escape a difficult situation.

Despite his comrades' misgivings, the DRVN President remained adamantly committed to a diplomatic solution. First, he believed – correctly, it turned out – that the Indochinese masses had grown tired of war and badly wanted peace. Indulging that desire, he thought, would endear his government and the Vietminh to those masses, enhancing the Revolution's long-term prospects. Second, the DRVN needed to temper "warmongers" in France and the United States calling for escalation of the war, and give Eisenhower no pretext to commit US combat forces in Indochina. Third, direct negotiations with France through an official channel would enhance the legitimacy of the DRVN government domestically and abroad, facilitating recruitment of new supporters and increasing the pressure on Paris and Washington to relent. Lastly, the Soviet Union and China were growing weary of the Indochina War. They favored its prompt conclusion, and Ho felt he needed to heed their desire. To be sure, the end of the Korean War in 1953 greatly dampened their enthusiasm for the conflict in Indochina. For Beijing, the Korean armistice offered an opportunity to finally start rebuilding and transforming along communist lines the Chinese state, which had been continuously experiencing war in one form or another for fifteen years by then. Considering the DRVN's dependency on Chinese material assistance, Ho would have been remiss to ignore Mao's wishes. Meanwhile, the succession crisis in Moscow triggered by the death of Stalin seemed to imperil the Soviet Union's commitment to the Vietminh.

Following consultations among them, spurred by the Korean armistice and the prospect of enhanced superpower cooperation, the big powers agreed to sponsor an international conference on Indochina, to open in Geneva right after the end of pre-scheduled talks on Korea beginning shortly. Ho welcomed the news, but took exception to the proposed format. The more parties were involved in the talks, he thought, the more interests would have to be accommodated, and the more difficult it would be for France and the DRVN to reach consensus on critical issues. Moreover, Ho feared that under the proposed format bigger powers might dominate the proceedings, and their interests trump those of the DRVN. Moscow and especially Beijing had dutifully supported the DRVN and the Vietminh to this point, but might decide to use the conference to further their own agendas, irrespective of the effects in Vietnam. After all, Geneva was an important stage, and this would be the first major international gathering attended by representatives from the PRC. Washington, for its part, had made no secret of its opposition to a negotiated solution of the Indochina War, and might scuttle the talks just to have a pretext to intervene militarily in it. Ho much preferred, as he had previously told Swedish journalists, bilateral talks with France.

Despite strong reservations about it, Ho accepted the proposed format in the end. Since the war had become internationalized, the peace process might as well be, he reasoned. Besides, Ho never missed an opportunity to talk with the enemy when the chips were down, as they were to some degree for his side at the time.

RAISING THE STAKES

Once clear that the future of Indochina would be decided at the bargaining table, Ho and the rest of the DRVN leadership sought to improve their battlefield situation to increase their leverage in Geneva and negotiate from a position of strength. They possessed limited negotiating experience, but enough to understand that success at the bargaining table was contingent upon success on the battlefield. After all, belligerents rarely won through talks what they could not secure in war. Subsuming military under diplomatic struggle, DRVN authorities undertook a series of bold military initiatives in late 1953 intended to tip the balance of forces in their favor before the opening of the Geneva talks. Specifically, they set out to thwart the French military strategy laid out in the so-called Navarre Plan. The brainchild of General Henri Navarre (1898–1983), Commander of French forces in Indochina, the three-stage plan called for beefing up the VNA and re-positioning

French units across Indochina; pacifying Cochinchina while maintaining a defensive posture in Tonkin and Annam and stopping Vietminh incursions into Laos; and, upon completion of those objectives, finishing off the Vietminh by going after its strongholds in Viet Bac and other parts of Tonkin.

Consistent with his plan, Navarre ordered the establishment of a large military outpost in Northwestern Tonkin to "choke" Vietminh forces operating in Laos, dependent on supplies and reinforcements from Viet Bac. Laos mattered to France for symbolic as much as practical reasons. Paris considered its government the friendliest among its colonial possessions, and thus a model member of the French Union. In October 1953, Paris and the Royal Lao Government in Vientiane signed a Treaty of Amity and Association by which France recognized the independence and sovereignty of Laos in exchange for the reaffirmation of its membership in France's global commonwealth. Failure to shield the Laotian government from external and internal threats thus risked compromising the French Union by raising doubts about its practicality among current and prospective members.

On 20 November 1953, the first of several French units parachuted into Dien Bien Phu, a remote valley of Northwestern Vietnam that commanded access to various routes into landlocked Laos. The Japanese had built an airfield there during World War II, another reason Navarre favored the site. Soon, the French garrison at Dien Bien Phu grew to over 12,000 troops and support personnel. At first, DRVN leaders did not know what to do about the remote outpost. That all changed on 18 February, when the big powers, meeting for a summit in Berlin, confirmed the Geneva Conference on Indochina would open no later than the first week of May. From that moment, crushing the garrison became the top priority of DRVN leaders, who reasoned that victory at Dien Bien Phu would almost guarantee a favorable outcome in Geneva, if not France's outright capitulation.

The DRVN leadership thus set out to annihilate the outpost, a senior Vietminh commander explained later, "to co-ordinate with the diplomatic activities then about to start in Geneva."[6] Ho told Vo Nguyen Giap, whom he put in charge of the campaign, that Dien Bien Phu represented "a very important battle not only militarily, but also politically, not only domestically, but also internationally."[7] Victory, Ho was certain, would cause a dramatic shift in the balance of power, in Tonkin at least, and convince Paris that it would lose everything if the war continued. The remote, heretofore unimportant but soon-to-be famous valley suddenly became the fulcrum on which the DRVN's prospects for success in Geneva – and in the Indochina War – rested.

The decision to challenge the French at Dien Bien Phu was a major gamble for Ho's regime, to say the least. It also created a logistical nightmare for Giap and the General Staff tasked with coordinating the campaign. As part of the preparations, the Vietminh recruited and otherwise conscripted no less than 255,899 *dan cong*, "patriotic workers" or "coolies" in derogatory Western parlance, to supply and sustain the 45,000 main force combatants to be deployed against the French garrison. Many *dan cong* were members of the Tai minority ethnic group, including several women, lured by promises of land. In the weeks leading up to the battle, *dan cong* used a combined total of 824 horses, 19,341 modified bicycles with a carrying capacity of 400 to 650 pounds each, 911 oxcarts, 820 horsecars, 11,000 watercraft, forty-one automobiles, and 551 wheelbarrows to move more than 26,000 tons of food and other supplies, plus thousands more tons of weapons and ammunition, over miles of treacherous, inhospitable, and mountainous jungle terrain. In retrospect, Giap would never have been able to sustain a lengthy siege of the enemy garrison without that support. *Dan cong* also helped Vietminh troops haul heavy artillery, namely, 105mm howitzers, weighing close to 5,000 pounds each, up the mountains surrounding the valley. Those guns and their positioning would give the Vietminh a critical advantage over the French after the battle began.

Increased assistance from China, no longer burdened by its involvement in the Korean War, vastly improved Vietminh capabilities at Dien Bien Phu. Mao was quick to recognize the merits of Ho's strategy, and supported his forces accordingly, sending them some 200 trucks, 10,000 barrels of oil, 100 cannons, 3,000 guns of various kinds, 2,400,000 rounds of ammunition, 60,000 artillery shells, and massive quantities of foodstuff. A good portion of the small arms and artillery pieces supplied by Beijing had been captured from rival GMD forces in the Chinese Civil War and from South Korean and UN/US troops in the Korean War, including the aforementioned 105mm howitzer guns. Since the Vietminh lacked the expertise to operate some of that equipment, Mao also dispatched specialized technicians, advisers, and artillery crews to provide training. Paris later claimed that the presence of Chinese gun crews at Dien Bien Phu had constituted direct military intervention in the Indochina War by China. Two Chinese generals were also on-site to counsel Giap as he planned his attack.

FIGURE 2.1 *Dan cong* delivering supplies to the front during the Battle of Dien Bien Phu, 1954. Courtesy of the Vietnamese Ministry of Foreign Affairs and National Archives Center 3, Hanoi.

BATTLE OF DIEN BIEN PHU

Giap originally intended to launch the assault on Dien Bien Phu on 25 January at precisely 5pm. His strategy, "lightning battle, lightning victory," called for an all-out attack on the French garrison to deliver victory expeditiously, in as little as two or three days. As often happens in war, things did not go as planned. The day before the attack was set to begin, Giap got word that one of his men had ventured too close to enemy lines during a reconnaissance mission, and been captured. Thinking the soldier might, under torture, reveal both the nature and timing of the attack, Giap decided to postpone it by twenty-four hours to maintain the element of surprise. When he woke up the morning of the 26th, Giap was no longer certain of his prospects for victory. This posed a problem, as Ho had personally insisted that no attack take place unless Giap could guarantee a win. Also, by now the number of enemy troops at Dien Bien Phu exceeded 14,000. Following consultations with his subordinates, and a conversation with Head Chinese Military Adviser Wei Guoqing (1913–89), Giap chose to put the attack on hold indefinitely, to the shock and disappointment of many of his troops. He explained later that this was by far the toughest decision he ever had to make as military commander.

Over the next two and a half weeks, Giap reassessed his entire strategy, eventually abandoning the "lightning" approach in favor of what he dubbed "steady attacks, steady advances." This would require more patience and time, possibly weeks instead of days, but greatly improve the odds for victory. As they awaited the launching of the attack, Vietminh forces consolidated their positions and, in accordance with Giap's instructions, embedded into the mountainside the heavy guns they had previously hauled up the ridges surrounding Dien Bien Phu to better protect them from enemy aerial and artillery bombings. That, it turned out, proved a brilliant decision.

Giap finally launched the assault on 13 March, at 5pm sharp. It began with an artillery barrage, followed by human-wave attacks on French positions reminiscent of Chinese tactics in the Korea War, and in fact recommended by the Chinese generals at Dien Bien Phu. After three days, Vietminh forces took the first fortified positions from the French, but at a staggering cost of more than 2,000 killed and 7,000 wounded. Concluding that such a high casualty rate was unsustainable, Giap suspended human-wave attacks and, by some accounts, sent both Chinese generals packing. He revised his strategy, again, settling on a "protracted war" approach. Telling his troops to prepare for a long fight, he ordered them to encircle the French and slowly tighten the "noose" around them by digging trenches and tunnels closer and closer to French positions as his gun crews rained artillery on them. Giap thought this revised plan was his best hope for success, though it could take several weeks if not months before his forces delivered final victory. As he explained later:

In striking surely and advancing cautiously, we could keep complete initiative, attack the enemy at any time and at any fronts as we liked; we would attack him only when we were sufficiently prepared and sure of victory, otherwise we would not attack or would delay the attack; we would defend only the positions which had to be defended and could be defended, otherwise we would not defend; after a battle, we would wage another one immediately if possible, otherwise we could take a rest to reorganize our forces and make better preparations for the next battle.[8]

Luckily for Giap, *dan cong* had delivered, and continued to deliver, to the front enough food, weapons, and ammunition to support a long fight.

As the battle raged, and they realized the Vietminh would not be easily defeated, the French dispatched Army Chief-of-Staff Paul Ély

(1897–1975) to Washington to beseech US military intervention. The idea took the form of operation *Vulture*, massive nighttime bombardments of Vietminh positions and supply lines in and around Dien Bien Phu by the US Air Force. American air crews had already flown supply missions in support of the French, but not combat sorties. President Eisenhower was lukewarm about the idea of military intervention, having only recently gotten US forces out of Korea and committed his administration to a "New Look" policy of nuclear deterrence and reductions in military spending. He agreed to come to the assistance of France, but only in concert with other countries, and Britain in particular. London, however, declined the offer for "united action," as the Americans called it. That was enough for the Eisenhower administration to scrap its plan for intervention. The same day the White House rendered its decision to Ély, 8 April, US Secretary of State John Foster Dulles (1888–1959) supposedly offered French Foreign Minister George Bidault (1899–1983) two atomic bombs for use against the Vietminh at Dien Bien Phu. Whatever the veracity of this story and the seriousness of the American offer, that, too, never materialized.

FALL OF THE FRENCH GARRISON

On 7 May 1954, less than twenty-four hours before the opening of the Geneva Conference on Indochina, Dien Bien Phu fell to the Vietminh. The battle had lasted fifty-five days. By the time it was all over, the French had suffered approximately 1,700 killed and 4,400 wounded. One woman, a nurse, and some 11,000 men, including the wounded, were taken prisoner (858 of the more seriously wounded were returned to the French in the ensuing days). By French estimates, some 1,600 troops went missing-in-action (MIA) during the engagement, many of whom deserted or rallied to the Vietminh. That was hardly surprising. The bulk of the garrison consisted of non-citizens of France, including legionnaires, Africans, and Indochinese. Some of these men were far less invested in the defense of French interests in Indochina than their metropolitan counterparts, and thus more susceptible to Vietminh propaganda urging them to abscond as the battle raged.

Several factors contributed to Giap and the Vietminh's success at Dien Bien Phu. Among the most notable was the use of heavy artillery, which caught defenders completely unprepared, and undercut both their capabilities and morale. According to wartime correspondent and historian Bernard Fall, the "real surprise" for the French was not that the Vietminh had artillery; it was, instead, that they were able to transport "a considerable mass" of it "across roadless mountains to Dien Bien Phu and to keep it supplied with a sufficient amount of ammunition to make the huge effort worth-while."[9] As this suggests, the French High Command underestimated its adversaries while overrating the capabilities of its own forces. Dien Bien Phu was not an "impregnable fortress" after all, as Navarre had alleged and US Vice President Richard Nixon (1913–94) reiterated during an earlier visit there.

Giap's victory over the French at Dien Bien Phu may have been unequivocal, but it was also horrendously costly. Vietminh forces suffered approximately 7,900 killed and at least 15,000 wounded during the battle. Thousands more *dan cong* died from exhaustion, dehydration, malnutrition, and diseases, their sacrifice largely forgotten. Tons of equipment were destroyed and munitions expended. In light of these results, public praise for the "momentous" triumph over the French at Dien Bien Phu by Ho and other DRVN leaders was echoed by private cautions against hubris and complacency. Truong Chinh, by now the Party Secretary, privately remarked shortly after the epic battle that, while the victory was important, it had done little to change the overall balance of forces between the two sides. Across the whole country and the rest of Indochina, he noted, Vietminh strength remained, at best, "only equal to the enemy's."[10] The balance of forces remained unchanged also partly because Paris, seemingly undeterred by the defeat at Dien Bien Phu, immediately dispatched more troops to Indochina. Left to run its course the war could easily take a turn for the worse, Truong Chinh, Ho, and other DRVN leaders thought, particularly if Washington decided to intervene. Since 1950 the United States had spent more than $3 billion in Indochina. By the time of Dien Bien Phu, it footed nearly eighty percent of the French war bill.

All things being equal, Ho and the Vietminh won a critical battle at Dien Bien Phu, but not the war itself. In fact, considering their losses, the arrival of French reinforcements, and Washington's unknown disposition vis-à-vis Indochina at the time, their battlefield situation was almost as precarious after the battle as it had been before. The outcome at Dien Bien Phu did, however, cast a big shadow over the talks about to get underway in Geneva. The DRVN also gained a significant bargaining chip in the guise of more than 10,000 new POWs, adding to thousands already in custody. For the DRVN's diplomatic struggle, at least, Dien Bien Phu was an important victory.

FIGURE 2.2 General Vo Nguyen Giap (center) assessing the situation in the immediate aftermath of the victory over the French at Dien Bien Phu, 1954. Courtesy of the Vietnamese Ministry of Foreign Affairs and National Archives Center 3, Hanoi.

GENEVA CONFERENCE

The Indochina phase of the Geneva Conference opened on 8 May 1954, a day after the fall of the French garrison. This was no coincidence. After agreeing to participate in those talks the previous year, Ho Chi Minh had instructed his military commanders to do what they could on the ground to improve the DRVN's prospects at the bargaining table, and closely coordinate their activities with the negotiations about to get underway in Switzerland. This fine calibration of military and diplomatic activities was intended to enable the DRVN to negotiate from a position of strength, and achieve the best deal possible, as previously noted.

In the immediate aftermath of Dien Bien Phu, some Vietminh commanders and Party members thought Ho ought to build on the momentum resulting from the successful campaign, forego negotiations, and keep fighting until total victory. To their dismay, Ho opted for caution, as he often did, and proceeded as planned. The triumph over the French had been stunning and dramatic, Ho acknowledged, but the cost had been exorbitant, and troops were tired. On top of that, at a time when those troops had barely enough to feed themselves, they had to sustain thousands of new French POWs. With Vietnamese opinion favoring the end of hostilities, Ho and the DRVN would have been hard-pressed to keep fighting. By 1954, the country had been at war more or less continuously for thirteen years, to say nothing of the yoke of colonial rule before that. While the prevalence of fatigue and war weariness among both combatants and the masses troubled Ho, his greatest concern remained the prospect of US intervention, which he thought was looming and sure to prove devastating if it materialized, especially now. In a letter to his forces after Dien Bien Phu, Ho warned that their triumph was "only the beginning;" the road ahead "may be long and hard" before "complete victory can be achieved," he wrote. For now a break in the fighting was not just preferable, it was imperative; if not to give combatants and civilians a chance to rest, then to preempt American intervention. The alternative was too risky, and Ho did not like risky.

At this juncture, the Eisenhower administration was in fact seriously considering intervention. After the fall of Dien Bien Phu, hawks in Congress pressed the President to take a firmer stance against communist expansion in Asia. For Eisenhower, however, the Korean War, marked as it had been by Chinese intervention, served as a potent reminder of the pitfalls of combatting communism too aggressively in that part of the world. Ultimately, the American President decided against intervention in Indochina, for the same reason he had refused to help the French before: he could not get other countries to support such a move. To his credit, however, he kept Ho guessing long enough to persuade him to not forego negotiations and to abandon, for now, his pursuit of total victory. A US Defense Department study revealed later that the "unpredictability" of American actions in Indochina that summer had been "fostered purposely" to confuse Vietnamese communists.[11] And confuse them it did.

The DRVN entered the Geneva Conference bent on reaching a deal with France, and cautiously optimistic about its ability to do so. Dien Bien Phu and the POWs gave it considerable leverage, as did the widespread unpopularity of the war in France. But DRVN authorities also faced certain constraints and liabilities of their own. French control of Laos and Cambodia remained essentially total, as it was in many cities and parts of Southern Vietnam. Then there was the lack of diplomatic experience of DRVN negotiators. The head of the delegation, Premier and Foreign Minister Pham Van Dong, was a seasoned revolutionary and highly capable man, who had represented the regime alongside Ho in the Fontainebleau talks of 1946. But neither he nor his colleagues in Geneva, or even Ho himself and decision-makers back in Vietnam for that matter, had ever been involved in a conference of this magnitude, on such an important stage. Besides the DRVN and France, participants included the governments of Britain and the Soviet Union, which jointly chaired the conference, as well as the United States, the PRC, the SOVN, and the pro-French, royal governments of Laos and Cambodia. The DRVN's biggest liability, however, was its desperate need to achieve a ceasefire.

Although they harbored no illusions about achieving all their goals, DRVN leaders hoped at least to achieve a comprehensive settlement providing for the end of hostilities, and which recognized Vietnam's territorial integrity and sovereignty as well as their government's legitimacy. They outlined these hopes in a "maximalist" proposal submitted at the opening of the conference. It called for: an immediate ceasefire; regroupment of military forces into demarcated areas; exchange of all POWs; recognition of the independence, sovereignty, and territorial integrity of Vietnam, Cambodia, and Laos; free general elections in each of these countries to form independent and sovereign governments and, in the case of the DRVN, affirmation of its legitimacy; and, withdrawal of all foreign forces from Indochina before the elections. Naturally, France rejected that formula. Leaders there wanted peace, but a peace they could live with, that would accommodate so far as possible their imperialist conceits. And so no sooner had the talks begun than they stalled. DRVN leaders needed peace as badly as Paris wanted it, but they, too, were not yet desperate enough to make the kinds of concessions necessary to break the deadlock.

SETTLEMENT

On 19 June 1954, Bao Dai, the largely ceremonial head of the SOVN, appointed Ngo Dinh Diem to lead his government. A Catholic from Central Vietnam, the forty-year-old Diem had previously served as Minister of the Interior in the Saigon government, earning a reputation as a hard-working, astute, fiercely nationalist, and resourceful administrator. Diem's appointment alarmed DRVN decision-makers. He had just returned from the United States, where he had spent three years studying in a seminary run by Cardinal Francis Spellman (1889–1967), an influential anti-communist Catholic cleric. During that time, the highly ambitious young Vietnamese had endeared himself to conservative and anti-communist American policymakers thanks to Spellman's extensive Washington connections, and personally urged some of them to do more in support of non-communist Vietnamese nationalists. Diem's American contacts, among them the fiery young Senator and fellow Catholic John

F. Kennedy (1917–63), were in fact the main reason Bao Dai selected him to be his new prime minister. With a familiar face at the helm of his government, Bao Dai reasoned, Washington was more likely to indulge his own aspirations in Geneva.

That stratagem was not lost on Ho, who interpreted Diem's return as presaging American intervention in the war and, at a minimum, interference in the Geneva process. And with that realization came another: the United States, not France, now constituted the DRVN's principal, most dangerous enemy. Suddenly, reaching a settlement with France became urgent for Ho. Without an agreement in Geneva, he thought, there would be no international limitations on what Washington could do in Indochina. Precluding American intervention thus became as compelling a reason to negotiate seriously for DRVN leaders as getting the French to stop fighting.

Owing largely to Ho, and his government's newfound compulsion to end the war with France before the Americans joined it, by the end of June the two sides had agreed on a framework for peace, calling for an Indochina-wide ceasefire, return of all POWs, temporary division of Vietnam into military regroupment zones, and national elections at an undetermined time leading to the country's reunification and complete independence under a single, fully sovereign government. Ironing out the specifics of the deal was trickier. The prickliest issue was the number and nature of the regroupment zones. The DRVN insisted on the creation of only two zones: a northern one for its forces and sympathizers, and a southern one for the French and their supporters. That would give Ho's government one contiguous area under its exclusive control. Conversely, Paris demanded a "leopard-spot" arrangement, that is, several disparate zones, to reflect its continued domination in all major cities and other regions, and prevent consolidation of the DRVN government's power.

The French eventually accepted the DRVN's partition proposal, contingent upon their retention of control over the urban enclaves of Hanoi and Haiphong, plus the Catholic-dominated Northern districts of Phat Diem and Bui Chu, which operated as a virtual theocratic state-within-a-state during the Indochina War. They also insisted on demarcating the two zones at the 17th parallel, to allow France to continue supplying landlocked Laos via Vietnamese Route 9 running just below that line. The DRVN rejected the idea of extended French control over portions of its regroupment zone, even their neutralization, fearing the French and, potentially, the Americans might use them to launch new attacks later. A second contentious issue was the deadline for reunification elections.

While France wanted no deadline, the DRVN demanded a delay of no longer than six months after the ceasefire. For Ho, an election guarantee represented a sure means to achieve national reunification under his government's exclusive control, as he had utmost confidence in his side's ability to prevail at the polls. The French privately shared that sentiment, which was largely the reason they refused to fix a deadline.

On 13 July, US Secretary of State Dulles made a pit stop in Geneva. The consummate and unrepentant cold warrior made quite an impression by refusing to shake the hand extended to him by PRC Premier and Foreign Minister Zhou Enlai during their first encounter. The impact on DRVN leaders of Dulles' sudden appearance and disposition was enormous, magnifying their fears of American intervention and solidifying Ho's resolve to end the war at once. During a special meeting of the VWP Central Committee held in Northwestern Vietnam on 15–7 July, which came on the heels of a secret conference between Ho, Giap, and Zhou at Liuzhou in Southern China, Ho stressed that, under current circumstances, finalizing a settlement represented the only way to avoid US intervention and protect the long-term interests of the Vietnamese Revolution. Secretary Truong Chinh, a loyal disciple of Ho at that time, seconded him on these points, claiming that the likelihood of American involvement was higher than ever. Getting a deal done on imperfect but reasonable terms, Truong Chinh argued, constituted their best chance to avoid war against an even more powerful enemy than France. Besides, he added, the proposed terms for a settlement were rather advantageous. The creation of only two regroupment zones would give the DRVN government jurisdiction over strategic locations, grant it direct access to considerable human and material resources, and enhance its legitimacy at home and abroad. The final resolution adopted at the conclusion of the meeting reflected Ho's and Truong Chinh's analyses and prescriptions. It also affirmed that Dien Bien Phu and other victories had for a period "changed the balance of forces between ourselves and the enemy in our favor," but ultimately done too little to affect the "strategic character" of the war. The resolution also cautioned that unless a negotiated settlement was achieved promptly, Washington would probably intervene directly and cause the balance of forces to "change to our disadvantage."

Only hours after the Central Committee meeting had adjourned, Pham Van Dong informed his French counterpart in Geneva that the DRVN accepted the 17th parallel as the partition line between the two regroupment zones. In return, the French consented to: a two-year deadline for national elections; the surrender of all areas, including Hanoi, Haiphong, and Catholic enclaves, north of the partition line; and, guarantees against the introduction of new foreign forces in Indochina. Ho deemed the latter concession a critical safeguard and deterrent against American intervention following the cessation of hostilities and the withdrawal of French forces. These concessions removed the last obstacles to peace, and the two sides signed the Agreement on the Cessation of Hostilities in Vietnam on 21 July 1954. Ominously, the American delegation made a point of noting Washington's objection to the Geneva formula. The SOVN, for its part, was not even party to it.

Historians have since maintained that the DRVN got the short end of the stick in Geneva: that it had to accept less-than-favorable terms because its interests got trumped by those of its own allies and other big powers, just as Ho had feared might happen. Admittedly, support for DRVN positions by both Moscow and Beijing was less than stellar as each big power was concerned more with successfully concluding the talks than helping DRVN negotiators and decision-makers secure what they legitimately deserved. During the negotiations both allies had, in fact, repeatedly urged the DRVN side to act in a conciliatory manner, even to abandon some of its core goals. Ultimately, however, Ho and the DRVN did what they did in Geneva, less because of pressure from those allies than their own trepidations about the possibility of American intervention. That, in the final analysis, most significantly conditioned their behavior in the talks. Unfortunately for Ho and his comrades, it was already too late: the United States was in Vietnam to stay.

Notes

1 Mark Atwood Lawrence, *Assuming the Burden: Europe and the American Commitment to War in Vietnam* (Berkeley: University of California Press, 2007), 31.
2 Quoted in Sophie Quinn-Judge, *Ho Chi Minh: The Missing Years, 1919–1941* (Berkeley: University of California Press, 2003), 254.
3 The First Red Scare (1917–20) resulted from the Bolshevik Revolution in Russia.
4 Lawrence, *Assuming the Burden*, 280, 282.
5 "So thao bao cao quan su o Quoc hoi lan thu 3 (12–1953)" [Preliminary Military Report to the Third Session of the National Assembly, December 1953], undated (December 1953); 1684: Bao cao thanh tich ve quan su trong 8 nam khang chien (Report on Military Achievements during the Past 8 Years of War) (1946–1954); Phong Quoc hoi; National Archives Center 3, Hanoi, Vietnam, 1–5.
6 Quoted in Tran Do, *Stories of Dien Bien Phu* (Hanoi: Foreign Languages Publishing House, 1962), 27.

7   Quoted in Cao Van Luong, "Chien thang Dien Bien Phu: thang qua cua y chi va quyet tam chien dau cua nhan dan Viet Nam vi doc lap, tu do va hoa binh" [The Dien Bien Phu Victory: Triumph of the Will and Determination of the Vietnamese People for Independence, Freedom, and Peace] in *Nghien cuu Lich su* [Historical Studies], no. 334 (2004), 20.

8   Vo Nguyen Giap, *Dien Bien Phu* (Hanoi: Foreign Languages Publishing House, 1984), 89.

9   Bernard B. Fall, *Hell in a Very Small Place: The Siege of Dien Bien Phu* (New York: Da Capo Press, 1966), 127.

10   "De hoan thanh nhiem vu va day manh cong tac truoc mat" [To Complete the Tasks and Promote the Work Ahead] in Dang Cong san Viet Nam, *Van kien Dang – Toan tap. Tap 15: 1954* [Party Documents – Collected Work. Volume 15: 1954] (Hanoi: Nha xuat ban Chinh tri quoc gia, 2001), 173–4.

11   "The Geneva Conference of 1954: Outcome & Significance for DRV, China, USSR, 1954"; Folder 03; Box 04; Unit 13 – The Early History of Vietnam; Douglas Pike Collection; The Vietnam Center and Archive at Texas Tech University, D-6.

3

Interwar Period, 1954–1965

CHOOSING PEACE

The signing of the Geneva accords marked an important milestone in the history of the Vietnamese struggle for independence. Excited as they were about peace, and the prospect of reclaiming jurisdiction over part of their country, DRVN leaders nonetheless had mixed feelings about them. Some thought the accords were unlikely to advance the revolutionary struggle, and might even set it back. Others, Ho among them, were cautiously optimistic their country would soon be reunified under communist authority, but remained concerned about a possible resumption of hostilities and American intervention in particular. Essentially, they hoped for the best but prepared for the worst. Despite these conflicting sentiments, Ho decided that it was worth giving peace, and the Geneva formula, a chance.

Consistent with the terms of the accords, DRVN authorities ordered Vietminh troops to cease fighting by the set deadlines (27 July in Tonkin; 1 August in Annam; 11 August in Cochinchina). They also instructed those below the 17th parallel to prepare for regroupment to the North within 300 days, as the accords mandated. Non-combatants, including communist cadres, could stay put. The authorities actually ordered most political operatives in the South to remain in place to disseminate their instructions, manage the regroupment of military personnel and their families to the North, and perform other organizational and propaganda tasks, such as exhorting the Southern population to insist that Saigon uphold its end of the Geneva deal. Approximately 85,000 cadres and Vietminh partisans stayed behind. An indeterminate number, possibly half, remained "active:" that is, they continued to take orders from Party leaders in the North. The rest saw no reason to remain engaged now that hostilities had ended, went back to their families, and became "inactive." The DRVN also handed back to France some 10,000 POWs, an equal number of whom, including two-thirds of the men captured at Dien Bien Phu, died in captivity. Some others refused to be repatriated, including Frenchmen but mostly colonial subjects from North Africa.

In violation of the accords, DRVN leaders kept a residual force of 10–15,000 seasoned troops in the South. However, those troops were under strict orders to take no action that could jeopardize the ceasefire; their presence was merely precautionary, in case the enemy resumed fighting. Interestingly, an unknown but good number of combatants stayed in the South against orders to regroup to the North. Leaving their homes, relatives, and ancestral lands behind to relocate to the North, where they had no roots or family, was one sacrifice they could not bring themselves to make. In a way, that was hardly surprising. Contrary to popular belief – informed as it has been by the myth of Vietnamese indomitability – Vietnamese are parochial and insular, even among themselves. This makes relocation from one part of the country to a distant other, and life in a new community, a very unattractive proposition. Still other Vietminh fighters in the South were so disheartened by Ho's decision to accept the accords, and consent to the country's partition and suspension of hostilities, that they decided to stop taking orders from his regime. Ho, they felt, had abandoned, even betrayed, them.

To be sure, Ho's decision to agree to and comply with the Geneva accords was a tough pill to swallow for Southerners who had fought France and its allies for nearly eight years only to find themselves with nothing to show for their efforts. Many were dismayed that the DRVN President had forfeited their hard-won gains in exchange for a vague pledge that France would support a national reunification referendum in two years. The "liberation" of the North was a positive development, but it mattered little to Southerners. Most dispiriting was Ho's insistence that fighters regroup to the North. That may have seemed sensible to a hardened, dedicated, and unattached revolutionary, but it was a lot to ask of the rank-and-file who just wanted to live in peace with their families on their ancestral land, under sovereign Vietnamese governance. Should the accords collapse and hostilities resume, which many thought was more than likely, their own families – if they did not regroup with them – and other relatives and friends would be at the total mercy of the enemy, with no means to protect themselves. Not only that, but regrouping the bulk of Southern Vietminh forces to the North would effectively eliminate their best leverage to encourage enemy compliance with the accords once the exchange of POWs was completed. From the perspective of many Vietminh combatants, and not just those in the South, the Geneva agreement had snatched defeat from the jaws of victory.

In the end, Ho's decision to endorse the Geneva formula proved even more controversial and divisive for his camp than his earlier decisions to dissolve the ICP in 1945 and accept the return of French forces in Tonkin a year later. Ho, it appeared to some of his detractors in the Party and government, seemed incapable of learning from his own mistakes. The DRVN President was well aware such attitudes existed among his followers, but was unmoved by them. In his own estimation, circumstances demanded strict adherence to the substance of the accords.

"NORTH-FIRST" POLICY

In October 1954, following completion of the French withdrawal from Hanoi, Ho's government relocated there and proclaimed the city its new capital. The domestic challenges the authorities faced at that point were daunting, to say the least. The Indochina War and the Japanese occupation before it had ravaged the Vietnamese economy, already chronically underdeveloped because of colonial rule. The transport infrastructure, where it still existed, was so pitiful as to be unusable. As a result of that and other factors, the food situation across the North was woeful. The situation was particularly bad in Tonkin, where the departing French took with them everything they could of any value, including factory machines and hospital equipment, destroyed what they left behind, and sabotaged power and water purification plants, out of spite or on orders. In that latter endeavor the French were assisted by an American "psywar" (psychological warfare) team, headed by Colonel Edward G. Landsdale (1908–87), a CIA operative, which also conducted its own "independent" sabotage operations, including contamination of the fuel supply of Hanoi's main bus company to wreck the engines of its vehicles.

No sooner had Ho's government assembled in Hanoi than it confronted malnutrition and even famine in areas under its jurisdiction. The socio-economic situation became precarious to the point of provoking anti-government demonstrations, including a revolt at Quynh Luu, in crisis-prone Nghe An Province. Local authorities there, supported by government troops, eventually put down the rebellion, but at great political and human cost. While such problems were largely legacies of the savage war Paris had waged to resume its *mission civilisatrice*, the burden was now on Ho's regime to redress them or lose domestic credibility and international legitimacy.

Years of war had certainly taken their toll on the economy, but the food shortages and resulting social unrest characteristic of the immediate postwar era in the North also had a lot to do with the land reform program launched by DRVN leaders in 1953. That program had run into serious and unending trouble as cadres charged with carrying it out abused their authority or simply proved unequal to the task. It disrupted food production and, most tragically, led to the execution of as many as 15,000 people, wealthy landlords and their family members for the most part, on charges of being enemies of the people. As villagers and even Party operatives occasionally took advantage of the campaign to settle old scores, many innocents were killed or driven to suicide. DRVN authorities eventually suspended the campaign, but not before terrible suffering and injustice had been visited upon the people, and great harm done to the rural economy and to the government's and Party's image.

The bloodshed and turmoil engendered by the land reform campaign plus the North's desperate economic situation prompted many Northerners to seek refuge in South. As previously noted, the Geneva accords allowed for the voluntary movement of civilians between the two zones until March 1955. Among those who left the North, besides the French, were members of ethnic minorities, devout Buddhists, as well as Catholics incited to do so by priests and other detractors of Ho's regime. Persecution awaited those who stayed, members of the Catholic clergy claimed, because DRVN leaders were communists intolerant of religion and suspicious of anyone thought to have collaborated with the French, which Catholics had ipso facto done by adopting their religion. Northern authorities did their best to counter assertions to that effect, insisting the Party and government harbored no ill feelings toward Catholics. But that had little effect. In the end, more than a million Northerners, nearly ten percent of the population, at least 500,000 of whom were Catholic, departed for the South. This mass exodus of civilians had no parallel in the South; only a negligible number of people there opted for voluntary relocation to the North. That incongruity was a major embarrassment for DRVN authorities. Its implications for the planned referendum on national reunification particularly troubled Ho.

Overwhelmed by domestic challenges threatening the very survival of their regime, DRVN leaders set aside concerns about national reunification and set out instead to rehabilitate and grow the Northern economy and infrastructure. A stronger economy and state apparatus would not only remedy pressing problems, but also make the North more self-sufficient and less dependent on foreign aid. That, in turn, would affirm the legitimacy of the government and prove invaluable should hostilities in the South resume. Thus, in 1955, Ho's regime effectively adopted a "North-first" policy. Southern liberation and national reunification remained critical goals, but under current circumstances their pursuit would have to wait. The proscriptions of Moscow and Beijing against renewal of hostilities validated, but did not account for, Ho's personal endorsement of the North-first policy. A more immediate stimulus was the adoption by North Korean leader Kim Il-sung (1912–94) of *Juche* ("self-reliance") as his regime's official political ideology that same year. Like Korea, Ho and his comrades gathered, Vietnam needed a strong "rear base," that is, a healthy North, to advance and meet its long-term objectives nationwide. China had served that purpose for part of the Indochina War, providing vital logistical support as well as safe havens for tired and wounded Vietminh troops. It even doubled as a staging area for major combat operations. Rehabilitating and strengthening the North would serve to create a "self-reliant economy" which would at once lessen the dependence on Beijing and create a safeguard against the renewal of hostilities in the South. And if events unfolded as DRVN leaders hoped, a strong and stable North would prove their own merits as nation-builders, vastly improving their prospects for victory in the upcoming national reunification referendum.

TROUBLES IN THE SOUTH

The decision to prioritize Northern reconstruction and development over Southern liberation did not sit well with Southern revolutionaries, already incensed by Ho's decision to accept the Geneva accords and the country's partition. Their gripes were not unreasonable. The North-first policy effectively gave the rival regime in Saigon free rein to do as it pleased in the South, and ignore key provisions of the Geneva accords, including holding consultative talks with Hanoi to discuss the planned referendum on national reunification. But that was far from the worst of it. Against all odds, Diem found ways to expand and consolidate his power. He even developed the confidence to defy and stand up to the French, who were more inclined to abide by the terms of the Geneva formula. In fact, one of Diem's first acts as Prime Minister was to sever all SOVN ties to the French Union. Such boldness owed much to the Americans, who agreed to directly assist his government and train his armed forces starting in 1955.

Since assuming the premiership in the summer of 1954, Diem had faced seemingly insurmountable challenges, from reorganizing and cleaning up the SOVN government's corrupt and highly inefficient bureaucracy to finding food, land, and jobs for the endless stream of refugees from the North. However, no challenge proved more daunting than quelling internal opposition to his rule, which included a faction within his own armed forces, a powerful criminal syndicate, and the paramilitary forces of two eclectic religious denominations, the afore-mentioned Cao Dai and the Hoa Hao. Following a lengthy but victorious battle against these "sects," Diem sensed the vulnerability of Southern communists, debilitated by regroupments to the North, and moved to crush them. In July 1955, on the first anniversary of the signing of the Geneva accords, he launched the "Denounce the Communists" campaign intended to achieve nothing less than the total eradication of their presence in the South. Diem's crowning achievement came in October, when he held a referendum of his own that resulted in Bao Dai's dismissal and his own investiture as both Head of State and Chief of Government of the new, fully sovereign and presumably democratic Republic of Vietnam (RVN). The ballot-counting was obviously rigged, with no less than 98.2% of registered voters allegedly casting ballots for Diem. Still, the exercise itself enhanced Diem's legitimacy by abolishing the French-sponsored SOVN and thus completely severing longstanding ties between Saigon and Paris. It also gave Diem even less reason to honor the Geneva accords. In fact, in the wake of the referendum, he declared that reunification elections would never happen under his watch as long as communists controlled the North.

Despite limited experience and resources, Diem somehow managed to overcome all challenges to his rule. No wonder, then, that the American press was soon referring to him as Washington's "miracle man" in Asia. By 1956, the United States supported Diem's regime to the tune of nearly $300 million annually. Diem's successes not only stunned Hanoi; they also amplified its own failings by suggesting his administration was more competent than Ho Chi Minh's. Most unsettling, they insinuated that the Southern system – guided as it was by Diem's "personalist" philosophy – was superior to the communist one in the North.[1]

PEACEFUL COEXISTENCE

Circumstances went from bad to worse for Hanoi when Soviet Premier Nikita Khrushchev (1894–1971), an ostensible ally, announced at the Twentieth Congress of the CPSU in February 1956 that henceforth Moscow – and the entire communist camp by extension – would espouse a policy of "peaceful coexistence" and "peaceful competition" with the capitalist West. The proclamation stupefied Hanoi, as it did the rest of the communist camp, because Khrushchev consulted with no one outside his inner circle before rendering his decision public. That decision, DRVN leaders thought, totally ignored realities in the Third World, and tacitly endorsed the status quo in Vietnam, Korea, and China, all of which remained fractured because of interference by capitalist countries, and the United States most notably. For many Vietnamese communists, Khrushchev's new line betrayed Marxist–Leninist orthodoxy because it disavowed violence as a means of resolving differences between their camp and the capitalist camp. Considering how the situation in Southern Vietnam was unfolding, taking the armed struggle option off the table might not only complicate but derail entirely the DRVN's national reunification project. Then there was Khrushchev's "secret speech," delivered right after the official closing of the Congress, when all foreign delegations had left. In that speech the Soviet leader denounced Stalin, his immediate predecessor, for his "crimes" against the Soviet people, including his rule by "cult of personality." When Hanoi got wind of the speech days later, it interpreted Khrushchev's condemnation of Stalin's personality cult as criticism of Ho Chi Minh's and other communist bloc leaders' own personality cults.

Despite strong private disapproval of Khrushchev's new line by some Vietnamese communists, Ho and the DRVN leadership publicly endorsed it because doing otherwise would have constituted a breach of communist etiquette and compromised Soviet–DRVN relations. Authorities also removed a large portrait of Ho from the façade of the municipal theater in Hanoi, where the National Assembly convened at the time, and stopped making public pronouncements in the name of "President Ho Chi Minh."

DOMESTIC LIBERALIZATION

The combined needs to improve domestic conditions, enhance the regime's legitimacy, match Diem's triumphs in the South, and mitigate the implications of peaceful coexistence prompted Hanoi to implement a series of bold domestic measures in 1956. Those were the most conciliatory and liberal it would ever adopt, attesting to the desperation of Ho's regime to turn things around. To begin, the regime formally ended the land reform campaign, and Ho personally apologized for its excesses. Shortly thereafter, to atone for its blunders, Hanoi launched another campaign, dubbed "Rectification of Errors," part of which consisted of reclassifying peasants, many posthumously, unfairly branded as enemies of the people, and returning property seized from them to their rightful owners or living relatives. These represented particularly meaningful gestures as the VWP was a Marxist–Leninist party and, as such, supposedly infallible, much as the papacy is supposed to be in the eyes of devout Catholics.

The Party itself underwent a transformation. During a Central Committee meeting that fall, those most closely associated with the land reform program were demoted, including Secretary Truong Chinh, its staunchest proponent. Until a suitable replacement could be found and properly vetted, Ho Chi Minh assumed the role of Party Secretary. Another consequential personnel change was the elevation of Le Duc Tho (1911–90) to head the powerful Party Organization Committee that dealt with all personnel matters. Born Phan Dinh Khai in the Northern province of Nam Dinh, Tho had been drawn to revolution by Phan Chu Trinh, whom he admired greatly. Radicalized by his involvement in various anti-colonial activities, including school boycotts, Tho joined the communist Revolutionary Youth League founded by Ho Chi Minh in China in 1925. He was twice detained by the French, in 1930–6 and 1939–44, which hardened him even more. His time spent behind bars was actually transformative: he came out of his second incarceration unequivocally committed to the liberation of his country and its transformation into a communist state, whatever the means, cost, and time it took. He eventually earned the nickname "Hammer" for his steely resolve and equally steely demeanor. During the Indochina War, Tho played a leading role coordinating Vietminh activities in the South, and distinguished himself for his bravery and inventiveness. He relocated to the North in 1955, a few months after the signing of the Geneva accords, and shortly thereafter joined the Politburo. He would soon play a critical and dominant role in state and Party affairs.

The changes did not end there. To win back public trust, DRVN authorities launched a domestic "détente," loosening their grip on the population. Consistent with the spirit of de-Stalinization just announced by

Khrushchev and *de rigueur* across the communist world, they suspended their exercise of arbitrary power and started promoting "democratic liberties" and "individual rights" for all citizens. They even freed political prisoners, and eased restrictions on travel and free speech. One of the consequential byproducts of the reforms was the appearance of two new literary journals, *Nhan van* ("Humanities") and *Tram hoa* ("Hundred Flowers"). Consisting of compilations of short stories, editorials, and other items, the journals became conduits for denouncing the dogmatism of Hanoi leaders, and push for even greater social and political change. To achieve the kind of real "popular democracy" Ho Chi Minh aspired to create, contributors to the journals insisted, the complete freedoms of speech, press, and association as well as the end of authoritarian rule were essential. Contributors demanded not the abolition of the system established in the North after July 1954, but its reform, "a fundamentalist return to the humanistic origins of Communist thought."[2]

Hanoi's rather sudden and radical departure from traditional communist governance was inspired by Khrushchev's peaceful coexistence policy, in the first instance, and similar campaigns then being undertaken in other communist states, in the second. China, to illustrate, launched the "Hundred Flowers" movement that same year, encouraging the masses and intellectuals in particular to freely and openly share their views on the communist system introduced there in 1949. In Poland, authorities turned a blind eye to the founding of the Skewed Wheel Club, an association of opposition leaders and artists based in Warsaw calling for political and economic liberalization and the end of Soviet domination. And in Hungary, Khrushchev's call for de-Stalinization prompted the resignation of hardline leader Matyas Rakosi (1892–1971) and the formation of intellectual forums to address the political, social, and economic challenges facing the country.

The DRVN's experiment in liberal governance was short-lived, proving as it did an abject failure and a nightmare for the authorities. Hanoi grossly underestimated the degree of frustration among the people, and the ability of its detractors, intellectuals in particular, to harness that frustration. Clamor for change undermined the regime's legitimacy and raised doubt about its ability to govern. Ho's sole consolation was to witness democratization efforts in other communist states also backfire. In line with the response by authorities in those states, starting in November 1956 the Ministry of Public Security initiated a harsh and methodical crackdown on public dissent. Among those targeted by the campaign were the editors of and contributors to *Nhan van* and *Tram hoa*, as well as dozens of others, university professors, artists, and journalists for the most part. The crackdown in the DRVN was not as bloody as those that occurred in parts of East Europe, especially in Hungary, and in China, but it was equally systematic and, ultimately, successful. It is possible that the experiment was a ruse engineered by Hanoi to encourage the enemies of communism to reveal themselves so they could be promptly and efficiently eliminated, that it was a means of entrapping dissidents. By some accounts, that was the primary rationale for launching the Hundred Flowers campaign in China, to "entice the snakes out of their caves," as Mao explained later. However, the bulk of the evidence – which remains limited – indicates that Ho and his regime genuinely believed democratization would appease and co-opt the masses at a critical juncture in the history of their new state; they simply miscalculated the consequences of their actions. One can only wonder how different the DRVN would have become had the regime's reformist zeal been sustained, and if that could have facilitated North–South reconciliation, and even prevented the Vietnam War.

LE DUAN

By 1956, Diem's stunning successes against challengers in the South, and the advent of the RVN, made clear to Ho and his comrades that the South Vietnamese President would never comply with even the most basic terms of the Geneva accords that applied to his regime. The evident failure of the Geneva formula, upon which Ho had cautiously pinned his hope for prompt and peaceful national reunification under his regime, distressed him. But it was hardly surprising. As much as he and other communist leaders had been hoping for the best, they had also been preparing themselves for the opposite, as noted earlier. What dumbfounded some, however, was Ho's abject refusal to modify the Party's strategy below the 17th parallel once that failure became obvious. His sustained commitment to the North-first policy, despite recent and extremely troubling developments in the South, particularly appalled Southern revolutionaries, who were just beginning to get over Ho's betrayal of them in 1954 and the North-first policy. In continuing to prioritize Northern reconstruction, and abide by the accords as Diem made a mockery of them, Ho effectively encouraged his rival to sustain his attacks on the Southern communist movement. His lackluster response to Diem's recent and terribly harmful initiatives in the South eventually prompted calls for a change of strategy from within the Party itself.

The most vocal exponent of change was Le Duan (1907–86), the forty-nine-year-old head of the Central Office for Southern Vietnam (COSVN) tasked with coordinating communist activities in the southern third of Vietnam, the former Cochinchina. Born Le Van Nhuan in Quang Tri Province in a working class family, Le Duan found employment as a railway official in the 1920s, which afforded him an opportunity to travel the country and witness, to his great frustration, the debilitating effects of French colonialism on his compatriots. He was drawn to communism, its structure and rigidity especially, at a relatively young age. He became a founding member of the ICP and an eager publicist of the individual and national salvation it promised. Responsible for ideological indoctrination in Tonkin, he was soon arrested by colonial authorities for subversion, and endured extreme deprivation, to say nothing of torture, during his subsequent incarceration. After his twenty-year sentence was commuted in the mid-1930s, the ICP appointed him head of its Trung Bo (Annam) branch. By then, Le Duan was more determined than ever to fight for the ICP's cause and for Vietnam's independence from France. He was arrested again in 1940, but released shortly thereafter, following the Japanese invasion of Indochina. After the outbreak of the war with France in 1946, the Party charged him with directing Vietminh activities in Cochinchina as head of the Nam Bo Executive Committee, COSVN's previous incarnation. Appointed in absentia to the Politburo in 1951, he stayed in the South after the country's partition in 1954, to act as its eyes and ears and help steer the Revolution there. Fighting the French for several years hardened him even more. Le Duan was as tough as Vietnamese revolutionaries came; a real agitator and demagogue. His revolutionary pedigree, commitment to Marxism–Leninism, and self-abnegation were beyond reproach.

Though he did his best to keep mum about it, at least in certain circles, Le Duan was absolutely revolted by Ho's decision to accept the Geneva formula and, after 1956, his passivity in the face of Saigon's obvious contempt for the peace accords and brutal crackdown on Southern communists. Unless the armed struggle below the 17th parallel resumed promptly, Le Duan thought, the entire Southern communist movement would be wiped out. As he reticently complied with instructions from Hanoi, he began encouraging his closest comrades in the South to adopt a more "forward" strategy to deal with Diem and the whole matter of national reunification. The current line espoused by Ho was simply untenable and entirely counterproductive, he believed.

TERRORISM

Moved to action by his own convictions, as well as encouragement from his peers, during the second half of 1956 Le Duan directly implored Ho and his comrades in the North to reconsider their revolutionary strategy, and endorse a more aggressive course of action predicated on active resistance, on armed struggle, in the South. Considering the unpopularity of Diem's regime and the international pressures confronting the United States at the time, victory, Le Duan claimed, would not take long. Such a call for revision of a basic strategy was bold, to say the least. Rarely did Party members, even ranking ones, take overt steps calling into question the current regime line. In Stalin's Soviet Union, as in Mao's China and Kim Il-sung's North Korea, such defiance often got people executed. But North Vietnam was different, in certain respects at least. While Hanoi sometimes dealt harshly with internal dissent, it never did so with the ruthlessness characteristic of those other regimes. In this instance, not only did Ho decide not to punish Le Duan, but he actually carefully considered his proposal. Le Duan was, after all, a member of the Politburo, just not its most compliant one. This episode is, in fact, emblematic of the extent to which Ho's regime tried to abide by the tenets of democratic centralism – the practice of rule by consensus among the ruling elite ("diversity in discussion, unity in action," according to Lenin), supposed to govern policymaking in all communist countries.

Following frenzied deliberations, in December 1956 the VWP Central Committee recommended, and the Politburo later approved, resort to violence by Southern revolutionaries, but on a very limited scale and in accordance with strict guidelines. Partisans could defend themselves, but not in ways that might provoke American intervention. At the limit, they could kidnap and hold for ransom or assassinate Saigon officials and other "tyrants," and bomb institutions and establishments associated with the Diem regime and the American presence. They were not authorized, however, to conduct actual military operations against Saigon's regular armed forces. Furthermore, Hanoi mandated that Southern revolutionaries who participated in what amounted to a campaign of domestic terrorism keep their ties to the Party secret, so that their actions appeared to be impromptu popular responses to the climate of fear created by Saigon, and not acts of aggression incited by Hanoi, which would be likely to elicit a dramatic American response. Possibly, this sanction for recourse to violence was prompted by the outcome of the Suez crisis of October 1956, which saw Western powers – France and Britain – and their Israeli allies back down in the face of the defiant stance adopted by President Gamal Abdel Nasser (1918–70) of Egypt (though in reality it was really American intercession that determined the outcome of the crisis). The sanction itself was a far cry from what Le Duan wanted, but at least it was something new and entailed the use of force.

In April 1957, in a move indicative of its growing concerns over the situation in the South, the Politburo recalled Le Duan to Hanoi and appointed him Acting Secretary of the Party. According to Le Duan's son, the appointment came at the insistence of Le Duc Tho, his former deputy in the South, who also wanted the Party to be more aggressive below the 17th parallel. The two men were actually "war buddies," a bond cemented by their respect and admiration for each other's revolutionary credentials, time spent in colonial jails, and commitment to Marxism–Leninism and Vietnamese liberation. Possibly, Politburo moderates engineered Le Duan's appointment to appease frustrated Southern militants. Whatever happened, Le Duan's promotion had no immediate effect on Hanoi's strategic priorities, as Ho and other moderates continued to dominate decision-making, and Le Duan's power base in the North Vietnamese capital was too small to permit him to press his views on other Party bosses. But an important die had been cast, the dramatic implications of which would not take long to become apparent.

TREADING CAUTIOUSLY

Consistent with Ho's wishes, throughout 1957 and 1958 Hanoi kept treading cautiously. It refused to escalate in the South, instead openly reiterating its readiness to engage in talks with Saigon, if not to salvage the Geneva accords then to explore the possibility of a new settlement between their two regimes. Pham Van Dong actually appealed directly to Diem, in a letter proposing that the two of them meet to discuss bilateral reductions of armed forces and resumption of commercial exchanges between the two halves of Vietnam. Diem never replied. Instead, he intensified his crackdown on communists and other dissidents. He even went after those formerly associated with the Vietminh who had stopped taking orders from its Northern leaders and been inactive since the signing of the Geneva accords.

Southern revolutionaries soon faced their "darkest days," as Diem's forces relentlessly pursued them – killing, capturing, or otherwise neutralizing thousands, along with their sympathizers. The onslaught was so systematic and effective that in time less than 5,000 active Party members remained, and no communist presence existed in large portions of the South. There was, however, a silver lining to all of this: Saigon's campaign was so sweeping and brutal that it directly impacted the lives of countless innocents who thereafter joined the communist movement just to get back at Diem. Perhaps most significant, it encouraged surviving, until now inactive veterans of the Vietminh to pledge loyalty to Ho's regime and resume their revolutionary activities on its behalf.

Despite the harsh clampdown on his partisans in the South, Ho remained steadfastly committed to economic development in the DRVN, to the North-first policy. In 1958, his regime unveiled a three-year economic plan (1959–61) calling for the abolishment of private farming in favor of communal farms, "agricultural cooperatives." The plan symbolically marked the end of the period of economic rehabilitation in the North and the beginning of its transformation into a communist state. Among other concrete objectives, the plan called for completion of the collectivization of Northern agriculture by the end of 1960. Agricultural collectivization was standard practice in aspiring communist states, which sought to streamline food production while eliminating individualistic, provincial, bucolic peasant thinking. First, the authorities expropriated land from the rich, and redistributed it among the poor. Then, once the situation had stabilized, and the rural economy was back on track, they collectivized. This first major step toward transforming the DRVN into a full-fledged communist state generated much discontent among peasants, many of whom had only recently been allotted their own parcel of land and could finally produce enough to live comfortably. In the name of communism, the government also commandeered private enterprises as it built new state-owned factories with outside money and counsel. By this time, state-owned and -operated enterprises accounted for nearly half of all manufacturing in North Vietnam. Because of shortages of investment capital and technical and managerial expertise, the authorities allowed some factories to remain under private ownership, and even encouraged wealthy Northern entrepreneurs to build new ones. Economic necessity in these cases trumped communist transformation.

SINO-SOVIET DISPUTE

As North Vietnamese leaders tackled pressing issues at home, problems were brewing next door in China. In 1957–8, Mao's commitment to "continuous revolution," a policy aimed at moving the Chinese Revolution forward through successive mass mobilization campaigns, brought about a sudden and drastic radicalization of Beijing's domestic and foreign policy. At home, Mao launched the Great Leap Forward (1958–62), an ambitious program of accelerated industrialization and communization. In support of that program, and also in response to the recent suspension of secret Sino-American ambassadorial talks in Warsaw, in August 1958 Mao triggered the second Taiwan Strait crisis by ordering sustained bombardment of islands controlled by Chiang Kai-shek's pro-American regime in Taipei. Shortly thereafter, China's "Great Helmsman" began publicly praising the merits of revolutionary militancy and encouraging national liberation movements throughout the colonial and semi-colonial worlds to fight more aggressively for the independence of their countries. Beijing manifested its intent to become the new vanguard in the struggle against imperialism and capitalism by dramatically increasing its assistance to communist insurgents battling British forces in the Malayan "Emergency" (1948–60). Some of that aid actually went through Vietnam. That all blatantly defied Khrushchev's policy of peaceful coexistence, and Soviet leadership of the communist camp by extension. The differences between imperialism and its victims were irreconcilable, Mao maintained; violent struggle represented the only way to achieve national liberation.

This hardening of Beijing's stance on Marxist–Leninist revolutionary strategy marked the end of China's "leaning-to-one-side" (i.e., the Soviet Union) policy and precipitated a long-simmering crisis in Sino-Soviet relations, over whether Beijing or Moscow was leader of the communist camp and fulcrum of world revolution, and over whether peaceful or violent methods should be employed to bring about revolutionary change. Before long, Mao was openly accusing Moscow of "big-power chauvinism," and denouncing Khrushchev for embracing "revisionism": that is, for abandoning "true" Marxism–Leninism and trying to reinterpret that perfect, scientific ideology. The ensuing split between the two communist powers had serious and long-lasting implications for Hanoi. Over the years, Vietnamese communist leaders had developed close ties to both China and the Soviet Union. Hanoi was, in fact, the only communist regime in the world close to and heavily dependent upon both powers at the same time. As noted in the previous chapter, during the Indochina War, China had provided vital political and material support, as well as advisers, while Moscow remained preoccupied by the situation in Europe. Since then, however, the Soviet Union had been supplying the bulk of the hardware and technical expertise in support of the DRVN's North-first policy. The Sino-Soviet dispute thus alarmed its leaders because it threatened these sources of supply, and the Vietnamese Revolution by extension. Should Hanoi ever have to pick a side in the dispute it would lose invaluable support from one of its benefactors, which it could not afford, especially at this critical juncture.

Equally dismaying, the split fueled squabbles among Vietnamese communists as the conflicting stances of Beijing and Moscow on world revolutionary strategies validated competing ideological currents within the VWP. As Vietnamese communists lamented the deterioration of Sino-Soviet relations, some blamed the Chinese, others the Soviets – effectively taking sides in their dispute. Even core leaders succumbed to the tendency. Acting Secretary Le Duan, and others who favored resumption of armed struggle, sympathized with China. They admired its boldness and radicalism, even found them inspirational. Ho, and other proponents of caution and of the North-first policy, predictably leaned toward the Soviet Union because peaceful coexistence vindicated, and to some degree informed, their own ideological stance. They preferred, for the time being, to advance Vietnamese interests through diplomacy, and to devote time and resources to growing and transforming the domestic economy, rather than to fighting. The Sino-Soviet dispute thus widened the existing, heretofore largely inconsequential rift between moderates and hardliners in Hanoi, between Ho's regime and its detractors. In time, it nurtured the coalescence of two major, competing factions within the VWP, a "hawkish" one under Le Duan and a "dovish" other under Ho Chi Minh.

RESOLUTION 15

In 1959, after more pleas for action from suffering Southerners and growing numbers of proponents of armed struggle in the North, the VWP Central Committee recommended to Ho and the Politburo that their strategy below the 17th parallel be revised. The recommendation took the form of a document, known as "Resolution 15" because of its adoption during the Central Committee's Fifteenth Plenum in January that year. Deploring the "wicked" policies of Diem and the Americans, and the attendant agony of the "poor and miserable people" of the South, the resolution called for adoption of "the general revolutionary law" guiding liberation struggles everywhere: armed insurrection. Political work – that is, propaganda aimed at rallying the masses – was necessary, but armed struggle in the form of sustained infantry attacks against the Southern regime's armed forces should supplement that effort. Resolution 15 also recommended the formation of a broad united front in the South, a new Vietminh, to bring together opponents of Diem's regime in an organization controlled by the Party. Hanoi, the Central Committee surmised, could sit by and wait no longer; its partisans in the South must be allowed to resort to military action and escape from their "darkest days."

In tone and substance, Resolution 15 echoed the sentiments of Le Duan and other hawks. In many ways, Le Duan was responsible for its endorsement by the Central Committee. The triumph of Fidel Castro (1926–2016) and his 26th of July Movement in Cuba – just days before, on 1 January – also bore on the Committee's recommendation to move to insurrectionary action in the South. The ousting of the pro-American dictatorship of Fulgencio Batista (1901–73) in Havana, and its replacement with a fiercely nationalist, anti-imperialist, leftist, eventually communist revolutionary regime under Castro, generated hopes that Vietnamese insurgents could inflict the same fate on South Vietnam's pro-US dictator. Best to strike while the revolutionary iron was hot, the Central Committee concluded.

Ho acknowledged the Central Committee's recommendation, but was reluctant to implement it as written because he still worried about the consequences of resuming armed struggle, and American intervention in particular. Washington's icy reaction to recent developments in Cuba attested to the need for caution, he thought. Ho also feared alienating foreign friends, especially Moscow, adamantly opposed to the resumption of war in Vietnam. His loyal disciple, and the head of the armed forces, General Vo Nguyen Giap, was similarly against renewing hostilities: the PAVN, the North's standing army, was undergoing modernization and restructuring at the time, and was thus unready for major combat operations.

Still, even Ho recognized that something meaningful needed to be done to address the situation in the South and the Central Committee's approval of Resolution 15. In the wake of the latter, he and the Politburo sanctioned the creation of "armed propaganda brigades" to engage in "self-defense activities." Their instructions to Southern revolutionaries said nothing of instigating a general insurrection in the form of coordinated and sustained attacks against Saigon's armed forces, as the Central Committee had recommended. This cautious, conditional endorsement of Resolution 15, which had Ho's stamp all over it, was meant to protect and grow the communist movement below the 17th parallel, not bring about Diem's demise. Better wait until more favorable circumstances existed before taking that bold and dangerous step, Ho thought.

FIGURE 3.1 Ho Chi Minh addressing the VWP Central Committee during its Fifteenth Plenum, January 1959. Le Duan is seated to Ho's right. Courtesy of National Archives Center 3, Hanoi.

Consistent with this reasoning, the Politburo explicitly prohibited its followers in the South from carrying out military operations against Diem's regular armed forces, the Army of the Republic of Vietnam (ARVN). They could only go after irregular forces: namely, local militias in remote villages. "Adventurist" actions, the Politburo's instructions warned, risked precipitating general hostilities. Those same instructions made no mention of the united front proposed by the Central Committee, ostensibly because Ho feared formation of such an organization might give Washington another pretext to intervene.

In support of its new policy, Hanoi dispatched to the South small arms and contingents of Southern combatants who had regrouped to the North in 1954–5, many of whom had been integrated into the PAVN after their arrival. By official account, the latter were "volunteer troops" returning to the South of their own free will; they had no affiliation whatsoever to the North's standing army. To maintain that pretense, they left as individuals, not unit members, and wore no uniforms or other paraphernalia linking them to the PAVN. Their main mission was to train, organize, and supervise Southern fighters, and ensure their compliance with the terms of Resolution 15, as Ho's regime had redefined them. Since they were born in the South and spoke with regional accents, these regroupees could relate to other Southerners more easily than Northerners. Most crucially, in the event of capture, Diem's security forces would never be able to prove they actually came from the North. Ho was prepared to help Southern insurgents, but only in limited and deniable ways, so as not to give Washington any reason to expand its commitment in the South or strike back against the North. That same concern about the United States accounted for Ho's abject refusal to commit for the time being actual Northern troops and complete units of the PAVN below the 17th parallel.

Hanoi shifted strategic gears in the South in 1959, but slowly and cautiously. Ho would have it no other way. All things being equal, the revised stance on the situation below the 17th parallel was intended less to defeat Diem's regime, than to appease increasingly disgruntled Southern revolutionaries and VWP members, without upsetting the status quo. Had it not been for pressure from Southerners, and the nagging and growing influence of Le Duan in particular, it is doubtful Hanoi's strategy would have changed at all that year. Unbeknownst to Ho and his disciples at the time, the strategic shift would trigger Vietnam's Fourth Civil War.

INSURGENCY

Arms and men sent by the North arrived in the South via a 10,000-mile-long network of roads, tracks, and waterways running through Laos and Cambodia. These had been developed during the Indochina War and christened the Ho Chi Minh Trail in 1959 because they were officially re-opened on 19 May that year, on the occasion of Ho's sixty-ninth birthday. The journey down the Trail, undertaken under the supervision of Group 559, which was responsible for its upkeep, was arduous and often deadly. Even before the United States began bombing it following the start of its military intervention in 1965, troops traveling on the Trail faced countless hazards. Mosquito- and water-borne diseases, poisonous snakes, inclement weather, exhaustion, and dehydration were among the most notable. The journey could take up to two months, depending on the season and other factors. One in ten individuals who undertook it died along the way.

Because bad weather – and, later, American bombs – frequently disrupted traffic on the Trail, Hanoi set up and used a second, maritime artery to move men and supplies into the deep South. That artery was the responsibility of Group 759, renamed Brigade 125 in 1964, which possessed twenty vessels initially. This "Ho Chi Minh Trail of the Sea" linked the ports of Do Son and Haiphong in the North to inlets and reception points in the Ca Mau Peninsula and Cambodia. Le Duan and other Party leaders typically traveled between the North and the deep South via this route, which incidentally did not run the length of the Vietnamese coast, but instead arched into the South China Sea to avoid detection by enemy naval forces patrolling territorial waters. The maritime infiltration route was actually the original trans-Vietnam supply artery, established during the Indochina War. The land route developed only after the French navy increased surveillance activities along the coastline. Until the imposition of a US naval blockade of the South Vietnamese coastline in 1965, the maritime artery was far more efficacious than the land trail.

Despite its conditional endorsement by the Politburo, Resolution 15 heartened Southerners, who assumed it presaged even greater changes in the future. A meeting of cadres burst into loud applause and chants upon hearing that Ho had finally authorized some form of military action in the South. Interestingly, but unsurprisingly, many Southern revolutionaries would take advantage of the weak Party apparatus below the 17th parallel and ignore the parameters imposed on their military activities by Northern leaders. To Ho's bewilderment, they launched guerrilla-style attacks against enemy forces, including Saigon's regular army, and even instigated "popular uprisings" wherever conditions permitted. The typical uprising took place within a single village or cluster of villages, spearheaded by armed partisans mobilized by and acting under the direction of local Party cadres or other agents. The partisans would kill those with direct ties to the regime in Saigon – namely, government officials and other civil servants – to deter others from collaborating with RVN authorities in the future. They would then create "people's councils" that assumed administrative responsibilities. If present, police and army barracks were raided for their armories. To win over the local population, land belonging to wealthy landlords or the government was seized and redistributed.

The timing of these uprisings, beginning as they did even before or within days after Hanoi's new instructions arrived, indicates that in several localities revolutionaries had grown so irritated with Ho's regime that they were already planning to take independent action. Clearly, Ho did not exercise absolute control over his followers in the South. Indeed, many of them would disregard the Politburo's injunctions against "adventurism" and regularly engage ARVN forces in combat. Within less than a year, a full-blown guerrilla war had engulfed the South, raising the specter of US intervention. Despite his best efforts to dodge them, Ho's worst fears were coming true.

While certainly substantial, gains made by Southern insurgents in 1959–60 turned out to be fleeting. As their aggressiveness and brashness increased, so did their exposure, and Diem's security and military forces made them pay. Capitalizing on that and the lack of coordination among insurgents, the ARVN gradually reclaimed territories previously lost. Sensing an opportunity to crush the communist movement once and for all, Diem instructed his security apparatus to make liberal use of a notorious new decree: Law 10/59, promulgated in May 1959 and mandating the death penalty for anyone who threatened the national security and stability of his Republic.[3] On the basis of his earlier triumph over the sects, Diem felt confident he could eradicate the communist menace to his regime within months. His confidence was boosted in November 1960 when John F. Kennedy (in office 1961–3) – a fellow Catholic, old acquaintance, and consummate cold warrior with a keen interest in the Third World – was elected President of the United States. The prospects of the Southern revolutionary movement, so bright for a brief moment, were gloomy once again. Ho had been right to urge caution below the 17th parallel, or so it seemed at the time.

THIRD PARTY CONGRESS

The VWP held its first national congress in nine years in September 1960. During the meeting, 576 assembled delegates, representing more than half a million party members in both halves of the country, reaffirmed the correctness of Hanoi's commitment to the North-first policy by rubber-stamping a five-year plan (1961–5) submitted by the Politburo. The plan called for improvement and acceleration of rural collectivization, and development of heavy industry in the DRVN "at all cost."[4] This was consistent with the state's second constitution of 1959, which defined the DRVN as a "people's democratic state led by the working class," and made communism its official ideology. The Politburo hoped the plan would improve living standards in the DRVN, still extremely poor and made worse by a terrible harvest in mid-1960. Conditions were so bad in certain regions that people starved. Out of desperation, some peasants abandoned their collectives and went searching for food and remunerated work elsewhere. In prioritizing economic development, the Politburo also sought to decrease its dependence on allies, and complete the transformation of the North into a "great rear base" of the Revolution in the South.

During the Congress, General Giap, in his capacity as Defense Minister, announced further reductions in the size and budget of the armed forces, underscoring the extent of Hanoi's commitment to economic development in the North, and its intention to not become embroiled in a major war in the South anytime soon.

The Congress was equally notable for its confirmation of Le Duan as Party Secretary, and thus head of the Politburo. His stock was rising in Hanoi, even though for now Ho continued to have the last word on strategic matters. The Congress also approved a new eleven-man politburo, which included Ho Chi Minh, Le Duan, Truong Chinh, Pham Van Dong, Pham Hung, Vo Nguyen Giap, Le Duc Tho, and Nguyen Chi Thanh. In addition to Le Duan and Le Duc Tho, two of these men – Nguyen Chi Thanh (1914–67) and Pham Hung (1912–88) – had fought in the South during the Indochina War. Not only did they share Le Duan's hardline views, but, like Tho, they also happened to be close personal friends of the Secretary.

Thanh, the only five-star general in the PAVN beside Giap, was a long-time collaborator of Le Duan. Born Nguyen Vinh in a poor peasant family from Central Vietnam's Thua Thien Province, he joined the ICP in 1937. Stints in colonial prisons turned him into a radical militant convinced that only armed resistance could save Vietnam from foreign occupiers. He played a crucial role in the August Revolution of 1945, and went on to head the Interzone IV Executive Committee, responsible for coordinating Vietminh activities in parts of Trung Bo following the outbreak of the Indochina War. It was then that he developed a close working as well as personal relationship with Le Duan, his counterpart in Nam Bo. Thanh's dogmatic commitment to the Revolution, and to Marxism–Leninism, so impressed the Politburo that in 1950 it appointed him Director of the PAVN's General Political Department (GPD), the organ responsible for ideological indoctrination in the armed forces, and welcomed him as a member a year later. After his promotion to five-star general in 1959, a nasty feud ensued between him and Giap. Like Le Duan, Thanh came to despise Giap for his presumably bourgeois lifestyle, elitism, and failure to appreciate the merits of ideological indoctrination in the armed forces.

Pham Hung, for his part, was from Vinh Long Province in the deep South. He began participating in revolutionary activities at the age of sixteen, and attended the founding congress of the ICP in 1930, when he was barely eighteen. He worked alongside Le Duan and Le Duc Tho in the Nam Bo Executive Committee during the Indochina War, becoming their close friend and trusted confidant. He even officiated at Le Duan's

FIGURE 3.2 The Third Congress of the VWP, December 1960. Ho Chi Minh (center) is flanked by delegates from the Soviet Union and the PRC. Pham Van Dong and Le Duan are seated first from the left, respectively. Courtesy of the Vietnam News Agency.

first marriage in 1948. Pham Hung regrouped to the North after the Geneva accords, and rose rapidly in Party and government ranks thereafter. He served as PAVN liaison to the International Commission for Supervision and Control in Vietnam (ICSC), tasked with supervising and monitoring implementation of the accords, before his induction into the Politburo in 1956. He held various important positions thereafter, including those of Deputy Prime Minister and Secretary of the Party Reunification Committee, which studied and made policy recommendations to the Politburo about the situation in the South. Disillusioned with Ho's moderate policies and refusal to do more for Southern compatriots, he began espousing militant views, becoming a staunch ally of Le Duan after the latter's recall to the North in 1957.

VIET CONG

The slowly shifting balance of power in Hanoi, recent setbacks suffered by Southern insurgents, and the perceived need to enhance Hanoi's control over the Southern revolutionary movement, prompted the Politburo to create, right after the Congress adjourned, a united front to bring together non-communist groups and individuals opposed to the Saigon government in the South, as propositioned earlier in Resolution 15. The resulting National Front for the Liberation of Southern Vietnam (NLF) was officially established in December 1960. According to its founding manifesto, the Front was an unaffiliated political organization that supported the end of American interference in Vietnamese affairs and the creation of a neutralist coalition government in Saigon to negotiate the terms of national reunification with Hanoi. In reality, the organization was intended to harness Vietnamese patriotism and nationalism, "the power of the Vietnamese masses" in communist parlance, in the furtherance of Party ambitions below the 17th parallel. It would allow Hanoi to centralize the heretofore fragmented opposition to Diem's regime, on the one hand, and more effectively control the Southern insurgency while concealing its hand in it, on the other.

North Vietnamese leaders were well aware that Diem's opponents in the South included not just communists but a wide variety of other groups and individuals, ranging from Buddhist clerics to student activists. Many Southerners who joined the NLF at this time did so for personal and ideological motives which had nothing to do with communism. In this sense, the NLF was essentially the Vietminh resuscitated under an exclusively Southern guise. Just as they had previously created a broad-based patriotic front to maximize their appeal among the masses and thus their chances for success in the resistance wars against Japan during World War II and France immediately thereafter, Vietnamese communist leaders established the NLF to rally individuals and groups from all political and socio-economic persuasions against Diem and his allies. The goal was to rid the South of foreign imperialists and their "lackeys," and thereby complete the first revolution, the bourgeois nationalist one. Under the circumstances, there was no reason to impose restrictions on those willing and able to participate in the effort. Once successful, then communist leaders could end their cooperation with "bourgeois" and other "reactionary" elements in and out of the NLF, and denounce and abandon them as "class enemies," as they had done in the North following its liberation in 1954. That process was the penultimate stage of the Marxist historical process in the colonial world, as previously noted, the stage of the "communist revolution," the triumph of which would usher the final stage, communism.

This strategy exemplified the shrewdness of Vietnamese communist leaders, specifically, their knack for manipulating Vietnamese nationalism and patriotism for their own ends. Most who joined the NLF did not suspect they were actually fighting for Hanoi, that its leadership answered directly to the VWP Central Committee. That leadership enjoyed some autonomy, but in the implementation of policies, not their making. The NLF's armed wing, the Liberation Armed Forces of Southern Vietnam (LAF), similarly answered to military authorities in the North. Its top brass consisted of those just returned from the North. The day-to-day activities of LAF troops, who numbered 10,000 by the end of 1961, were coordinated by communist cadres and organs such as COSVN, now under Le Duan's successor, Nguyen Van Linh (1915–98).

In retrospect, creating the outfit that became known as the "Viet Cong" in the West – from the Vietnamese *Viet Nam Cong san*, possibly *Viet minh Cong san*, or "Vietnamese/Vietminh communist" – was a stroke of genius on Hanoi's part. Its existence supported the premise that the conflict in South Vietnam was a domestic dispute in which foreign powers, the United States in particular, had no business intervening. That would give Hanoi a major propaganda advantage over Washington during the Vietnam War, as the two battled for hearts and minds there and around the world. The NLF eventually established its own Foreign Relations Commission – which took orders from Hanoi, of course – for the express purpose of exporting its message and mustering sympathy for its cause worldwide.

GUERRILLA WARFARE

The rise of the Viet Cong helped the Southern communist movement survive and even thrive in places. Emboldened by the fall of the pro-American, "reactionary" government of Syngman Rhee (1875–1965) in South Korea in April 1960, Southern insurgents stepped up their attacks later that year, their capabilities bolstered by increased assistance from the North. In January 1961, the Politburo called for acceleration of the struggle in the South, and to that end authorized escalation of both political and military activity. LAF units scored a number of important victories that year, resulting in the "liberation" of significant portions of the countryside and creation of the first bona fide Viet Cong "revolutionary bases." While the North functioned as the "great rear base" of the Vietnamese Revolution in general, revolutionary bases or liberated zones in the South became the backbone of the war effort there, serving as staging areas for attacks on enemy forces, food production units, supply depots, and safe havens for tired and wounded troops. Hanoi leaders insisted, with considerable success, that their forces in the South treat civilians with respect and refrain from stealing or confiscating from them, because to do otherwise would undermine the political struggle and drive civilians into the arms of the enemy. Thus, whenever circumstances allowed, they purchased or offered fair compensation for whatever they obtained from the people in those zones, as Vietminh forces had done during the Indochina War.

Again, however, Diem proved equal to the task. Savage counterattacks by his armed forces during 1962 reversed Viet Cong gains of the previous year. The introduction of large contingents of US military advisers, secretly authorized by Kennedy to participate in combat, in conjunction with an influx of sophisticated military hardware, including helicopters, from the United States the year before markedly enhanced ARVN capabilities and effectiveness. Thus began the era of "Special War" (*chien tranh dac biet*), according to Vietnamese communist periodization. The Strategic Hamlet program, launched around the same time, also contributed to the improvement of Saigon's fortunes. Unlike the previous and somewhat similar Agroville program of 1959, this latest effort involved no mass relocations of peasants; instead, it called for creation of security perimeters around existing villages in contested areas and well-trained self-defense forces to protect them. Assignment to these villages of competent government officials, who answered directly to Saigon and were charged with instituting land and other reforms as necessary, made the program popular and successful for a time. According to Diem, strategic hamlets existed to combat three enemies at once – communism, discord, and underdevelopment – and did just that at first. They seriously compromised Viet Cong efforts to enlist new recruits, and limited insurgents' access to food, medication, tax revenue, and other items necessary to sustain their activities. According to historian Edward Miller, the program and related policies were so successful that they engendered "hopes of victory" in Saigon. Diem himself came to believe that he could defeat the Viet Cong within one year: that is, by the end of 1963. He even turned down American offers to dispatch combat forces, thinking that would delegitimize his government and prove counterproductive to the realization of his objectives.

A PARTY DIVIDED

Diem may have been deluded by his prospects for victory, but his successes in stymying the Southern insurgency unnerved Hanoi and fueled intra-Party tensions, already high. Growing numbers of Party members complained that Ho was doing too little to support their compatriots in

the South. They were especially bothered by his fear of American intervention and insistence that the situation there could somehow still be
resolved diplomatically. People everywhere revered Ho, his most irascible
critics recognized, but he had lost touch with the evolving needs of the
Revolution at home. Those critics introduced the "theory of two mistakes" to make their case. Twice already Ho had seriously compromised
the Vietnamese struggle for national unification and independence, the
critics maintained: first, during the Fontainebleau talks of 1946; then, in
Geneva in 1954. If Ho had been naïve for thinking he could negotiate
with colonialists in 1946, he had been thoroughly misguided to make
the same mistake again during the Geneva Conference. Assuming, as Ho
did in 1962, that Hanoi's differences with Saigon and Washington could
still be resolved diplomatically seemed just plain foolish to his detractors within the Party. Had not Diem and the Americans demonstrated
time and again their total contempt for diplomacy and the peace process?
Had they not repeatedly violated the 1954 accords, despite Hanoi's best
efforts to hold its end of the bargain?

This indictment of Ho's leadership and judgment, and by extension of
Hanoi's Southern strategy, by members of his own party was a very serious
matter that jeopardized the future of the Vietnamese Revolution. Unity
of thought and purpose was always a near-sacred tenet of Vietnamese
communism, and an obligation for its leaders if they hoped to be victorious in the end. It ensured discipline within the Party, and facilitated
collaboration with other communist parties around the world. In more
ways than one, the growing divide between hawks and doves in Hanoi
mirrored the contemporaneous tension between hardliners and moderates in Washington grappling over whether or not to "escalate" American
involvement in Indochina despite Diem's own reservations.

A series of dramatic events in 1962–3 emboldened hawks in Hanoi,
and consequently aggravated their spat with Ho and other doves. The first
was the outcome of the Algerian War of Independence (1954–62). After
an arduous eight-year struggle, Algerian "freedom fighters" had expelled
the French and secured the complete independence and sovereignty of
their country. Their victory, Vietnamese hawks thought, attested to the
merits of daring, persistence, and violence. The continuing radicalization
of Chinese foreign policy – and Beijing's decision to extend unqualified
support for armed struggle to Vietnam, announced during a May 1963
visit to Hanoi by CCP Vice Chairman Liu Shaoqi (1898–1969) – similarly roused Vietnamese militants. So did the collapse of the multilateral
Geneva accords on Laos, signed the previous year, which were supposed

to have ended the civil war in that country by creating a neutral coalition government. Negotiating with the United States and its local clients, Vietnamese hawks inferred from the failure of the Laotian "experiment," was futile: only war could solve the differences between the two camps. Militants also felt that Khrushchev's decision to back down in the Cuban crisis of October 1962 and remove nuclear-tipped Soviet missiles from the island had been tantamount to a betrayal of his allies in Havana and of national liberation struggles across the Third World. That, in turn, discredited peaceful coexistence in their eyes and validated their own stance on revolutionary violence. Ultimately, however, no event was more important than the Battle of Ap Bac in January 1963 in emboldening Vietnamese supporters of armed struggle. During this one-day battle, a grossly outnumbered Viet Cong force defeated ARVN regulars backed by US advisers. For hawks in Hanoi, that outcome proved communist forces could not only hold their own against but actually defeat Saigon's troops in large-scale military operations.

With support from key allies within the Party's upper echelon – namely, Le Duc Tho and Nguyen Chi Thanh – Le Duan evoked Ap Bac and the other favorable circumstances just mentioned to persuade other members of the Central Committee and the Politburo of the suitability of armed struggle to bring about the "liberation" of the South and its reunification with the North. Many lent a sympathetic ear. After all, it had been nearly a decade since Ho had agreed to the Geneva accords, promising national reunification within two years. By now, the Northern economy had been rehabilitated, and its communist transformation was proceeding more or less apace. Conditions in the countryside, deplorable for some time, were finally starting to improve. The PAVN had not yet completed its modernization and reorganization, but substantial advances to these ends had been made. And, while Moscow remained opposed to the resumption of hostilities in Vietnam, Beijing had given its blessing and promised substantial material aid, even troops if necessary, to help Hanoi achieve its revolutionary goals. If Southern guerrillas could defeat ARVN troops in major combat, as Ap Bac demonstrated, surely PAVN regulars could crush them.

The rift between hawks and doves inside the Party widened through the summer of 1963. In the South, the so-called Buddhist crisis, marked by widespread protests against Diem's regime and the self-immolation of monks, rocked the RVN's foundation. Party hardliners thought the turmoil there presented a golden opportunity to escalate the armed struggle, perhaps even to topple Diem's embattled regime. But Ho refused to act. Then, on 1 November, a group of South Vietnamese generals staged a coup against Diem, abetted by Washington. The next day, the bodies of Diem and his brother and closest adviser, Ngo Dinh Nhu (1910–63), were found in the back of an armored vehicle. A new government, a military junta, was soon proclaimed in Saigon under ARVN General Duong Van Minh (1916–2001). In the aftermath of this startling turn of events, hawks in Hanoi could no longer be restrained. Tensions in the South finally had come to a head; the same was about to happen in the North.

NINTH CENTRAL COMMITTEE PLENUM

The coup in Saigon set in motion a chain of events in Hanoi that culminated in a coup of a different kind there, one that would bear heavily on the onset of American intervention in 1965. Immediately following Diem's overthrow, the VWP Central Committee held a special session to discuss the latest developments in the South, which few in Hanoi saw coming. Diem had been facing mounting domestic challenges, Vietnamese communists knew, but also demonstrated remarkable resiliency – and success – in the face of adversities seemingly more threatening than the Buddhist crisis. The South Vietnamese President had been a formidable adversary, to say the least. And that was largely the reason the Central Committee, after getting over its initial shock, celebrated his ouster. However, the investiture of a military junta in Saigon raised new concerns. The South Vietnamese armed forces had close ties to the United States. That, plus the (correct) suspicion that Washington had had a hand in the coup, suggested that the new regime would be supported by, and beholden to, Washington to a much greater degree than its predecessor. It might even welcome the deployment of US combat forces to help consolidate its power and suppress its enemies, which Diem had resisted, as noted earlier.

It suddenly became apparent to the Central Committee that the Vietnamese Revolution was at a crossroads. Hanoi could do nothing while waiting on events below the 17th parallel. Alternatively, it could send peace feelers to the new regime to test its intentions and attitude toward negotiations. Finally, it could launch an invasion of the South before the junta had a chance to sort out its options and consolidate itself. The debate over what to do was the spark that exploded the dispute between doves and hawks in Hanoi. The former maintained it was best to wait and see what happened in Saigon before settling on a course of action, and perhaps even entertain the possibility of negotiating with the new regime; but the latter insisted on taking advantage of the prevailing chaos there and dramatically escalating combat operations in the South to achieve total victory within months if not weeks.

True to form, Le Duan led the charge against temperance, making a strong appeal, his brawniest to date, for war during a speech before the assembled Party elite. He even harshly, albeit circuitously, criticized Ho and his supporters for still believing the situation in the South could be solved peacefully, diplomatically. There was no better time than the present, Le Duan argued in his speech, to pursue the liberation of the South and national reunification. Failure to seize the opportunity afforded by recent developments domestically and internationally would only hurt the long-term prospects of the Revolution. In a bid to ward off rash action, Vo Nguyen Giap reminded Le Duan and his comrades, in an address of his own, that the North's armed forces remained unprepared for major combat against Southern forces, which enjoyed the full backing of the United States. Giap's entreaties were in vain. In the end, moderates failed to contain militant ambitions, and the hawks carried the day. The concluding statement by the Central Committee, "Resolution 9," as it became known, called for immediate and drastic escalation of armed struggle in the South: that is, for the onset of "mass combat operations."

That escalation would have two objectives: destroying the Strategic Hamlet program and, most crucially, annihilating Saigon's armed forces before the United States could get enough troops and military might into Vietnam to make a difference. Essentially, Resolution 9 amounted to a declaration of war against Saigon. Implicitly, it repudiated Ho Chi Minh's leadership, which was not lost on the veteran leader. According to a document from the Russian archives, this turn of events so unsettled Ho that he told the Soviet ambassador he intended to retire from politics the following year. He never really did, but his role in the Party changed dramatically thereafter.

The Central Committee's Ninth Plenum occasioned the most significant revision of Party strategy since the 1954 decision to negotiate an end of the war with France. It marked a decisive turning point in the history of the Vietnam War. For Hanoi specifically, it constituted a point-of-no-return that eventuated in the onset of war against the United States a little over a year later. To be sure, authorities in Saigon and Washington played significant roles in shaping the events that culminated in direct US military intervention in Vietnam. In hindsight, however, no policy choice was more consequential than the Central Committee's decision to endorse Resolution 9, which gave the green light for "big war" to achieve Southern liberation and national reunification.

LE DUAN TAKES CHARGE

The Central Committee's recommendation to change strategies below the 17th parallel was a harbinger for change in the balance of power in Hanoi: essentially, for a bloodless, quiet palace coup. The outcome of the Ninth Plenum effectively discredited Ho and the dove faction. That left the door wide open for Le Duan and his chief lieutenants to assert their dominance over the Party. Indeed, in the days that followed, the latter rallied their supporters and condemned moderates for setting back the reunification struggle with their caution and betraying the ideals of the Vietnamese Revolution and Marxism–Leninism. Le Duan thus seized the mantle of power from Ho, who had neither the political capital nor willingness to resist him, and put his own personal stamp on the Party thereafter. By early 1964, Le Duan had become North Vietnam's new paramount leader.

Le Duan's first order of business was to consolidate his own authority, to centralize power by assuming responsibilities his predecessor had delegated to others. As part of that effort, he instigated a "rectification campaign" in February, aimed at purging influential doves from Party ranks lest their thinking poison others and undercut his own authority. Le Duan personally led the charge against those he variously labeled "revisionists," "pacifists," and "rightist deviationists," while Le Duc Tho, as head of the Organization Committee, facilitated their "reassignment" and replacement with trustworthy hawks. Even Ho and Giap fell victim to the purge. While both men kept their titles, they lost all influence over decision-making. To ensure their compliance with and loyalty to the new order, and possibly also to preclude a counter-coup, Le Duan went after their power base in both the Party and armed forces. He did so by demoting, incarcerating, and otherwise forcing into exile Ho and Giap's closest allies and most stalwart civilian and military devotees. Ranking doves who survived the purge were cowered into distancing themselves from the disgraced leaders, or voluntarily retired.

Within weeks, Le Duan and the hawks' dominance of the Party was absolute. Besides Le Duc Tho, the other central figures in the new regime were Le Duan's other "war buddies" from his days in the South, Nguyen Chi Thanh and Pham Hung. Suspicious of everyone outside their clique, the bond between them cemented by stints in French prisons, service in the South during the Indochina War, faith in Marxist–Leninist orthodoxy, and scorn for feebleness, these men claimed for themselves and their allies all key positions in the Party and government; so much so that their domination of policymaking lasted for the next twenty-three years!

Soon, an unprecedented air of repressiveness descended upon Hanoi and the rest of the North. Those bold or foolish enough to speak against the new regime, including several veterans of the Indochina War, had to answer to the Ministry of Public Security and its head, the dreaded Tran Quoc Hoan, who was quick to pledge allegiance to Le Duan. The DRVN thus became a quintessential Stalinist police state, a totalitarian political entity whose regime used all available means to monitor the activities of its citizens, quash dissent – actual, potential, or imagined – and intimidate the masses into passive submission. After 1964, historian Christopher Goscha has contended, no other party to the war matched Hanoi's ability to "control, rectify, and destroy those who defied its leadership in their cultural production and quest for individual liberties."[5]

PATRIOTIC INTERNATIONALISM

The new regime's leadership style was brittle, resolute, and uncompromising. It ruled through intimidation and fearmongering, intentionally arousing public concern and alarm to foster acquiescence in and support for its policies. Marxism–Leninism, as its core members interpreted it, was its ideological compass. Fiercely independent in his thinking and decision-making, Le Duan heeded the often-conflicting counsels of Moscow and Beijing only as the needs of the day and the volume of aid received dictated. His reserved demeanor and bland appearance concealed a zealous, fanatical commitment to national liberation and reunification. As battle-hardened veterans of the Indochina War, he, Tho, Thanh, and Pham Hung were imbued with a strong desire to secure the South's liberation by any means necessary, and at whatever cost. All were keen to succeed where Ho and the "old guard" had failed. Upon assuming the American presidency, Kennedy had vowed to "bear any burden" and "pay any price" to protect America's national security. The new regime in Hanoi was prepared to do the same to meet its own ends in Indochina, and would eventually do just that, literally.

Central as Marxism–Leninism was to Le Duan and his cohorts, a syncretic adaptation of that ideology actually conditioned their behavior and decisions. It mixed an obsession with national liberation and reunification under communist authority with a desire to serve as inspiration, model, and even vanguard for revolutionary and protest movements everywhere. "The Vietnamese revolution was, at heart, a communist revolution," historian Tuong Vu writes, and Hanoi's new sheriffs "as a group were internationalists no less than their comrades in the Soviet Union and China." For them, "a successful proletarian revolution in Vietnam was a step forward for world revolution, which was to occur country by country, region by region."[6] All things being equal, "patriotic internationalism" best captures the ideological and political leanings of Le Duan's new regime. It accounted for Hanoi's unbridled commitment after 1964 to defeating its domestic enemies, and thus preserve Vietnam's territorial integrity and secure its complete sovereignty, on the one hand; and actively contribute to the worldwide struggle against imperialism and capitalism, and become an exemplar of the possibilities of national liberation and socialist solidarity, on the other. For Le Duan in particular, national liberation was a means to even greater, nobler ends: liberation of all oppressed masses, social advancement of the underprivileged, and the demise of imperialism and global capitalism.

Over the years, Vietnamese communist leaders had repeatedly iterated their commitment to "world revolution," and just as often publicly repeated the central role of the Vietnamese Revolution in the latter. To be sure, the Cold War, to say nothing of the Sino-Soviet dispute, created countless challenges for Hanoi. However, the ongoing process of decolonization in the Third World, and the growing sense of solidarity among and between national liberation and protest movements, also created opportunities. Le Duan believed that his people, having gained international notoriety for their contributions to decolonization through their war against France and their dramatic triumph at Dien Bien Phu, were in an ideal position to lead the charge against American imperialism, and inspire others to do the same. Back in 1959, Party leaders had expressed confidence that "the victory of the Vietnamese Revolution" would have "an enthusiastic effect on the movement of popular liberation in Asia, Africa, [and] Latin America," and precipitate "the disintegration of colonialism throughout the world."[7] They had even dispatched military instructors to Egypt to train insurgents to fight in the Algerian War of Independence and expedite that disintegration. It was arguably Le Duan's greatest aspiration to make all of this culminate under his watch.

The men in charge in Hanoi after 1964 were not communists in the classical sense; nor were they mere nationalists, as is often assumed by American historians of the Vietnam War – they were an amalgam of elements. They sought to co-opt all ethnic groups, not just ethnic Vietnamese, for the sake of freeing and reunifying their country. That made them patriots. They also cared deeply about the fate of revolutionary and other progressive movements elsewhere. In fact, they considered it their duty to contribute to the global revolutionary process, to the final triumph of communism, by rousing opponents of capitalism, imperialism, and neo-colonialism everywhere. And that made them internationalists.

TONKIN GULF INCIDENT

The complexion of the struggle in the South changed dramatically following Le Duan's ascent as paramount Party leader and Ho's sidelining. Consistent with his "go-for-broke" mentality, as political scientist David Elliott labels it, Le Duan immediately boosted assistance to Southern guerrillas, who had already shifted the focus of their attacks to Saigon's main force units. Within weeks, the frequency and intensity of Viet Cong combat operations increased dramatically, generating new instabilities in the South. In January, Saigon was rocked by yet another coup and change of leadership, the second in less than three months. In fact, there would be three more regime changes in the South before 1964 was over.

Le Duan's willingness to accept the risks inherent in carrying out Resolution 9 stemmed largely from ideological factors. He understood the vicissitudes of international communism, but was also convinced that capitalism and imperialism were on the strategic defensive worldwide, as the forces of revolution successfully asserted themselves. Promoted by Beijing, revolutionary militancy was gaining increasing currency in the communist camp, despite Moscow's injunctions against it, and among national liberation movements across Asia and Africa in particular. Chinese radicalism, in both domestic and foreign affairs, now resonated through the Third World, and that thought shored up Le Duan's audaciousness and confidence. In time, Hanoi under Le Duan would actually prove more radical, more dogmatic, more "Chinese" than the Chinese themselves.

As the situation below the 17th parallel spiraled out of control, policymakers in Washington grew alarmed, and scrambled to find a solution. President Lyndon Johnson (in office 1963–9), who succeeded Kennedy following his assassination in Dallas in November 1963, and his closest advisers, most of whom Johnson had inherited from his predecessor, felt that the United States had too much invested already in a non-communist South to let its government succumb to what it considered communist aggression. In the Cold War context that conditioned the new President's thinking, "losing" South Vietnam was not an option. The damage to the credibility of the United States, the Democratic Party, and him personally would be too great. Vietnam already had gained worldwide notoriety as a Cold War crucible; the United States simply could not abandon it without "losing face," as a phrase then current went.

The White House thus responded in kind to the escalation of hostilities in the South, heaping upon Saigon massive quantities of military hardware and deploying more advisers, whose numbers reached 23,000 in 1964. It also increased logistical support to South Vietnamese commandos engaging in acts of sabotage against the North, which included infiltrating spies, disseminating disinformation, and blowing up such facilities as power plants and radar installations. This program of covert actions, known as OPLAN-34A, had actually begun in 1961. It expanded dramatically in 1964, thanks to so-called DESOTO patrols by US destroyers conducting electronic surveillance and intelligence-gathering off the North Vietnamese coast. Enemy patrol boats occasionally harassed these ships, but no gunfire was exchanged.

That all changed on 2 August 1964, when the *USS Maddox* came under fire from patrol boats responding to the destruction of a North Vietnamese radio transmitter the night before. Presumably, the order to attack the American ship came directly from Le Duan. Two days later, that same vessel and another destroyer, the *USS Turner Joy*, reported being shot at again by the DRVN navy. Though evidence of that second attack was circumstantial at best, it was enough to move the US Congress to adopt a measure called the Gulf of Tonkin Resolution, which authorized President Johnson to "take all necessary steps, including the use of armed forces," to "promote the maintenance of international peace and security in southeast Asia." The resolution essentially gave Johnson a blank check to wage war in Vietnam. In its tone, substance, and meaning, it mirrored Hanoi's Resolution 9. In fact, it answered circumstances set in motion by that resolution.

NORTHERN TROOPS JOIN THE FIGHT

Shortly after the Tonkin Gulf incident and ensuing congressional action, Le Duan and the Politburo convened to decide their next move. Implementing Resolution 9 had produced tangible gains in the South, most notably by disrupting the Strategic Hamlet program. Unfortunately, it had fallen way short of dealing Saigon's armed forces a crushing blow. Viet Cong forces, 100,000-strong by now, including 30,000 regular troops, inflicted sizeable losses on the ARVN during the first half of 1964, but not nearly enough to alter the balance of forces below the 17th parallel. But whereas Hanoi could be patient before, that changed after Congress passed the Gulf of Tonkin Resolution. Time suddenly became of the essence for DRVN leaders. Le Duan understood better than anyone that fulfilling the goals of Resolution 9 would be significantly more difficult once US forces arrived in significant numbers. Hoping to pre-empt that prospect, in September 1964 he and the Politburo fatefully chose to deploy combat units of the DRVN's own armed forces, the PAVN, to the South. According to an official Vietnamese history of the war, they effectively set in motion the process by which they would "mobilize the entire Party, the entire population, and the entire armed forces:" that is, "concentrate all our capabilities," to "bring about a massive change in the direction and pace of expansion of our main force army on the battlefield, to launch strong massed combat operations at the campaign level, and to seek to win a decisive victory within the next few years."[8]

The Politburo thus settled on total war to achieve Southern liberation and national reunification. By its own calculations, it had a short window of opportunity, two years at the most, before Washington committed "the full force of US military might to the Vietnam War." The reason for this interval, Le Duan believed, was that the domestic and international situations would prevent the Johnson administration from acting earlier. Internationally, antiwar sentiment was rising; at home, Johnson faced re-election in November. Before the American President could act, the presence of sufficient numbers of well-equipped professional soldiers from the North would surely bring about the swift collapse of Saigon's armed forces. The key to all this was timing.

That same month, September, the Politburo dispatched to the South a retinue of ranking Party and PAVN officials, including Nguyen Chi Thanh, with orders to increase the military pressure on Saigon. Thanh would actually replace Nguyen Van Linh as head of COSVN, attesting to Le Duan's sense of urgency, determination to exercise greater control over combat activities in the deep South, as well as to the totality of his commitment to war below the 17th parallel. Thanh's command of COSVN largely ended Southern autonomy in deciding certain military matters. The ranking cadres accompanying him were experienced in building and deploying main force units, in military leadership, and in combat command. Upon arrival in the South they set out at once to improve the quality of local cadres and strengthen the LAF, whose numbers needed to grow and were organized at the regimental but not the divisional level.

It was not lost on members of the Politburo, and Le Duan in particular, that committing PAVN combat units to the struggle in the South at that juncture was a huge gamble. American decision-makers had shown relative restraint in their support of Saigon to this point, but their reaction to the deployment of thousands of Northern troops to the South, if and when it came, might not be so restrained. It might even include an invasion of the DRVN. But even that latter prospect was not enough to dissuade the Politburo, whose willingness to assume such risks was reinforced by two events in 1964 that had nothing to do directly with the American threat. The first was the "voluntary retirement" in mid-October of Soviet Premier Khrushchev, who, it turned out, was ousted by his peers in a bloodless coup, not unlike the one that had just taken place in Hanoi and resulted in Ho Chi Minh's marginalization. Khrushchev had staunchly opposed escalation in Vietnam, fearing it might lead to another crisis between his country and the United States. Le Duan welcomed news of Khrushchev's ouster, presuming it portended the end of the policy of peaceful coexistence, and thus a change in Moscow's policy vis-à-vis his country. The second event was the successful testing of a nuclear bomb by China on 16 October. Beijing's possession of "the bomb" boosted the popularity of Chinese revolutionary prescriptions, and thus Hanoi's confidence in its own ability to prevail in the South. It was also likely to make Washington much more hesitant to invade the DRVN, or so Le Duan thought. In retrospect, if ideology and experience had conditioned Hanoi's decision to settle on total war in September 1964, these fortuitous circumstances validated that choice.

VIETNAM WAR BEGINS

The first PAVN units began marching South via the Ho Chi Minh Trail in October, reaching their destinations a little over a month later. No sooner had they arrived than Hanoi decided to launch a major offensive to take place in two phases between December 1964 and March 1965. The intention was to confront and destroy main force ARVN units, and expand liberated areas, especially in the Central Highlands and along the Cambodian border. Success in those endeavors would dramatically alter the balance of forces below the 17th parallel, imperil the Saigon government, and set the stage for victory before Washington could intervene. Failure, on the other hand, would likely mean war against the United States as early as the following year. The fate of the offensive hinged, not just on the capabilities of the armed forces, but also on the willingness

of the Southern masses to rise against the Saigon regime once they realized that the North had entered the war with sufficient force to win it.
The ambitious campaign was meant to mark the dawn of a new era in
the Vietnamese Revolution, "the era of combining guerrilla warfare with
conventional warfare, combining military attacks with uprisings conducted by the masses." This was tantamount to unconditional endorsement of Resolution 15 of 1959, and so much more.

The results of this "Winter–Spring Campaign" turned out to be mixed
for Hanoi. Despite numerous local successes, Saigon's armed forces were
only dented, and certainly not devastated, as originally intended. Also,
there was no popular uprising, not even an inkling of it. Perhaps the
most consequential event in the campaign occurred on 7 February 1965,
when overzealous Viet Cong guerrillas attacked an American air base at
Pleiku in the Central Highlands, killing eight US servicemen and wound-
ing more than a hundred. Coming on the heels of another raid on a US
airfield at Bien Hoa, outside Saigon, the previous October that killed four
Americans and wounded thirty, the attack on Pleiku became the prover-
bial last straw for Washington decision-makers. American intervention
on a massive scale began shortly thereafter.

Le Duan would thus lose his first major gamble; Vietnam's American
War was about to get underway. Unfortunately for communist forces,
it would not be the last time their leaders erred and they paid the price
for it. As 1964 gave way to 1965, Hanoi was at war in and with the
South, and preparing for American intervention and an onslaught against
the North. "The capital has become a city of war," a foreign diplomat
reported following a visit there in mid-December. "Anti-aircraft guns
have been positioned on rooftops, and people are busy digging trenches
in the streets."[9] Although Americans at the time did not know it yet, the
Vietnam War had begun.

Notes

1   Personalism, formally endorsed by the Diem government, was a hazy politi-
    cal ideology that rejected liberalism and communism and sought to promote
    Asian traditions as it extolled the virtues of Western values.
2   Peter Zinoman, "NhanVan-Giai Pham and Vietnamese 'Reform Communism'
    in the 1950s: A Revisionist Interpretation" in *Journal of Cold War Studies*,
    Vol. 13, no. 1 (2011), 98.
3   Law 10/59 mandated a "sentence of death, and confiscation of the whole of
    or part of his property, with loss of rank in the case of army men," for those
    who commit or attempt to commit "crimes with the aim of sabotage" or oth-
    erwise threaten "the security of the State."

4 Heavy industry, considered essential to achieve affluence and greater autarky in communist states, generally referred to large-scale manufacturing of capital goods and extraction of raw materials. It usually involved such activities as steelmaking, machine tool (industrial machinery) manufacturing, chemical and electrical plants building, and coal and iron mining. Heavy industries produced goods for industrial, not "end" or individual, consumers.

5 Christopher Goscha, *Vietnam: A New History* (New York: Basic Books, 2016), 369.

6 Tuong Vu, *Vietnam's Communist Revolution: The Power and Limits of Ideology* (New York: Cambridge University Press, 2017), 7.

7 "Nghi quyet Hoi nghi Trung uong lan thu 15 (mo rong): Ve tang cuong doan ket, kien quyet dau tranh giu vung hoa binh, thuc hien thong nhat nuoc nha" [Resolution of the Fifteenth Plenum (Expanded): On Strengthening Unity, Resolutely Struggling to Maintain Peace and Unify the Country] in Dang Cong san Viet Nam, *Van kien Dang – Toan tap. Tap 20: 1959* [Party Documents – Collected Works. Volume 20: 1959] (Hanoi: Nha xuat ban Chinh tri quoc gia, 2002), 67.

8 Military Institute of Vietnam (trans. by Merle L. Pribbenow), *Victory in Vietnam: The Official History of the People's Army of Vietnam, 1954–1975* (Lawrence: University of Kansas Press, 2002), 137.

9 Quoted in French Mission at the United Nations to Ministry of Foreign Affairs, Paris, 19 December 1964; 313; Asie-Oceanie: Vietnam Conflict; Archives Diplomatiques de France, La Courneuve, 1.

4

American War, 1965–1968

AMERICANIZATION

In March 1965, the United States responded to the onset of major combat operations and the killing of US personnel by communist forces in South Vietnam by initiating sustained bombing of the North, and, days later, deploying the first of hundreds of thousands of combat troops to the South. In time, forces from South Korea, Australia, Thailand, New Zealand, and the Philippines joined the American effort to curb communist aggression in Indochina and protect the regime in Saigon.[1] This sudden Americanization and partial internationalization of hostilities marked for Hanoi the end of the "Special War" era and the onset of the period of "Limited War" (*chien tranh cuc bo*). Though it had anticipated that scenario if communist forces below the 17th parallel failed to meet the goals outlined in Resolution 9 expeditiously, Le Duan's regime still found it unsettling because it underscored the inability of those forces, which included nearly 10,000 PAVN soldiers by the time the Americans landed, to do what was expected of them, as well as the resilience and competence of South Vietnamese troops. Giap, it seemed, had been right to point out that PAVN and communist forces generally were not ready for "big war."

Hanoi predicated its strategy in the American War on the now familiar tripod of three "modes of struggle," the same as had been used in the Indochina War. The military struggle aimed to attrit enemy forces and protect the human and material assets of the Vietnamese Revolution. Specifically, it aimed to annihilate the ARVN, while coping with its Western allies and limiting the amount of damage those foreign troops could inflict on communist forces. The second mode, political struggle, concerned the use of propaganda to recruit fighters and partisans and fuel popular opposition to the Saigon regime. It was a struggle for South Vietnamese hearts and minds that challenged the enemy in the political and moral realms, considered absolutely vital by Hanoi in the new context. One of that struggle's critical components after 1965 was clandestine proselytization among Saigon's armed forces to encourage desertion and undermine overall morale, *binh van* in Vietnamese communist parlance. For much of the American War, the balance between military and political activities maintained by communist troops and agents in the South depended on the area where they operated. In sparsely populated "mountain-jungle" (*rung nui*) regions, the Central Highlands in particular, they prioritized military struggle; in more populated "lowland-rural" (*dong bang*) areas, especially in Nam Bo and the Mekong River Delta, they maintained an even calibration between military and political action; finally, in cities, where their movement was weakest and exposure made them most vulnerable, communist agents conducted secretive political work almost exclusively.

The third leg of the tripod was diplomatic struggle. Its goal was to garner popular support for the Vietnamese war effort and opposition to American intervention and the regime in Saigon overseas. This globalization of the political struggle aimed to manipulate world opinion and muster sympathy for the anti-American, anti-Saigon cause outside Vietnam, including in the United States. The dark horse that eventually became a crucial part of Hanoi's overall strategy and a central factor in its ultimate triumph, the diplomatic struggle had two critical components after 1965. The first consisted in praising the merits and righteousness of the "Anti-American Resistance for National Salvation," as Hanoi officially called it, and appealing to the spirit of "proletarian internationalism" and "Third-Worldism" (*tiers-mondisme*) to obtain maximal material assistance from "comrades" in the communist camp and "friends" in the Afro-Asian bloc and Latin America. That assistance, Hanoi believed, was essential for efficiently prosecuting the war in the South and defending the North against US air raids. The second component consisted in bringing worldwide attention to the situation in Vietnam, with a view to encouraging international condemnation of American intervention, isolating Washington and its allies diplomatically, and thus limiting their policy options in Indochina. Inspired by their own experience in the Indochina War and the recent triumph of Algerian revolutionaries, whose "diplomatic revolution" had facilitated achievement of their larger strategic goals, Hanoi concluded that, the more the international community condemned US involvement in Vietnam the greater would be the pressure on Washington decision-makers to end it. Skillful use of diplomacy by the Vietnamese and the Algerians during their respective wars against France had demonstrated that Western military power could be partially neutralized by international opinion and the political and moral opprobrium of the global community. The aim was to shame the enemy into abandoning his designs.

Through the diplomatic struggle, communist leaders hoped, not only to exploit "contradictions" between the United States and other countries, but also to drive a wedge between policymakers there and their own people, as they had tried to do against France before. They recognized adverse public opinion and antiwar sentiment as potentially great vulnerabilities of Washington leaders, and key to derailing their efforts to prosecute the war in Vietnam. "People's diplomacy," introduced at the Second Party Congress in 1951, could serve them especially well in this new context. By their reading of American political history, presidential administrations could only do as much as the people allowed them to do; that is, public opinion could validate a policy just as easily as it could force its repudiation. Hanoi also recognized, however, that those administrations always endeavored to shape public opinion to their own advantage. Armed with these understandings, it devised strategies and tactics intended less to attrit US forces – to kill as many troops as it could – than to destroy the willingness of the American people to support the war, of Congress to finance it, and of the White House to prosecute it. "The emphasis was not on military defeat of the United States," David Elliott has fittingly written of Hanoi's approach, "but, rather, on exhausting the strategic possibilities open to it." The core element in that approach was to "defeat the 'aggressive will' (*y chi xam luoc*) of the United States – a psychological objective more than a military one."[2]

Le Duan's regime had done its homework on Washington. It knew that the commitment to contain communism around the world, formalized through the Truman Doctrine of 1947, and honored by every president since, might convince the Johnson administration to get more deeply involved in Vietnam. But it also knew, largely on the basis of its interpretation of the recent war in Korea, that any presidential administration would have a tough time sustaining a war in Vietnam without popular and congressional approval. The centrality of that diplomatic front in Hanoi's strategic calculus – it eventually became more important than the ground war in the South – demonstrated a commendable awareness of the inferiority of its military capabilities vis-à-vis the United States, and how to compensate for it. Therein lies what was arguably the most distinctive aspect of Hanoi's war effort, the most revolutionary – and meritorious – dimension of its strategy: it aimed to defeat the United States by using circumstances outside Vietnam to deny Washington the ability to win.

PEOPLE'S WAR

To meet the aims of the war effort, DRVN authorities initiated a mass mobilization campaign in North Vietnam in April 1965. That they did not do so sooner demonstrates how sure Le Duan's regime was of itself that the United States would not dare deploying combat forces in Vietnam until at least 1966. Known as the "Three Readinesses," the campaign urged men to be ready to fight, join the armed forces, and perform other tasks as necessary. As part of it, the government adopted a new military service law mandating mass conscription of males aged eighteen to forty, indefinite extension of service for those already in the armed forces, and reenlistment of officers and enlisted men recently discharged for budgetary reasons. An unscrupulous few used their family's wealth or political connections to evade the draft. Most were not so lucky. By the end of the year, nearly 300,000 additional troops had been mobilized, two-thirds of them under twenty-six years of age. That brought the total number of servicemen in the PAVN to 400,000. Local militia forces similarly grew, from 1.4 million in 1964 to two million in mid-1965. The guiding principle behind these measures was "Let the Entire People Fight the Enemy and Take Part in National Defense."

Another campaign, the "Three Responsibilities," directed women to replace men on farms and in factories, and otherwise support the war effort however they could. Authorities conjured the Trung Sisters and Lady Trieu, folk heroines who had led rebellions against the Chinese some 2,000 years before, to inspire females to enthusiastically contribute to the anti-American struggle. Thousands of young, mostly single "long-haired warriors," as they became known, would go on to participate in the defense of the North, work on the Ho Chi Minh Trail, and serve as medics and nurses in the South, distinguishing themselves for their valor. Despite finding themselves in harm's way, women were empowered by the war, assuming more visible and important roles in Vietnamese society. Soon, females made up to seventy-five percent of the Northern workforce, and more than half the members of local self-defense units and militias. By 1967 they comprised forty-eight percent of officials in People's Village Councils, the Party's arm at the village level, compared to twenty-one percent when the American War began, and sixteen percent in 1961.

Unlike most Americans, who had no direct ties to the war, practically the entire North Vietnamese population contributed to it in one capacity or another. Children evacuated to the countryside assisted host families by performing various chores as needed, contingent upon their abilities. Artists, including musicians, singers, and actors, traveled to the front to entertain troops and sustain their morale. The fatherland had been invaded by the United States, Hanoi told the masses, and it was every-one's duty to contribute to its defense. Authorities did not hesitate to use coercion when necessary. Families whose members were reluctant to back the war effort, whose sons or fathers sought to evade the draft, to illustrate, received reduced food rations. For Le Duan, the war against the United States was an existential struggle akin to that the Soviet Union had waged against Nazi Germany in World War II. As Stalin had mobilized and led his people to victory against impossible odds, the VWP Secretary would now do the same for his nation.

PAVN SOLDIERS

The Northern soldier deployed to the South in the early phases of the war was between twenty-one and twenty-eight years old, from a peas-ant family, and not an only son, as Hanoi generally exempted such peo-ple from combat duties. After basic training, he underwent specialized military and political training, lasting up to three months and designed explicitly for those going to the South. There, his superiors told him, he would be fighting Americans. Nothing was ever said about fighting other Vietnamese, even though among themselves his leaders had determined that "on the military front, we must above all bring about the annihi-lation of the puppet [i.e., South Vietnamese] armed forces," as iterated earlier in this chapter. As a consequence, troops deployed to the South were often surprised and a bit disoriented when they realized that they were also fighting other Vietnamese, and doing so for much of the time, at least in some areas. The deception was sensible: soldiers would be more motivated going into battle against a foreign enemy than against their own compatriots. It was specifically to reduce the moral conundrum of having to kill other Vietnamese that communist authorities sought to dehumanize their Vietnamese rivals by labeling them "lackeys" and "puppets" of the Americans.

Despite undergoing extensive ideological indoctrination, the average Northern soldier was by no means a devout communist. He did, however, firmly believe in the righteousness of the cause he served. To him, battling Americans below the 17th parallel was not just a way of protecting his family, but a moral duty to his country on behalf of his embattled Southern compatriots. His willingness to serve for these purposes was a way of carrying on the heroic tradition that defined the Vietnamese character, or so his superiors persuasively argued. He was so well-programmed, so well-indoctrinated, that he was prepared to die to uphold that tradition, as he was for the cause of the anti-American war. He considered his chances of eventually returning home to his family alive slim, although, as one study put it, "he obviously would rather be anything than dead." His motto was "Use Weakness to Defeat Strength, Use Rudimentary Weapons to Defeat Modern Weapons, and Use a Drawn-out Struggle to Defeat a Swift Offensive."[3]

Unlike his American counterpart who served a one-year "tour of duty" in South Vietnam, the typical Northern soldier was there for the long haul: that is, indefinitely, for as long as his own physical and mental condition allowed and his superiors determined. His only ways back home were dead, severely maimed, mentally damaged – or victorious. Still, he accepted the constraints he faced and did not see in them reason to give up by going AWOL (absent-without-leave) or surrendering to the enemy. Besides death, his biggest fear was to be left behind on the field of battle, dead or wounded. Death meant his body would never be returned to his family, that he would receive no proper burial and his soul would wander aimlessly for perpetuity. To be seriously wounded and left on the battlefield implied that he would either die in agony or be captured by the enemy and tortured before facing execution. These and related anxieties prompted some Northern soldiers to defect, to go over to the enemy. However, relative to the total number of Northerners who served in the South during the war, defectors were few. By American estimates, they amounted to no more than 2,200 individuals.

COMMUNIST MILITARY ORGANIZATION

Communist forces in the South were divided into three groups. Each group had its own, unique capabilities and responsibilities. Main or Regular Forces were responsible for "national defense," and answered directly to Hanoi. They consisted of professional soldiers of the PAVN and LAF troops trained in the North, for the most part. These forces were highly mobile and often on the front lines of major combat operations. They sported the best, most sophisticated weaponry available. Regular troops were extremely well-disciplined and effective in combat, much as American Marines were. Local or Regional Forces were second-line "defense troops," generally operating within their home provinces, like National Guard units in the United States. They took orders, not straight from Hanoi but from so-called Interzone Committees, as well as COSVN. The combat readiness and effectiveness of local troops varied greatly. They supported Regular Forces in combat, and otherwise engaged enemy forces in ambush-style attacks. Lastly, Popular Forces consisted of "village defense" militias. They did not wear uniforms and were poorly armed, poorly trained part-time guerrillas who worked the fields, or performed some other form of labor, during the day and fought or laid booby-traps at night in platoon-size units (ten to fifteen people). Militiamen – and the women among them, in particular – became the poster children of the communist war effort in the South, even though they rarely engaged US troops in battle. Despite their limited capabilities, militias provided invaluable services, less by fighting than by collecting intelligence for and providing logistical assistance to Regular and Local Forces. Their contributions would in fact prove critical to the success of communist armies in the Vietnam War.

Recognizing the importance of maintaining order, discipline, and strong numbers among its armed forces, Hanoi placed a premium on organization, indoctrination, and mobilization – that is, on political work – among those forces. It assigned one political "commissar" to each military outfit down to the platoon level, if conditions permitted. The commissar shadowed and served as political counterpart to the outfit's military commander. He – commissars were almost invariably male – lectured soldiers on the merits of their struggle and the inevitability of victory during the latter's downtime, with a view to bolstering morale and improving combat effectiveness. He doubled as unit counselor and chaplain, assisting soldiers grappling with personal issues, including emotional problems, and mediating disputes among soldiers, and between soldiers and their officers. The political commissar kept spirits high in challenging times, and in some units even became a father figure of sorts. He essentially "personalize[d] the impersonal Party," acting as "living breathing proof" that distant leaders in Hanoi genuinely cared about those fighting and sacrificing for their cause.[4]

The political commissar supervised "self-criticism sessions," a Party tradition intended to promote investigation, assessment, learning, adaptation, and, ultimately, egalitarianism and improvement within its ranks, through frank exchanges of opinions among members of the same group or organization. During the American War, such sessions afforded any member, irrespective of rank, of a PAVN or LAF unit opportunities to openly express their thoughts on the unit's performance and leadership. Frequently held immediately after combat operations, self-criticism sessions proved invaluable in enhancing the effectiveness and adaptiveness of communist forces in the South. Political commissars also helped administer villages in "liberated" areas of the South and recruit fighters and sympathizers on behalf of the Viet Cong. All communist activities in Southern villages "were aimed at controlling the peasants and channeling their resources for the war," noted one American wartime study. The resulting "effective combination of an extensive village-level organization and a favorable peasant-insurgent relationship" constituted "one of the enduring strengths" of communist forces, and a key contributing factor to their eventual triumph.[5]

Following the war's Americanization, Southern peasants answered the call of communist political agents and volunteered to join the Viet Cong for a variety of reasons. As historian David Hunt and other studies have demonstrated, a majority did so because they believed it was the right thing to do; or, they or members of their immediate family had been mistreated, possibly harmed or tortured, by representatives of the regime in Saigon, its armed forces, or American troops. Peer pressure from friends, relatives, or fellow villagers accounted for the decision of others to enlist, as did the desire to dodge the RVN draft and the promise of more land for their families. Some just sought to escape the drudgery of village life, or a difficult living situation, or else were swayed by recruiters promising them adventure, the chance to shoot guns – even to meet beautiful women and handsome men. Interestingly, a number of Southern females joined the Viet Cong seeking emancipation, to evade traditional obligations such as marrying someone chosen for them by their relatives, and for whom they felt no affection. While several women fought for the Viet Cong, others became political agents, who calculatingly used their femininity and nobility as non-traditional "long-haired" revolutionaries to recruit males.[6]

EARLY STAGES

Although the war in Vietnam became Americanized in March 1965, it took some time for the United States to build up its military capabilities in the South. In fact, it was not until July 1965 that the Johnson administration committed the first sizeable contingent of US troops, more than one hundred thousand of them, to South Vietnam. By then, there had been yet another coup in Saigon, in June, that brought to power a military-led National Leadership Council under Lieutenant General Nguyen Van Thieu (1923–2001) as Head of State. Through the spring and summer of 1965, therefore, the war remained a predominantly Vietnamese affair.

The first major encounter between US and PAVN forces took place in fall 1965 at Ia Drang, in the Central Highlands. The battle began on 14 November and lasted four days. It saw the heaviest fighting to date, and the casualties to show for it. When it was over, the Americans had lost about 250 killed, and the North Vietnamese in excess of 1,000 dead. In an assessment reflecting its willingness to tolerate excessive losses in pursuit of its goals, Hanoi considered the engagement a "victory," demonstrating that "our main force troops had high combat morale and a high resolve to defeat the Americans."[7] Meanwhile, it persisted in its efforts to decimate the ranks of ARVN forces, which it still considered the biggest key to victory. By year's end, communist forces in the South totaled 221,000, those of the United States numbered 175,000, and those of Saigon exceeded half a million.

As communist forces became aware of the dangers of taking on enemy units in large battles, they settled into a protracted war approach, favoring smaller operations that included ambushing isolated US platoons roaming the Vietnamese countryside looking to kill them in "search-and-destroy" operations, the brainchild of US Commander in Vietnam General William Westmoreland (1914–2005). They became partial to fighting in the remote Central Highlands and the Mekong River Delta, which made it more challenging for the United States to bring the full might of its military power to bear on them. To prevail in a war against such a powerful foe, Vietnamese communist forces and their leaders had to be shrewd, cunning, resourceful, disciplined, and adaptive.

The Viet Cong base in Cu Chi District outside Saigon was a testament to all these things. A popular tourist attraction nowadays, it consisted at the time of an underground tunnel complex running several miles right next to a major US air base. The installation included such facilities as nursing stations, an operating room, kitchens, as well as dining, resting, and storage areas – all of them situated beneath layers of dirt. Perhaps most importantly, it allowed guerrillas to operate right under the nose of American forces, to engage them unexpectedly with lethal consequences, and then to disappear quickly. "Lightning attacks" eventually became standard practice for communist forces, and a defining aspect of the Vietnam War. In most instances during the conflict, it was PAVN and

LAF troops waiting in ambush who instigated firefights. They usually retreated and vanished before their enemies could call for air or artillery support, after just a few minutes. Fundamentally, communist forces followed a strategy of evasion during the war, remaining hidden, as in Cu Chi, or constantly moving around, as in the Central Highlands, until ready to engage the enemy at a time and a place of their own choosing. These practices dictated the order of battle in the South, and thus the overall tempo of the war.

This all proved terribly frustrating for US forces, ill-prepared for such combat initially. In its efforts to annihilate hard-to-find communist units, while minimizing American and allied casualties, the US Military Assistance Command, Vietnam (MACV), the organ managing the ground war in the South under the aforementioned General Westmoreland, became keen on bombing suspected enemy positions and strongholds. While the tactic succeeding in killing, maiming, and otherwise demoralizing scores of communist troops, the attendant collateral damage drove neutral civilians into the arms of the Viet Cong. According to one study, "conditional on how strong the Viet Cong presence was in any hamlet [small cluster of houses] at one point in time, the addition of more bombs increased the likelihood that the Viet Cong was able to maintain or increase its level of control in subsequent periods."[8] Beyond that, indiscriminate killing of innocent Southern Vietnamese, from thousands of feet up in the air, served as a powerful propaganda tool in Hanoi's public diplomacy and domestic propaganda campaigns.

AIR WAR AGAINST THE NORTH

As its forces cut their teeth against US troops below the 17th parallel, Hanoi braced for a possible invasion of the North by American and South Vietnamese forces. That contingency had long been a concern of communist leaders, who prepared for it by building massive earth works that included bunkers and underground structures at more than 120 sites in eight provinces. The invasion never materialized, boosting hopes for victory and enabling Le Duan's regime to send ever-increasing numbers of Northern troops to the South. Still, sustained US bombings of the DRVN mandated the retention of large numbers of soldiers in the North to maintain law and order and answer the air raids. Those raids usually targeted the Northern infrastructure, including railroads and bridges, power plants and fuel storage facilities, factories, radar sites, and military bases.

Washington thus aimed to dislocate the DRVN economy while sapping its war-making capabilities, and pressure Hanoi to relent in the South.

The air raids exacted a psychological toll on the population, disrupting and threatening the lives of everyone. However, their predictability – and advance warnings provided by Soviet ships, monitoring American air and naval activities from just off the North Vietnamese coast – helped attenuate their impact. Terrified by the bombings at first, Northerners eventually learned to adjust their lives to the realities they imposed. Despite causing a loosening of government control over social life and domestic economic activity, the air war bolstered anti-American sentiment in the North, facilitating mobilization of human and material resources by the authorities. One anthropologist has noted that, as the frequency and intensity of American raids against the North increased between 1965 and 1968, "the solidarity among villagers increased in support of the war effort, both in terms of resources and manpower."[9] Washington's rationale for conducting the raids – that the North was being punished for its military and political activities in the South – was completely lost on Northern civilians, and DRVN propaganda made sure it stayed that way. In sum, the bombings baffled Northerners, who saw them as something they had to endure for no sensible reason. Fear turning to anger stirred patriotic fervor, and made people eager to contribute to the effort to defeat the United States in the South. In more ways than one, the bombing validated Hanoi's claims that the United States was a nation controlled by "warmongers" bent on turning Vietnam into an American colony.

To defend itself against US bombings, the DRVN assembled over time a rather impressive, but not always effective, air defense apparatus built around advanced radar systems, its own air forces, heavy anti-aircraft guns, and Soviet-made surface-to-air missiles. Air defense forces, bolstered by the presence of Chinese anti-aircraft artillery units, scored notable victories over the Americans in the skies above North Vietnam, but not enough to persuade Washington to halt its attacks. They did, however, shoot down enough enemy warplanes to make US decision-makers fret over the number of American airmen killed or captured flying missions over the North. Well aware of the value of POWs as sources of information, propaganda tools, and leverage in potential peace talks, DRVN authorities mandated civilians to immediately report downed US airmen to local security forces, apprehending them beforehand only if circumstances allowed. Vile as they were, no harm should come to these "pirates," Hanoi insisted, and medical assistance had to be rendered if

FIGURE 4.1 Children helping firemen to put out a fire caused by American bombs, 1966. Photo by Nguyen Ba Khoan, courtesy of his family and National Archives Center 3, Hanoi.

necessary. Rumor in Vietnam today has it that, in a number of isolated instances, angry villagers, acting alone or in mobs, were unable to restrain themselves when faced with an opportunity to punish their tormentors. Instead of following official procedure, they beat or hacked to death the unfortunate soul who parachuted close by, before disposing of the body somewhere safe to avoid discovery, and thus punishment by the government. This may have been the fate of a handful of US military personnel, still listed as MIA. It nearly befell John McCain, now a Senator from Arizona, after his plane was shot down over Hanoi in 1967.

HANOI'S PROPAGANDA MACHINE

While Americans could judge the merits of the war for themselves, thanks to a free press, the North Vietnamese masses never had that opportunity. All the information they had was vetted and manipulated by their government to maximize popular support for the war and stave off opposition to it. Those – very few – individuals who expressed dissent toward the war or the regime were dealt with in ways that deterred others to do the same. If we never speak of popular opposition to the war in North Vietnam as we do in the United States, it is not because it was non-existent, or that Hanoi's cause was more righteous than Washington's; it is because the DRVN's propaganda and security apparatus preempted it. Hanoi's monopoly over information meant that most Northerners could never appreciate the war's complexities, its human and material cost, and the role of their own leaders in precipitating, escalating, and prolonging it. They embraced the opportunity and obligation to serve their country because they were convinced, and remained convinced, that the Americans, like the French before them, wanted to control and exploit their labor and resources. The skillful management of this narrative by Hanoi's Ministry of Culture (formerly the Ministry of Propaganda) and other outfits was a fundamental aspect of Hanoi's strategy in the war.

Northerners kept themselves apprised of the state of the war through newspapers, news reports broadcast over loudspeakers, or the radio. Since the government controlled all outlets, everyone got the same news all of the time. Thanks to that control, the masses saw, heard, and read only what the authorities wanted them to know. They thus understood that the South was a vast graveyard for US troops, hundreds of whom fell to communist bullets each week, and the North a perilous place for US warplanes, dozens of which were shot down each month. Under those circumstances, victory was inevitable. Though communist military strategy below the 17th parallel aimed first and foremost at annihilating South Vietnamese army units, the authorities obscured that fact, as noted above. Instead, they characterized the war as a patriotic national struggle against American imperialism. After all, it was much easier to muster enthusiasm and support for a struggle against foreign aggression than against domestic rivals in Saigon. Better to be fighting an anti-imperialistic war than a fratricidal civil war.

To serve their ends, DRVN authorities continually evoked the, presumably unswerving, spirit of resistance of their people manifested in bygone eras. They cleverly used history as a building block of their domestic propaganda effort, perpetuating the myth of Vietnamese indomitability in the face of external aggression addressed in Chapter 1. They did this variously to motivate soldiers, rally popular support for their policies, and improve morale when times were tough. Fighting the Americans, authorities asserted, was in fact the "moral obligation" of the heirs to a millennia-old tradition of combatting foreign invaders "for national independence and salvation." Romantic belief in traditional heroism was as much an inspiration to resist the Americans as it was a cause for the war's prolongation.

To communicate and spread its message, the central government relied heavily on such "mass organizations" as the Vietnam Women's Union, the

Vietnam Youth Union, and the Vietnam Fatherland Front (VFF), established in 1955 specifically to promote national unity, loyalty to the state and Party, and resistance to foreign aggression and internal subversion. The "emulation" campaigns organized by these groups for their respective constituencies and, in the case of the VFF, for the entire nation, were essentially efforts to manipulate and harness nationalism and patriotism and shape popular perceptions of the war while downplaying its internecine dimensions. In the end, those campaigns contributed notably to Hanoi's success in the American War. And that may well have been the silver lining for Hanoi in the Americanization of hostilities. The American presence on the ground in the South, and in the skies above the North, helped significantly to rally the Northern masses behind the war effort, and retain their support for it year after year.

Because of Hanoi's absolute control over information, Northerners never got a real sense of the nature of the war, and of its cost in Vietnamese lives lost or irreversibly shattered. Combat deaths were rarely reported, and never in a timely fashion. A soldier may have been dead several years before authorities finally notified his family. In fact, most families learned of the death of loved ones only after the war ended in 1975. Those seriously wounded in the line of duty were often prohibited from returning home to avoid undermining morale. They had to wait out the rest of the war in sanctuaries in Laos, Cambodia, and Southern China. References to casualties in the media usually took the form of stories about an individual "martyr," a brave soldier who saved others by, for example, shielding them from enemy gun fire with his own body. Such stories of voluntary sacrifice and heroism, accurate as they may have been, functioned to glamorize the war effort and assure Northerners that those fighting in the South were in good hands, surrounded by comrades determined to keep them safe and alive. On rare occasions a family received a letter from a relative deployed in the South, hand-carried by a fellow soldier recalled to the North; there was no mail delivery system between the two halves of Vietnam during the war. But even such correspondence was unlikely to provide accurate information about realities, since North Vietnamese soldiers were under strict orders to reveal nothing "sensitive" about their circumstances, defined by the authorities as pretty much anything they were involved in. Besides, circulating news of hardships undermined civilian morale, which was a crime. Most families suspected, but could never know for sure, that their relatives in the armed forces were actually in the South. By army regulation, soldiers slated for deployment there were not allowed to tell loved ones where they were headed, even if they knew: only that they were going away, somewhere, possibly abroad, on an important mission. Since they could not write freely or honestly about their experiences, or else did not want to give their families false hope for their imminent return, most did not write at all.

Independent sources of information about the war were, to all intents and purposes, non-existent. A handful of foreign publications were allowed into the country, mostly from other communist states. But even those were censored, despite the fact that they were usually intended for non-Vietnamese – mainly, foreign diplomats in the capital. To illustrate how complete the censorship was, censors literally cut out of each copy of every foreign newspaper and magazine any item or portion of an item deemed objectionable. Foreign journalists and other visitors, usually prominent antiwar activists, occasionally traveled to the DRVN by invitation from the authorities, but those visits were so meticulously planned and supervised that they afforded no opportunity for meaningful exchanges between visitors and local civilians. Few of these guests would have criticized anything they saw or experienced anyway; all were granted access in the first place because of their sympathetic views on the American War or their ties to friendly political organizations.

Despite limited pertinent experience, resources, and technological savviness, North Vietnamese authorities proved expert manipulators and fabricators of information. That expertise allowed them to dictate the narrative of the war – irrespective of its realities, to control and steer their own people's attitude toward it, and even to shape perceptions of the conflict across the rest of the world, including in the United States.

DOMESTIC RESTRUCTURING

After the American War began, Hanoi remained committed to economic development and communist transformation in the North. Now more than ever, the DRVN needed to be a solid rear base for the resistance in the South, its leaders thought. To that end, both manufacturing and agriculture had to produce at optimal levels. Authorities circulated a new slogan, "Producing while Fighting," to impress upon people the importance of maximum efforts and outputs in factories and fields. This was difficult for everyone. Dislocating the DRVN economy was a central aim of the American air war, and US bombers regularly targeted industrial plants. Facilities located within populated urban cores generally escaped direct attack as Washington sought to minimize collateral damage to avoid international outcry; but those elsewhere were attacked repeatedly. And although the bombings never targeted farming as such, each fly-over disrupted production by forcing a work stoppage. Peasants constantly worried that enemy planes would destroy irrigation and protective dikes and flood their fields and homes, but that never occurred on a systematic scale.

At the time the American War broke out, the Northern economy was still based on subsistence agriculture. Peasants had little need for manufactured goods and similar products. Still, bombing-related disruptions of industrial production were damaging because they stopped the clock on development. Since the end of the war against France, more than a decade before, DRVN leaders had sought to rehabilitate and then modernize the economy while reinventing society. Now, that effort and hard work were imperiled. In addition, as the disruptions mounted, Hanoi became ever more dependent upon allies and friends. Its fight for independence could lose all meaning if the price of victory was reliance on others for even basic commodities. Besides, Le Duan's regime understood only too well that the more economic, military, and other aid it accepted from the Soviet Union and China, the more entitled leaders there would feel to tell it how to conduct its business. That was a potential source of trouble as Le Duan was never going to allow those allies to dictate or even meddle in the conduct of the Vietnamese Revolution. Advice would be considered but accepted only when it seemed consistent with his regime's pursuit of its own objectives. Ever grateful for and dependent on the support of allies, Hanoi was never beholden to them.

To alleviate the impact of the bombing on the industrial sector, DRVN authorities mandated localized, dispersed production. Regional manufacturing of goods for local consumption, with export of surplus production, was the best way to support the nation against an enemy that bombed roads, bridges, and rail lines almost at will. In time, dispersed workshops and small factories replaced large industrial plants. Several provinces became self-sufficient, capable of providing "on-the-spot supplies" for essential needs. Factories deemed indispensable, or whose operations could not be parceled out, were relocated to areas Washington was unlikely to attack, such as downtown Hanoi and Haiphong. Following the evacuation of its teachers and pupils to the countryside, to illustrate, the National Music School building in the capital housed a displaced factory. Despite its best efforts to remain self-sufficient, the DRVN could never have sustained its war effort without a massive influx of outside aid.

REFUSAL TO NEGOTIATE

Then and since, much has been made of missed opportunities for peace after the American War began. By some accounts, the conflict could have ended much sooner than it did, and without nearly as much bloodshed, had the United States in particular seized one of these opportunities. Those accounts ignore an essential point: namely, what peace meant to decision-makers in Hanoi during the war. For Le Duan, peace entailed not just the absence of war, but total victory: that is, the unconditional departure of the Americans and their foreign allies, surrender of the Saigon regime, and reunification of Vietnam under communist governance. Anything less than that was unacceptable to him. The Party Secretary never had any intention of indefinitely suspending hostilities unless Washington and Saigon accommodated all his regime's demands, tantamount to capitulation. Compromise was weakness to him. It implied failure to achieve core objectives – the totality of them. However eager or sincere Washington's desire to end the war through negotiation may have been, a diplomatic solution resulting from give-and-take negotiations had no chance in the middle and late 1960s: Le Duan was consumed by thoughts of total victory, and confident of its imminent realization.

Several factors informed Le Duan and his regime's stance on negotiations. The first and most significant was the specter of Geneva. A little over a decade before, Ho Chi Minh and other DRVN leaders had shown good faith and assented to a diplomatic resolution of the war with France. The prospect of peacefully achieving within two years what fighting had failed to deliver in eight had been alluring. Unfortunately, it proved illusory. Because of that mistake, Hanoi was no further along in its effort to reunify the country now than it had been a decade before. In fact, things were worse: the Americans had replaced the French. In retrospect, achieving the goals of national liberation and reunification seemed more plausible in 1954 than it did in the mid-1960s. If only the DRVN had kept fighting the French after Dien Bien Phu, Le Duan thought, the nation would already have been reunified under Hanoi's governance, and it would not have to fight the Americans now. How could Ho have shown so little grit, been so shortsighted, at so critical a juncture? That was hindsight, to be sure, and hindsight is always 20/20. But whatever its merits, that reasoning shaped the thinking of North Vietnamese leaders on matters of diplomatic negotiations after 1965.

A second reason Le Duan's regime frowned upon negotiations was a lesson it inferred from the Geneva experience: imperialists and their lackeys could not be trusted. That is, they agreed to negotiations and sometimes even to settlements, but only to deceive, to buy time to gain military advantage. (That, of course, was something Hanoi itself would do later, as prescribed in Mao's approach to "people's war.") Accordingly, only defeat on the field of battle would convince Washington to get out of Vietnam. In a speech to the National Assembly in April 1965, DRVN Prime Minister Pham Van Dong explained that, in the aftermath of the Geneva accords, "the US imperialists gradually [sought] to replace the French colonialists in South Vietnam, set up the Ngo Dinh Diem puppet administration, wiped out one by one opposition groups, and carried out ruthless and wicked repressions against the people." The Americans had shown no respect for the Geneva accords or for the rights of the Indochinese peoples under those accords, and they now "drowned in blood all patriotic forces aspiring to independence, democracy, and peaceful national reunification" in Vietnam. Negotiations with that kind of enemy were not just pointless, they were foolish and even dangerous. "Popular violence is the only way to oppose the violence of the imperialist aggressor," Dong concluded.[10]

The belief of core leaders in the merits of violence, and in "just struggle," constituted a third reason Hanoi refused to negotiate early on. Le Duan, Le Duc Tho, Nguyen Chi Thanh, and Pham Hung were all hardened communists, imbued with a dogmatic faith in the centrality of armed struggle to achieve revolutionary goals. Though their "brand" of communism was distinctive in its own ways, their views on revolutionary change were essentially those of Mao. For them as for Mao, war was the only means of securing strategic objectives in the face of imperialist aggression; it was also the only means of sanctifying the national liberation struggle. In this sense, any compromise to end the war against the United States would betray the very ideals that inspired the Vietnamese Revolution in general and the struggle for national reunification in particular. Le Duan and the others who now decided policy in Hanoi would have never gone for that. The Secretary had been calling for armed struggle since 1954. For nearly a decade his pleas had fallen on the deaf ears of a leadership dominated by Ho and other doves, who saw little merit in national liberation and reunification achieved by force, and who cowered before the prospect of war with the United States. These soft men had been sidelined by Le Duan and his ilk, who were finally calling the shots on national policy. There was no way those men would now abandon their longtime willingness to use of violence to expedite Southern liberation and national reunification.

A fourth reason Hanoi forewent diplomatic negotiation was its commitment to patriotic internationalism, and thus its hope to serve as inspiration and example for other national liberation movements in Asia, Africa, the Middle East, and Latin America. That end demanded that it defeat the United States unequivocally. A secret Party document revealing this conviction notes that "proletarian internationalism" drove the anti-American effort in Vietnam; accordingly, compromise would let down not just the Vietnamese people, but everyone elsewhere invested in "world revolution." To be, as Le Duan and his closest comrades were, committed communists also meant that they were self-confessed internationalists. Unlike other nationalists who considered ethnicity the defining element in their ideology, North Vietnamese leaders thought social class trumped national identity. As "real" communists, their allies were all members of the proletariat, of working and peasant classes, irrespective of ethnicity or nationality. Their enemies were the exploiters of all such groups, domestic and foreign. Driven by such convictions, North Vietnamese leaders saw their revolution as a vanguard movement with the potential to rouse oppressed masses around the world. Achieving a decisive triumph over the United States, they thought, would do just that. "We have to establish a world front that will be built first by some core countries and later enlarged to include African and Latin American countries," Le Duan vowed. Vietnamese communists had a special role to play in class struggles throughout the colonial and semi-colonial world. "Final victory" in their "sacred struggle" would mean "not only an immense step forward in the Vietnamese revolution but also an active contribution to strengthen the world revolution." Fighting the Americans until final victory in Vietnam, Le Duan repeated to Chinese premier Zhou Enlai, was indeed the "moral obligation" of his people and of his regime.[11] He even bragged that he accepted the possibility of an "enormous bloodletting" to fulfil that mission.

Finally, Hanoi renounced diplomatic negotiations to avoid alienating its supporters in the South. Revolutionaries and their sympathizers there had already been betrayed once before by Party leaders. The possibility of another compromise agreement, mandating a halt to the armed struggle they had only recently resumed, and leaving Saigon in charge of certain areas, was inconceivable. On the one hand, it would have lent damaging credibility to speculations that emerged when Ho was still in charge: that the North cared little about people in the South, that it was even prepared to accept a permanent division of their country. As noted earlier, many Southerners interpreted Ho's North-first policy after 1954 as proof that they would always be nothing more than a "sacrificial animal" in the eyes of Northern authorities. On the other, Le Duan and his closest collaborators had personally invested too much in the Southern revolutionary movement to risk impeding its progress. After years of distress and neglect, that movement was finally gaining strength and momentum. Negotiating with the enemy under such circumstances was sure to demoralize Southerners and compromise, if not altogether terminate, Hanoi's control over the Viet Cong.

Unlike Ho, Le Duan was prepared to pull out all the stops to achieve Southern liberation. His regime "made the unity of the country one of [its] reasons for fighting and living," one scholar has noted.[12] Accordingly, it had nothing to negotiate. But even though Le Duan's regime saw no merit in genuine negotiations, it shrewdly recognized the short-term political advantages of *looking like* it wanted to negotiate. To that end it publicly welcomed initiatives by third parties to jump-start peace talks. Among those offering their good offices after 1965 were France, Britain, Canada, Italy, Poland, Romania, Ghana, the Soviet Union, and the UN. However, none of those initiatives – no less than 200 during the war – achieved anything: Hanoi invariably came up with excuses not to talk, or else conditions that American decision-makers, with good reason, found unacceptable.

To maintain the pretense of openness to negotiations, shortly after the war's onset the DRVN Foreign Ministry put forth a four-point proposal to end the war diplomatically. Its positions included:

1. Unilateral withdrawal of American forces and support personnel from Indochina.
2. Cessation of all attacks against the North.
3. Settlement of political issues pertaining to the South by the people there preceded by replacement of the regime in Saigon with a provisional coalition government dominated by neutralists and communists.
4. Respect for the sovereignty and territorial integrity of Vietnam consistent with the terms of the 1954 Geneva accords.

Seemingly a legitimate and reasonable platform upon which to negotiate a sustainable peace, the plan actually required the United States to meet the first two points before talks could even begin! In this sense, it was not a workable proposal. Le Duan would have peace, but only on his terms.

RELATIONS WITH ALLIES

Hanoi's anti-American strategy, including its refusal to negotiate with Washington, delighted Beijing, which expressed its support and gratitude by extending generous military and economic aid. China would in fact provide the bulk of the small arms and ammunition used by the PAVN and LAF against the Americans and their allies in the South, as well as fighter-jet aircraft (MiGs 17, 19, and 21) to the DRVN's People's Army Air Force, flown from bases in Southern China for their protection. Beijing also sent tens of thousands of troops from its own People's Liberation Army (PLA) to assist the DRVN with various war-related tasks, including the aforementioned anti-aircraft gun crews. In 1967, the peak year, more than 170,000 Chinese military personnel were stationed in North Vietnam.[13] Combat engineers supported the construction of defensive positions for use in case the United States decided to invade the North, previously mentioned, and helped maintain and improve road and rail links along their common border. Other troops, including anti-aircraft artillery units, beefed up North Vietnamese air and coastal defenses. Chinese crews reportedly downed 126 US planes during the war. Combat units, including field gun and mortar regiments, also operated above the 21st parallel (Hanoi did not allow them south of the Red River). The presence of these units boosted North Vietnamese morale, and served as a first-line defense should the United States invade the DRVN. Because of the long history of troubled relations between the two countries, and to help relations between its own troops and their hosts, the Chinese High Command issued each PLA soldier serving in North Vietnam a "discipline handbook," which described proper behavior while stationed there. In addition, Chinese troops in the DRVN had to wear either PAVN or workers' uniforms, or civilian clothes, not only to avoid detection by the Americans but to show deference toward the local population.

Several factors from the appeal of proletarian internationalism and Asian solidarity to its own national security concerns influenced Beijing's response to the situation in Vietnam, including its decision to generously assist Hanoi's war effort. Arguably the most consequential was the Sino-Soviet dispute. Just as Washington came to the rescue of the regime in Saigon in 1965 to prove the seriousness of its commitment to the Truman Doctrine and the containment of communism, Beijing provided ever-increasing support to Hanoi to demonstrate its revolutionary superiority over the Soviet Union. The North Vietnamese had effectively disavowed peaceful coexistence, and were waging a war of national liberation that chipped away at American power. Success in that struggle would boost Mao's revolutionary credentials, enhancing his appeal among Third World revolutionaries while undermining the attraction of Moscow's more cautious example. For Mao, Vietnam was a laboratory, and the war there an experiment to prove the correctness of his views on national liberation, and thus on the most effective way of addressing the world struggle between capitalism and communism.

By the mid-1960s, Beijing deemed the Soviet Union, not the United States, its foremost enemy. In its strategic calculus, Soviet heresy – the "revisionist" condemnation of violent revolution for the sake of East-West détente – was tearing apart the communist camp and endangering the future of global communism. It was, in this sense, even more dangerous than capitalism and American imperialism, both of which threatened communism from outside, not within. Furthermore, Moscow's soft, accommodationist stance concerning the capitalist world now stood in stark contrast to Mao's own. In the circumstances, Hanoi's decision to fight the Americans in the South almost compelled Beijing to lend the Vietnamese all the help it could. Interestingly, however, although Mao pressed Hanoi to fight, he did not want the war to get out of hand. He preferred a limited conflict that bogged down and "bled" the Americans, roused Third World revolutionaries, and ran no risk of devolving into a larger war involving his country. Taking on the US military directly, as his forces had done during the Korean War, was an experience Mao did not want to repeat.

Ironically, the same Sino-Soviet dispute also spurred Moscow to provide copious amounts of aid to the DRVN despite Hanoi's ideological proximity to Beijing and belligerent strategy in the South, that went against the tenets of peaceful coexistence. The Soviet Union had minimally contributed to the Vietminh's effort during the Indochina War. After the signing of the Geneva accords, however, it developed much closer ties to Ho Chi Minh's government, providing invaluable technical expertise and assistance for the rehabilitation and communist transformation of the North's economy and society. Moscow leaders felt Hanoi deserved their support because the Vietnamese had suffered greatly during the Indochina War; and, perhaps most important, Ho had in effect embraced peaceful coexistence thereafter. After hawks seized power in Hanoi and sidelined Ho, and then decided to revise VWP strategy in the South, Le Duan himself went to plead for military aid from the Soviets. An angry and disapproving Khrushchev turned him down. Hanoi was wrong to instigate a war to bring about national reunification; international conditions were not propitious for that, Khrushchev scolded his North Vietnamese counterpart. Instead of fighting, Hanoi should find a diplomatic solution to its differences with Saigon and Washington.

Following Khrushchev's ouster from power in late 1964, and especially after Americanization of the war the following year, Moscow's stance toward Vietnam changed. It still urged Hanoi to pursue a negotiated settlement, but finally agreed to provide military and other assistance. It did this both to help North Vietnam defend itself against US air raids and prove its reliability as an ally and leader of the communist bloc, openly questioned by China. International prestige mattered to Soviet leaders. Breaking ranks with Hanoi would not only "arouse contempt among other communist states," a wartime intelligence analysis observed, but also "risk their prospects for a substantial future role in Southeast Asia." The systematic elimination of Indonesian communists – hundreds of thousands of them – by right-wingers who seized power in a coup in Jakarta in 1965, one of the biggest blows to international communism during the Cold War, likewise conditioned Moscow's decision to render more aid to the Vietnamese starting that year, particularly as the coup in Indonesia came in the wake of similar, albeit less bloody, occurrences in Brazil and Bolivia the year before. Much as the discord with Beijing affected its strategic calculations, Moscow still needed to hold its own against the United States in that contest of will. All else being equal, had it not been for the Sino-Soviet dispute and larger Cold War considerations, Moscow, like Beijing, would never have supported the Vietnamese to the degree, and for as long as, it did.

The Sino-Soviet dispute was a real blessing in disguise for DRVN leaders. Because of it, each Moscow and Beijing desperately sought Hanoi's constancy, support, and approbation. The North Vietnamese leadership thus found itself in the highly enviable position of being locked in a metaphorical love triangle, courted by two suitors at once. Well aware of that, Hanoi turned the competition between the two powers to its advantage. It publicly kept a certain distance from both, even as it privately claimed to have a special, intimate relationship with each. It effectively played one against the other to squeeze maximal assistance from them. The would-be puppet thus became the puppeteer. Most notably, North Vietnamese leaders capitalized on Soviet fears of their alignment with Beijing to secure advanced weapons systems, including surface-to-air missiles, and technicians to operate them. In this and other ways, the Sino-Soviet dispute created circumstances without which Hanoi would never have been able to hold its own against the United States and its South Vietnamese allies.

Although it was no secret it favored Beijing's revolutionary prescriptions, Le Duan's regime carefully avoided public comment on that and the Sino-Soviet dispute in general. Its pretense of impartiality and neutrality in the dispute kept both sides guessing about its true loyalties, to a degree at least, which allowed the DRVN to keep receiving assistance from both. To maintain that pretense, DRVN Foreign Ministry officials, including diplomats stationed abroad, were under strict orders never to raise the matter of the dispute, in either formal or informal discussions with foreign officials and dignitaries, especially Chinese and Soviet ones; and they were always to speak with equal appreciation of the contributions of both Beijing and Moscow to global communism, world peace, and the Vietnamese reunification struggle when circumstances warranted. Party and government officials were strictly forbidden from commenting on the state of Sino-Vietnamese and Soviet-Vietnamese relations, unless their comments had previously been vetted by their superiors.

The vagaries in the relationship between Hanoi and its allies attested to an important reality of international relations during the Cold War: namely, that big powers did not always have their way with "satellite" states. In fact, the latter sometimes exercised more influence over the former, as Nasser's Egypt, Castro's Cuba, and the Shah's Iran demonstrated. The United States, the Soviet Union, and China were surprisingly vulnerable to the caprices of international politics during the Cold War. Some of Washington's friends thought its fear of communism inordinate; some of Moscow's allies questioned its commitment to peaceful coexistence; and some of Beijing's loyalists thought its break with Moscow unhelpful. These disagreements meaningfully conditioned the foreign policies of the United States, the Soviet Union, and China, respectively. Allies depended on them, foes were supposed to fear them, and the rest of the world watched all of them, often nervously. For these big powers, prestige and credibility, the main currencies of international politics, counted as much as actual power. They were indispensable for deterring enemies, reassuring allies, and otherwise advancing their own interests in the Cold War. That reality was not lost on leaders in the DRVN and other undersized states. In this sense, the latter were often much more than pawns in superpower games; they influenced their own destinies in usually significant ways. Hanoi was a truly independent actor in the Sino-Soviet rivalry, and in the Vietnam War. While the events that unfolded in Indochina during the 1960s and 70s were certainly tragic, they were just as certainly not solely the product of big power intercession and tampering.

Much as Hanoi benefited from the Sino-Soviet dispute, the tension between Beijing and Moscow was also a major headache for it. For instance, Chinese leaders periodically denied Moscow access to their territory for physically transferring aid to the DRVN, thus causing long delays in the delivery of Soviet military and other supplies, which had to come by sea instead of air or rail. The tensions were also troubling because they kept getting worse. Collapsing Sino-Soviet relations made ever-present the possibility of an aid cutoff, if one ally or the other grew tired of Hanoi's balancing act, and insisted that it take a side in the dispute. Even a minor reduction in aid would have imperiled Hanoi's anti-American struggle. Foreign aid, in conjunction with decentralization of industrial production, kept the DRVN economy afloat; Soviet arms transfers bolstered its air defense capabilities; and Chinese aid enabled communist forces to hold their own against American troops and their allies below the 17th parallel.

DIPLOMATIC STRUGGLE

As their handling of the Sino-Soviet dispute exemplifies, DRVN leaders were keen observers of, and active participants in, international politics. They had to be, in order to meet the goals of the diplomatic struggle upon which they relied to offset the disparities between their political and military capabilities and those of their enemies. Despite limited means and qualified personnel, Hanoi was surprisingly successful in establishing and maintaining constructive diplomatic contacts with the outside world, as well as a meaningful diplomatic presence – for itself and the NLF – on all major continents. DRVN and NLF diplomats and missions abroad served several important purposes. They enhanced the political legitimacy of both organizations while validating their claims to be, respectively, the sole representative government of the Vietnamese people, and the sole representative body of Vietnamese living below the 17th parallel. Equally important, they gathered information, propagandized for the cause of Vietnamese independence and reunification, and collected and distributed documentation about the "criminal behavior" of US troops and their leaders in Indochina. To these ends, diplomats developed close partnerships with host governments and their intelligence communities, such as the *Stasi* – the Ministry for State Security, the national security service – in East Germany, which taught DRVN authorities how to spy on their own people, and also on the diplomatic corps in the North Vietnamese capital. They also regularly hosted activists who opposed the American war in Vietnam, as well as representatives of "progressive" constituencies, such as student and women's associations from the United States and other Western countries, with a view to shaping the Western political imagination, and the American one in particular. Communist diplomats serving overseas were voracious readers of local and national newspapers, from which they collected pertinent clippings they then forwarded to Hanoi (whose archives today abound with them).

Arguably, the most important function of DRVN and NLF diplomats overseas was to engage in public diplomacy, specifically, to disseminate information about the war which highlighted the justness of the struggle of the Vietnamese people, and the American role in their victimization. There was nothing objective about this endeavor: it was propaganda that sought to shape public perceptions of the conflict, pure and simple. Still, this propaganda proved remarkably persuasive in the absence of other, more objective sources of information, and Washington's failure to effectually counter it in particular. Hanoi would come to excel at marketing its own struggle, not only in Vietnam but around the world. It proved especially adept at recruiting influential antiwar activists to spread its message, and through them creating a transnational network of opposition to the American War. *New York Times* correspondent Harrison Salisbury (1908–93), movie star Jane Fonda (b. 1937), and famous essayist Susan Sontag (1933–2004) were among the Americans it co-opted to spread its message. By invitation of the DRVN government, each visited the North during the war, and thereafter wrote and spoke favorably of Hanoi and the NLF's efforts, as they denounced Washington's war against them. Le Duan's regime considered personal or "people's diplomacy," as it called it, and such "citizen diplomats" to have "the potential to significantly shape the political discourse in the United States and the decisions of American policymakers," according to historian Judy Tzu-Chun Wu.[14] Indeed, most guests returned to the United States emboldened by their experience among the North Vietnamese, and eager to do even more for the antiwar cause.

Vietnamese communist policymakers had learned to appreciate the merits of public diplomacy, and the value of propaganda, during the war against France. But their biggest inspiration was the success of the recent international public relations campaign conducted by the Algerian National Liberation Front (*Front de libération nationale [Algérie]*, or FLN) in its triumphant war against France. The FLN had mounted a truly impressive campaign to rally world opinion in support of its liberation struggle against French colonialists. That campaign had effectively weaponized propaganda – and with it, diplomacy – turning both into assets to support the armed struggle. This was not the first time diplomacy, customarily an antidote to war, had been used as an instrument of war. But rarely had that end been achieved so successfully. The FLN had even managed to have its struggle take center stage at the UN, despite not being a member of that organization. That, and related initiatives, globalized concerns over the Algerian War, and dramatically increased pressure on France to abandon its claims to Algeria. In doing all that, the FLN drew on the resources and influence of the Afro-Asian bloc, the Non-Aligned Movement, and the Third World generally. It even received substantial military assistance from the communist camp, even though none of its leaders was communist.

ENGAGING THREE CIRCLES

From the Algerian experience, the Vietnamese learned the merits of appearing to be all things to all people, to appeal to as many demographics as possible to secure maximal political and moral support from each. During the Vietnam War, Hanoi's diplomacy targeted three "circles" in particular. The first was other communist parties: not just those in the Soviet Union and China, but also East Europe, North Korea, and Cuba, whose support was solicited on the grounds that the Vietnam War was an integral part of the global revolutionary struggle against capitalism and imperialism on behalf of proletarian internationalism. Hanoi used the confidentiality afforded by party-to-party contacts, governed by the golden rule of "what-is-said-among-communist-parties-stays-among-communist-parties," to more or less honestly present its circumstances, problems, and needs, and request the assistance necessary to cope with them. Le Duan's regime, always wary of outsiders, generally trusted its communist allies, to a degree, at least. Communist solidarity, the VWP Secretary believed, obligated fraternal parties to do all they could to help comrades in need, especially those in Hanoi's circumstances. Exploiting party-to-party contacts on this basis helped Le Duan obtain the bulk of the military hardware his forces used – and needed – to fight the Americans.

The second "circle" in this quest for support comprised non-communist, nationalist regimes in the Third World, including members of the Non-Aligned Movement. Here, the efforts of diplomats and other officials from the DRVN Foreign Ministry – a government, not a Party, organ – took center stage. Admittedly, ranking members of the North

Vietnamese government, especially the Foreign Ministry, were also invariably members of the VWP. That was, in fact, a requisite for government service at high levels. However, in engaging and soliciting support from Third World governments, Foreign Ministry officials downplayed their communist credentials, as they did Hanoi's intimate ties to the communist bloc. After all, other than Yugoslavia, all of the major non-aligned countries had non-communist governments. Some even banned national communist parties from participating in their state's political life. The communist credentials of DRVN representatives were of course known, but those representatives emphasized their nationalist credentials instead.

Foreign Ministry officials solicited political and moral support from Third World countries – including Algeria, Egypt, and newly-independent sub-Sahara African states – by casting Hanoi's war as a struggle for national reunification and self-determination, which resonated deeply in such places. They characterized the American intervention in Vietnam as a neo-colonial crusade. The presence of American forces in the South, and bombings of the North, they maintained, constituted crimes against the Vietnamese people, and a denial of their right to independence and the protection of international law. A special DRVN government agency, the American War Crimes Investigative Commission, compiled numbers and produced detailed, though quite exaggerated, reports on "illegal," "immoral," and "criminal" American activities in Vietnam. Fundamentally, these government-to-government contacts were intended to enhance the DRVN's legitimacy as a polity and, by extension, expose the unlawfulness of the regime in Saigon, and the criminality of decision-makers in Washington. These efforts made members of the UN General Assembly, particularly African and other Asian states, sympathetic to Vietnam's plight and antagonistic toward Washington. Government-to-government contacts were Hanoi's best chance to replicate the success of the Algerian revolutionaries, and were thus taken quite seriously by DRVN authorities.

The third and final "circle" in the DRVN's search for outside support consisted of non-state actors such as student, women's, and labor unions, particularly in the West. That circle was the purview of the NLF and its Foreign Relations Commission, acting as they always did under Hanoi's secret instructions. The Front's "guerilla diplomacy" was a critical component of Hanoi's diplomatic strategy. It served specifically to turn Western publics against their own governments supportive of American policy in Vietnam, and against the US government specifically. As a non-state actor, the NLF could ignore formal diplomatic channels (even though it possessed its own foreign affairs department and diplomatic missions abroad) and readily engage interest groups and individuals. The Front became a dynamic element in various transnational causes, most notably national liberation, women's rights, and student/youth activism, the tide of which crested in the 1960s and 70s. "Its public diplomacy," historians Mark Philip Bradley and Viet Thanh Nguyen have written of the NLF, in fact "built upon and deepened an emergent global symbolic theater of quasi-state diplomacy."[15]

Posing as a purely nationalist and emancipatory organization, the NLF found favor with broad segments of the international community, particularly grass-roots, left-leaning, non-communist organizations. As a participant in the fight against foreign domination in Indochina, it also gained sympathy from liberation movements throughout Asia, Africa, and Latin America. The NLF's struggle against the "tyranny" of the Saigon regime and its manipulative outside backers resonated among disenfranchised, marginalized, and ideologically disaffected groups the world over. In tone, and ostensibly in substance, the NLF's action program was consonant with the platforms of resistance movements around the world, whether revolutionary fronts in the Third World or counter-cultural and progressive action groups challenging the status quo in the First. In time, the NLF became a symbol of defiance against the state, of opposition to the international order dominated by the *pax Americana*, and of rebellion against policies perceived, rightly or wrongly, to be unjust by certain non-conformist factions.

AMERICAN ANTIWAR MOVEMENT

By virtue of its roots in this broad-based appeal, the NLF could even charm and marshal sympathy from organizations and individuals inside the United States. Its struggle captured the political imagination of Americans dissatisfied with the status quo at home and struggling for their own brand of justice. The NLF became an icon for American radicals, who often adopted its flag as a symbol of their own resistance effort. It nurtured that sympathy by hosting antiwar and social activists, as well as academics, from the United States at its missions abroad and even in "liberated areas" of South Vietnam. The more the Front reached out to and engaged its own supporters in the West, Hanoi correctly estimated, the more they spoke and wrote favorably of its purposes. That, in turn, facilitated the mobilization of larger numbers of Americans against their government's intervention in Southeast Asia. Female Viet Cong warriors, rare as they were in reality, became objects of special adulation in American feminist circles because they attested to the possibilities of social emancipation. Radical African American civil rights activists, for their part, shared a sense of commonality and kinship with the Vietnamese resisting the American intrusion upon their country. They chanted "No Viet Cong Ever Called Me Nigger," a mantra misattributed to the American boxer Muhammad Ali, at rallies to suggest the absurdity of fighting noble revolutionaries overseas while racism thrived at home.[16] The militant Black Panther Party even proposed sending members to South Vietnam to fight alongside the Viet Cong, as it did to other places struggling for national liberation. Meanwhile, pacifist religious organizations sent to both the DRVN and NLF medical and other supplies purportedly intended for civilians and children. Quakers and Mennonites were especially active in these respects, as well as in protesting the war at home.

NLF propaganda, like that of the DRVN, never failed to note that the gripe of the Vietnamese was not with the American people, but with Washington policymakers. In that alone, they had much in common with disaffected groups in the United States. Their propaganda invariably characterized Americans in flattering terms, as peace-loving and progressive, but their leaders as duplicitous and imperialistic. Differentiating between the "desire for peace of the American people" and the "warmongering tendencies" of Washington policymakers allowed the NLF to appeal directly to the American masses without contradicting the line of argument espoused by the authorities in Hanoi that the United States was the source of all evils in Vietnam. Admittedly, various elements contributed to the rise of antiwar sentiment in the United States, but the successful spread of the image of the NLF as a hapless victim of Washington's criminality warranted some reciprocity. The NLF looked magnanimous; American policymakers seemed maniacal. That, to no insignificant degree, helped turn American opinion against the war.

In retrospect, few factors did more to encumber Washington's efforts to prosecute the Vietnam War than the resulting domestic opposition to it. Public diplomacy may not have singlehandedly won the war for Hanoi, but it certainly played a seminal role in shaping its outcome. The antiwar movement never rallied a majority of the population in the United States, but it was vocal and well organized, and featured prominently on the front pages of newspapers and during network television evening news broadcasts. It raised troubling questions about the legitimacy and effectiveness of the American intervention, roused opponents of the administration, including otherwise sympathetic moderate civil rights leaders and their supporters, and widened the credibility gap between the Oval Office and the people. The antiwar movement became emblematic of a growing malaise in American society, characterized by a mounting lack of trust in the competence of the federal government. It also incited, even as it seemed to validate, foreign criticism of American policy in Indochina. After all, if Americans themselves – a meaningful segment of them, at least – stood in opposition to the war, why should others abroad not do the same? The net effect of these trends was to alienate many Americans from their own government. This result was far from absolute, but it was sizeable and meaningful enough in time to topple an American president.

DIVIDENDS OF INTERNATIONALISM

Hanoi's wide-ranging public diplomacy campaign reflected its views of its own stake in the shifting currents of international relations in the mid-1960s. The Cold War had divided the world into two hostile blocs, and made the situation in South Vietnam after 1965 a major expression of that hostility. Recognizing that fact, Le Duan concluded that success in the war against the United States would tip the worldwide balance of power in favor of the cause of national liberation and communism. This conviction – informed as it was by his patriotic internationalist worldview, addressed in the previous chapter, and combined with the fact that Hanoi and the NLF had to conduct their diplomacy from a position of relative weakness – made Le Duan and other DRVN leaders accomplished practitioners of international politics. Throughout the American War, they never thought strictly in terms of their own interests, narrowly defined; they remained internationalists through-and-through.

The war against the United States, Le Duan believed, was an integral part of a worldwide struggle against imperialism that aimed to improve living conditions in Asia, Africa, and Latin America. In his own thinking, the prospects of the American War were inextricably linked to those of the rest of the non-capitalist world. By that rationale, defeating the Americans would not only satisfy Hanoi's own vital interests but also those of other oppressed nations. It would turn Vietnam into a "solid outpost" of communism and national liberation in Southeast Asia, serving to agitate and support national liberation and communist movements everywhere. Hanoi, in Le Duan's own eyes, had a unique calling in the world.

Hanoi's conscious effort to inspire others to fight imperialism, even as it attempted to rally them in support of its cause, paid dividends. Its "determined stance in the face of American technological might," historian Michael Latham writes, "became an appealing symbol of determined resistance and the power of popular revolutionary war." [17] In January 1966, Fidel Castro hosted the Tricontinental Conference in Havana to promote national liberation and communism in Asia, Africa, and Latin America. Some 600 participants – representing more than eighty sovereign governments, national liberation movements, and other organizations – attended the thirteen-day event. In a stirring "message to the Tricontinental," Ernesto "Che" Guevara (1928–67) – an architect of the Cuban Revolution who had just left Cuba to lend his expertise to other Third World revolutionary movements – noted that "every people that liberates itself is a step in the battle for the liberation of one's own people." Vietnam, he said, "teaches us this with its permanent lesson in heroism, its tragic daily lesson of struggle and death in order to gain the final victory." In that country, "the soldiers of imperialism encounter the discomforts of those who, accustomed to the standard of living that the United States boasts, have to confront a hostile land; the insecurity of those who cannot move without feeling that they are stepping on enemy territory; death for those who go outside of fortified compounds; the permanent hostility of the entire population." "How close and bright would the future appear," Che famously concluded, "if two, three, many Vietnams flowered on the face of the globe, with their quota of death and their immense tragedies, with their daily heroism, with their repeated blows against imperialism, forcing it to disperse its forces under the lash of the growing hatred of the peoples of the world!"

The meeting in Havana spawned the Organization of Solidarity with the People of Asia, Africa and Latin America (commonly known by its Spanish acronym OSPAAAL), which staunchly supported Hanoi and the NLF's anti-American war thereafter. Che's message, published a year later under the title "Create Two, Three ... Many Vietnams, That Is the Watchword," became a rallying cry for revolutionary organizations and movements all around the world, increasing Vietnam's international profile and the notoriety of its anti-American resistance. Even French President Charles de Gaulle jumped on that bandwagon, condemning US military intervention in Vietnam and calling for Washington to end the war at once, in a much-publicized speech in Phnom Penh, the Cambodian capital, in September 1966.

STALEMATE

Between 1965 and 1967, just under 20,000 US troops, and nearly twice that number of ARVN soldiers, died in Vietnam, attesting to the efficacy of the PAVN and LAF. Those forces were obviously not simple, unorganized peasants compelled by circumstances to pick up a gun in defense of their homeland. As previously noted, all main, and most local, forces were well-trained, -disciplined, and -equipped. At the time, however, the image of peasants, often women, in black "pajamas," forced to fight – an image originated and cultivated by communist authorities themselves – shaped the American imagination of the war. This amplified the negative psychological impact of news of casualties suffered by American forces, who seemed unable, not only to defeat such "primitive" enemies, but even to defend themselves against those enemies. Paradoxically, certain reports and pictures of communist casualties, victims of US military might, underscored the inequity between the two armies, and fueled anti-war sentiment in the United States. Vietnamese guerrillas were heroes, if they were not victims, and vice versa. "The underdog status of these Vietnamese villagers underscored the message that the entire war conveyed to the American public," notes one historian. Communist forces "lacked the technological weaponry of the U.S. military, but they were winning the war or at least fighting the United States to a stalemate."[18] Such images were actually valuable propaganda tools that ennobled Hanoi's anti-American resistance.

As the resistance made headway in the South, the resourcefulness of leaders and the valiance of people above the 17th parallel mitigated the impact of US bombings. Work units, some supported by Chinese troops, repaired road and rail arteries promptly in most cases, thereby minimizing disruption to the movement of troops and supplies to the South. Schoolchildren regularly contributed to such tasks. These initiatives were necessary, not only to help defeat the United States, but also to divert attention from the harsh realities of life in wartime. Over time, as Northerners grew accustomed to the rigors of war, they accepted their wartime fate with quiet resignation, developing a new sense of what it meant to live a "normal" life.

Ultimately, however, all that valiance, all these successes, could not change the balance of forces, nor make Vietnamese in both halves of the country impervious to the war's lethality and destructiveness. In the North, the bombing inflicted a heavy toll on the economy, while claiming the lives of thousands of civilians and maiming scores more. As for the war in the South, it had for all intents and purposes stalemated by the end of 1967, despite the heavy casualties inflicted on enemy forces and mounting domestic challenges to the regime of Nguyen Van Thieu in Saigon. Challenges to Thieu's authority included a long-standing and nasty rivalry with his own Prime Minister, Nguyen Cao Ky (1930–2011), a flamboyant former Chief of the Vietnamese Air Force; growing religious animosities resulting from Thieu's preferential treatment of Catholics (Thieu himself had converted to Catholicism in 1958) that culminated in the "Second Buddhist Crisis" and a temporary loss of central government control over the cities of Da Nang and Hue in spring 1966; a widening chasm between advocates of civil liberties and military hardliners calling for the imposition of martial law in response to the Buddhist uprising; and a presidential election in September 1967 that Thieu won with a modest thirty-four percent of the popular vote. Hanoi and the NLF, however, were unable to capitalize on those challenges to Thieu's rule, and the attendant polarization of Southern society.

As Hanoi infiltrated more men and supplies into the South, and the Viet Cong enlisted new recruits, the United States brought in more troops, and Saigon dragooned more young men into its armed forces to counter them. By mid-1967, 277,000 PAVN and LAF regulars were battling 1,334,000 allied troops, including 448,000 US military personnel, in the South, a 1:5 ratio. The war grew deadlier and more destructive, but the military balance essentially remained the same: that is, highly unfavorable for communist forces. Losses inflicted upon American and ARVN units were notable, as previously related, but paled in comparison to those suffered by communist forces. During the same 1965–7 period, the PAVN and LAF lost an astonishing 230,000 killed. Troops kept fighting with determination and discipline, but the staggering decimation of their ranks, in conjunction with the slow pace of progress in the war, and the inability to take advantage of the sectarian infighting in the South, raised serious concerns in Hanoi.

The Pacification program, managed jointly by American and South Vietnamese authorities, and formally known as Civil Operations and Revolutionary Development Support (CORDS) after May 1967, also hurt the communist effort below the 17th parallel. As Washington's answer to Hanoi's political struggle, CORDS specifically targeted the NLF's political infrastructure and sought to rally Southern opinion in support of Thieu and his regime. Core initiatives included the *Chieu hoi* ("open arms") program, designed to counter Hanoi's *binh van* efforts and encourage defection of communist troops and cadres, some 75,000 of whom, mostly Viet Cong, had absconded by 1967. That program also assigned US advisers to train local militias, promoted rural development and land redistribution initiatives, and assisted internally displaced persons. Arguably, the most effective and controversial CORDS initiative was the Phoenix program. Modeled on a "counter terror" effort mounted by the French during the Algerian War, it employed "hard interrogation" techniques and targeted assassinations to neutralize Viet Cong cadres and sympathizers. Despite its controversial nature, it exacted a major toll on the Viet Cong's political apparatus, resulting in the death or incarceration of tens of thousands of operatives.

GOING FOR BROKE, AGAIN

By summer 1967, Le Duan was losing patience with the results of the war. A few months earlier, in January, the Central Committee had given him its blessing to devise a stratagem to bring about "decisive victory" within two years. In June, the Secretary proposed a new initiative, one he hoped would create the possibility of a major triumph over the enemy and bring the war to a prompt and successful conclusion. The only way to force Washington to withdraw from Vietnam, Le Duan surmised, was to show political leaders there that they could not win. On orders from the Politburo, and with direct input from Le Duan, the PAVN General Staff devised a plan for delivering that kind of message. The plan called for a "general offensive," sudden enough to catch the enemy off-guard, and powerful enough to inspire a "general uprising" by the Southern population. Essentially, the General Staff sought to combine military and political struggle to foment mass popular uprisings and eclipse Saigon's authority. Its plan specifically called for major synchronized uprisings in cities and towns across the South to end Saigon's authority over them. Unable to rule populated areas, Thieu's regime would collapse, and the Americans would have to disengage.

The military parts of the plan involved concerted attacks by main force units and local guerrillas on urban settlements in the South, which, according to Le Duan, constituted the enemy's "rear base" and "nerve center." The main targets were the South's largest cities, Saigon, Hue, and Da Nang. Though a variety of objectives would be achieved through the attacks, their central military aim was to "crush every large puppet army unit." That aim was consistent with Resolution 9 of 1963, which continued to guide Hanoi's war strategy. The military plan also mandated direct strikes on US forces, especially in remote regions, less to annihilate them than to pin them down, keep them away from cities, and prevent them from coming to the rescue of embattled ARVN units. The siege of the isolated US garrison at Khe Sanh, to begin ten days before the start of the general campaign, was integral to that plan. If that 7,500-strong encampment happened to fall to communist forces, in a sort of replay of

Dien Bien Phu, Washington might follow the French example: accept a negotiated settlement and withdraw the rest of its forces. But that was not the chief reason for the attack there. Le Duan had long believed that striking forcefully at the South Vietnamese armed forces, while keeping their American counterparts bogged down elsewhere, represented the likeliest way to exploit the vulnerability of the former, while neutralizing the might of the latter. Should that occur, it would be enough to change the strategic balance in the war, and deliver victory.

In October 1967, the Politburo convened to discuss the timing of the proposed campaign. After careful consideration, it agreed on a launch date to coincide with lunar New Year's Day, 30 January 1968: a date sure to surprise the enemy and optimize the campaign's impact. That day – Tet – is Vietnam's most celebrated holiday. Festivities last several days as many urban dwellers rejoin relatives in the countryside to celebrate. Communist military planners were convinced they would catch the enemy off-guard, since heretofore the two sides had observed an informal truce during that period. The timing of the campaign would also allow communist forces to take advantage of the vulnerability of South Vietnamese units depleted by troops and officers taking leave to be with family. Hanoi had a keen sense of history. As related in Chapter 1, Emperor Quang Trung had taken advantage of the New Year celebrations in 1789 to defeat a Chinese army occupying Hanoi and secure the independence of Vietnam.

Le Duan's regime also had a keen sense of the American political calendar. The proposed offensive would take place at the start of a presidential election year. Officials in Hanoi had spent a great deal of time studying the American system of government and its political culture, as noted earlier. They appreciated the central role presidents played in shaping foreign and military policy, exercising as they did almost imperial authority over both. They also recognized, however, that in an election year presidential hopefuls needed to pander to public opinion on such matters, especially during wartime. That encouraged them to shape policy agendas according to the needs and demands of specific constituencies to improve their prospects for victory. As those agendas were being formulated, Hanoi would endeavor to sway American opinion in favor of the candidate who seemed to offer the least resistance to the realization of its own goals.

That was no small feat, to be sure. Nonetheless, DRVN leaders attempted to do just that in 1964, would do so now in 1968, and then try their luck again in 1972. What they would do now was dramatically escalate hostilities, not just to the point of altering the balance of forces in the South, but also generating a political tsunami in the United States. In other words, Hanoi intended to use the American system against itself, for its own benefit. Despite its own lack of experience with liberal democracy, it demonstrated a sharp understanding of its workings, plus an aptitude for taking advantage of the vulnerabilities of American politicians to the vicissitudes of domestic opinion. That was a major reason Hanoi was able to compensate for its relative military weakness against Washington throughout the war.

In the days prior to the offensive, guerrillas, assuming the identity of merchants or relatives of residents, infiltrated Southern cities. Weapons came separately, concealed in foodstuff cargoes or in the coffins of fake funeral processions, among other means, and then stored at designated safe locations, usually a sympathizer's private residence. In early January, the Central Committee gave final sanction to the campaign, ratifying Resolution 14, which called for communist forces to initiate major combat operations later that month. To make sure the element of surprise was not compromised, instructions withheld the exact day and time of the start of the attack. Meanwhile, the Politburo directed military commanders to make final preparations for the assault on American forces at Khe Sanh and elsewhere. Failure was not an option; only success on the field of battle could guarantee that Southerners would join in mass demonstrations – the hoped-for general uprising – against the Saigon regime and the American presence, which represented the most critical component of the entire effort.

ANTI-PARTY AFFAIR

As Hanoi made final preparations for the so-called Tet Offensive, Le Duan instigated a purge of untrustworthy Party members. Purges had become frequent under his regime, obsessed with discipline and unity of thought. However, this one, spurred by rumors of an internal plot against Le Duan and his fellow hardliners, implicated people at the highest levels, like that of 1964. This particular instance was triggered by the mysterious death in July 1967 of Nguyen Chi Thanh, a core member of the regime who doubled as head of COSVN. While initial reports indicated that Thanh had died of a heart attack after a day of heavy drinking in Hanoi, Le Duan suspected that someone loyal to Giap, Thanh's arch-nemesis in the PAVN, had poisoned him, and that the death presaged an effort to overthrow his regime. Possibly, this was all a sham, and Le Duan fabricated the rumor of an impending coup again him to create a convenient pretext for clamping down on internal dissent and amassing even more power on the eve of the Tet Offensive, upon which so much was riding. Whatever actually happened – the truth remains unknown – in the wake of Thanh's death the Politburo ordered the secret purge of dozens of upper-level members, and others known or presumed to harbor "anti-Party" – that is, moderate, dovish – views. That included those who preferred negotiations with the United States over escalation of the war, and otherwise favored caution over boldness. To ensure COSVN's proper functioning following Thanh's death, Le Duan selected none other than Pham Hung, another member of his inner circle, to take over its leadership. Pham Hung would hold that position until the end of the war in 1975.

Events in China, where the Cultural Revolution (1966–76) was currently exalting radical tendencies and punishing "revisionists" and others charged with "deviationist" thinking, may also have encouraged Le Duan to carry out the purge and embrace ultra-leftist tendencies. That, plus the fact that those he targeted had close personal and ideological ties to the Soviet Union, risked compromising his regime's relations with Moscow. However, the Secretary was confident that, because of their own dispute with China, which reached new heights in the late 1960s, Soviet leaders would probably not press the issue, nor do or say anything that might undercut their relations with Hanoi. The purge was, after all, an internal VWP matter. Besides, the second Arab-Israeli War, popularly known as the Six-day War, of June 1967 was preoccupying the Soviets because of the disastrous performance of their Arab clients. In the end, Le Duan won that wager. Moscow was not pleased by his actions, but passively accepted them. The episode demonstrated one more of the ways North Vietnamese decision-makers were not afraid to assert and maintain their autonomy vis-à-vis their big power sponsors during the Vietnam War. Ho Chi Minh, whose health was starting to fail by then, could only watch from the sidelines as the regime he had previously led prepared for its biggest gamble since Dien Bien Phu, in 1954.

TET OFFENSIVE

On 21 January 1968, communist forces began laying siege to the American garrison at Khe Sanh, pounding it with heavy artillery before launching sustained infantry attacks against it. Unlike French forces at Dien Bien Phu, the Americans at Khe Sanh controlled the surrounding hilltops, maintained continued access to air-dropped supplies, and enjoyed the protection of massive airpower – including raids by B-52 strategic bombers. That enabled the defenders to hold out for a total of seventy-seven days.

As that battle unfolded, on 30 January the cities of Da Nang, Nha Trang, Pleiku, Ban Me Thuot, Hoi An, Qui Nhon, and Kontum all came under attack. According to one source, the command of Interzone V, under whose jurisdiction these cities fell, never received word that the general offensive, originally supposed to start that day, had been postponed at the last minute for twenty-four hours. Fortunately for Hanoi, neither Washington nor Saigon realized that these attacks presaged the imminence of a much larger, general offensive. Intelligence reports noted augmented enemy infiltration and troop build-ups in the northern panhandle of South Vietnam, and even warned of possible attacks in and around Quang Tri Province, but none hinted at an offensive on the scale about to take place.

During the early morning hours of 31 January, a small *Peugeot* truck and an old taxicab pulled up in front of the US embassy in Saigon. Out of the nondescript vehicles surged nineteen guerrillas, who proceeded to blast their way through the outer wall of the compound and place it under siege. Within hours, eighteen of the intruders were dead, the remaining one wounded and taken captive. This unsuccessful but astonishingly bold raid was the opening shot of the Tet Offensive, a colossal, unprecedented effort involving some 84,000 communist troops, who attacked a total of 100 urban centers, including all large cities and provincial capitals in South Vietnam. In several places it took some time for ARVN and US forces to realize an attack was underway; the sound of shots fired by communist forces was drowned out by the cacophony of exploding firecrackers ushering in the New Year. In Saigon itself, besides the US embassy, guerrillas raided the Presidential Palace, Tan Son Nhut Air Base/ Airport, and the headquarters of both the South Vietnamese police and MACV. They also attempted to take over the national radio station, but were overcome as they were about to air a pre-recorded message urging the population to rise against American "imperialists" and their Saigon "lackeys."

The generalized attack caused shockwaves, not just in South Vietnam but around the world. At a time in the war when American and South Vietnamese forces had made so much apparent progress, the scope and nature of the offensive seemed unfathomable. The jolt in the United States was amplified by the fact that, just weeks before, President Johnson had to

great fanfare launched his so-called Success Offensive – a major public relations effort to rally domestic opinion behind the war, by exalting the merits
of the American intervention in Vietnam and, more crucially, its progress.
By the widely-publicized account of MACV's General Westmoreland, military and political conditions in the South had improved so much recently
that "the end" was beginning to "come into view," and victory was "within
our grasp." In light of the optimism generated inside the United States
by that assessment, among others, the series of widespread, coordinated,
and surprise attacks constituting the Tet Offensive exploded the myth of
American progress in the fight against Vietnamese communist forces. That
in turn shattered the credibility of the Johnson administration, the military brass, and the President himself, and called into question the whole
project of the American military enterprise in Vietnam.

This initial reaction was soon shown to be vastly overdone, from a
strictly military standpoint, but its effects persisted long enough to sow
doubt in the minds of people of many political persuasions: that defeating
Hanoi and the Viet Cong in a reasonable amount of time at an affordable
cost – short of dropping a nuclear bomb on the North Vietnamese capital – was out of the question. The storming of the American embassy in
Saigon became the symbol of these fears and concerns. If even the safety
of that piece of real estate – sovereign US territory under international
law – and of its occupants could not be guaranteed after nearly three
years of American effort, involving more than half a million troops at a
cost of more than 25,000 US dead, how could all of South Vietnam and
its people ever be fully pacified?

As this and related questions were still being pondered, the moral position of Washington collapsed before the lens of an unscrupulous photo-
journalist. A man, presumed to be Viet Cong, wearing a checkered shirt
and a pair of shorts, hands tied behind his back, was brought before
National Police Chief Nguyen Ngoc Loan (1930–98).[19] Loan proceeded
to slowly unholster a .38 caliber revolver, signaled bystanders to move
back, brought the gun to the man's head, and pulled the trigger. This episode, entirely caught on camera, generated massive press coverage, and
prompted further questioning of the virtues of working in tandem with
such men as Loan. After the incident, Walter Cronkite (1916–2009), the
most influential US television news anchor at the time, told his audience
of millions that it seemed "more certain than ever that the bloody experience of Vietnam is to end in a stalemate." President Johnson's endeavors
in Indochina were failing. Hanoi had seemingly scored the unequivocal
victory it had sought.

REALITIES OF TET

Politically and diplomatically, the Tet Offensive paid huge dividends for Hanoi. It galvanized antiwar sentiment across the United States and the West, and demonstrated that communist forces were much better organized, disciplined, and capable than Washington had ever assumed. The final military tally, related below, mattered less to global media audiences, whose thinking on the American war effort had become conditioned more by iconic images and acerbic analyses, both of which the Tet Offensive generated in abundance, than actual statistics. Thus, from a psychological standpoint, the offensive was a major strategic victory for Hanoi and, in light of subsequent events in the United States, a watershed moment in the history of the Vietnam War. That victory would in fact vindicate in the eyes of its own people and armed forces Hanoi's decision to undertake such a daring, risky, and, ultimately, costly wager. Elsewhere, the false but enduring assumption that psychological victory had been their principal objective all along made North Vietnamese leaders look like wizards who seemed to have inflicted a mortal blow on Washington and Saigon's ability to carry on the war. All things being equal, the Tet Offensive's greatest impact was on perceptions of the war in the United States and around the world.

As it turned out, the offensive was an unqualified, unmitigated military disaster for Hanoi. What Le Duan thought was a "sure thing" turned into a nightmare for communist forces. The raid on the American embassy was, again, emblematic of what happened. Taking advantage of the element of surprise, the attackers quickly secured their assigned target. However, they could not hold on to it when American and South Vietnamese forces counterattacked, and lost everything, including their lives. Some of the local victories in the Tet Offensive were meaningful, to be sure, but none translated into long-term gain. In the aftermath of the main offensive, Hanoi tried to recoup its losses by launching two follow-up efforts, "mini Tets," in March and again in May. Consisting primarily of further concerted attacks on Southern cities, they produced no significant gains – only more casualties, especially the May campaign.

Looking back upon the entire effort, it is clear that Le Duan had again grossly overestimated his prospects for victory. The general uprising he predicted, and upon which success in the 1968 campaign rested, never materialized. Once the initial wave of attacks had subsided, South Vietnamese forces quickly regrouped and, with US reinforcements, fought back successfully. The masses felt no incentive or compulsion to rise against Saigon and the Americans. As a direct result of the offensive, Saigon for the first time ordered a general mobilization that dramatically expanded the size of its armed forces. As to the human cost of the offensive for Hanoi, it exceeded 40,000 troops killed and untold numbers of others wounded. According to conservative estimates, perhaps 165,000 civilians also died during the campaign, and between one and two million were displaced from their homes.

Most of the communist troops involved in the offensive, and therefore most of the casualties, belonged to the LAF. In fact, the failed Tet gambit decimated its ranks. Because the offensive had been planned and coordinated by Hanoi, this subsequently led to speculation that Northern leaders had consciously used Southerners as sacrificial lambs to fight and be killed, in order to spare their own forces and ensure their total domination of national politics once reunification was realized. The speculation is on its face preposterous. To be sure, the bulk of the troops in the Tet Offensive were Southern, but that was because the nature of the campaign required it. In preparation for the attack, combat and other personnel infiltrated cities. Northerners were ill-suited for that because they lacked familiarity with local geography and, most importantly, their accent could have easily alerted local authorities to their presence, compromising the entire campaign. Besides, the Southern masses were more likely to be roused by calls for a general uprising – the fundamental objective of the campaign – issued by fellow Southerners whom they might even know personally.

In the final analysis, the use of Southerners was sensible policy, a product of the strategic necessity of fighting in Southern cities, and not duplicitous intent. The decimation of Viet Cong ranks did nothing to improve Hanoi's prospects for military victory, and in fact constituted a huge setback. For Le Duan and other Hanoi leaders with Southern ties, the loss of so many Southern compatriots, many of whom they knew personally having previously struggled alongside them, was especially tragic.

The challenges confronting Hanoi in the South after Tet were compounded by a sordid event attributed to its forces, and which would haunt it for years afterwards. During their month-long occupation of Hue, the old imperial capital, communist troops, most of them from the North, summarily executed some 2,800 people on charges of being enemies of the people. Victims included members of the South Vietnamese government and armed forces, as well as hospital staff, teachers, and others with only indirect ties to the regime in Saigon. A number of foreigners, among them missionaries, were also killed. Victims' bodies were dumped in mass graves, later investigation revealing some were buried alive. Admittedly, atrocities were commonplace during the war; communist forces had a habit of summarily executing "traitors," to punish them and to deter others from associating themselves with, or otherwise supporting, the regime in Saigon. However, this instance of violence stands out because of the number of victims, their status, and the methods used to kill them. It was also eerily reminiscent of the barbaric behavior exhibited later on a much larger scale by the genocidal Khmer Rouge in Cambodia.

Disclosure of the Hue massacre shortly after South Vietnamese and US forces reclaimed the city called into question the intentions and purposes of Hanoi and the NLF. Many Southerners linked to the regime in Saigon had been drafted into the armed forces, or else depended on it for their livelihood. That is, their ties to it were not voluntary, but necessary or obligatory. The killings in Hue were not only misguided, but made a mockery of communist propaganda that theirs was the side of freedom and justice. They also spawned rumors that similar bloodbaths would ensue if and when communist forces defeated the Saigon regime. Those rumors not only motivated South Vietnamese soldiers to fight harder, but also produced a wave of eager volunteers for the army, just as Saigon issued its general mobilization order. In the waning days of the war, they fueled panic among Southerners, encouraging many to flee the country. In retrospect, few events did more than the Hue killings to undermine the communist political struggle in the South.

The Tet debacle had a sobering effect on Le Duan. It tempered his impetuousness and bellicosity, and encouraged him to think and act more pragmatically thereafter. It also chastened his revolutionary zeal and, for a period, shook his confidence in the ability of the forces under his command to realize their objectives as he defined them. Thereafter, the Secretary developed a new appreciation for diplomatic struggle, which his regime would come to rely upon more heavily to advance their cause after 1968. "Inwardly," historian Lien-Hang Nguyen has written, Le Duan knew that the Tet Offensive had failed, and that he "would have to shift tactics to save the revolution."[20] For the second time in four years, he had gambled big, and lost big. It was time for a new approach.

Notes

1   In addition, an estimated 35,000 Canadian nationals served in Vietnam, including a sizeable contingent of native Americans. They were mostly volunteers who enlisted in the US armed forces since Ottawa refused to join the allied coalition.

2 David W.P. Elliott, "Hanoi's Strategy in the Second Indochina War" in Jayne S. Werner and Luu Doan Huynh (eds.), *The Vietnam War: Vietnamese and American Perspective* (Armonk, NY: M.E. Sharpe, 1993), 70.

3 Konrad Kellen, *A Profile of the PAVN Soldier in South Vietnam*, RAND Memorandum RM-5013-1-ISA/ARPA, June 1966, 48, 59.

4 Douglas Pike, *PAVN: People's Army of Vietnam* (New York: Da Capo Press, 1986), 165.

5 R. Michael Pearce, *The Insurgent Environment*, RAND Corporation Memorandum RM-5533-1-ARPA, May 1969, ix–x.

6 David Hunt, *Vietnam's Southern Revolution: From Peasant Insurrection to Total War, 1959–1968* (Boston: University of Massachusetts Press, 2008).

7 Military Institute of Vietnam (trans. by Merle L. Pribbenow), *Victory in Vietnam: The Official History of the People's Army of Vietnam, 1954–1975* (Lawrence: University of Kansas Press, 2002), 159.

8 Matthew Adam Kocher, Thomas B. Pepinsky, and Stathis N. Kalyvas, "Aerial Bombing and Counterinsurgency in the Vietnam War" in *American Journal of Political Science*, Vol. 55, no. 2 (April 2011), 201–18.

9 Hy Van Luong, *Revolution in the Village: Tradition and Transformation in North Vietnam, 1925 – 1988* (Honolulu: University of Hawaii Press, 1992), 201.

10 "Government Report Submitted by Prime Minister Pham Van Dong, April 1965" in *Against US Aggression: Main Documents of the National Assembly of the Democratic Republic of Vietnam, 3rd Legislature – 2nd Session, April 1965* (Hanoi: Foreign Languages Publishing House, 1966), 15, 54.

11 Quoted in Stein Tønnesson, "Tracking Multi-Directional Dominoes" in Odd Arne Westad et al. (eds.), *77 Conversations Between Chinese and Foreign Leaders on the Wars in Indochina, 1964–1977*, Cold War International History Project Working Paper no. 22, 1998, 33–4.

12 Philippe Franchini, *Les guerres d'Indochine, Vol.2: De la bataille de Dien Bien Phu à la chute de Saïgon* [The Indochina Wars, Volume 2: From the Battle of Dien Bien Phu to the Fall of Saigon] (Paris: Éditions Pygmalion/ Gérard Watelet, 1988), 189–90.

13 A total of 320,000 Chinese troops served in North Vietnam during the Vietnam War. They suffered 1,300 casualties, including 300 killed.

14 Judy Tzu-Chun Wu, *Radicals on the Road: Internationalism, Orientalism, and Feminism during the Vietnam Era* (Ithaca: Cornell University Press, 2013), 8.

15 Mark Philip Bradley and Viet Thanh Nguyen, "Vietnam: American and Vietnamese Public Diplomacy" in Geoffrey Wiseman (ed.), *Isolate or Engage: Adversarial States, US Foreign Policy, and Public Diplomacy* (Stanford: Stanford University Press, 2015), 119.

16 Ali actually said: "My conscience won't let me go shoot my brother, or some darker people, or some poor hungry people in the mud for big powerful America. And shoot them for what? They never called me nigger, they never lynched me, they didn't put no dogs on me, they didn't rob me of my nationality, rape and kill my mother and father… Shoot them for what? How can I shoot them poor people? Just take me to jail."

17   Michael E. Latham, "The Cold War in the Third World, 1963–1975" in Melvyn P. Leffler and Odd Arne Westad (eds.), *The Cambridge History of the Cold War – Volume II: Crises and Détente* (New York: Cambridge University Press, 2010), 276.

18   Tzu-Chun Wu, *Radicals on the Road*, 153.

19   According to subsequent reports, the man in question was a Viet Cong Sapper Captain suspected of having executed one of Loan's subordinates in the police force, his wife, and their four children. South Vietnamese Marines had just captured him when Loan found out what he had done and, in a fit of rage, shot him.

20   Lien-Hang T. Nguyen, "Negotiating While Fighting or Just Fighting?," paper presented at *Colloque International: "Guerre, diplomacie et opinion. Les négociations de paix à Paris et la fin de la guerre au Vietnam (1968–1975)"* [International Seminar: "War, Diplomacy, and Perspective: The Paris Peace Talks and the End of the Vietnam War (1968–1975)"], Paris, 13–14 May 2008, 1.

5

American War, 1968–1973

On 30 March 1968, President Johnson declared on American television that he would not seek another term in office. The Vietnam War had claimed its most famous victim. In his address, Johnson also announced an indefinite suspension of the bombing of North Vietnam above the 20th parallel, thinking that might encourage Hanoi to agree to peace talks, consistent with the so-called San Antonio formula.[1] The American leader was obviously baffled by the course events had taken. South Vietnamese and US forces had made what he had thought were impressive gains in recent years. General Westmoreland's famous "body counts" of dead Vietnamese communist soldiers indicated allied forces were killing enemy troops faster than Hanoi and the Viet Cong could replace them. But no matter how many of their comrades died in battle, communist forces found both the resolve and new recruits to keep fighting. The air war against the North, for its part, had had punishing effects, but failed to shake the confidence of communist leaders, at least as far as Johnson could tell, and stem the flow of men and supplies into the South. Whatever US bombs destroyed above the 17th parallel seemed to be always promptly repaired or replaced. Aid from the Soviets and Chinese kept flowing into the North, and from the North into the South, with no apparent end, or even reductions in sight. The war, Johnson concluded, had turned into a quagmire. The United States needed to get out of it. Since victory was no longer an option, the only decent way out of it was through negotiation.

Johnson's television address came as a great relief to Hanoi, and provided a much-needed boost to its confidence. It gave it a reason to remain optimistic about the war in the long run, if it played its cards carefully. The Tet Offensive had not been in vain after all. Perhaps most significantly, and fortuitously, Johnson's address rendered credible Hanoi's grossly exaggerated and fabricated claims that the campaign had unfolded exactly as planned, and been an unmitigated strategic triumph. That bolstered morale among the masses and strengthened their faith in their leaders and determination to win. In a most sensible assessment, political scientist Tuong Vu has written that Johnson's "major mistake" in the aftermath of the Tet Offensive was to de-escalate the war. "Having authorized half a million American troops to be sent to Vietnam, the commander-in-chief abandoned the effort just when his enemy was desperate to break the stalemate, went for broke, and suffered massive losses."[2] These diverse considerations effectively enabled Hanoi to snatch victory from the jaws of a deeply disappointing defeat. The task now was to deal with a mortally wounded United States.

The counter-cultural movement that swept across the United States and much of the rest of the West, and reached its zenith during this time, also gave Le Duan's regime cause to see its prospects in positive terms. Characterized by vociferous denunciations of, and angry protests against, traditional sources of political, social, and cultural authority by progressive groups, the movement destabilized Western societies and governments, including those supportive of the American effort in Vietnam, through general strikes, mass demonstrations, and even acts of domestic terrorism. This happened as the Johnson administration, which remained in office until January 1969, faced the widening schism between established authority and authorities, on the one hand, and a militant protesting citizenry, on the other.

Less than a week after Johnson's address, on 4 April, the iconic leader of the contemporaneous civil rights movement, Martin Luther King (1929–68), was assassinated. At once, race riots broke out in more than 100 American cities. Much of this mayhem bore directly on Washington's ability to respond to the situation in Vietnam in the months after Tet. In August 1968, groups that included the National Mobilization Committee to End the War in Vietnam, Students for a Democratic Society (SDS), and the Youth International Party – all of them major, nationwide protest groups – disrupted the Democratic Party's National Convention in Chicago (26–9 August). Their protests morphed into large-scale rioting, and a bloody crackdown by police and national guardsmen ensued. In Hanoi's eyes, such episodes of radicalism and activism in support of anti-establishment causes manifested explicit opposition to capitalism, imperialism, and the American role in Vietnam. They also presaged a dramatic socio-political reorientation in North America and West Europe. History, Hanoi surmised, was entering a new era.

Whatever their actual circumstances, student demonstrations in France, race rioting in the United States, surging separatist sentiment in French Canada, and radical militancy in West Germany – each in its own way encouraged Le Duan's regime to continue the struggle against the United States and its allies in Vietnam, to not give up despite recent setbacks and the slow pace of progress. Each also made the regime feel like time was on its side.

POST-TET STRATEGY

The Tet Offensive thus turned out to be a major psychological victory for Hanoi. But the war was far from over, and communist decision-makers could not gloss over the reality of the appalling losses their side suffered in the campaign. The Viet Cong was in particularly bad shape. The loss of hundreds of highly-skilled and experienced political operatives compounded that of thousands of fighters, and disrupted day-to-day operations, while greatly impairing recruitment and training of replacement combatants thereafter. North Vietnamese forces fared slightly better, but still suffered far more casualties than anticipated. For the first time, Le Duan confronted the reality that defeating the Americans and their South Vietnamese allies might take much longer – and cost a lot more, in terms of both material and human resources – than he had anticipated.

Le Duan's gross miscalculations, and the resulting cost borne by his forces, did little to undermine his stature in Hanoi. The man behind the offensive came out of it largely unscathed, his authority as dominant as before, if not more. There were reasons for this. First, the purges of the previous year had rid the Party and government of actual and potential detractors, allowing the Secretary to centralize power to an unprecedented degree. Second, unlike his American counterpart, Le Duan did not have to answer to his people, only to a Politburo stacked with his staunchest allies. Lastly, the absolute control over information exercised by the DRVN government enabled his regime to obscure the devastating effects of the Tet Offensive, made easier by the reaction to it: in the United States generally, and Washington specifically. Indeed, that reaction validated in the eyes of many in the North Le Duan's boldness and competence as a military leader, as suggested in the previous chapter. Dissident antiwar organizations, critical of his hardline policies, sprung up in certain cities, including the capital, but were promptly quelled by the Ministry of Public Security.

In light of these circumstances, and the situation in the United States and elsewhere in the Western world, Le Duan faced no significant external pressure to rethink his regime's strategy or goals after Tet. He understood, however, that it could not sustain hostilities at previous levels, nor continue following an aggressive military strategy, in light of the losses recently suffered. Accordingly, beginning in mid-1968, Hanoi scaled back armed struggle in the South, and instructed its forces to exercise greater caution and patience. Caution and patience had never been the Le Duan regime's strong suit, but circumstances compelled it to think and act more pragmatically and less impetuously. Ideology still guided its strategic thinking thereafter, but now it subordinated dogma to realistic assessments of the new military and geostrategic situation it confronted. That shift signaled the abandonment of the Maoist revolutionary model, closely followed since Le Duan had become paramount leader in 1964. His regime's goals remained the same after mid-1968, but its tactics to meet them changed, for a period at least.

During the second half of 1968, on orders from Hanoi, communist forces in the South suspended major combat operations, and went back to waging low-intensity guerrilla warfare, as they had before 1964 and the introduction of Northern forces into the South. "The enemy's cumulative losses during his Tet and follow-up offensives," wrote Robert Komer, head of the Pacification program in South Vietnam at the time, "were a major factor in forcing him to revert to a protracted war strategy in 1969–71."[3] This paring down of military activity was accompanied by renewed emphasis on political struggle to enlarge and strengthen the Viet Cong, whose recruitment methods became more coercive in the post-Tet era. Hanoi also used the opportunity afforded by Johnson's de-escalation of the war to rest and regroup its own forces, recall battered units to the North for refitting, deploy fresh troops to the South, and otherwise rebuild the PAVN's capabilities. In a move attesting to the extent of the PAVN's decimation in the Tet Offensive and the difficulties North Vietnamese leaders faced in replenishing its ranks, Hanoi drafted growing numbers of young men from groups it had until now avoided tapping because of their questionable allegiance to the DRVN: namely, ethnic minorities and Catholics. Under current circumstances, achieving "economy of forces" became the strategic priority of Le Duan's regime. By official account, the communist struggle entered the phase of "fighting while consolidating" its forces.

PROBLEMS WITH ALLIES

Unfavorable circumstances outside Vietnam also encouraged Hanoi to proceed cautiously after 1968. The Cultural Revolution in China, which began in 1966, threatened to spill over into North Vietnam. The havoc it occasioned was so great that DRVN officials who traveled to Beijing recalled fearing for their lives there more than they ever had at home, even during US bombings. By the late 1960s, the chaos in China was disrupting aid deliveries to Vietnam. Not only that, but members of the "vanguard" of the Cultural Revolution, young and fanatical Red Guards, attempted to infiltrate the North in hopes of making their way to the South to go fight the Americans. Hanoi barred them. Not only might these revolutionaries radicalize young Northerners and destabilize the DRVN, just as they were destabilizing China, but the sudden appearance of Chinese nationals carrying guns in the South might prompt the United States to resume bombing the North above the 20th parallel, and possibly even invade it.

Relations with Moscow, for their part, continued to be troubling. Soviet leaders had never been fond of Hanoi's aggressiveness in the South, and despite keeping mute about it, had been deeply offended by the purge of so-called pro-Soviet elements in the VWP in 1967. They had also been dismayed by the Tet Offensive, and disappointed at having had no prior knowledge of its projected scope. After Tet, relations between Moscow and Hanoi reached their lowest point in years. In light of the beating its forces had just taken, and the shortfalls in Chinese aid because of the Cultural Revolution, Hanoi could not afford any loss of Soviet support. Fortunately for Hanoi, the reduction of military activity in the South, as necessary as it was for other reasons, had the appearance of accommodating Soviet desires concerning de-escalation, and assuaged the apprehensions of Soviet leaders about the situation in Vietnam. This apparent accommodation was especially appreciated because, at the time, the Soviet Union was being widely criticized for its invasion of Czechoslovakia to suppress the Prague Spring reform movement (January–August 1968), which had been calling for democratization and economic decentralization. Extremely unpopular worldwide, the invasion generated an outpouring of condemnation, even from within the communist camp. Beijing denounced it particularly harshly, partly because it considered the invasion a warning, a veiled threat of what might happen to China itself if Mao kept defying Moscow. Moved by both necessity and feelings of communist solidarity, Hanoi not only refused to criticize the Soviet invasion, but even praised Moscow for its efforts to preserve the unity of the communist camp. Apparently satisfied, the Soviets kept pouring aid into North Vietnam.

PEACE TALKS

Taking into consideration the pressing needs to preclude escalation of hostilities in the South and improve relations with Moscow, Hanoi accepted a request for peace talks from the Johnson administration in April 1968. The decision may have also been prompted by the onset of the aforementioned Prague Spring in Czechoslovakia, which rocked the communist world, stole the global spotlight from the war in Vietnam, and impressed upon Hanoi leaders the limits of Soviet tolerance for waywardness among its allies. In the event, the decision breached a heretofore inviolable principle of the anti-American resistance, and a lesson learned from past experience: that Hanoi would talk with its enemies only from a position of absolute strength, in order to avoid the pitfalls of compromise that had ensnared its negotiators in Geneva in 1954, and do so only after Washington had *unconditionally* suspended *all* acts of war against the North.

Hanoi's willingness to talk suggested it had decided to change its revolutionary goals. But that was not the case. In internal communications, the Politburo labeled the talks "contacts" (*tiep xuc*, in Vietnamese), not "negotiations" (*thuong luong*). This bit of legerdemain, of wordplay, was intended to obscure or make light of the previously basic policy, and preempt a backlash from radicals within the VWP. In a secret memorandum, the Politburo explained that it had agreed to "contacts" with Washington to discuss conditions for later "negotiations," including the unconditional cessation of bombing and other acts of war against the North. In other words, the leadership agreed to talk about talks – to a pre-negotiation, as it were – and nothing more; certainly not to give-and-take bargaining. That decision did not mark a shift to a "fighting-while-negotiating" strategy, as many American historians of the war have advanced. Despite the trying circumstances it faced, Le Duan's regime still had no interest in meaningful negotiations, or in any political settlement that involved compromise on its part. It merely wanted to satisfy the urgent needs noted above.

Feigning interest in ending the war diplomatically would, Le Duan thought, buy his regime much-needed time and space to address post-Tet problems. He knew Washington was less likely to escalate the bombing of the North, or the war in the South, when peace talks were ongoing. Beyond that, talking with the Americans would please Moscow, which kept urging Hanoi to end the war diplomatically, while appealing to a growing segment of world opinion calling for peace, thereby further-ing the diplomatic struggle. Finally, an apparent willingness to negoti-ate would mask Hanoi's continuing commitment to total victory, while ratcheting up the pressure on Washington to scale back its own condi-tions for a settlement. Since Hanoi intended to blame Washington for the inevitable failure of the talks, the Johnson administration would thereby be further discredited and isolated. In view of President Johnson's rather abject capitulation, Hanoi's agreement to talk might even encourage him to abandon the US military intervention altogether.

There were other, less obvious but nonetheless meaningful consider-ations in Hanoi's calculations. The agreement to talk stood a good chance of driving a wedge between Washington and Saigon. In Hanoi's calcula-tions, South Vietnamese President Nguyen Van Thieu would feel slighted by his exclusion from the talks, and by the Johnson administration's deci-sion to proceed without him. Furthermore, the exclusion of Saigon would imply that it was a lesser actor in the conflict; that Washington was, in fact, running the war against Hanoi. This would bear out Hanoi's con-tentions that Washington had caused the war and recruited the regime in Saigon as a "puppet" to assist it. Conversely, Washington's formal diplomatic engagement of Hanoi would insinuate that the United States recognized the legitimacy of the DRVN as a sovereign political entity. That recognition would improve the prospects of the diplomatic strug-gle, enabling Hanoi to obtain greater political and moral support from the international community. Unless the United States proved sufficiently desperate to accept a settlement on Hanoi's terms, which even Le Duan knew was a long shot, there would be no serious negotiations.

The talks opened in Paris in May 1968, just as massive anti-government protests engulfed France. Unlike the protests, the talks produced nothing of substance, settling as they immediately did into perfunctory exercises in mutual recrimination and criticism. It did not help that they were semi-public, open to the press. This was not diplomacy in the traditional sense; it was speechifying aimed at manipulating public opinion. But that suited Hanoi's purposes just fine. Lingering problems in the South soon prompted Le Duan to err on the side of caution and agree to open another, private negotiating channel with Washington. Closed meetings between DRVN and American diplomats began in June 1968, and allowed for more candid, constructive dialogue, while reinforcing the impression that

Hanoi was genuinely interested in a settlement. But they too led nowhere at first.

PLAYING FOR DE-ESCALATION

Recognizing the lead-up to the American presidential election in November as "an opportune time" to encourage the Johnson administration to further de-escalate the war through additional concessions, in the fall Hanoi changed its demeanor and started conducting the talks in a conciliatory manner, even hinting publicly at the possibility of finalizing an agreement within weeks. Appeasing antiwar activists in the United States, Le Duan gathered, represented Johnson's best bet to help the Democratic Party retain the White House against the hawkish Republican candidate and former Vice President under Eisenhower, Richard Nixon. Hanoi's apparent moderation encouraged Johnson to do just that. On 1 November, the American President ceased all bombing of North Vietnam, thinking that would induce Hanoi to negotiate in earnest and agree to end the war before year's end. The opposite happened: taking Johnson's gesture to mean that the American President was in fact desperate to end the war, Hanoi hardened its stance. If Johnson wanted a deal so badly, Le Duan surmised, he might decide to make further concessions. Johnson failed to do that, and his party lost the election. In all this, Hanoi was toying with Washington, and winning.

At Washington's insistence, Hanoi agreed to allow representatives of the South Vietnamese government to join the semi-public talks, which continued even after the private talks had begun. But its agreement was conditional on the NLF also having a seat at the table. As it turned out, Hanoi only consented to this *quid pro quo* because it was convinced that the positive political ramifications of doing so outweighed the negative ones. To date, Thieu had adamantly refused to recognize the NLF's legitimacy as a political movement; in his eyes, it was a terrorist organization. Its participation in the expanded talks would thus compel Saigon to at least indirectly accept the Front as a legitimate political and diplomatic entity. That in turn might not only serve the political and diplomatic struggles, but also create new "contradictions" between Washington and Saigon since their discussions about the Front's participation in the talks would surely be contentious. Thieu eventually agreed to Hanoi's proposal, but in a testament to the touchiness of the matter, and to Thieu's own reservations about NLF participation, it took the two sides no less than three months just to agree on the shape of the table they would use for their talks.[4] Once that was finally settled, the talks began. It was not long before they proved even more pointless than the bilateral ones had been, as far as the cause of peace was concerned, at least.

No sooner had the Johnson administration announced the end of sustained bombings than Hanoi issued orders to comprehensively rehabilitate the economy and repair the transport infrastructure in the North. As previously noted, DRVN authorities had mandated economic decentralization and encouraged localized production following the onset of US air raids in 1965. Although successful in minimizing the impact of the raids, this policy had impeded economic growth and development. Facilities that could not be moved, such as power plants, had for the most part been destroyed, and had to be rebuilt. The same was true of major roads, bridges, and rail lines. The immediate goals of the new effort were to grow the economy, improve logistical capabilities, and stymie increased dependence on allies. Longer-range goals included restoring and developing the central industrial base of "national industries," essential to resume the North's evolution from "a backward agrarian country into a communist society without undergoing the phase of capitalist development." Le Duan cherished Lenin's axiom – that heavy industry was an indispensable foundation for communism – and revered Stalin as a nation-builder and leader. He firmly believed that developing heavy industry remained key to achieving greater economic self-sufficiency and, eventually, autarky.

The economic and related initiatives undertaken by the DRVN, starting in late 1968, proceeded relatively smoothly. They won widespread support from the masses, who thought they signaled the imminent end of the war. Living standards noticeably improved thereafter. Carrying out economic rehabilitation in the North, while scaling down military activity in the South, was reminiscent of the "North-first" policy of the post-1954 era. On the flip side, the end of US bombings, and gradual improvement of the quality of life in the North, caused a decline in the patriotic fervor of the masses, believed by Hanoi authorities to be responsible for a spike in criminal activity, including theft and corruption.

VIETNAMIZATION

On 6 November 1968, Richard Nixon (in office 1969–74) was elected 37th president of the United States, assuming leadership of the country – and command of the American war in Vietnam – the following January. The ascent to power of this ardent cold warrior, much of whose political career had centered around denouncing the evils of communism, and hounding its sympathizers at home, sounded alarm bells in the North Vietnamese capital. During his campaign, Nixon had promised "peace with honor," encouraging the idea that he would end hostilities soon. However, he never specified what "honor" entailed. That, too, concerned Hanoi.

In Nixon, Le Duan would find his match. Just as the North Vietnamese leader was obsessed with victory as he defined it, so Nixon would seek peace only on his own terms. Toward this end, he too was prepared to be methodical and act as he deemed necessary. Each man was wedded to specific ideas and ideals, the realization of which both turned into a personal quest. Each was uncompromising on the matters dearest to him, less because he feared looking weak than because he was convinced he was right: so, each leader believed that the objectives he was pursuing in Indochina were sound, correct, and legitimate – even imperative. As failure was not an option for either, both were prepared to make sacrifices as necessary, whether in human, material, or political terms. Le Duan and Richard Nixon were true believers – in themselves, and in their ability to eventually prevail in the titanic battle they were about to undertake. That battle conditioned the course of the Vietnam War after 1969, and decided its outcome. It is one of the most bizarre lacunae in the history of that war that Nixon never knew how much power Le Duan yielded in Hanoi: that he was in fact his nemesis, the architect of the policies that eventuated in the American defeat of 1975.

Nixon's first major decision concerning Vietnam came in June 1969, when he ordered the withdrawal of 25,000 US troops from the South by the end of the upcoming August. The news astonished Hanoi, which assumed it portended unilateral and unconditional American disengagement from Indochina. A little over a month later, on 25 July, Nixon confirmed that a phased withdrawal of all US ground forces was indeed underway. During the same news conference from Guam, the American President laid out a new plan for Vietnam; part of his so-called Nixon Doctrine, which reaffirmed his administration's commitment to the containment policy without significant troop deployments overseas. The plan called for substantial increases in training and equipment for South Vietnamese forces to enable them to assume full responsibility for the security of their own people and government. "Vietnamization," as it became known, aimed to offset the consequences of the departure of American troops from the South. On the surface, it resembled France's "yellowing" policy of 1949–50, discussed in Chapter 1. Vietnamization was intended to serve two specific objectives: strengthening the ARVN through increased conscription, improved training, and massive arms transfers; and expanding, as well as escalating, the Pacification program. Basically, Vietnamization meant a gradual return to the pre-1965 situation, when Saigon held primary responsibility for the military effort against communist forces below the 17th parallel, and the United States played a supporting role.

Publicly, Hanoi celebrated Vietnamization: as symbolizing the bankruptcy of the American effort in Vietnam, the end of the "Limited War" phase, and the dawn of a new era of "indigenization" of hostilities (*Viet nam hoa chien tranh*). Antiwar activists, and other detractors of Nixon's Vietnam policy in the United States and around the world, agreed with that assessment. The United States, Vietnamization and related developments suggested, was packing up and finally exiting Vietnam. Privately, however, Le Duan and his regime found Vietnamization deeply unsettling for one reason: it portended the return of "pure" civil war in the South. To be sure, the American War had always had an element of civil conflict, given the collusion of Saigon and its armed forces with the United States. The problem was that, after four years of war, increased Vietnamese-on-Vietnamese violence would cause even more bad blood between Southerners on each side, on the one hand, and between Northerners and Southerners, on the other. The more Vietnamese killed each other, Hanoi surmised, the more difficult national reconciliation would be after hostilities ended. That, in turn, would defeat the purpose of reunification. What would be the point of Vietnamese finally coming together under a single government if lingering hatreds and feelings of mutual recrimination continued to divide and separate them? Enmity and polarization, sure to result or increase from prolonged civil conflict, would not only compromise postwar reconciliation, but also reconstruction and economic development. They would also tarnish Vietnam's image as a model of the possibilities of national liberation.

More pressingly, expansion of the South Vietnamese armed forces, a core aspect of Vietnamization, would hamper Viet Cong recruitment efforts, which were already challenging. For obvious reasons, anyone with relatives in the ARVN, already a large segment of the Southern population, was loath to join the fight against it and the United States. Vietnamization would also invalidate Hanoi's characterization of its struggle as a resistance against outside aggression, a central tenet of its self-image that could potentially critically undermine the political and

diplomatic struggles. Denied its ability to style its war effort as a nationalist enterprise against foreign imperialism, Hanoi would lose moral
legitimacy at home and abroad. In more ways than one, the Americans
were copying the French: in 1949–50, at the height of the Indochina War,
France had created the SOVN, and expanded its "national" armed forces
with a view to indigenizing the military effort against the Vietminh.
Finally, as the war in the South became de-Americanized, owing to
Vietnamization, the onus for its continuation would fall on Hanoi. In
their efforts to rally domestic and world opinion, DRVN authorities had
insisted all along that the United States must disengage from the South
to enable Southerners to decide their own fate for and by themselves. As
Washington complied with that exigence and pulled out its troops, Hanoi
would become prisoner of its own rhetoric and face mounting pressure to
do the same with its forces below the 17th parallel.

PROVISIONAL REVOLUTIONARY GOVERNMENT
FOR SOUTHERN VIETNAM

Despite the best efforts of its cadres to find new recruits, the NLF could
not recover from the Tet Offensive, nor could the LAF regain its pre-Tet
strength. In fact, the overall quality of LAF troops noticeably declined
thereafter as new recruits, who would typically first gain experience in
village militias, went straight to Main or Regional units. Stepped-up
pacification efforts by the enemy added to the stresses on communist
forces, causing the death, capture, or defection of thousands more cadres
and troops. In the first months of 1969 alone, more than a thousand
Northern cadres serving in the South were killed or captured. The number of new fighters recruited by the NLF in the Mekong River Delta fell
from 16,000 in 1968 to barely 100 a year later. In Western Cochinchina,
the number of combatants dropped from 85,000 in late 1968 to less than
21,000 two years later. At that rate, Southern guerrillas risked becoming inconsequential in their own liberation struggle. In light of such setbacks, communist control of the countryside decreased dramatically after
1968, resulting in the loss of several revolutionary bases and attendant
revenue, access to supplies, and ability to conduct military operations.
Cumulatively, the population living under communist jurisdiction in the
South fell from over four million to less than one million between 1968
and 1970. "History had come to a tough period," a North Vietnamese
general said of the situation.[5] Had Washington decided to escalate its war
instead of curtailing it in the wake of the Tet Offensive, it likely could

have dealt communist forces in the South a fatal blow, as related earlier. Luckily for Hanoi, that did not happen.

The overall situation in 1969–70 was the bleakest it had been since the "dark days" of 1957–8 for communists and their sympathizers. Just as Nixon had recently redefined US goals and strategy, Le Duan was at a point where he contemplated doing the same for his side. But the Secretary was hesitant; visions of victory still consumed him. Following lengthy deliberations, the Politburo decided that Northern troops would henceforth bear the brunt of the fighting. It even ordered PAVN commanders to indefinitely "loan" some of their own troops to the LAF so its units could remain operational. Thus, as the war effort on one side was de-Americanized and South-Vietnamized, on the other it became de-South-Vietnamized and North-Vietnamized. A major upshot of this was that Northern and Southern Vietnamese troops engaged and killed each more frequently, exposing latent, age-old tensions between their two regional communities, and compounding one of Hanoi's long-term challenges.

To offset the growing military irrelevance of the Viet Cong and the potentially disastrous impact of Vietnamization, Hanoi decided to give the NLF expanded political and diplomatic responsibilities by enhancing its appeal at home and elevating its profile abroad. Having the Front participate in the four-party talks in Paris had been part of that effort. So, too, was the selection of the widely respected Nguyen Thi Binh (b. 1927) to act as its chief negotiator in those talks. The grandniece of renowned nationalist leader Phan Chu Trinh, Binh was a member of the NLF Central Committee and a veteran diplomat in the Front's foreign service. Among other postings, she had served as head of its permanent mission in Algiers. Intelligent, articulate, and worldly, she was experienced and at ease in diplomatic circles. She also knew how to play the diplomatic game. Indeed, it was not uncommon for her to show up dressed impeccably in a form-fitting *ao dai*, Vietnam's traditional female dress, and make a striking impression at press conferences and during interviews. After 1969, she became a media sensation as well as a diplomatic star, singlehandedly transforming popular perceptions of the Viet Cong in the West. The "VC," she demonstrated, were more than a collective of anonymous men and women in black pajamas fighting Americans with rudimentary weapons. They were also educated, sophisticated, and possessed a keen sense of their own political purposes. As a female, Binh could also use "the language of sisterhood and motherhood" to connect with women elsewhere, nurture their interest in US policy in Vietnam,

FIGURE 5.1 Nguyen Thi Binh visiting with antiwar demonstrators in England, 1969. Courtesy of the Vietnamese National History Museum, Hanoi.

and contribute to building "a global antiwar movement among diverse sisters."[6] Her leadership of the NLF delegation in Paris, sanctioned by Hanoi, was a stroke of genius that bore huge dividends on the diplomatic front. But it was all window dressing. In reality, Binh and the NLF had no authority of their own in the negotiations; their positions were dictated by Hanoi, and North Vietnamese advisers wrote all of Binh's position papers. Of course, no one other than Binh herself and her immediate entourage as well as leaders in Hanoi knew this.

To further raise the status and visibility of the NLF, in mid-June 1969 Hanoi announced the formation of the Provisional Revolutionary Government of the Republic of Southern Vietnam (PRG). Sanctioned by the Politburo, the new entity was a coalition of mostly members of the Viet Cong and the People's Revolutionary Party (PRP), the VWP's Southern branch, under President Nguyen Huu Tho (1910–96), the Chairman of the NLF's Central Committee and a longtime communist. Meant to challenge the legitimacy of the Saigon regime in the South and overseas, the PRG actually had no independent decision-making powers, and no influence in the conduct of the war; that remained the prerogative of authorities in Hanoi, though that, too, remained secret. The PRG's purpose was to raise the political and diplomatic struggles to a new level and rally support for the anti-American resistance at home and abroad, particularly in the West where, thanks to "Madame Binh," the Viet Cong was suddenly enjoying unprecedented popularity.

At once, the PRG sought diplomatic recognition. Non-aligned and non-communist Third World states extended recognition almost immediately, assuming that might spur efforts to end the war diplomatically. In retrospect, it served only to prolong it. Despite appearances, these ostensibly dramatic maneuvers were never meant to improve the prospects for a negotiated settlement. Hanoi merely sought to buy time and support for its anti-American resistance. The PRG and the other new groupings were not instruments of peace but weapons of war, means of facilitating and expediting the fulfillment of Hanoi's strategic objectives. Like DRVN participation in the Paris talks, creation of the PRG served the pretense that America's enemies were seriously committed to peace and negotiations, and that Viet Cong and other Southern entities were legitimate, democratically constituted, and representative political groups.

SECRET TALKS

Nixon's commitment to peace with honor, to winding down American involvement in Vietnam while preserving US prestige and credibility as a superpower in the Cold War, plus the stalemated war in South Vietnam encouraged Le Duan's regime to make more resourceful use of peace talks to advance its interests. Intent as ever to delude American policymakers into thinking it wanted a diplomatic settlement, in the summer of 1969 Hanoi accepted an offer from Nixon to open a new negotiating channel. That channel had the peculiarity of being secret, meaning that no one would even be aware of its existence except Nixon, Le Duan, and their most trusted advisers. Nixon's own Secretaries of State and Defense would not even know about the existence of that channel! With the media and the public unaware of these talks, each side would be able to speak frankly and openly, and let the other know of its concerns on all issues without fear of public or diplomatic backlash, or so Nixon thought when he made the proposal to the North Vietnamese.

It took some time to iron out the logistics, but eventually the secret channel was open. The opening was facilitated by French leaders, with aid from private citizens, who let the negotiators use their homes outside the French capital for their meetings. The first secret encounter took place on 4 August 1969 at the apartment of a common acquaintance, a retired French diplomat. Nixon's adviser for national security affairs, Henry Kissinger (b. 1923), represented the United States, while Xuan Thuy (1912–85), a ranking member of the VWP who had been Hanoi's Minister of Foreign Affairs between 1963 and 1965, represented the DRVN. Although the meeting produced nothing substantial, the exchange between Kissinger and Thuy was cordial and constructive enough to convince the two sides to meet again. Soon, none other than Le Duan's war buddy, and number two man in the Politburo, Le Duc Tho, joined the secret talks, attesting to their growing importance in the Secretary's own eyes. For the first time, Washington would be talking directly with power brokers from the Party, not mere representatives from the DRVN government. Meanwhile, the semi-public four-party talks continued, but less as a venue for negotiation than a means of guarding the secrecy of the backchannel talks – where "real" discussions took place – and as a forum for publicly spewing propaganda. In Hanoi's view, the semi-public talks remained important as a vehicle for "win[ning] the sympathy of the people of South Vietnam, especially the ones in urban areas," and for "influenc[ing] the anti-war public opinion in the US that includes not only the people at large but also the political, business, academic, and clerical circles." Interestingly, even the officials involved in those talks were unaware of the existence of the parallel secret channel.

The involvement of Kissinger and Tho underscored the value Nixon and Le Duan attributed to the secret channel, and the similarities in the two men's personalities. Like Le Duan, Nixon trusted few people. As the latter entrusted his representation to his chief foreign affairs adviser, so the former chose Tho, whom he trusted more than anyone else in Hanoi, to be his eyes and ears in Paris. Also, as Nixon and Kissinger created an executive structure in Washington that enabled them to personally dictate the conduct of the war – Nixon playing the lead role as decision-maker, while Kissinger shaped and implemented policy – so Le Duan and Tho assumed the same functions, respectively, in Hanoi. Nixon's White House and Le Duan's regime were mirror images of each other, in some critical respects at least.

Nixon's determination to curtail US military involvement in Vietnam presented Le Duan with an opportunity to curb the DRVN's own military effort. Ending the American War altogether would have alleviated many of the problems and other challenges facing his government, communist forces fighting in the South, and civilians on both sides of the 17th parallel. By this time the return of peace on any terms was the forlorn aspiration of millions of Vietnamese. However, securing peace at that juncture would have entailed at least some compromise on Hanoi's part, and Le Duan would have none of that. Still opposed to any actual bargaining as long as he could hope for total victory, his regime played for time. Agreeing to secret talks and then protracting them endlessly was part of that strategy, predicated on a calculation that Nixon would not escalate the war as long as their discussions continued. So, the backchannel remained open, even as Hanoi refused to compromise on anything substantive, fearing that might jeopardize its ability to win everything later. Banking on Nixon's obvious yearning for a settlement, and hopeful that mounting domestic and international pressure would force him to concede significantly, Le Duan's regime temporized.

As it did so, it closely monitored the progress of Vietnamization and the phased withdrawals of US forces from the South. As long as the status quo endured and hostilities remained muted, communist forces could fortify themselves as Hanoi and the PRG/NLF sustained their efforts to secure political and other forms of support from outside. In the words of Nguyen Khac Huynh, a veteran Vietnamese diplomat involved in the Paris talks, Hanoi was carrying out "diplomacy and peace talks" to rally "international friends" and embolden "the anti-war movement of the American people." The ultimate goal of these efforts, Huynh confessed, was to "corner Nixon."[7] In January 1970, the Central Committee agreed that, since it was impossible under current circumstances to use war to advance the Revolution, Hanoi must "broaden" and "diversify" the resistance by making stronger appeals for international support and communist solidarity, while continuing to expose the magnitude of American "crimes" in Vietnam. For the time being, military endeavors had to take a back seat to the diplomatic struggle.

DIPLOMATIC SETBACKS

A series of events in 1969–70 unsettled Hanoi, shook its confidence in the efficacy of its tactics and strategies, and encouraged it to continue exercising caution in the South, while also prompting the Central Committee to adopt the stance just mentioned. The first was the brief but vicious Sino-Soviet Border War of March 1969, which could easily have escalated into a major conflict as Moscow thought Beijing was bracing for an invasion of the Soviet Union itself. Hanoi had by this time learned to live with the rift between its key allies, and even turn it to its advantage, as noted earlier. However, the Border War took that rift to new and dangerous heights, with potentially devastating consequences for Hanoi and the rest of the communist bloc. Already, North Vietnamese leaders worried that a time might come, and soon, when either Moscow or Beijing, or both, decided to distance themselves from the war in Vietnam, and turn inward to address pressing problems of their own. The Border War confirmed the validity of those worries.

A second unsettling development, tangentially related to the first, was the growing tension in Sino-Vietnamese relations. Hanoi's participation in peace talks with Washington upset Beijing leaders, who assumed that their Vietnamese comrades had decided to abandon Marxist–Leninist orthodoxy, and Maoist ideas on revolution specifically, in favor of Moscow-style revisionism and "defeatism." Hanoi's assurance that it sought no diplomatic solution with Washington – that it was using the talks for probing purposes only, and remained as committed as ever to total victory – did nothing to alleviate Chinese suspicions. As a result, relations between the two allies, close but often troubled, soured. In 1969–70, Beijing trimmed down military and political support to the DRVN, withdrawing the bulk of its troops from North Vietnam. This disappointed Hanoi, which badly needed continuing Chinese aid in the wake of the Tet debacle. Mao would eventually recognize that he had been too rash in this, and even apologize for not heeding Hanoi's reassurances; but the damage had been done. Le Duan and his entourage would not soon forget Beijing's veiled criticism of their handling of their own affairs, to say nothing of the mess Mao had made of things by carrying out his Cultural Revolution at such an inopportune time. Relations between the two leaderships were never the same afterwards.

The death of Ho Chi Minh from heart failure on 2 September 1969, twenty-four years to the day after he had proclaimed the independence of Vietnam and the founding of the DRVN, capped what may well have been the most challenging year for Hanoi in the American War. Ho's passing came as no surprise to North Vietnamese policymakers: he had been battling bad health for years. Also, as Ho had exercised no influence over decision-making for over five years, his death had no meaningful bearing on the power structure in the capital. It was, however, devastating for the diplomatic and political struggles. Owing to his political exploits, personal history, and charisma, Ho had achieved national and international eminence like no other Vietnamese ever had, or would. He had endeared himself to millions at home and abroad, and become the venerable face of the struggle for Vietnamese independence and reunification. His lifelong fight against imperialism, and for self-government in Indochina, had made him an iconic figure worldwide. Many of his hardline peers had considered him too soft, but he remained a communist through-and-through, a reality obscured by his impeccable nationalist credentials. Third World leaders idealized him, national liberation fighters were inspired by him, Western liberals empathized with him, and millions of his own people revered him. For the communist world, beset with problems stemming from the Sino-Soviet dispute, Ho had been a powerful source of solidarity, and perhaps its best hope for defusing Sino-Soviet tensions and restoring its unity.

Aware of Ho's world stature, Le Duan's regime had cultivated and exploited the cult of his personality in pursuit of its own ambitions. His death thus deprived it of arguably its most valuable asset for rallying the rest of the world behind its effort to defeat the United States. Ho had been especially effective in securing assistance of all types from abroad. According to historian Ang Cheng Guan, his passing critically "weakened" Hanoi's diplomatic struggle, and its "finely calibrated relations with Moscow and Beijing" in particular.[8] Indeed, each major ally tolerated Hanoi's relations with the other because it sought to co-opt the rest of the communist camp; and it could not do that without being on good terms with Hanoi, and thus with Ho, the poster figure of communist and Third World revolutionary defiance. Ho's stature had been a powerful enticement to assist the DRVN, for both Moscow and Beijing; especially when Ho himself relayed the request, as he often did, on behalf of Le Duan's regime. That was the chief reason Le Duan kept him around after sidelining him in 1964. Ho remained an indispensable public relations tool, a hugely important source of legitimacy for the Party. His death could hardly have come at a worse time for Hanoi.

MY LAI MASSACRE

Le Duan's regime did catch an important break in late 1969, which offset some of its stresses. This was the disclosure, in November, of the killing of somewhere between 350 and 500 South Vietnamese villagers, including women and children, by US troops, at a place called My Lai. The event had taken place more than a year earlier, on 16 March 1968. News of the slaughter captured television and newspaper headlines worldwide. In fact, the American and world press featured accounts and gruesome photographs of it for weeks. The My Lai massacre, and the attention it received, galvanized opposition to the war in the United States, which had lost some steam after Nixon was elected president promising "peace with honor." It also returned the international spotlight to Vietnam, creating fertile grounds worldwide for Hanoi's diplomatic struggle. Exposure of the massacre in fact dominated Vietnamese communist efforts to win hearts and minds abroad thereafter. A good portion of propaganda materials disseminated overseas through DRVN and NLF missions consisted of photographs documenting the My Lai incident and other war crimes actually or allegedly perpetrated by US forces. Those materials were intended to disgrace Washington, and corroborate communist claims that the American War was in fact a neo-colonial crusade of the worst kind. They also vindicated Hanoi's narrative of the anti-American struggle as a national resistance war while undermining Washington's counter-narrative that its forces were in Indochina to defend freedom and democracy from communist subversion and brutality.

Owing partly to the shrewdness with which Hanoi handled this campaign, and to the receptiveness of foreign audiences, it no longer mattered that US troops in Vietnam acted professionally the vast majority of the time, and certainly no less so than did their enemies. The propaganda implied that the Americans always behaved callously and savagely in Vietnam. The net effect of all this was to make Washington policymakers, as well as US forces, accountable to world opinion for their actions. Hanoi made sure of that, just as it made sure the case was made that American forces in Vietnam were fighting not just Vietnamese troops but history itself. The gist of Vietnamese history embedded in Hanoi's propaganda was a tale of repeated victimization by foreign aggressors and of inevitable triumph over them. Casting the United States as the latest in a long line of invaders generated sympathy for Hanoi's "resistance war," a patriotic struggle that enabled Le Duan and other communist leaders to pose as determined nationalists and seize the moral high ground. American decision-makers were never as competent as their Hanoi counterparts in rationalizing their actions and manipulating public perception of their purposes and policies; that is, they could never develop and cultivate the kind of broad-based, global political awareness communist leaders could. Communist forces also committed crimes and atrocities, the most notorious of them taking place in Hue in 1968, but the United States could not turn that to its long-terms advantage. Besides, those forces usually enjoyed the benefit of the doubt: they were in their own country and ostensibly fighting for their own freedom and independence.

In South Vietnam, reports of the My Lai massacre, and other incidents of wanton violence by US forces against civilians, became important recruitment tools for the NLF among appalled, fearful, and incensed civilians. They made urban dwellers, usually wary of the Front, more receptive to its message. Intellectuals in particular had a habit of reproving the Viet Cong's use of violence against other Vietnamese, insisting that the country had had enough of war and should solve its problems by non-lethal political and diplomatic means instead. But American war crimes changed the thinking of some of them, by diverting attention from Hanoi's role in instigating and prolonging the war and giving credence to NLF claims that it existed to protect Southern Vietnamese from foreign invaders and their local agents. That increased the Front's appeal among conservatives and non-communist nationalists in the South, who otherwise shied away from the Viet Cong because of its suspected ties to Hanoi.

CAMBODIA & LAOS

Heightened Sino-Soviet tensions and Ho's death generated anxieties in Hanoi that even the windfall of My Lai could not attenuate. Those anxieties drove DRVN leaders to tread cautiously through 1970–1, even to reassess their priorities. Concern turned to alarm in March 1970 when, in a bold and unexpected move, US forces in South Vietnam invaded Cambodia. Nixon was supposed to be winding down the war, Hanoi thought, not expanding it. Just days before the invasion, it had been stunned to learn that Prince Norodom Sihanouk (1922–2012), Cambodia's longtime neutralist ruler, had been overthrown in a coup. For a long time, Sihanouk had turned a blind eye to its use of his territory to move soldiers and supplies to the South. Now, he had been ousted in a coup staged by pro-American elements led by his own Prime Minister, General Lon Nol (1913–85), who assumed leadership of the country thereafter. Hanoi suspected that Nol, an anti-communist to the core, had conspired with the Americans against Sihanouk, and then invited them to invade his country.

There is no evidence supporting that suspicion, but Nol's control in Phnom Penh created a new, significant stumbling block for Le Duan's regime that went well beyond the matter of using Cambodian territory to infiltrate men and supplies into the South. As previously noted, Vietnamese communist decision-makers always considered the whole of Indochina to be a single political and military theater, believing that Vietnam would never achieve reunification and genuine independence unless Laos and Cambodia were also free of any foreign, imperialist presence. At least some of the leaders in the latter states shared these views.

Thus, shortly after his overthrow, Sihanouk formed a new government-in-exile in China, and agreed to collaborate with the DRVN, the NLF, and Laotian communists of the Pathet Laos revolutionary front in the struggle against American imperialism in Indochina. This delighted authorities in Hanoi, who at the same time feared that the new Cambodian regime might compromise their use of the Ho Chi Minh Trail.

The American incursion into Cambodia came dangerously close to seizing COSVN headquarters, and capturing caches of secret Vietnamese documents on strategy and tactics. This would have set back by months resistance activities in the deep South, by exposing cadres secretly operating among civilians, spies working in Saigon, and revealing other sensitive information. But that did not materialize. COSVN personnel managed to elude advancing American forces, take classified materials with them, and destroy what they could not carry. The invasion made Le Duan reel when he realized how far Nixon was prepared to go to get peace with honor, buoy Thieu's regime, and improve the prospects of Vietnamization. Soon, Hanoi was publicly denouncing Vietnamization as another ruse engineered by Washington to conceal its intention of expanding the war.

Arguably the most consequential benefit of the Cambodian episode for Hanoi was the widespread negative response to it in the United States. Coming at a time when the war was supposed to be winding down, the invasion sparked massive protests nationwide. During demonstrations at Kent State University in Ohio, four were killed and nine wounded after National Guard troops opened fire on student protestors. Eleven days later, two more students died and twelve others were wounded in a similar incident at Jackson State College in Mississippi. A public relations nightmare for the White House, those tragedies were a boon for Hanoi as they widened the credibility gap between US decision-makers and their own people and energized the antiwar movement.

Less than a year later, in February 1971, South Vietnamese troops supported by American airpower carried out another major military incursion, into Laos. Thanks to information collected by spies embedded within the Saigon regime, and to local and Western media reports detailing its timing and location, this operation came as no surprise to Hanoi. In fact, communist forces had enough advance warning to boost their presence in the area, fielding a force of 36,000 heavily armed PAVN regulars against the invaders. Hanoi thus hoped to crush ARVN troops and expose the futility of Vietnamization.

It did just that. PAVN forces inflicted heavy losses on ARVN units, compelling their withdrawal in a total rout. Widely circulated photographs of South Vietnamese soldiers frantically hanging onto the skids of helicopters to escape the combat zone amplified the impact of the communist victory. A testament to Hanoi's resourcefulness and cunning more than ARVN weakness, this outcome was the first real test of Vietnamization. It profoundly embarrassed Washington and humiliated Thieu, who won a second presidential term in a rigged election later that same year. The ensuing cynicism and despair among the Southern populace raised serious concerns, domestically and abroad, about Saigon's ability to defeat its enemies once the Americans were completely gone. It also provided a much-needed morale boost to communist troops, whose victory over South Vietnamese forces in Laos had actually been quite costly. American bombardment of communist positions, and the sometimes gritty performance of ARVN troops, caused some 10,000 communist casualties, by Hanoi's own account, no less.

WASHINGTON BETWEEN HANOI & ITS ALLIES

In 1970–1, the United States remained Beijing's foremost capitalist enemy, but the Soviet Union had become the greatest threat to China's national security and ideological position in the communist camp. To balance their vulnerabilities against Moscow, Chinese leaders reached out to Washington. Sensing an opportunity to satisfy certain of its own interests against its neighbors to the North, and in the Cold War generally, Beijing responded to the easing of trade restrictions by the Nixon administration by agreeing to resume previously suspended ambassadorial-level talks in Warsaw. Through the intermediary of the Pakistani government, the two sides began working toward higher-level contacts and normalization of relations. In a goodwill gesture, in April 1971 Beijing invited the US national table tennis team, then participating in a tournament in Japan, to visit China. This "ping pong diplomacy" eventuated in a major breakthrough: a secret visit to Beijing by Henry Kissinger that July. During his stay, Nixon's national security adviser met Mao and Premier Zhou Enlai. Together, they discussed future relations between their countries and, most important for Nixon, the war in Vietnam. The talks were extraordinarily constructive, and paved the way for a gradual rapprochement between the two governments.

No sooner had Kissinger left Beijing in July 1971 than Zhou Enlai arrived in Hanoi, to discuss the implications of the pending change in Sino-American relations with Vietnamese leaders. Doing his best to put a positive spin on it for his hosts, Zhou told them the change was so promising that Mao had agreed to host Nixon for a summit in Beijing the following year. The North Vietnamese were as outraged as they were stunned. Washington was clearly trying to pry Beijing from them by appealing to its instinct for self-preservation. Any dealings with the United States aimed toward détente between the two powers would cripple, not only Vietnam's position in its struggle against the Americans in the South, but also the entire global revolutionary process, Pham Van Dong grumbled. Zhou explained Beijing's reasoning for seeking rapprochement with Washington, vowing that it would have no effect on China's support for Vietnam's reunification struggle. His reassurances fell on totally deaf ears. In fact, the Vietnamese were convinced that Zhou was lying, that Beijing had already struck a deal with Washington wherein the Americans would relent on Taiwan in exchange for Chinese collaboration in bringing the Vietnam War to a close. Like Hanoi, Beijing was obsessed with national reunification and territorial integrity. As the former was fighting to liberate the South, the latter longed to reincorporate Taiwan into the state it controlled. Nixon was clearly shrewd enough to know this, which was the reason DRVN leaders suspected he had made the offer of recognizing Taiwan as a part of China, in exchange for Beijing's cooperation in ending the war in Vietnam on decent terms for the United States. After all, if anyone could appreciate the appeal of such an offer, it was North Vietnam's own leadership, which sought for the South exactly what their Chinese counterparts wanted for Taiwan.

As Beijing had rejected Hanoi's rationale for agreeing to peace talks with the United States in 1968, Hanoi now denounced Chinese motives for pursuing rapprochement with Washington. Beijing's dealings with the Nixon administration, Le Duan and other leaders thought, amounted to nothing less than a betrayal of their revolutionary struggle. How could Beijing agree to host Nixon, personally responsible for the death and suffering of millions of Vietnamese? Mao was mocking their struggle, as well as the larger principles of communist solidarity. Welcoming the American President also implied that China was distancing itself from the war in Vietnam, losing interest in the liberation and reunification struggle of the Vietnamese people. Such an entreaty might well encourage other friends and allies to do the same. Hanoi concluded that China's rapprochement with the United States was "a torpedo," aimed directly at its anti-American resistance.

Despite its protestations, Le Duan's regime had to acquiesce in Beijing's engagement of Washington; it simply could not allow relations with

China to sour further. Denouncing Chinese duplicity in public risked, not only offending Beijing, but also being interpreted there as indicative of Hanoi's own alignment with Moscow in the Sino-Soviet dispute, with devastating consequences for Sino-Vietnamese relations. The Vietnamese were fighting "a big imperialist country," Le Duc Tho observed; it was unwise to upset an indispensable ally, and the careful balance maintained between Moscow and Beijing. To make matters worse, in August 1971 severe flooding damaged crops in parts of the North, causing losses that could only be offset by foreign, including Chinese, food imports. Privately, Le Duan's regime kept pressing Beijing to reconsider its engagement of the United States, most notably by extolling the virtues of communist unity to Chinese envoys visiting Hanoi. "Our Vietnamese people with all their thoughts and their whole soul," the regime pleaded on one occasion, "aim at strengthening the martial unity with the fraternal communist countries, the international communist movement, the national libera-tion movements in Asia, Africa, and Latin America and the nations of the whole world."[9] It was all to no avail. Beijing continued on the path of rapprochement with Washington, even as it sustained its assistance to the DRVN and claimed to remain committed to its final victory.

Circumstances went from bad to worse for Hanoi when Moscow announced, in October, that it had also extended Nixon an invitation to visit the Soviet Union and discuss reconciliation between their two coun-tries. This, too, came as a bombshell, causing disbelief and new levels of unease in the North Vietnamese capital. What was the communist world coming to? This latest development was dismaying because it suggested that both communist giants were now weary of the Cold War, and thus of the Vietnam War as one of its most acute manifestations. Equally dis-concerting, it demonstrated just how wily Nixon could be. He had only recently increased the pressure on Hanoi militarily by going after the sanctuaries of its forces in Cambodia and Laos, and diplomatically by courting China. Now, he was upping the ante by flirting with Hanoi's other indispensable ally in obvious hopes of estranging it as well from the DRVN. Nixon's message to Hanoi was clear: collaborate and play ball in ending American involvement honorably, or face the punishing military and diplomatic consequences of obstinacy.

Nixon, Hanoi leaders gathered from all this, was taking advantage of cleavages within the communist camp to tear it apart. It was as if he had stolen a page from their own playbook by exploiting contra-dictions between one's enemy and that enemy's friends and allies. This was "choking warfare" at its best, as one Vietnamese analyst put it: an

FIGURE 5.2 Le Duan and Mao (center, holding hands) in Beijing, May 1970. They are flanked, from left to right, by DRVN Ambassador to the PRC Ngo Thuyen, CCP Politburo Standing Committee member Kang Sheng, CCP Vice Chairman Lin Biao, DRVN Deputy Minister of Foreign Trade Ly Ban, PRC Premier Zhou Enlai, and CCP Politburo member and PLA Chief of Staff Huang Yongsheng. Courtesy of the Vietnamese Ministry of Foreign Affairs and National Archives Center 3, Hanoi.

existential threat to Hanoi's war effort.[10] Nixon was positioning himself between Moscow and Beijing in an attempt to play each against the other and, ultimately, meet his purposes in Vietnam. He effectively made them compete in a geo-political game, the goal of which was inducing Hanoi to wind down the Vietnam War on terms most advantageous to Washington. The prize for the winner was improved relations with the United States, and the security and economic benefits that came with that. Essentially, Nixon aspired to get Hanoi's closest allies to sacrifice North Vietnamese interests for the sake of their own. As closer ties developed between Washington and each of the communist giants, tensions built between Hanoi and the latter. Would either or both of them demand that Hanoi end its war or face an aid cut-off? Even the first of these proposals was distasteful to the extreme for Le Duan's regime.

UNRAVELING OF SINO-VIETNAMESE ALLIANCE

Chinese leaders welcomed Nixon to Beijing in February 1972. The visit went without a glitch, and at the end of it the two governments introduced the fruit of their recent discussions, the Shanghai Communiqué. By its terms, the United States recognized Taiwan as part of China, albeit under a different political system. The two governments also pledged to keep working toward the normalization of their relations. This confirmed what Hanoi had suspected all along: a deal had been struck between Nixon and Mao at Vietnam's expense. Indeed, Beijing would soon start leaning on Le Duan's regime to wrap up the war and be more accommodating in the Paris talks. It never, however, went so far as to threaten an aid cut-off if Hanoi ignored it. Its "encouragements" were unequivocal, but understated, falling far short of what Nixon expected of Beijing's leaders. In this sense, Mao carried out his end of the bargain with Nixon, but not with the enthusiasm or in the manner the American President had hoped.

Le Duan and other DRVN leaders nonetheless deeply resented Chinese meddling in their affairs, and their audacity to discuss their own war with Nixon. Beijing had become complicit in Nixon's gambit to achieve peace with honor in Vietnam. In contravention of the most basic principle of communist solidarity, it had acted in its own interest at the expense of the interests of an ally. "The basis for all of China's actions is Chinese nationalism and chauvinism," grumbled one DRVN official. Others speculated that China had never been genuinely interested in their revolution, but simply wanted the Vietnamese to pin down the United States in the South and make its soldiers bleed to weaken and humiliate it. Beijing had manipulated and exploited the Vietnamese all along, they claimed, using them as pawns in a geo-strategic game to enhance its own power and prestige. To further its own goals, Beijing was prepared to support the war in Vietnam "to the last Vietnamese." The CCP had fallen from communist grace, Beijing's detractors in Hanoi thought; it no longer deserved recognition as a revolutionary vanguard. "The current Chinese leaders are not revolutionaries," a dejected Le Duan exclaimed privately, but "traitors to the interests of the revolutionary forces of the world." At this low point in the fortunes of the anti-American resistance, Beijing was currying favor with Washington. What had happened to its earlier boastings of being as close to the Vietnamese as "lips to teeth" in the struggle against American imperialism and Soviet revisionism? Who were the revisionists now?

The Soviets were no less duplicitous and unreliable, in Hanoi's reckoning, intending to roll out the red carpet for Nixon in Moscow less than three months after the Chinese had done the same in Beijing. But because of the closeness of their relationship in recent years, Le Duan's regime found Beijing's behavior much more frustrating and unsettling. Soviet–American détente was disgraceful, but it amounted in Vietnamese eyes to no more than a renewed commitment to the policy of East–West peaceful coexistence, introduced more than a decade and a half ago by Khrushchev. Since then, Hanoi had made its peace with Moscow's revisionist tendencies inasmuch as those tendencies had never precluded Soviet support for the DRVN in the American War, since 1965, at least. But China's *volte-face* was so sudden and complete as to look like apostasy: a complete disavowal of all that Marxism–Leninism, proletarian internationalism, and Sino-Vietnamese amity represented. "In Hanoi's eyes," historian Chen Jian has contended, "Beijing's dubious behavior had formed a sharp contrast with the revolutionary discourse of anti-imperialism and anti-revisionism that Beijing's leaders had fashioned throughout the Vietnam War years."[11] The extent of North Vietnamese vexation was obvious in the unguarded comments made by a DRVN official to a foreign counterpart. In flagrant violation of his own government's injunctions against off-the-cuff comments on relations with allies, the official blurted that Chinese leaders had failed properly to understand and practice communism because they were just a bunch of "peasants and artisans" with neither class nor intellectual refinement! Disappointment with China ran so deep that some in Hanoi wondered whether Beijing might sabotage national liberation movements and other progressive causes it had only recently encouraged, just to gratify Nixon. It might do that, these cynics thought, by becoming a voice against Third World revolutionary movements once it gained admission to the UN as a permanent member of the Security Council, another matter Mao had broached with Nixon during their recent summit, and which Beijing cared about greatly.

Sino-American rapprochement also distressed Hanoi more than Soviet-American détente for historical and geographical reasons. "If there is a special relationship in the history of Asian communism," historian Christopher Goscha writes, "it is the one linking Vietnamese Communists to their Chinese counterparts."[12] China and Vietnam were neighbors. Both were non-Western, Third World nations whose geographies, histories, and cultures were closely intertwined, as related in Chapter 1. As the smaller and thus more dependent of the two in this virtual condominium, Hanoi always expected more from China than it did from the Soviet Union. It was also always more affected existentially by what Chinese leaders said and did in their domestic and foreign affairs than by the words and deeds of other governments, including Moscow. Until recently, the Chinese had not disappointed the Vietnamese, nor let them down when the latter needed them. They had played the leading role in assisting the DRVN during the war against France. As everyone knew, "There would have been no victory at Dien Bien Phu without the 105mm guns supplied by China."[13]

After the ensuing Geneva accords, and creation of the DRVN as a bona fide state, Beijing helped Ho Chi Minh's government consolidate itself and rebuild and reorganize along communist lines the domestic economy. When Le Duan decided to go to war in the South in 1964, Beijing quickly pledged moral and material backing, and unconditionally supported his quest for total victory and reunification thereafter. Moscow had not even agreed to provide small arms. The Soviets proved more forthcoming after the onset of the American War, but kept pressing Hanoi to accept a diplomatic solution, and indefinite partition of Vietnam by extension. Of the two allies, China had clearly been the better and more accommodating one. And that may have been what sealed the fate of their alliance after Nixon began his machinations. No matter how much Beijing helped Vietnam, it could never do enough. "If Beijing and Hanoi had not been so close, they would have had fewer opportunities to experience the differences between them," Chen Jian concluded. "Too intimate a tie created more opportunities for conflict."[14]

SPRING OFFENSIVE

In spring 1972, Le Duan decided, somewhat surprisingly given the relative weakness of communist forces in the South, to go for broke again and mount another general offensive against the South. This was a presidential election year in the United States, and the Secretary could not resist the temptation of undertaking a bold military initiative at such a time. Unlike the Tet Offensive, this campaign would consist of a conventional-style invasion of the South, involving armored and heavy field artillery units; like the Tet Offensive, it would be an all-out effort to turn the war permanently to Hanoi's advantage. The new campaign's central objective, as Le Duan envisioned it, was to rout and demoralize the ARVN by crushing its main force units. "The time had come to lay all cards on the table" and finally "sweep away the Saigon forces and regime" all the way to Saigon, he believed. Tanks and heavy artillery were highly vulnerable to aerial bombing, but if the situation remained favorable they would secure "total victory" expeditiously, within ten to fifteen months. At a minimum, the VWP Secretary expected communist forces to easily conquer the northern third of South Vietnam, cutting it off completely from Saigon and severely disrupting enemy pacification efforts there. To defend invading PAVN columns against US air strikes, Hanoi ordered

Northern air defense units, idle since the suspension of the bombing of the DRVN in 1968, to join them.

The Spring (or Easter) Offensive had other immediate purposes beyond influencing the 1972 US presidential election and tipping the military balance in the South. Foremost among these was disrupting Sino-American rapprochement and derailing the Moscow summit between Soviet leader Leonid Brezhnev (1906–82) and Nixon upcoming in May. By now, Nixon's bold foreign policy initiatives were enhancing his political position domestically, and by extension weakening the American antiwar movement upon which Hanoi depended to constrain the American President's war effort. Encouraged by these developments, Kissinger had hardened his stance in the Paris talks. Only escalating hostilities could blunt those threatening trends, Le Duan thought. To be sure, doing so now might put Hanoi's diplomatic struggle, it public diplomacy, at risk by signaling that it was more committed to war and military victory than to actual peace, but that was a risk Le Duan was prepared to assume. All things being equal, the proposed campaign laid bare Hanoi's eagerness to break the military and diplomatic impasse before Chinese and Soviet leaders divorced themselves entirely from the war. Interestingly, both allied leaderships were aware Hanoi was planning an offensive in the South, but had no idea of its extent and timing; Le Duan knew they would never approve of the sort of effort he envisaged. Besides, he did not want to risk losing the element of surprise.

Although it was being pressed by circumstances, Hanoi nonetheless remained confident in its prospects for success in the attack. The year before both the Soviet Union and China had increased their military assistance to the DRVN, substantially bolstering the capabilities of its forces. The United States had less than 100,000 troops left in the South, and there was no way Nixon would dare deploying more in a presidential election year. He could respond to the offensive by resuming sustained bombings of the North, but would face major political risks doing so at this juncture. He might compromise, if not altogether stop, the process of Sino-American rapprochement. He might also prompt Moscow to cancel the upcoming summit, thus halting the burgeoning détente between their two countries. Either or both of these possibilities would seriously hurt his prospects for reelection. And then there were the domestic implications of resuming the bombing, sure to fire up the antiwar movement. To placate public opinion generally and antiwar sentiment specifically in a politically critical year, Nixon would have to limit his response to the invasion, Hanoi concluded. In retrospect, the rationale was sensible.

Still, the offensive was a very risky calculation. Not everyone in Hanoi was in favor of it; ranking members of the Party and armed forces, including committed hardliners, opposed it at first. Hanoi's previous go-for-broke campaigns, in 1964 and 1968, had both failed to meet their intended goals. Another flop at this stage of the war might very well, in conjunction with mounting diplomatic uncertainties, devastate the long-term prospects of the Vietnamese Revolution. The Viet Cong, for its part, remained weak, its guerrillas still lacking the numbers and strength to effectively support, logistically and militarily, invading forces from the North. But none of these concerns were enough to make Le Duan change his mind: his fixation on victory was unshakable, and made him oblivious to such peril.

Code-named *Nguyen Hue*, after the leader of the army that had defeated the Chinese invasion of 1789, the offensive got under way on 30 March 1972 when five PAVN divisions comprising 120,000 men crossed into the South from bases in the North and sanctuaries in Laos and Cambodia. The attack went well at first, but then ran into unex-pectedly stiff resistance from ARVN forces. That was not the worst of it for Hanoi. Within days, Nixon ordered massive sustained bombings of Northern supply lines into the South, and of the DRVN itself, an oper-ation code-named *Linebacker*, after the President's love of football. The United States also took the unprecedented step of dropping mines into North Vietnamese harbors to disrupt the flow of foreign aid arriving by ship. To Hanoi's consternation, neither Moscow nor Beijing meaningfully protested Washington's daring response. In fact, even as the bombing and mining crippled the North, both powers sustained their diplomatic engagement of Washington. Most outrageously, Moscow refused to can-cel the upcoming Brezhnev–Nixon summit. It would not even postpone it.

The tame response of the Soviets and Chinese to the resumption of the bombing of the North effectively helped Nixon's reelection chances. Adding insult to injury, the Soviets turned down a request for assistance from Hanoi in de-mining North Vietnamese harbors, citing concerns about a direct confrontation with the United States; but pos-sibly, too, because of fury at DRVN leaders for launching a campaign so obviously aimed at derailing East–West détente. Hanoi interpreted these reactions to Washington's actions to mean that both the Soviet Union and China now valued their relationships with the United States more than they cared about the fate of Vietnam: it seemed they pre-ferred to work with the Americans, rather than join the Vietnamese in defeating them.

FAILURE, AGAIN

Facing punishing air strikes, spirited resistance by ARVN forces, mounting material and human losses, and waning allied support, the invasion soon ran out of steam, and Hanoi felt compelled to call the whole thing off in early June. As historian Lien-Hang Nguyen later wrote, Le Duan's regime "had to accept that its objective for the 1972 Spring-Summer offensive to alter the military balance of power on the ground and to thwart superpower obstruction from above failed."[15] Yet again, Le Duan had miscalculated, grossly overestimating the capabilities of his forces while underestimating the resilience of ARVN troops. Above all, he completely misread Nixon, failing to gauge even remotely accurately his reaction to the offensive. Obviously, Le Duan did not really know his enemy, just as he did not understand how far Nixon was willing to go to secure a decent peace. Communist forces, and the Northern masses, paid a terrible price for his latest blunder.

The Spring Offensive proved an indubitable debacle for Hanoi. It achieved few meaningful gains, and produced horrendous losses for communist forces. According to conservative estimates, those forces suffered in excess of 100,000 casualties, including 40,000 killed, mostly North Vietnamese. The enemy lost 10,000 killed and 33,000 wounded and missing, mostly from the ARVN. Communist losses matched those of the Tet Offensive four years earlier, with none of the gains then made off the battlefield. What is more, most territory seized by communist forces during the early stages of their attack was eventually reclaimed by South Vietnamese forces. The PAVN also lost more than 250 tanks, approximating the total number committed to the campaign. Some 25,000 civilians died in the offensive, and nearly a million more were internally displaced. Communist combat units, or what was left of them, ran on fumes thereafter, as US bombings continued disrupting supply lines long after the campaign had ended.

DECLINING MORALE

These setbacks and hardships, coming as they did after seven years of war, made war-weariness almost pervasive in communist ranks. Northern soldiers were remarkably well-trained and -disciplined, but their steadfastness was reaching its limit. An increase in the overall number of Northern forces in the South was just about the only positive outcome of the Spring Offensive. That meant little at the time, but would impact the military balance in the South after the last US troops left. The campaign also momentarily energized the Viet Cong, spurring the resurgence of guerrilla activity in parts of the South, the implications of which would similarly go without note until after the end of the American War.

In the North, the resumption of the bombings on an unprecedented scale devastated the infrastructure, which the authorities had spent the better part of the past four years rebuilding and improving. New laser-guided bombs increased the precision of US air raids, evident in the complete destruction of most bridges and miles of rail lines in just a few days after the bombings began, greatly impairing aid deliveries from China and the movement of goods and supplies within the North and between North and South. Hanoi's decision to redeploy air defense units to protect the PAVN invading force did nothing to help the situation. The mining of harbors similarly disrupted the flow of external aid and domestic economic activity, hurting agriculture and causing food shortages despite strong harvests that year. Almost all industrial plants save those in Hanoi were destroyed. The bombing was so disruptive that, on average, people performed productive labor for only four to five hours each day. All of this meant the imposition of new privations on the masses, who had been getting used to living somewhat normal lives again. The psychological cost thus proved as elevated as the physical one. One DRVN official actually considered these latest "tests" faced by the North and its people "the toughest of the entire war."

In the aftermath of all this, apathy toward Hanoi's political and social goals became widespread in the North, especially among the young, whom authorities accused of "primitive selfishness." Labor discipline became looser, with increasing number of employees arriving to work late, leaving early, or not showing up at all. The most basic of life's comforts disappeared, the vibrant black market becoming the only place where certain items such as toothpaste and razor blades could be obtained, but at grossly inflated prices. After all these years spent fighting and suffering and eking out a living, the end, it seemed, was still not in sight for the people of North Vietnam. That thought consumed and disconcerted many, increasing general wariness of the government, of the information it fed them, even of its handling of the conflict. Indeed, subtle calls for ending the war at once, by any means and on any terms necessary, became more prevalent among the Northern masses. With good reason, they had had enough. The dreary, somber, even depressing urban landscapes depicted in the paintings of Bui Xuan Phai (1921–88) clearly conveyed one man's displeasure with the effects of prolonged conflict. The sudden popularity of "yellow music" – sentimental, romantic, pre-war tunes, banned by the authorities, who sanctioned only "red," or revolutionary, music – similarly attested to a general lassitude among the people.

A divide opened between the people, tired of wartime austerity and longing for the return of peace, on the one hand, and Le Duan and other leaders, still consumed by visions of total victory, on the other. The divide became threatening enough to prompt the fearsome Ministry of Public Security to launch a "counter-counterrevolutionary" campaign to silence or otherwise deter any public, open criticism of the Party line. In a stunning assessment of the situation, a Soviet analyst concluded that the challenges now confronting Hanoi were such that it would never win the war: that it was, in fact, "destined" to suffer "irremediable defeat."

DIPLOMATIC SOLUTION

Hanoi's next move confirmed the relative accuracy of that assessment. By official account, in calling off the Spring Offensive in mid-June 1972, Le Duan's regime effectively shifted from a "strategy of war" to a "strategy of peace." That is, it decided to forego for the time being total victory, and end the war through negotiations instead. This constituted the most important revision of general strategy since the 1963–4 decision to use "big war" to defeat the regime in Saigon, and its foreign supporters, and bring about national reunification. It was also a key moment in the history of the American War, marking the beginning of its end.

Having settled on this new course, Hanoi's first task was to set the parameters for an acceptable agreement that promised peace now without ruining the prospects for total victory later. Le Duan's regime did not seek a permanent agreement; only an interim one, although that fact had to remain secret. The approaching presidential election in the United States loomed large in this calculus. DRVN leaders thought Nixon might indulge them in his eagerness to complete a deal before Americans went to the polls in November, and thus guarantee his own reelection. That Le Duan went along with this idea and, most likely, proposed it himself, showed how badly his forces had been hurt by the Spring Offensive, how effective US bombings had proven, and how desperate his regime was for the cessation of hostilities. Paradoxically, Le Duan was opting for the same solution now that Ho had pursued in 1954, and which Le Duan himself had vehemently condemned at the time. Admittedly, circumstances now and then were markedly different. Nonetheless, it is a testament to the extent of his own exasperation that Le Duan endorsed the same strategy he had so aggressively opposed two decades earlier.

The parallel does not end there. Like Ho back then, Le Duan was prepared in 1972 to suspend armed struggle short of achieving basic revolutionary objectives not because of the pressure of allies – though he would conveniently blame Beijing for having to do that – but because conditions of his own making in the South and in the North left his regime no alternative. To be sure, consenting to suspend the war was a momentous decision, for a leadership so accustomed to acting "psychologically" as if it "feared peace more than the continuation of the war," as an American diplomat put it. But as Ho had done in 1954, Le Duan had to make the pragmatic choice in 1972 and pursue a negotiated end to the war against a mighty Western adversary.

In mid-June, just as Le Duan's regime was setting on the new strategic course, a high-level Soviet delegation arrived in Hanoi to urge leaders there to drop their demand for the removal of South Vietnamese President Nguyen Van Thieu as a condition for a diplomatic settlement with the United States. Shortly afterwards, Chinese envoys came to ask the same of DRVN leaders. If Hanoi allowed Thieu to stay in power, the Chinese said, "the US will be surprised because they do not expect that"; in successful negotiations, "surprise is necessary." Such entreaties irritated Le Duan, who saw in them evidence of Moscow's and Beijing's collusions with Washington to put the "Vietnam problem" to rest. To nudge and reassure Hanoi, and in a vain effort to convince DRVN decision-makers that their respective governments remained steadfastly committed to the Vietnamese Revolution, both the Soviet Union and China increased their aid to record levels in 1972.

That fall, Le Duan and the rest of the Politburo swallowed their pride and decided to drop the demand for Thieu's removal. As much as they hated to admit it, their allies were right. Besides, the gesture was necessary to restore momentum in the negotiations, which were at an impasse, and get the Americans to accept a settlement that would meet Hanoi's most pressing needs. During their next meeting, in France in early October, Le Duc Tho surprised Henry Kissinger by presenting a complete draft agreement, the first such proposal ever advanced by either side. The draft was especially notable for making no allusion to Thieu's fate, and calling instead for creation of a government of national concord in Saigon through negotiations between the PRG and Thieu's government *after* a general ceasefire.

FIGURE 5.3 Le Duc Tho (standing) and Xuan Thuy (sitting, second from left) enjoying some down time with other members of the North Vietnamese delegation to the Paris talks. Courtesy of the Vietnamese National History Museum, Hanoi.

With that concession, Hanoi abandoned its quest for a comprehensive peace settlement, and for the first time signaled its willingness to accept a two-stage solution: first, an agreement covering military issues only leading to a ceasefire within days after its signing, which Washington had insisted upon all along; and, second, a settlement of political matters, including the political future of the two Vietnams, to be arranged by the Vietnamese parties themselves in separate, subsequent talks after the ceasefire had come into effect and the United States had pulled the last of its forces. Kissinger recognized right away that Tho's draft constituted a major breakthrough, as Hanoi had always insisted that it would never accept a diplomatic settlement that left fundamental political problems unresolved beyond the suspension of hostilities.

After some haggling, the two men reached a tentative settlement based largely upon Tho's proposal. The substance of that settlement obligated the United States to: end completely its military involvement in Vietnam; recognize the legitimacy of the PRG; accept the presence of PAVN forces in the South after a ceasefire; acknowledge the right to self-determination of the South Vietnamese people; and, pay for postwar reconstruction in Indochina, including North Vietnam. Hanoi, for its part, had to return all American POWs, accept the continued existence of Thieu's regime in Saigon, and negotiate the future of South Vietnam with the aforementioned government of national concord after its formation. Washington conceded more than Hanoi to achieve this tentative deal, but its terms still fell far short of what Le Duan's regime had always maintained were its minimal aspirations. The American War, it seemed, was coming to an end.

ELUSIVE PEACE

Peace, it turned out, was not "at hand" just yet, despite Kissinger's declaration to that effect during a 26 October press conference, and Hanoi's own resigned outlook. The proposed terms proved unacceptable to South Vietnamese President Thieu, who categorically and defiantly rejected the draft settlement after Kissinger visited Saigon to brief him on it. Since winning re-election in October of the previous year, Thieu had been manifesting increasingly imperious, dictatorial tendencies. Only recently he had limited press freedoms and begun a crackdown on political opponents. In his defense, since he had been kept in the dark about the terms of the draft settlement, and even the substance of Kissinger's talks with Tho, he had cause to balk. What self-respecting leader would not have done the same? Thieu's rejection of the draft settlement, and Nixon's refusal to override or ignore that rejection – to "go-it-alone" with the North Vietnamese, as Kissinger kept urging the American President to do – prompted Nixon to request another round of talks with Hanoi, to make the document palatable to Saigon. Sensing a growing rift between Saigon and Washington, and hoping to capitalize on it, Hanoi elected to stall. With the American presidential election just around the corner, it figured that, if push came to shove, Nixon would ignore Thieu's recalcitrance and accept the agreed-upon draft. Hanoi therefore informed Washington of its refusal to reopen the talks, convinced that Nixon would not want to face reelection without a deal, any deal.

The American President, it turned out, was unfazed by the gambit. Once again, Le Duan and his regime had miscalculated. Just days later, to their consternation, Nixon won a landslide victory. How many more times could DRVN decision-makers miscalculate, and still hope to achieve the liberation of the South and national reunification? Armed with a new four-year mandate, what would Nixon do next, they wondered? Would he make them regret their temporizing? Or would he continue working with them toward a diplomatic settlement? Reluctant to test Nixon's mettle, Le Duan accepted his offer for another round of discussions in late November. Owing to Hanoi's intransigence, and Washington's insistence on amending the agreement to mollify Thieu, this latest round of talks was inconclusive, and the two sides recessed the negotiations indefinitely. As much as it remained committed to a negotiated end to the war, Hanoi feared that accommodating Nixon, by making fresh compromises, might make it look weak or desperate, energize Nixon, and encourage him to introduce new demands. After the abortive November talks, Tho returned to Hanoi to brief the Politburo on developments in Paris. In his estimation, Washington preferred to continue the war rather than settle it. Under the circumstances, Hanoi's best bet was to do nothing, to wait for Congress, the American public, and the international community to pressure Nixon into ending the war on the terms already agreed upon.

In a last-ditch effort to salvage the agreement and terminate the war before the end of the year, Tho and Kissinger met one more time in Paris during the first week of December. Kissinger submitted what he described as Nixon's "utmost proposal": a return to the October agreement with six seemingly minor changes to meet the least troublesome of Thieu's objections. Tho agreed to five of the proposed changes, but balked at the sixth, which had to do with the demilitarized zone (DMZ) at the 17th parallel. The wording Kissinger proposed, Tho said, could be interpreted to mean that the partition line between the two Vietnams was a political boundary, not a provisional demarcation between two regroupment zones, as stipulated in the 1954 Geneva accords. Hanoi could never accept any language in any official document suggesting the existence of two separate Vietnamese states. Vietnam was not Korea or Germany, Tho maintained; it was one sovereign state, with one legal government. The regime in Saigon, and the "Republic of Vietnam" it claimed to preside over, had no legitimacy in international law. Also, Tho believed that Kissinger's wording would allow Saigon to reopen the issue of Northern military withdrawal from the South during subsequent talks between the Vietnamese parties and, beyond that, make it illegal, and thus more difficult, to rotate and re-supply PAVN troops in the South after the ceasefire. What good was an agreement allowing Northern forces to remain below the 17th parallel if those forces could not be kept ready for combat?

Close as Tho and Kissinger came to agreement, the December negotiations ended in failure because of this single issue. The substance and the wording of the final agreement mattered a great deal to DRVN leaders. This was not just another piece of paper in their eyes, as some historians have maintained. Vietnamese communist leaders had a long history of taking diplomatic agreements, particularly internationally sanctioned ones, seriously. Le Duan and his comrades understood that Washington, the international community, and even their own allies, would hold them accountable to whatever terms they agreed on, just as they understood that Washington might try to use those terms to give legal justification to a decision to re-intervene militarily after the withdrawal of the last of its forces. Each word in the agreement could be used against them, once they formally accepted that agreement. Le Duan's regime understood this so well that, in late 1972, it rejected a reasonable deal – and a chance to end the war – over just a few of those words.

LINEBACKER II

One of the war's strangest and most remarkable episodes unfolded immediately after the December negotiations recessed. Per previous agreement with Kissinger, Tho returned to Hanoi to consult with the rest of the Politburo and see if there was any chance he could make his colleagues change their mind about the latest American proposals. Tho's plane landed, at Noi Bai Airport on the outskirts of the capital, around noon, local time, on 18 December. Within an hour, Tho was back at his private residence, where the other members of the Politburo awaited him. According to the unpublished account of Nguyen Khac Huynh, a senior member on Tho's staff, Tho supplicated Le Duan and others present to accept the American wording on the DMZ. That, Tho argued, was better than risking indefinite prolongation of the war. He also repeated Kissinger's warning that Hanoi faced "grave dangers" if no agreement was reached, as Nixon had promised to undertake "whatever action" was necessary to meet his objectives in Vietnam before the new Congress convened in January 1973.

Le Duan rejected Tho's entreaties at first, but then changed his mind. Accepting the proposed language and the rest of the draft agreement, he reasoned, might create problems later, but at least it would bring hostilities to an end now, allowing his regime to remedy pressing problems at home and among its forces in the South. The DRVN could hardly sustain the war at this point; if its complexion changed, if Nixon decided to escalate it, as Kissinger had threatened, it could lose everything. Growing domestic and international pressure to end the war at once might make it difficult for Nixon to do that, but then again the American President had shown that he was not easily deterred. The dilemma was a real one.

By the time the meeting at Tho's house adjourned, around four o'clock in the afternoon, the Politburo had unanimously agreed to do as Tho had suggested, and concede on the language in the agreement concerning the DMZ. Unfortunately, before it could relay its decision to the White House, it was already too late; Nixon had reached the end of his tether. At 8pm, Hanoi time, that same day, the United States commenced its most savage bombing of the North to date. And with that, an opportunity to end the war before the (Western) New Year died.

When Nixon learned of the outcome of the December round of talks, he was livid. He thought he had gone as far as he could to secure a settlement, but Hanoi had remained hung up on details and technicalities. Communist decision-makers, he reasoned, were playing him. Intent as ever to achieve peace with honor – and not be taken for a fool – he turned to the only course he thought the stubborn North Vietnamese leadership might respond to sensibly: bombing. This time, however, he envisioned no ordinary campaign, but the most intense and concentrated effort ever undertaken against the DRVN. Nixon would go after, not just all of the usual targets, but also sites in and around Hanoi and Haiphong, the North's largest and most important urban center and port, respectively, previously off-limits to American bombers. It was now Nixon's turn to go for broke. Some historians have erroneously claimed that the bombing was intended to reassure Thieu before Washington signed a deal with Hanoi which he, Thieu, found objectionable; but that claim has no basis in fact. Nixon ordered operation *Linebacker II*, as this latest bombing campaign was labeled, for the sole purpose of compelling Hanoi to sign a peace agreement on the terms last proposed by Kissinger, and nearly accepted by Tho just days before. Nixon considered waiting a little longer before commencing the bombing, but in the end concluded that Hanoi would not budge, that Tho would not make the Politburo change its mind about Kissinger's latest proposals, that his promise to Kissinger to try and sway his comrades in Hanoi was just a stalling tactic.

On 17 December, American planes dropped more mines in North Vietnamese ports. The following evening, the bombing itself began. Its scale was, admittedly, unprecedented. Over the next twelve days (18–29 December, with a thirty-six hour truce on Christmas), B-52 strategic bombers, each capable of carrying a payload approximating one hundred 500-pound bombs, flew more than 700 sorties over North Vietnam, while smaller aircraft flew an additional 1,200. Together, they dropped over 20,000 tons of bombs, a large portion of which fell in and around Hanoi and Haiphong. The resulting physical destruction was staggering: 1,600 military installations, miles of railway lines, hundreds of trucks and railway cars, eighty percent of electrical power plants, and countless factories and other structures were taken out of commission.

As with the previous *Linebacker* campaign, the December bombings effectively nullified the economic progress that had been made in the North since Johnson suspended air raids in 1968. The *Linebacker* bombings crippled the North's vital organs, obliterating the results of its communist transformation, and its ability to sustain the war in the South by extension. Had the bombing lasted any longer at the same intensity, a Soviet diplomat commented, the North would have become "a wasteland." DRVN air defense forces fired nearly 900 Soviet-made surface-to-air missiles at US planes, shooting down fifteen B-52s and several other aircraft, but depleting their stock of the weapons in the process. All things being equal, those forces fought valiantly. Their record is especially impressive, given that the bulk of their effectives, some two thirds of them, had been redeployed to defend troop columns in the Spring Offensive, as previously mentioned, and never returned.

"DIEN BIEN PHU OF THE SKIES"?

The impact of the December bombings in the North was as numbing as it was stupefying. An effort of such magnitude, coming so late in the war, stunned both leaders and the populace. Nixon, it seemed, was indeed a "madman" whose mania knew no bounds, as some of his detractors claimed. The terror that gripped the population during the air raids was magnified by the destruction of Bach Mai hospital on the southern edge of Hanoi, as well as the razing of Kham Thien Street in a residential neighborhood. Officially, the "Christmas bombing" claimed the lives of 1,318 civilians in Hanoi and 305 in Haiphong. The numbers were low relative to the physical destruction because most residents of both cities had previously been evacuated to the countryside; only essential personnel had stayed behind. Beijing and Moscow, for their part, aggressively denounced the bombing – but did nothing more. Equally disappointing for DRVN leaders was the public outcry in the United States, surprisingly understated in their own view.

The bombing proved too much for Le Duan, and everyone else in North Vietnam. On 26 December, as the bombing was ongoing, Hanoi informed the White House that it was prepared to resume negotiations once the B-52 raids stopped. Nixon obliged. Le Duan, it turned out, was prepared to put his people through hell to see the Revolution through to completion, but he would not have the country destroyed and his communist project in the North compromised. Besides, hard as he and his colleagues tried to uphold popular confidence in the government, and belief in the merits of the anti-American resistance, their pleas and promises were starting to ring hollow.

Ever the masterful manipulators of information, DRVN authorities did their best to spin an abject defeat into a stunning imaginary victory. According to the narrative they presented to their own public in the immediate aftermath of the suspension of the December bombings, the story of the events of late December 1972 was a tale, not of massive loss and destruction, but of heroic resistance by Northerners. By official account, air defenses shot down not fifteen B-52s, as the Americans claimed, but a much more impressive number of thirty-four. They also performed innumerable other feats of spirited defense and heroism which, in conjunction with similar triumphs by other outfits, had contributed to this remarkable triumph of the Vietnamese people. In fact, the toll on the US forces had been such that it had forced Nixon to beg Hanoi to resume the peace talks, and to unilaterally and unconditionally end the bombing. The entire enterprise had been so costly for the United States as to amount to its own "Dien Bien Phu of the Skies," DRVN authorities claimed, a contention so embellished as to be outrageous.

It is as much a testament to the delusions of anti-American and antiwar sentiment generated around the Vietnam War as it is to the effectiveness of Hanoi's propaganda, that such views still have credence among Vietnamese, including scholars, today. The Vietnamese government still commemorates the anniversary of this "great victory," which allegedly brought about the end of the American War soon thereafter. Shockingly, many American scholars have accepted Hanoi's version of the outcome of this last major battle of the Vietnam War.

Notes

1 During a speech in San Antonio, Texas, in September 1967, Johnson offered to suspend the bombing of North Vietnam in return for a pledge from Hanoi to agree to negotiations and not take advantage of the suspension to infiltrate more men and supplies into the South. Hanoi did not respond.

2 Tuong Vu, *Vietnam's Communist Revolution: The Power and Limits of Ideology* (New York: Cambridge University Press, 2017), 294.

3 Robert W. Komer, *Bureaucracy at War: U.S. Performance in the Vietnam Conflict* (Boulder, Colo.: Westview Press, 1986), 147.

4 Hanoi proposed a square or lozenge-shaped table, with each of the four delegations on its own side. Washington rejected that proposal at Saigon's

insistence because it conferred equal legitimacy upon the NLF. The Americans countered with a two-side arrangement, the Americans and South Vietnamese on one side, and the other two parties on the other. Hanoi rejected it because it did not give sufficient exposure to the NLF. After three months of haggling the two sides accepted a Soviet recommendation to use a large round table for negotiators and two small rectangular tables situated on opposite sides of the round table for note-takers.

5   Van Tien Dung, *Cuoc khang chien chong My: toan thang* [The Anti-American Resistance: Total Victory] (Hanoi: Nha xuat ban Su that, 1991), 47–8.

6   Judy Tzu-Chun Wu, *Radicals on the Road: Internationalism, Orientalism, and Feminism during the Vietnam Era* (Ithaca: Cornell University Press, 2013), 200, 218.

7   Nguyen Khac Huynh, "Les pourparlers de Paris 40 ans après – un regard rétrospectif et réflexions," paper presented at *Colloque International: "Guerre, diplomacie et opinion. Les négociations de paix à Paris et la fin de la guerre au Vietnam (1968–1975),"* [International Seminar: "War, Diplomacy, and Perspective: The Paris Peace Talks and the End of the Vietnam War (1968–1975)"] Paris, 13–14 May 2008, 2–3.

8   Ang Cheng Guan, *The Vietnam War from the Other Side: The Vietnamese Communists' Perspective* (New York: RoutledgeCurzon, 2002), 142.

9   Quoted in "Information on the Visit of the Vietnamese Party-Government Delegation in Beijing," 5 December 1971; archivna edinitsa [hereafter a.e.] 33; opis 22p; Arkhiv na Ministerstvoto na Vunshnite Raboti (Archive of the Ministry of Foreign Affairs, Sofia) [hereafter AMVnR], 303. Document translated by Simeon Mitropolitski and provided by Lorenz Lüthi of McGill University.

10 Hoc vien Quan he quoc te, *Ngoai giao Viet Nam hien dai: Vi su nghiep gianh doc lap, tu do, 1945–1975* [Contemporary Vietnamese Diplomacy: For Delivering Independence and Freedom] (Hanoi: Nha xuat ban Chinh tri quoc gia, 2001), 256.

11 Chen Jian, "China, the Vietnam War, and the Sino-American Rapprochement, 1968–1973" in Odd Arne Westad and Sophie Quinn-Judge (eds.), *Third Indochina War: Conflict between China, Vietnam and Cambodia, 1972–1979* (London: Frank Cass, 2006), 59.

12 Christopher E. Goscha, "Vietnam, the Third Indochina War and the Meltdown of Asian Internationalism" in Westad and Quinn-Judge (eds.), *Third Indochina War*, 157.

13 British Consulate-General, Hanoi to Southeast Asia Department, London, 18 November 1965; FO 371/ 1805283; National Archives of the United Kingdom, Kew, 1.

14 Chen Jian, *Mao's China and the Cold War* (Chapel Hill: University of North Carolina Press, 2001), 236.

15 Lien-Hang T. Nguyen, *Hanoi's War: An International History of the War for Peace in Vietnam* (Chapel Hill: University of North Carolina Press, 2012), 255.

6

Civil War, 1973–1975

Though their efforts to turn a dismal defeat into a public relations victory had been remarkably successful after Tet, in the aftermath of the December bombing North Vietnamese leaders understood that they could not continue the war without mortgaging their country's future and compromising the Revolution generally. After all, the North was supposed to be the great rear base of the liberation struggle in the South; without it, that struggle was doomed to fail. To this point, Vietnamese from both halves of the country had fought valiantly, but their efforts could not deliver the decisive victory Le Duan so badly wanted.

In retrospect, that was not surprising. The Secretary had miscalculated too many times, repeatedly overestimating the capabilities and tactics of his own forces, while underestimating those of his enemies. Perhaps most egregiously, and tragically for communist troops, he had completely failed to gauge Nixon's resolve to salvage America's honor and avoid a humiliating defeat in Vietnam. In light of such flagrant and costly miscalculations, it was almost miraculous that Hanoi was still in the fight by 1973. That, to no insignificant degree, was due to Le Duan's own determination: his stubborn, blind faith in the ultimate triumph of the anti-American resistance and the Vietnamese Revolution. It was also due in part to the DRVN's propaganda machine, whose masterful handling of information was critical to maintaining the illusion, at home and abroad, that Hanoi's war effort was righteous and, most important, unfolding successfully, as planned. But even Le Duan and his regime had a breaking point, and they had reached it.

In accordance with the terms of the secret pact that ended the bombing, Kissinger and Tho met again in Paris in early January 1973. Their meeting opened on an ominous note, when a livid Tho entered the room and pounded his fist on the table, exclaiming that Washington had had no right to attack the North as savagely as it had in late December, especially in view of how close the two sides were to a settlement. Tho ranted for minutes, as Kissinger listened, impassively. When Tho was done, Kissinger asked understatedly if they should end the war once and for all. After Tho had cooled off, the two men set out to iron out the remaining differences and settle other outstanding issues. It soon became obvious that each man had come to Paris with orders to bring the negotiations to a prompt and successful conclusion. Hanoi's yearning for a ceasefire became evident when Tho informed Kissinger that Hanoi agreed to the disputed language on the DMZ that had scuttled the talks back in December, resulting in the Christmas bombing. While many historians consider this concession to have been no more than a cosmetic change of a trivial point, it was in fact a substantive matter for Hanoi, for reasons detailed earlier. Indeed, the DRVN would not have suspended the talks over that one issue, setting itself up for the devastating December air raids, had it felt otherwise.

As DRVN leaders understood only too well, the language Tho had now formally accepted would create potential obstacles should they decide to resume fighting after the ceasefire took effect. But that was in the future, and right now they needed a suspension of hostilities at all cost. Tho's acquiescence confirmed Hanoi's longing for peace. That concession, and Tho's readiness to agree to end the war, were the dividends redeemed by Nixon's ruthlessness. That same concession and readiness also constituted as close to an admission of Hanoi's own poor judgment – in rejecting the DMZ language back in December only to accept that same language a month later – as it ever came to acknowledging during the Vietnam War.

In addition to yielding on the DMZ issue, Tho also agreed to the continued presence of a small contingent of US advisers in the South after the ceasefire, as well as to making the release of political prisoners held by the Saigon regime – a matter of great importance to the NLF – conditional upon the reduction of PAVN forces below the 17th parallel. These, too, were meaningful concessions. The former allowed the United States to maintain a symbolic military footprint in Vietnam, while the latter compelled Hanoi to recall at least some of its forces from the South, or risk disappointing its Southern allies. Only recently a DRVN Foreign Ministry official had confided that "the ceasefire can only be guaranteed with the total withdrawal of all American troops from South Vietnam and termination of all interference and participation in Vietnam from the side of the USA, as well as termination of all support whatsoever of the Saigon regime." The terms Tho accepted did not meet that standard. "Since the Hanoi Politburo's aim from the summer of 1972 had been to settle an agreement without further damage to their war effort," Lien-Hang Nguyen correctly surmised from all this, its compromises in the January talks were "a horrendous testament to the failure of that goal."[1] In exchange for Tho's concessions, Kissinger agreed to the withdrawal of all US combat forces from the South within sixty days after the ceasefire, as well as to the indefinite suspension of all acts of war by the United States against the North. Essentially, these terms reestablished the *status quo ante bellum*, the state of affairs that had existed before the war's Americanization in 1965. Vietnam was going right back to where it had been nine years earlier.

PARIS PEACE AGREEMENT

By the time Tho and Kissinger left Paris, they had finalized a draft peace settlement each thought his government could live with. The key provisions of that settlement, which on the surface resembled the October draft agreement but in fact contained substantive differences that only a close reading of the document could reveal, called for:

- US recognition of the sovereignty and territorial integrity of Vietnam;
- a ceasefire in place, followed by an immediate end to acts of war against the DRVN by the United States;
- withdrawal of US and all other foreign forces from Vietnam within sixty days;
- deactivation and removal of mines in DRVN waterways and harbors by the United States;
- dismantlement of all US military bases;
- creation of a Four-Party Joint Military Commission (FPJMC) with representation by the United States, the DRVN, the RVN, and the NLF/PRG to determine the specifics of the troop withdrawal;
- creation of a Two-Party Joint Military Commission (TPJMC) of RVN and NLF/PRG representatives to delineate the areas controlled by the military forces of each party in the South;
- return of all POWs;

- release of all political prisoners detained by Saigon, contingent upon the partial withdrawal of PAVN troops from the South;
- consultations between the PRG and Saigon leading to the creation of a National Council of National Reconciliation and Concord of three equal segments (nationalists [i.e., Thieu loyalists], communists, and neutralists), to organize free elections under international supervision to determine the future of the South;
- national reunification at an indeterminate period through peaceful means and cooperation between North and South Vietnam;
- US postwar reconstruction aid to Vietnam, including the DRVN;
- formation of an International Commission of Control and Supervision (ICCS, a reconstituted ICSC), consisting of members from Poland, Hungary, Indonesia, and Canada, to monitor implementation of the agreement, document and report violations, and adjudicate disputes between the parties.

Pleased by its terms, Nixon promptly endorsed the draft agreement. Thieu, the reason Hanoi and Washington had had to reopen the talks after reaching a tentative deal back in October of the previous year, initially rejected that deal as well. He changed his mind only after some strong-arming by Nixon, and the American President's personal assurances that the United States would not tolerate and forcefully respond to significant violations of the agreement by Hanoi or the Viet Cong. Le Duan hated the new draft settlement, but he knew it was the best his side could get under the circumstances. Nguyen Thi Binh and the NLF/PRG, for their part, accepted it because Hanoi said it had to.

Unlike the Geneva accords, the Paris agreement did not mandate the regroupment of belligerent forces in clearly delineated zones. Instead, it sanctioned a "leopard-spot" arrangement, whereby forces from each side would remain in areas of the South they controlled and administered as of the time the ceasefire took effect. Hanoi itself had insisted on this arrangement, which became the purview of the TPJMC after the ceasefire took effect, for a number of reasons. First, it would encourage Saigon to respect those provisions of the agreement directing the Vietnamese parties to resolve outstanding political issues in negotiations among themselves after the withdrawal of Americans forces. Second, the continued presence of communist troops in pockets across the South implied the United States and, most significantly, Thieu's regime recognized the existence in South Vietnam of two administrations, two armed forces, and two zones of control, and thus the legitimacy of the PRG, the NLF, and the LAF.

Third, the presence of both large and small zones of communist control below the 17th parallel ensured that Hanoi would be able to respond expeditiously should the agreement collapse and fighting resume. Lastly, the leopard-spot arrangement would prevent Saigon's armed forces from expanding their territorial control unopposed, as they had managed to do following the regroupment of Vietminh forces to the North in 1954–5.

Still, the leopard-spot model was a peculiar and chancy arrangement. Most problematically, it did not specify who had jurisdiction over what portions of the South; that was to be decided by the TPJMC *after* the ceasefire. That made contestation of control of areas immediately after the ceasefire more likely, and violations of one side's areas by the other more difficult to ascertain by supervisory authorities of the ICCS. In fact, in the days leading to the signing of the peace agreement, scheduled to take place in Paris during the last week of January, the two sides aggressively jockeyed for control of territory in the South, seeking to expand the areas under their control at the expense of the other before the ceasefire took effect. The resulting "land grabbing" schemes actually caused hostilities to flare briefly, but significantly. Each side signaled control of an area by blanketing it with its own flag. Hanoi took this "Battle of the Flags" seriously, but its troops were less than enthusiastic about attacking enemy positions when peace was just around the corner. "Nobody wanted to die in the last days of the war," a North Vietnamese soldier recalled.[2]

HOPE & TREPIDATION

The two sides signed the agreement in the French capital, as scheduled, on 27 January 1973. With the stroke of a pen, literally, Hanoi consented to suspend hostilities in return for de-Americanization of the war in the South. Because the governments in Hanoi and Saigon still refused to acknowledge each other's legitimacy, their representatives signed the agreement on separate pages. That, plus the recent escalation of hostilities occasioned by the Battle of the Flags, did not bode well for implementation of the agreement's political provisions, or for the prospects of peace in general for that matter.

By accepting the Paris agreement, Hanoi was giving up on total victory, for now at least. That Le Duan resigned himself to its terms attested to his own sense of despair. To be sure, he acceded to it only out of necessity. His regime could have easily obtained an agreement on similar terms back when Johnson was still President, but had not even entertained the possibility because the Secretary remained at that point consumed by visions of victory. Now, however, conditions in both halves of the country, and internationally, had become so unfavorable that Hanoi had to suspend its quest to defeat and humiliate the United States. It was a supreme irony that the man who had built his political career on attacking Ho, and other doves within his own party, now found himself capitulating – for that is what he thought he was doing – to an agreement whose terms could only be described as moderate given the circumstances on the ground in both halves of Vietnam in early 1973.

Despite reservations about the terms and implications of the peace agreement, Hanoi welcomed the suspension of hostilities. That, and the pending withdrawal of US forces, would give its forces a chance to rest, tend to their wounded, and regroup. It would also boost their sagging morale. Communist troops were still reeling from the effects of the disastrous Spring Offensive. Many were, in fact, at the end of their tether. Unlike their ARVN counterparts, who had enjoyed robust support from their American allies, PAVN and LAF troops had always fought their own battles, with lesser resources. They were exhausted and, in light of recent events, demoralized. A good portion of them had not seen or heard from their families in years, some for as long as a decade. And it was not just their spirit that was dwindling. Their capabilities were also sapped. Suspension of hostilities would thus allow them to recuperate, as well as consolidate and fortify areas under their control.

The end of the bombings of the North provided parallel advantages for the people there. The previous year's experiences, culminating in the dreadful B-52 raids on Hanoi and Haiphong, had crushed morale. Long separation from children, parents, and other relatives and friends evacuated to the countryside for their own protection, caused great anxiety among those who had stayed behind in places like the capital. Indeed, the latter constantly worried about the well-being of loved ones despite being in harm's way themselves. Vietnam is, after all, a Confucian country. Its people have high esteem for their families, and adults are expected to look after their elderly parents as they do their own children. The inability to meet filial as well as parental obligations troubled "stay-behinds." The carnage they had witnessed, plus other hardships and privations they endured, exacted an enormous psychological toll that added to their emotional burden. The Paris agreement and the resulting end of air raids thus lifted spirits across the North, fostering a sense of relief that a nightmare was finally over. Agricultural production, back to subsistence levels, and industrial output, at the point of near-collapse, could also finally recover. Dependence on Chinese and Soviet allies, now more or less absolute, and dangerously so in light of their recent behavior, could be lessened. For air defense forces, the end of the bombings was an existential relief. Their supplies of assembled surface-to-air missiles were exhausted, as were the troops themselves.

In sum, communist troops in the South, and civilians and air defense forces in the North, were utterly spent by 1973, and the Paris agreement promised to offer them relief and reprieve. At a minimum, the agreement would buy them precious time to recover. The post-Paris agreement situation was certainly not to Hanoi's disfavor. How to proceed from the current nadir was the next question Le Duan's regime had to answer. National reunification under its rule was impossible at that juncture. But the bombing had stopped, the Americans were leaving, and Hanoi's military and political presence in the South remained substantial. The future would belong to whoever could best deal with these new, conflicting circumstances.

Cautiously optimistic about their prospects, DRVN leaders nonetheless shared a profound sense of trepidation about the agreement. To begin, it offered no guarantee of national reunification under their authority. If this was a victory for their side, as they officially claimed, it was a bittersweet one. The impending withdrawal of the last American troops was a major breakthrough, but even without them the balance of forces in the South continued to favor Saigon. Its army of more than a million regular and paramilitary troops was the fifth largest in the world; and recent, accelerated military aid deliveries from the United States had made it even more dangerous and lethal. North Vietnamese military analysts acknowledged among themselves that Saigon's armed forces were in much better shape in 1973 than their own forces, and fretted over the implications of that disparity for the immediate future. Washington had agreed to pull out the remainder of its forces, but not without making sure South Vietnam could defend itself. And from the looks of things, it was poised to do just that.

The agreement, mandating as it did the de-Americanization of the conflict, also stood to rob Hanoi of one of the centerpieces in its propaganda campaigns, at home and abroad. That was no minor loss considering the critical role information and its manipulation had played in the national liberation strategy. Characterizing its struggle as an anti-American, anti-imperialist resistance had obscured Hanoi's commitment to Marxism–Leninism and enabled North Vietnamese leaders to pass themselves off as ardent nationalists, earning countless accolades domestically and internationally as a result. It had also obscured the fact that the war in the South was part civil war, fought against other Vietnamese. This obfuscation had markedly enhanced Hanoi's ability to rally supporters at home, mobilize opinion on its behalf abroad, isolate Washington and Saigon diplomatically, and secure material and diplomatic support from practically everywhere. Without the American presence, Hanoi's struggle for Southern liberation and national reunification lost much of its luster, even its *raison d'être* in the eyes of some of its supporters.

Lastly, but no less disconcerting, the Paris agreement unnerved Hanoi because it might generate expectations among its allies that peace in Vietnam was here to stay, and that DRVN authorities would do their utmost to abide by its letter and spirit indefinitely. Even before the agreement was signed, both Moscow and Beijing had insisted that Hanoi not violate the terms of any ceasefire it concluded with Washington; it should wait at least a few years before resuming hostilities, and then do so only if forced to by circumstances, when diplomatic efforts had been exhausted. This was one of the reasons Le Duan had never wanted a diplomatic settlement of the war in the first place, and precisely the situation he had wanted to avoid: dependence on allies to such an extent that his regime's freedom of action might be compromised by them. Waiting years before resuming the struggle for national reunification meant losing revolutionary momentum. The conundrum was a real one.

GIVING PEACE A CHANCE

Le Duan's regime did its best to comply with the spirit of the agreement at first, calculating that the advantages of doing so outweighed any benefits from doing otherwise. Most pressingly, it hoped to elevate the domestic and international standing of the PRG, to show that it was a legitimate, respectable, trustworthy political organization, and enhance its legal status through involvement in various diplomatic undertakings having to do with promotion and implementation of the accords. To that and other ends, Hanoi ordered its forces in the South to suspend all combat activities the moment the ceasefire took effect, and obey the "five no's": no attacking enemy garrisons; no retaliating against enemy attacks; no encircling enemy outposts; no using artillery; and no creating or expanding liberated areas. The struggle would continue, it told its forces, through political means only. The regime essentially espoused now the same strategy in the South that Ho's government had adopted back in 1954 after signing the Geneva accords, minus the recall of forces to the North.

In Le Duan's own estimation, there was an infinitesimally small possibility that Thieu would respect the peace agreement, in which case his regime might well be able to achieve its goals below the 17th parallel without resuming armed struggle and running the risk of enflaming the Americans and disappointing its allies. Most likely, however, Thieu and his forces would not honor the agreement, and a resort to violence would become necessary for communist forces, if only to protect themselves. Self-defense would give Hanoi a reasonable pretext to resume fighting, affording an opportunity to complete the liberation of the South sooner rather than later. According to political scientist William Turley, "the communists decided to respect the Paris agreement precisely because they assumed that Thieu was determined to obstruct it."[3] Either way, Hanoi would not lose. For now, however, it was better to stop fighting, remain vigilant, and prepare for the possible resumption of hostilities than to act impetuously, with all the risks that that entailed. The North Vietnamese top military brass endorsed these prescriptions, reckoning their forces would be unable to launch another offensive campaign for another three to five years.

Hanoi's decision to suspend hostilities, accept a negotiated settlement and thus the status quo, and abide by the basic provisions of that settlement received mixed reviews among partisans in the South. The majority welcomed peace, irrespective of its terms. After nearly a decade of "big war," the killing and destruction would finally end. The war, the members of that majority felt, had dragged on too long and been too costly in material as well as human terms; national reunification could wait. Some, who had joined the Viet Cong after the arrival of US forces in 1965, saw no reason to remain in that organization now that the "imperialists" had decided to pack their bags and go home. If fighting did resume, they would be taking on other Vietnamese exclusively, and that was not what most had in mind when they volunteered to fight. And so they quit the resistance, and returned to civilian life.

A radical minority of Southern partisans objected to the ceasefire. They believed that the Paris agreement, like the truce negotiated in Geneva some two decades earlier, unnecessarily delayed Southern liberation, and would be used by the enemy to consolidate his forces in preparation for new attacks. Diplomacy had proven counterproductive for their side before, and there was no reason to believe things would be different this time. Had VWP leaders not learned anything from their own history? How could Le Duan, of all people, go along with this idea, and become complicit in another betrayal of the Revolution in the South? Once more, radicals thought, the South had been abandoned by a distant Northern leadership in the furtherance of strictly Northern interests. Conditions were challenging, they acknowledged, but not to the point of requiring the cessation of hostilities, and indefinite postponement of Southern liberation and national reunification. At best the agreement would cause a letdown in revolutionary fervor among the masses and the armed forces; at worst, it would make the partition of Vietnam permanent.

Some Southern radicals, torn between loyalty to Hanoi and their own desire to see the South liberated at once, refused to lay down their weapons, but did their best to conceal their insubordination from their superiors. Yet others simply ignored orders against fighting, and deliberately taunted the enemy to sabotage the ceasefire. Such behavior exasperated Hanoi, which feared violations of the ceasefire and other provocative acts by radicals might delay the withdrawal of US forces, or worse, prompt Nixon to renew the bombing of the North.

KISSINGER IN HANOI

In early February, Henry Kissinger traveled to Hanoi by previous arrangement between the two sides. The purpose of his visit was to iron out certain matters relating to implementation of the peace agreement, as well as to explore the possibilities of normalizing relations between the United States and the DRVN, and thus open a new era in Vietnamese–American relations. Discussion topics included American reconstruction aid for Vietnam and the framework for normalization, which at that point the two sides thought they could achieve within months. Normalization seemed less far-fetched then than it does in retrospect. Immediately after signing of the Paris agreement, a number of Western governments, among them France and the United Kingdom, proceeded to normalize relations with Hanoi and formally recognize the DRVN. They did so to encourage communist leaders to respect the ceasefire agreement, as well as to serve other, narrower interests. That was evidently also Kissinger's purpose in visiting Hanoi. Normalizing relations, like the promise of reconstruction aid, was a carrot dangled by the Nixon administration to entice North Vietnamese leaders to honor the Paris agreement and fulfill other goals, including erasing memories of national humiliation.

During his stay in Hanoi, Kissinger visited the National History Museum. While there, according to a story Vietnamese historians love to relate, Kissinger paused in front of a plaque featuring the famous poem read by Ly Thuong Kiet to his troops before they defeated the Chinese in 1079, related in Chapter 1. After reading the poem in translation, Kissinger turned to his hosts and, melodramatically, confessed that: if the United States had been more aware of Vietnam's long history of resistance against foreign aggression, if it had understood the weight that Kiet's words carried, it would never have gotten involved militarily in their country. Kissinger's deference delighted his hosts, who interpreted it as an apology for the war the United States had waged against their country. For a brief moment, it seemed, peace might have a chance after all.

COMPLACENCY

DRVN authorities took advantage of the end of US bombings and the return of peace to tend to the badly damaged transport infrastructure, the poorly functioning economy, and their dejected population. Excellent rice harvests in 1973 helped their fortunes immeasurably. Meanwhile, PAVN units in the North were reconstituted and returned to full strength, as those in the South were sent desperately needed supplies. The pace of progress in these developments surprised even Le Duan.

In that Hanoi was extremely lucky, because the end of the American War brought with it expectations of a better life among Northern civilians, which DRVN authorities knew they would have to satisfy to some degree, or risk losing legitimacy. Henceforth, Hanoi had to assume responsibility for the hardships its people endured; it could no longer blame American bombs. Northern civilians had tolerated the war and its rigors while their lives were threatened by bombings, but became more demanding and far less indulgent once an actual agreement promising their end was signed. Convinced that this time peace was here to stay, they manifested unprecedented concern about their own well-being, and quickly lost interest in the unfinished business of reunification with the South. The pervasiveness of such sentiments worried the Politburo, which understood only too well that there was no guarantee peace would last, nor that the bombing would never resume. The more people convinced themselves that the war was over, the more difficult it would be to rally them should heavy fighting resume. That was, after all, how things had played out following the signing of the Geneva accords: until the bombing of the North began in 1964–5, Northerners had shown little enthusiasm for their government's efforts to liberate the South by force.

Within days after peace returned, foreign correspondents in Hanoi noticed a palpable sense of relief among the people. That feeling was accompanied by a marked decline in the patriotic fervor that had theretofore animated and energized civilians. Clearly and understandably, foreign correspondents in the DRVN noted, many Northerners had grown tired of making sacrifices and lost all sense of revolutionary purpose once the American War ended. As the sense of emergency abated, banal problems re-emerged: trafficking of ration cards, theft from government warehouses and cooperatives, and so on. The black-market economy thrived as the formal sector suffered.

Such problems were not new, but their scale reached new levels after January 1973. Worker absenteeism in both factories and on collective farms, rare during the war, became rampant, hampering production and thus economic growth. War fatigue, or the "obvious relief from the stresses of conflict and the wartime need to work tirelessly to safeguard the country's defences," as one observer put it at the time, was officially cited as the primary cause of this upsurge in "disgraceful behavior."[4] The tendency of individuals to act increasingly self-servingly paralleled the let-down in their revolutionary discipline. All of this not only went against Marxist–Leninist ideals, but also threatened the social unity and order needed in case the war resumed. If Hanoi hoped to eventually bring about Southern liberation and national reunification, it would have to find a way to balance popular expectations of peace with its own sense of self-restraint and what remained to be done before "real" peace could come.

A parallel headache for the authorities was the fact that Northern soldiers in the South also experienced a loss of enthusiasm for sacrificing after learning of the Paris agreement. Now that the bombing of the North had ceased, and their families were safe, many PAVN troops lost their personal motivation to serve in the armed forces. Their superiors reminded them that the struggle for national reunification was not over; still, the rank-and-file could not help feeling an emotional letdown after the ceasefire, a loss of the revolutionary zeal that had previously animated and inspired them. These troops were "deluded by illusions of peace," an official Vietnamese history comments.[5] PAVN soldiers in the South maintained their discipline and continued to follow orders, forging ahead with the consolidation of liberated areas, addressing problems as they encountered them, promoting the well-being of civilians as best they could to win more hearts and minds. But it came as a great disappointment to them that they could not return home to their families right after the Paris agreement; they had to stay put and wait around to see if peace would hold.

As Hanoi developed a better sense of the effects of the agreement on its forces, it instructed military commanders to impress upon their troops that the war was not over, that Washington might renew the bombing of the North any day, and that Saigon would likely not observe the cease-fire and might even be plotting to resume major attacks on communist positions across the South once conditions permitted. The purpose of this was to convince troops that their nation still needed their strength and courage; that their mission, their patriotic duty, remained unfulfilled. New PAVN recruits deploying to the South after the last US troops had pulled out in March 1973 were still told they were going to fight foreign enemies. Owing to the authorities' continued total control of information, these troops had no way to dispute or even question those fabricated claims.

INTERNATIONAL REACTION

It was not just at home that interest in completion of Vietnamese liberation waned after signing of the Paris agreement; foreign friends and allies felt the same. Third World governments and progressive organizations in the West had enthusiastically lent their moral, political, and sometimes material support during the American War. They had done this because they opposed what they saw as Western neo-imperialism, and supported the right of oppressed peoples to independence. American military intervention, the media coverage it received, and Hanoi's own efforts to expose its criminality had turned Vietnam into a *cause célèbre*. Indeed, in time it became fashionable in various political circles to support, in one way or another, the Asian David combatting the American Goliath.

Most supporters and donors totally lost interest in Hanoi's reunification struggle following news of its imminent de-Americanization. Le Duan's regime had been right about that: with the end of US military involvement, the situation in Vietnam lost much of its relevance, meaning, and appeal internationally, even though the fate of Vietnam as one country remained undecided. Almost overnight, the Vietnamese conflict was displaced by new objects of leftist, counter-cultural, or anti-American concern. Foreign "friends," it was now clear, had cared more about opposing the US presence in Vietnam than about helping Hanoi and the Viet Cong bring about their country's reunification. The withdrawal of American forces from Vietnam made banal Hanoi's reunification struggle internationally. The Vietnamese still faced important challenges, but they were no more daunting or singular than those confronting other Third World nations. As Vietnam lost its notoriety as a Cold War crucible, the Middle East, Chile, and Portuguese Africa took center stage in the international political arena and imagination.

The winding down of the Cold War itself – symbolized by Sino-American rapprochement, Soviet-American détente, and, now, the end of the American War in Vietnam – was another factor that robbed the situation in Indochina of its international prominence. By 1973 the Cold War had ceased largely to be a possible source of nuclear confrontation between the superpowers, thanks to Nixon's diplomatic engagement of main rivals. Admittedly, the Yom Kippur (or Ramadan) War later that same year, in October, precipitated a standoff between Moscow and Washington, but only briefly and inconsequentially. As an iconic symbol of the dangerous Cold War era, the Vietnam War had to be put to rest to give détente and rapprochement a better chance.

Even Moscow and Beijing cut their assistance to the DRVN after January 1973, effectively suspending shipments of tanks, heavy artillery, and shells. They did this in the spirit of détente: in the interest of developing full-scale relations with the United States, as well as to incentivize Hanoi to embrace peace with Washington just as they, the Soviets and the Chinese, were doing. Besides, the allies thought, respect for peace would boost both the DRVN's and the PRG's prestige globally. They slashed their aid, too, for good measure, to deny Hanoi the ability to resume armed struggle and compromise détente and the imminent end of the Cold War. Le Duan deeply resented these actions by the communist giants. Artillery shells were in very short supply among communist forces, and thus desperately needed. But he accepted the cuts with quiet resignation – he had no choice.

Hoping to make his allies reconsider their decision, Le Duan traveled to Beijing and then to Moscow to discuss Hanoi's unfinished business in the South. Vietnam's struggle for national reunification, he told each leadership, was not over; it had merely entered a new phase. His regime still needed their unqualified support, materially at least. Despite Le Duan's insistence, both governments refused to provide military aid beyond current, diminished levels. Each also categorically refused to condone resumption of hostilities by Hanoi, even if it found itself pressed by circumstances; it should focus instead, they both said, on building up and strengthening the capabilities of its forces and rehabilitating the Northern economy. To the latter end, Moscow agreed to an economic and technical aid agreement with the DRVN, wrote off part of the North Vietnamese debt, and extended direct economic assistance to the PRG.

Beijing's rebuke and insistence that Vietnamese reunification could wait several years particularly frustrated Le Duan. For a country that was itself still territorially divided, into Taiwan and the mainland, China's stance was mindboggling. Le Duan and other DRVN leaders concluded, not incorrectly in retrospect, that Beijing preferred the Balkanization of Indochina, and the continued existence of two Vietnams, specifically because it feared that the political vacuum resulting from American disengagement from the region might be filled by the Soviet Union.

PEACE UNRAVELS

If Le Duan's regime was initially committed to peace, at least in the short term, the same could not be said of Saigon. Despite acceding to Nixon's demand to sign the Paris agreement, Thieu had no intention of respecting its provisions; although, admittedly, no signatory to the agreement especially liked nor fully complied with them. Hanoi, to illustrate, secretly infiltrated new troops into the South, hesitated to provide full accounting of POWs it held, and showed bad faith in talks addressing the South's political future. But it was Saigon that manifested the least interest in upholding the settlement, and did the most, overtly, to derail it from the onset. Thieu followed a "four no's" policy: no giving up territory; no coalition government; no negotiations; and no tolerance for communism or neutralism. In doing this, he may have had a number of motives. He may have felt that, if he could let everyone know that the promised peace was a pipedream, the threat he perceived from it would vanish. Or, since he felt certain Hanoi and the Viet Cong had no intention of respecting the agreement, he might provoke them into violating it, in which case Washington might halt the withdrawal of its forces and keep fighting for the preservation of his government, and of a non-communist South. Once the last American troops were gone, Thieu may have reasoned, they would be unlikely ever to return, despite Nixon's eager personal reassurances to the contrary. Thieu had two months after the ceasefire came into effect – the period Washington required to withdraw its forces – to prove that the ceasefire was unworkable and force Nixon to honor his reassurances. Whatever his actual calculations on these matters, Thieu had nothing to lose by criticizing and undercutting the agreement as he did not believe in the kind of peace it promised.

With little or no incentive to respect the ceasefire, but many reasons to sabotage it, Thieu ordered his armed forces in parts of the South to keep fighting: specifically, they should do what they must, irrespective of the terms of the peace agreement, to take back territories lost in the Battle of the Flags. Within less than a month after the ceasefire came into effect, entire regions were engulfed in heavy fighting. By early March, monitors from the ICCS, the organ created by the Paris agreement to supervise its implementation, were reporting that the ceasefire was not working. Caught largely off guard by Saigon's aggressiveness, and unable to put up a stiff resistance due to their battered condition and Hanoi's directives to stand down after the ceasefire, communist forces lost scores of troops and chunks of territory, including most areas just recently liberated. In only a few weeks, large swaths of land passed from communist to RVN control. In spite of Saigon's transgressions of the agreement, Hanoi maintained its composure and stuck to its post-agreement strategy. But it was becoming increasingly clear that that strategy was not suited to the circumstances.

In an effort to save the crumbling Paris agreement, the United States took the lead in organizing a weeklong international conference to discuss its implementation. The conference, mandated by the agreement itself to encourage compliance with its terms, convened in late February 1973. In attendance were the four signatories to the agreement, plus representatives from the Soviet Union, China, France, and Britain, as well as the UN and the ICCS. The "final act" of the conference committed all parties to "solemnly acknowledge, express their approval for, and support" the agreement. That was about all that that meeting achieved. In the absence of trust – an indispensable ingredient of peace – between the signatories to the Paris agreement, peace in Vietnam never had an honest chance.

Later in March, the United States withdrew what remained of its combat forces from the South, as Hanoi released the last American POWs. Undeterred, Saigon kept fighting, and refused even to discuss the elections mandated by the agreement to establish a new government below the 17th parallel. Having recovered US prisoners, Nixon made no effort to restrain Thieu. The United States also refused to dismantle its military bases, as it was supposed to do according to the language in the agreement, handing them over to Saigon instead. Equally infuriating for Hanoi, no sooner had the last US troops withdrawn than Washington ignored the reparations it had promised in the peace treaty. Kissinger sent an aide to Paris to discuss the matter with North Vietnamese representatives, but Hanoi found American conditions unacceptable. Concluding that abiding by the substance of the agreement was futile, during a 27 March meeting the Politburo decided to resume large-scale infiltration of men and supplies into the South, and ordered its forces in both halves of the country to prepare for the renewal of major combat operations.

RESOLUTION 21

In July 1973, the American Congress voted to prohibit further US combat activities in Indochina. The same month, the VWP Central Committee met to discuss challenges and opportunities below the 17th parallel. In light of Saigon's flagrant violations of the ceasefire, the Committee determined that it was pointless, and even counterproductive, to think the Paris agreement would work, to keep hoping for peaceful resolution of differences with Thieu; the struggle for the South could triumph only through violence. Despite the US Congress' recent decision to bar further US combat operations in the region, the Committee worried that Nixon, who had proven impervious to congressional and public pressure in the past, might redeploy combat troops or, more likely, renew the bombing of the North. But Hanoi could not afford to wait any longer. The challenge confronting the Central Committee was coming up with a plan that would stop the advances of Saigon's armed forces, without sounding alarm bells in Washington and incensing Moscow and Beijing.

After assessing the possibilities of the situation, the Central Committee passed Resolution 21, calling for resumption of armed struggle to preserve existing positions in the South and reclaim those recently lost to the enemy: that is, to "resolutely counterattack." That seemed reasonable enough, the Committee thought, and should meet the pressing objectives just mentioned. Large-scale military operations to "roll back" Saigon's control beyond the areas specified in Resolution 21 were discouraged: they might serve as a pretext for US re-intervention, with all the negative ramifications that that entailed. Until Hanoi could be certain that the Americans were never coming back, it had to exercise restraint. Implementing the plan for limited action would test Washington, gauge its reaction to escalating hostilities in the South, and give Party leaders a clearer sense of what to do next.

Resolution 21 authorized communist forces in the South to counter Saigon's aggression, by official account to "strike back" at its acts of war, but not to pursue military victory just yet. Those forces were to defend their positions, while preserving and growing themselves for the bigger, decisive fight later. The resolution also stressed continued political work among the masses, and diplomatic struggle internationally. In its tone and substance, Resolution 21 was reminiscent of Resolution 15 of 1959. Much had changed since then, but Hanoi's fear and uncertainty surrounding American intentions were just as palpable now as they had been back then, for many of the same reasons. Resolution 21 further directed that the armed forces in the North undergo new training, chiefly to prepare for urban warfare, hitherto a bane for communist forces but likely to be necessary in the near future.

Within days after the adoption of Resolution 21, ICCS monitors noted that Hanoi, undeterred by not "one scintilla by the Paris Agreement," had resumed large-scale infiltration of PAVN troops and supplies into South Vietnam. Within weeks, the South was engulfed in war. As had been the case with Resolution 15, communist forces in the South took liberties with carrying out Resolution 21. The resolution's "cautious formulation," as David Elliott put it, was "enough to give the green light to commanders in the South to take more aggressive measures as they saw fit."[6] Soon, PAVN and especially LAF units, were doing much more than defending their positions; they were making military incursions deep into areas under enemy jurisdiction, initiating violence for not just self-defense but also offensive purposes, in contravention of the substance of Resolution 21.

The drastic escalation of hostilities during the second half of 1973 made Hanoi leaders tense with worry. They feared the reaction of remaining friends, and the prospect of American re-entry into the war. The Politburo reminded commanders in the South to proceed cautiously and tactically, to avoid attention-grabbing offensive operations, and to concentrate military activities in areas as far removed from Saigon as possible – in the Central Highlands, for example. Beyond rhetoric, there was little else it could do. Once more, Southerners were leading Northerners, it seemed, usurping Hanoi's authority below the 17th parallel, pointing the armed struggle in their own direction. In November 1973, in a nod to Southern belligerence, Le Duan confessed his regime had been mistaken to trust in the Paris agreement.

GAINING CONFIDENCE

That same month, the US Congress adopted the War Powers Act over Nixon's veto. The new law limited presidential authority to deploy US military forces overseas without prior assent from Congress. Upon hearing it, Hanoi cheered. It saw the act as a clear legal sanction against the resumption of US combat operations in Indochina that would make it nearly impossible for Nixon to reintroduce forces in Vietnam whatever transpired in the South. Around that same time, the Watergate scandal, which broke in 1972, started grabbing newspaper and television headlines, threatening Nixon's political future. By the end of 1973, the scandal was consuming Nixon, sapping his resolve to resume US combat operations in Vietnam. He became increasingly detached from the war, leaving its management and supervision to advisers, including Kissinger, who were less emotionally and personally invested in the preservation of American honor in Southeast Asia. The scandal, and the resulting congressional inquiry into it, made it difficult, the Politburo concluded, for Nixon to perform his duties as President, and impossible for him to resume combat operations in Vietnam. His political fate, it seemed, was sealed. Gradually, Le Duan's regime began to disregard Nixon in its strategic calculations.

By 1974, the military situation in the South had improved for Hanoi. Its forces were recovering from setbacks suffered the previous year, and recapturing the territories they had lost as a result. That, in conjunction with cuts in US aid to Saigon's armed forces, slowly tilted the balance of forces in their favor. A new confidence began animating communist forces, buoyed by stepped up deliveries of men and material from the North, and renewed military assistance from Moscow resulting from a Soviet-DRVN agreement on military aid signed a few weeks earlier. As part of their aid package, the Soviets dispatched more than 400 military specialists to North Vietnam, plus a fresh batch of surface-to-air missiles. Moscow's continuing dispute with Beijing, and desperation to win over Hanoi, largely accounted for its newfound largess.

And then developments involving China raised alarm bells in Hanoi. In January, with no prior warning or explanation, Chinese forces clashed with an ARVN garrison in a contested region of the Paracel Islands, in the South China Sea, the East Sea to the Vietnamese. Saigon begged for American assistance, but Washington turned it down and even sought to restrain Thieu's response because it did not wish to compromise its budding reconciliation with Beijing. Though these islands had for years been under Saigon's effective control, Hanoi recognized them as sovereign Vietnamese territory, like the rest of the South. China's attack and eventual occupation of the islands – ongoing to this day – thus constituted a violation of the DRVN's own territorial integrity, and an insult to its leaders. Equally offensive and troubling for Hanoi was Beijing's increasingly close relations with the Khmer Rouge in Cambodia, an ostensibly communist faction at odds with Hanoi for some time by then, and which had in fact recently murdered several North Vietnamese cadres operating on Cambodian soil. In sum, China's Indochina policy deeply alienated DRVN leaders, and made them nervous about the future of Sino–DRVN relations. It was partly to militate against rising Sino–Vietnamese tensions that Hanoi moved toward closer and more formal alignment with the Soviet Union. That only aggravated the row with China, and perpetuated the vicious circle of recrimination and counter-recrimination that wrecked socialist unity and solidarity generally and the Sino-Vietnamese alliance specifically.

Encouraged by the changing fortunes of its forces and pressed by crumbling relations with Beijing, in March 1974 Hanoi ordered its forces to prepare for another general offensive and uprising. Through the spring, PAVN soldiers and what remained of the Southern guerrilla movement mounted raids against ARVN positions, especially in the Central Highlands, to test the waters and their own capabilities. They were surprisingly successful. Thanks to Northern reinforcements, by the summer most PAVN combat units in the South were operating at full or near-full strength, and with a renewed sense of optimism and purpose. In July, Le Duan predicted that a "big and decisive victory" could be secured within three years. Then, on 9 August, Nixon resigned as President of the United States. Hanoi reckoned that his successor, Gerald Ford (in office 1974–7), would not reengage the United States militarily in Vietnam. This was too risky an initiative for an incoming president who had not been elected, possessed little foreign policy experience, and lacked political capital. Besides, Congress and the American people would never support it. The effects of an economic recession resulting from an oil embargo by Arab states in the wake of the Yom Kippur War made a new American military venture in Vietnam even more unlikely. The feeling in Hanoi, expressed by one official there, was that at this point the United States would not return to Vietnam "even if you offer them candy."

In fall 1974, from 30 September to 8 October, the Politburo met to review these new and improved circumstances, and plan an appropriate response. Le Duan and other leaders, now overcautious in view of their past overconfidence, estimated that, if circumstances remained favorable, they might be able to complete the liberation of the South in one final "showdown" by the end of 1976. The balance of forces was finally in their favor. Thieu's growing tribulations, and declining approval ratings, in the South buoyed their optimism. Drastic cuts in economic aid from the United States, plus the decline in economic activity following the departure of American troops, had caused the South Vietnamese economy to contract dramatically in 1973–4. That, in turn, fueled popular disenchantment with Thieu, as did the rampant corruption in his government and armed forces, and a spike in the price of oil and other basic commodities. Growing numbers in the Catholic clergy, traditionally staunchly supportive of the regime, turned against Thieu, and denounced him for failing to stem the tide of graft and improve the lives of Southerners. Beyond all that, war fatigue and weariness made apathy rampant among the Southern populace.

ANOTHER GENERAL OFFENSIVE

In light of the recent successes of its own forces and Thieu's plunging stock, as well as the disappearance of Nixon from its own strategic calculations, the Politburo decided to deliver a *coup de grâce*, by proceeding with the general offensive proposed back in March. Militarily and politically, conditions were as good as ever for such a move. Even the weather was ideal. The launch of the general offensive would coincide with the onset of the dry season, when downpours were less frequent and combat much easier. This time, Le Duan thought, boldness would surely pay off.

The objectives of the new campaign were nothing less that total annihilation of enemy forces and conquest of all major cities, including Saigon. This time, however, the assaults on cities would be in sequence – not simultaneous, as in the Tet Offensive – and the attack on each urban center would occur only after its periphery had been "pacified." Hanoi was not going for shock and awe, as in earlier campaigns; it intended instead to seize and, most crucially, maintain effective control of targets, one after the other. This was another go-for-broke effort, but in such inviting circumstances that success seemed guaranteed. Interestingly, not all Northern military commanders were as confident of success as Le Duan. Some of them believed their forces were still unready for such an ambitious plan. Local guerrilla units were too weak and disorganized to be relied on, and Saigon's forces were actually much stronger than Le Duan seemed to think. The Secretary and the Politburo took those reservations under consideration, but ultimately chose to ignore them.

The plan developed by Le Duan and his advisers called for extensive use of mechanized units, including tanks, which meant that road conditions had to be optimal. A more delicate task was to make available to forces on the ground the hardware and other supplies they needed when they needed them. Reductions in foreign arms deliveries meant that certain items were in short supply, including ammunition for large guns such as cannons, mortars, and heavy machine-guns. To remedy that problem, Hanoi created a new organization, the General Technical Department (GTD), to coordinate the collection, repair, and distribution of weapons of all types, from hand grenades to armored vehicles, and also to manufacture explosive devices and replacement parts for tanks and other vehicles, as well as guns. Among the GTD's most important functions were inventorying, refurbishing, and distributing military and other hardware captured from the enemy for use by communist forces. In preparation for the general offensive, the GTD repaired and refitted thousands of field radios, telephones, and generators, previously seized from ARVN forces, which markedly enhanced the communications capabilities of both PAVN and LAF units.

To accelerate the infiltration of men and supplies into the South, Hanoi also invested heavily in the restoration and improvement of the Ho Chi Minh Trail, badly pummeled by American bombs in 1972. Engineering units also completed a gas pipeline, running along the border inside of Laos and Cambodia down to Bu Gia Map, some ninety miles northeast of Saigon. More than a thousand miles long, and fitted with concealed fueling stations every ten miles or so, the pipeline facilitated the movement of vehicles, and thus of people and supplies, into the South. Considering how vulnerable it was to air attack, its existence was a measure of Hanoi's confidence that the Americans would not return.

All that preparation paid off. In November–December 1974, as the campaign got under way, communist forces scored a series of rapid and relatively painless victories. On 13 December, they launched an attack on Phuoc Long Province, located north of the South Vietnamese capital and near the Cambodia border. That effort was specifically intended to test American intentions, to see whether Washington would intervene in support of its allies in a critical battle, and secure key transportation routes for a final assault on Saigon. The results were unequivocal: communist forces crushed their opposition, achieving the "liberation" of the entire province on 6 January 1975. Despite repeated pleas for assistance by Thieu, during and after the battle, Washington did nothing. The Ford administration approached Congress about the possibility of another aid package in the form of material and financial support for its embattled ally, but to no avail. In late December 1974, a North Vietnamese intelligence estimate concluded that, on the basis of the American reaction, for now the United States would undertake no dangerous action against the DRVN, or its forces in the South, to save the Saigon regime. Washington was out for the count; Thieu and his armed forces were on their own.

The liberation of Phuoc Long eased the resupply of communist units in the deep South. In its aftermath, the Politburo endorsed a proposal by Le Duan to complete the liberation of the South not by the end of 1976, as originally projected, but before the onset of the next monsoon season, in April 1975. This was ambitious, to be sure, but the situation seemed so favorable, Le Duan argued, that it was best to take advantage of this "opportune moment" and launch "the strongest and swiftest attack possible" to achieve "a complete, total victory." The triumph that had eluded Hanoi so often in the past seemed finally to be at hand.

FINAL PUSH

In March 1975, communist forces assaulted the strategically important city of Ban Me Thuot, in the southern Central Highlands. Military planners estimated that enemy forces there were weaker and more vulnerable than elsewhere. Their assessment proved correct: Ban Me Thuot fell within days, along with the rest of the southern third of the Central Highlands. As communist forces prepared to move against their next targets, including Pleiku, home to a large ARVN airbase, Thieu decided to evacuate the rest of his forces, including elite Airborne and Marine divisions, from the region and redeploy them along the coast, as well as to areas just north of Saigon. He ordered the redeployment to consolidate the defense of what was left of his country and, specifically, to form protective rings around areas of greatest strategic importance, such as the capital, until his forces had regained enough strength and momentum to retake Ban Me Thuot, and other lost positions in the Central Highlands.

It was at this point that everything began to unravel for Thieu. Southerners, including members of his own armed forces, interpreted his decision to redeploy elite divisions, and surrender the Central Highlands, as presaging the surrender of the rest of the South to communist armies. That effectively doomed his regime. ARVN soldiers, a good portion of them conscripts with little interest in sacrificing their lives in a hopeless cause, lost what little will they had left to fight, and either surrendered, defected – or simply shed their weapons and uniforms and went home. They were encouraged in this by Southern mothers recruited by communist forces to broadcast radio messages imploring ARVN soldiers to stop fighting. Those who remained loyal to the regime did their best to follow orders, but the precipitate withdrawal from the Central Highlands compelled them to abandon vast quantities of weapons and equipment, thus diminishing what fighting capabilities they had left. In fact, what began as an orderly retreat from the Central Highlands quickly turned chaotic, with South Vietnamese soldiers literally running for their lives to escape fast-approaching communist forces.

The hardware left behind by the fleeing ARVN forces included everything from tanks, armored personnel carriers, trucks, and heavy artillery to rifles, pistols, and hand grenades. The quality and quantity of enemy materiel captured by communist forces was such that it offset both their battlefield losses and shortfalls in weapons deliveries from abroad. To illustrate, in an earlier series of raids over one five-day period, North Vietnamese forces overran an ARVN district headquarters and its peripheral outposts and police stations, seizing more than a thousand weapons of various types, including four 105mm howitzers plus their 7,000 shells. Days later, they used those same artillery pieces and shells to win a series of battles in which they seized 10,000 more shells, instantly compensating for what they had just expended and actually shoring up their inventory. Communist forces were thus able to take advantage of their own momentum, as well as the panic on the other side, to crush the remnants of Thieu's army and give it no chance to regroup. They added to the confusion and mayhem by occasionally going into battle wearing ARVN uniforms, slightly altered so that only communist forces could differentiate between friendly and enemy combatants. In a twist of irony, the generous assistance lavished upon the South Vietnamese regime by the United States just before and after the signing of the Paris agreement helped seal the doom of the regime it was intended to save.

The disarray in the South Vietnamese armed forces demoralized Southern civilians who still supported Thieu or otherwise dreaded a communist takeover because of their ties to his regime. Approximately seventy percent of Southerners were either employed by, or had close relatives working or fighting for, the Saigon regime in 1975. Many of them feared they would be killed or tortured if communist forces triumphed. After all, those forces had set a terrifying precedent in Hue back in 1968, during the Tet Offensive, when they murdered some 2,800 civilians whose only crime was to have ties to Thieu's regime. Who was to say such a bloodbath would not happen again? According to a rumor floating around in the South in 1974–5, able-bodied Southern women who had lent no support to the communist war effort would have their fingernails plucked out one-by-one if ever captured by Northern soldiers. They would be thus punished, the rumor went, for being "bourgeois reactionaries," more concerned about their physical appearance than the liberation of the country. In the midst of this final campaign, local guerrillas in one district displayed in a market square the bodies of militiamen loyal to Saigon they had just killed in combat. Their intention was to convince enemy troops to lay down their weapons and civilians to rally against

Saigon to avoid dying unnecessarily, as these men had. In reality, such acts reminded Southerners of the abominations communist forces were capable of committing, and alarmed them about what would come next.

By the end of March, broad swaths of the South were under communist control, and the Saigon regime was disintegrating. Events unfolded so rapidly that Hanoi leaders had a difficult time adjusting to the resulting circumstances. As communist forces completed their sweep of the Central Highlands, the Politburo met twice to discuss the situation in the South. On 25 March, Le Duan and the Politburo gave their final sanction for taking Saigon and complete the liberation of the South within a month. Le Duan entrusted none other than Le Duc Tho to go to the South, to personally supervise what he hoped would be the final campaign of the Vietnam War.

The next main targets of communist forces were the coastal cities of Hue and Da Nang, the South's second largest city. Their fall was spectacularly fast, and cut off the northern half of the South from Saigon. In less than a month, communist armies had scored their biggest victories of the entire war. The 1974–5 general offensive was indeed the "strongest and swiftest attack" launched by Hanoi in the South, as Le Duan had hoped it would be. It was also its most successful, by far. The offensive exceeded even the expectations of Le Duan, who always demanded more than his forces could deliver. At long last, brashness was paying off. By early April, close to half of the entire South Vietnamese population, some eight out of nineteen million people, lived in areas controlled by communist forces. By then, too, the South Vietnamese army had become a shadow of its former self, having lost nearly half of its troops and weapons in just a few weeks. These developments completely "transformed the situation," as an official communist history states.[7] Hanoi could now launch the final attack on Saigon.

SAIGON FALLS

Immediately after the fall of Hue and Da Nang, the last major battle of the war, the so-called *Ho Chi Minh* campaign, began. Supervised by Tho, but directed by PAVN General Van Tien Dung (1917–2002), it aimed to seize Saigon and force the capitulation of the regime there. Spearheaded by tanks – and involving bombing raids on enemy positions using captured aircraft, including at least one flown by a defector from the South Vietnamese air force – the battle unfolded at lightning speed. As communist forces approached Saigon, they learned that the Cambodian capital of

Phnom Penh had fallen to the Khmer Rouge. On 21 April, Thieu resigned as RVN President, and fled the country. Thousands, mostly members of the elite, followed him, boarding the last flights out of Tan Son Nhut Air Base/Airport outside Saigon, which closed to civilian airlines on the 26th (US military planes continued to fly people out of there for the next three days). Tran Van Huong (1903–82), a former prime minister, replaced Thieu, only to step down himself less than a week later, at which point ARVN General Duong Van Minh, who had briefly replaced Diem in the aftermath of the November 1963 coup, assumed the presidency. Highly respected in both halves of Vietnam for his patriotism, moderate views, and distinguished career, Minh offered to negotiate an end to the war. Hanoi turned him down.

Over the next few days, remaining American personnel prepared to evacuate the South Vietnamese capital and other sites. Concerned about setting off a general panic in the South, the Ford administration refused to organize an early evacuation of its diplomatic corps. Staff at the US embassy in Saigon nonetheless went on a frenzy, destroying any sensitive materials and equipment they would not be able to take with them once the order to leave came. At the secret behest of Washington, relayed through the Soviets, Hanoi presumably ordered its forces to slow down their advances on the capital, to allow the Americans to complete their evacuation, thus avoiding a complicated and hazardous situation for both governments.

Meanwhile, panic set in among the population, particularly those with close ties to the regime and the United States who had missed the last flights out of Tan Son Nhut. Fearing harsh retribution from communist troops in the event of their victory, thousands of government officials, ranking members of the armed and security forces, religious leaders, doctors, teachers, artists, and other members of the intelligentsia prepared to flee the country with their families. Lower-level personnel from both the government and armed forces, and Catholics, also sought to leave. These prospective refugees sold what they could, exchanged as much of their Vietnamese currency for gold and US dollars, gathered the most valuable possessions they could carry with them, and attempted to contact any American they knew, hoping they could facilitate their departure from Vietnam.

Just before noon on 30 April, a tank bearing the NLF flag, but actually belonging to the PAVN, crashed through the main gate of Independence Palace in Saigon, the South Vietnamese President's official residence. Newly-invested President Minh offered the surrender of his government,

FIGURE 6.1 PAVN tanks in the streets of Saigon hours after the surrender of the South Vietnamese regime, 30 April 1975. Courtesy of National Archives Center 3, Hanoi.

only to be told that he had nothing left to surrender. Flanked by communist troops, he went on national radio and called on all remaining ARVN forces to lay down their weapons (possibly, Minh's message was pre-recorded by communist cadres). Some unit leaders disregarded the order, but they and their men were soon neutralized. As this unfolded, frantic Southerners attempted to reach the safety of US warships, anchored off the South Vietnamese coast, by any means they could find, including army helicopters. More than 120,000 Southerners left their country on or just before that day, accompanied by some one thousand remaining US personnel. In a scene emblematic of the national humiliation suffered by the United States in Vietnam, and forever embedded in the national psyche, some of the last Americans, along with their closest Vietnamese collaborators and their families, ungracefully departed by helicopter from the rooftop of not the US embassy, as is usually assumed, but a hotel in the South Vietnamese capital.[8]

Interestingly, the first communist troops to enter Saigon were in no mood to celebrate just yet. In fact, many were terrified. They feared and actually braced for a repeat of the Tet Offensive, when they had seized Southern cities with relative ease only to be expelled and decimated in subsequent enemy counterattacks. Veterans of the 1968 campaign were especially unnerved by that possibility. To their great relief, there was no response by the enemy. This time, only peace ensued.

Thus ended the Vietnam War. Hanoi won; Saigon and the United States lost. Le Duan finally had his moment of triumph – and vindication for the millions of lives lost or shattered because of the war he had so desperately wanted, and been instrumental in precipitating more than a decade before.

Notes

1   Lien-Hang T. Nguyen, "Between the Storms: An International History of the Second Indochina War, 1968–1973," Ph.D. dissertation, Yale University, 149–50.

2   Quoted in David W.P. Elliott, *The Vietnamese War: Revolution and Social Change in the Mekong Delta, 1930–1975* [concise ed.] (Armonk, N.Y.: M.E. Sharpe, 2007), 409.

3   William S. Turley, *The Second Indochina War: A Concise Political and Military History* [2nd ed.] (Lanham: Rowman & Littlefield, 2009), 206.

4   "Communist Carrot" in *Far Eastern Economic Review*, 11 June 1973, 18–9.

5   Military Institute of Vietnam (trans. by Merle L. Pribbenow), *Victory in Vietnam: The Official History of the People's Army of Vietnam, 1954–1975* (Lawrence: University of Kansas Press, 2002), 335.

6   Elliott, *Vietnamese War*, 17.

7   Military Institute of Vietnam, *Victory in Vietnam*, 394.

8   Most Vietnamese who fled around the time of the fall of Saigon were taken to Guam, and from there relocated to the United States. Interestingly, some 1,500 of them had a change of heart after arriving in the small Western Pacific island and sailed themselves back to Vietnam.

Epilogue: Legacies

REUNIFICATION & RE-EDUCATION

Two weeks before the fall of Saigon, on 17 April 1975, the Khmer Rouge seized power in Cambodia. In December, the People's Democratic Republic of Laos was proclaimed, under pro-Vietnamese communist leader Prince Souphanouvong (1909–95), completing the "liberation" of Indochina. Following a largely ceremonial consultative conference between PRG and DRVN representatives, Northern and Southern Vietnam were formally merged into the Socialist Republic of Vietnam (SRVN) on 2 July 1976. According to its constitution, recycled from the DRVN's 1959 constitution, the SRVN was a "people's democratic state," a euphemism for communist state, led by "the working class," a euphemism for the Communist Party. National reunification under communist governance, the main thrust of the anti-American resistance, fulfilled a fundamental objective of the Vietnamese Revolution launched forty-five years earlier. In 1980, the SRVN adopted its first original constitution, confirming its proud membership of the communist bloc, and marking the apogee of Le Duan's power.

Formal reunification of the country was much easier to achieve than national reconciliation and unity. Southerners proved extremely wary of the new regime responsible for their well-being, and reluctant to buy into the socio-political and economic order it supported. The relationship between Hanoi and those who had previously served in Thieu's government and armed forces, and otherwise supported his regime or worked with Americans, was especially fraught with distrust. As noted in the previous chapter, during the latter stages of the conflict Vietnamese communist authorities had estimated that more than seventy percent of Southern households had direct or indirect ties to the Saigon regime. Years of war, pitting Northerners against Southerners, and the dire consequences of Vietnamization in particular, created a lot of bad blood between the two. Mutual acrimony and mistrust persisted long after hostilities ended.

Mistreatment of former enemies by the victors was particularly detrimental to national reconciliation. Contrary to rampant rumors at the time, there was no bloodbath, no mass killings of Saigon loyalists following the fall of that regime. Summary executions of RVN government, armed forces, police, and other personnel occurred, but were rare and unsanctioned by communist authorities. There was, however, a mass incarceration of as many as one million Southern "reactionaries," only a handful of whom were ever formally charged or tried in court, in more than eighty "re-education camps" spread across the country. By official account, Hanoi aimed only to "reform" those individuals to facilitate their rehabilitation into "new society," a practice introduced in the North in 1961 to deal with unrepentant former members of the French colonial government and armed forces. The reality proved much starker. Re-education camp detainees received a mandatory "education" centered on history and communism. They also had to write their life history, and confess as well as atone for their crimes, which included supporting the Saigon regime, colluding with the Americans, opposing the Vietnamese Revolution, and committing national treason. Detention lasted anywhere between a few weeks to several years, depending on one's former activities, response to "treatment," and family connections. Many spent over a decade in the camps. As part of their "therapy" detainees performed hard, often dangerous "productive labor," such as clearing mine fields. They endured sleep and food deprivation as well as frequent beatings. Malnutrition, maltreatment, and diseases claimed the lives of more than 150,000 detainees. These Vietnamese "gulags," a reference to the unforgiving Siberian prison camps where Stalin sent his real and imagined enemies, were veritable death camps.

Healing the physical and emotional wounds of war among Northern civilians was no easy task either. Many Northerners blamed Southerners for causing and prolonging hostilities by colluding with the United States. That, in conjunction with the fact that Vietnam had no real tradition of national unity and been partitioned for so long, further encumbered national reconciliation. Long after the war ended, Northerners continued to look down upon, and speak disparagingly about, their Southern compatriots. Tensions between Northerners and Southerners remain palpable to this day. Northerners also felt a great deal of anger and resentment toward their own government and leaders, though few dared express such sentiments openly. Close to a million of them served in the South between 1965 and 1975. Most fought multiple years; countless never returned. As previously mentioned, during the war DRVN authorities rarely notified families of the confirmed death of a relative to sustain morale and support for the war at home. Shortly after the war ended, however, the government had to inform those families. It was only at that point, when they received official word that their loved ones, like those of so many other households, would never be coming home, that Northerners began to get a real sense of the war's actual cost. Realization that the government had deceived them – and known for years of the death or disappearance of their fathers, sons, mothers, and daughters but chosen to withhold that information – compounded the exasperation and ire of bereaved families.

So it was that the exhilaration resulting from the war's end in both halves of Vietnam quickly gave way to gloom, sadness, and despair. Vietnam holds nationwide celebrations and commemorations on 30 April each year. For those Vietnamese who lived through the war, they are merely stark reminders of the war's appalling cost, of the sacrifices their families had to make, and of the personal losses they suffered.

ECONOMIC WOES & EXODUS

A few months after reunification, in December 1976, Vietnamese communists held their Fourth Congress, the first in sixteen years. Le Duan was reappointed Secretary and, to mark the dawn of a new era in Vietnamese politics, the VWP was rebranded the Communist Party of Vietnam (CPV). More meaningfully, the Congress adopted a new five-year plan (1977–81) stressing expedited reconstruction along socialist lines, integration of the South into the socio-political and economic order already in place in the North, and completion of nationwide communization. That meant the immediate expropriation of all private property and the collectivization of farming in the South. Many of the objectives outlined in the plan, it turned out, were too ambitious. "Drunk with pride in their success in war," political scientist Tuong Vu has written, "Vietnamese leaders set highly unrealistic goals and employed draconian tactics in their quest to develop socialism 'in five, ten years.'"[1] Predictably, those goals were never met, but resort to draconian measures by the authorities lasted well into the 1980s.

Hanoi faced a mountain of challenges at the time which, insofar as the authorities were concerned, warranted the application of harsh measures. The war was over, but much remained to be done before people could enjoy the fruits of peace. Merely repairing and rebuilding what had been damaged and destroyed during the conflict seemed impossible. Millions of bomb craters, as well as land mines and other unexploded ordnance, littered the countryside. The latter killed and badly injured people, especially peasants and children, long after the fighting stopped. And they still do. At the last count, undetonated explosives had claimed more than 40,000 lives, nearly the number of Americans killed in the war itself.

Improving economic and living conditions and returning to normalcy was made all the more difficult by the exodus of many of the best and brightest Southern minds just before and after collapse of the Saigon regime. And while the SRVN would receive generous assistance from other communist states and the Soviet Union in particular after 1975, including an army of technical and other experts, the rest of the world, seemingly so concerned about the fate of the Vietnamese during the period of US military intervention, largely forgot about them after it ended. Always quick to denounce the destruction of factories, schools, and hospitals by American bombs during the war, the international community was largely absent when time came to rebuild them afterwards. Japan and a handful of West European states were the only capitalist countries to maintain trade relations with Vietnam after its reunification under communist governance. But even that was not enough to ward off the threat of famine in certain Northern cities, including the capital, in spring 1978.

Agent Orange, a carcinogenic herbicide, as well as other chemical substances used by the United States during the war to deprive enemy forces of crops and jungle cover, poisoned the soil in parts of Southern Vietnam, making food production in affected areas either impossible or dangerous for farmers themselves or consumers of their produce. As many as four million Vietnamese were directly exposed to and suffered illnesses because of Agent Orange. Thousands of children were born with horrific birth defects because of their parents' exposure to the toxic chemical. Labor hours lost because of those effects, and the cost of providing and caring for victims, compounded the economic woes of the SRVN and its people.

Another important challenge was demobilizing, rehabilitating, and finding jobs for more than two million soldiers whose services were no longer needed once hostilities ceased. Many were young men who had spent their entire adult life fighting for one side or the other, and possessed little or no professional or technical skills. Some were looking forward to putting the past behind them and to start living normal lives; others simply could not. Emotional, psychological, and physical wounds hampered their reintegration into civilian life. Post-traumatic stress disorder (PTSD) is not a diagnosable condition in Vietnam. However, if close to a quarter million Americans who served in the war were subsequently diagnosed with the mental illness, a significantly larger number of Vietnamese combat veterans presumably suffered the same affliction. Some of the more than 1.5 million Vietnamese combatants maimed in the war eked out a living begging on street corners, or performing whatever menial work they could find after it ended. Several wounded veterans from the North turned to smuggling goods from China and other countries. Owing to their military service, SRVN authorities usually turned a blind eye to their activities.

While most veterans, especially former members of the South Vietnamese armed forces, were left to fend for themselves after hostilities ended, Hanoi rewarded demobilized PAVN soldiers who had distinguished themselves by their valor and leadership with lucrative managerial positions in Southern and some Northern state-owned enterprises (SOEs). These "heroes of the Revolution" made terrible bosses. Lacking pertinent knowledge, training, and interpersonal workplace skills, they proved incompetent and highly ineffectual. Their presence at the helm of sometimes very large and important firms slowed the pace of Vietnam's recovery and contributed to its serious economic problems, including underperforming SOEs, lasting well into the 1990s. The attendant domination by Northerners of the Southern civil service, including the security and education sectors, added to the frustrations of people there. The presence of and privileges enjoyed by these "carpetbaggers" was especially irksome for those who had fought for and otherwise supported the NLF during the war. A majority felt Hanoi simply turned its back on them once peace returned and it no longer needed their services. The government's decision to rename Saigon "Ho Chi Minh City" did nothing to alleviate Southern feelings of vexation and destitution.

The economic situation remained so bad through the 1980s that the government had to institute a system of rationing, as had existed in wartime. But whereas the North Vietnamese population had rarely if ever experienced shortages of necessary commodities during the war, they became regular occurrences throughout that decade. Other features of life in the "subsidy era," as the Vietnamese call it, included queuing for hours each week to obtain basic allotments of vital items; spartan living conditions in a politically repressive atmosphere; and extreme dependence of foreign aid, especially from the Soviet Union. The total embargo on trade imposed by Washington after the fall of Saigon and strictly enforced afterwards exacerbated those misfortunes. In the absence of healthy manufacturing and agricultural sectors, cheap labor became one of Vietnam's chief exports. Workers went to other communist countries, which also trained them and other specialists. Remittances from overseas relatives, including in time from those resettled in the West, became a lifeline for countless families.

The dire economic situation, plus discrimination and maltreatment by the authorities, prompted more Vietnamese to flee their country. As many as one million people left during the late 1970s and 1980s, some by land but most by rickety fishing vessels, prompting the international community to label them "boat people." While leaving was a challenge in itself, it was nothing compared to the dangers awaiting them on the high seas, including dehydration, starvation, and drowning, as well as rape, capture, or death at the hands of pirates who abounded in coastal waters. Under the best of circumstances, asylum-seekers would be picked up after a few hours or days by passing cargo ships. Most, however, were at sea for anywhere between a few weeks to a few months before reaching safe havens in Thailand, Malaysia, Singapore, Indonesia, the Philippines, or Hong Kong. Unsurprisingly, many did not survive the voyage. The UN estimates that 300,000 boat people perished at sea. Some survivors resorted to or witnessed cannibalism, pushing them to suicide later.

SOVIET-VIETNAMESE TREATY & CAMBODIAN INVASION

In November 1978, Vietnam entered into the Treaty of Friendship and Cooperation with the Soviet Union. By the terms of that agreement, valid for twenty-five years, Hanoi pledged to support Moscow in "strengthening relations of unbreakable friendship, solidarity and fraternal mutual aid" between their two countries, and "steadfastly develop political relations and deepen all-round cooperation." Most critically, it consented to "vigorously counteract all the designs and machinations of imperialism and reactionary forces." The treaty represented more than a cementing of ties between the two governments; it formalized Hanoi's alignment with Moscow and repudiation of China. As previously discussed, throughout the American War Vietnamese communist leaders had successfully struck a careful balance between their two major allies in order to retain the constancy of each. The Soviet-Vietnamese Treaty of 1978 ended that policy. It led to an influx of Soviet advisers and technical experts into Vietnam and the forging of a "special" bond with Moscow. That, in turn, made Vietnam an enemy of China.

The decision to align with Moscow was largely Le Duan's. The Chinese may have provided the revolutionary prescriptions that informed his views and policies during the American War, but their behavior during its late stages and after had irrevocably offended him. As previously noted, Le Duan and his regime always expected more from the Chinese than from other allies, including the Soviets. In their eyes, Beijing's inability to meet their expectations and its failure to unfailingly support their strategic positions had caused the rift between their two governments. China's decision to sustain rapprochement with Washington, even to collude with it against the Soviet Union in places like Angola and Mozambique after 1975, was the last straw. Tired of Beijing's shenanigans, convinced that the differences with it were irreconcilable, and calculating that Hanoi had less to lose than to gain from closer alignment with Moscow, Le Duan entered into a strategic partnership with Soviet leaders. Not everyone in Hanoi was happy about that decision, however. A pro-Chinese faction inside the CPV lamented Le Duan's decision, but there was nothing it could do to reverse it.

Deng Xiaoping (1904–97), who emerged as paramount leader of China following the death of Mao in 1976 and a nasty succession crisis, set out to make Hanoi pay for its perfidy. In late 1978, following the old adage that "the enemy of my enemy is my friend," Beijing dramatically increased political and material support to the rabidly anti-Vietnamese Khmer Rouge in Cambodia. Led by a bloodthirsty maniac named Pol Pot (1925–98), the Khmer Rouge were once close allies of Hanoi, but the two had a falling out shortly before their respective triumphs, largely the result of Vietnamese aspirations to control the Cambodian Revolution and Pol Pot's refusal to abide them. By the first half of the 1970s, the Khmer Rouge began to assert its independence and take its distance from Hanoi. Its leaders claimed that the Vietnamese were greedy imperialists – not unlike the French – who had "stolen" the Mekong River Delta from the Cambodian people two centuries earlier and now sought to dominate the rest of the Indochinese Peninsula. Pol Pot had collaborated with Vietnamese communists, and tolerated their meddling in Cambodian affairs, because he needed their support to liberate his country. Once certain of victory, he expelled and even killed some of Hanoi's cadres and troops in Cambodia, as noted earlier.

Shortly after defeating Lon Nol's pro-American regime and seizing the capital, Phnom Penh, in 1975, Pol Pot and the Khmer Rouge went on a genocidal rampage. Seeking to institute "true" communism, they turned the Cambodian clock back to the "Year Zero." They ordered the evacuation to the countryside of everyone living in cities, resettling many in rural work camps doubling as correction and re-education facilities. Meanwhile, specialized outfits rounded up, tortured, and summarily executed those deemed irredeemably corrupted by foreign influences and thus "irreformable": namely, members of the educated urban elite, including anyone known to wear glasses or speak foreign languages. This "sui-genocide" (genocide of one's own people tantamount to collective suicide), in conjunction with the cleansing of Vietnamese and other ethnic minorities, as well as other Khmer Rouge abuses and the economic dislocation they produced, claimed no less than two million lives, approximating a quarter of the country's population. As they were hard at work reinventing Cambodian society, the Khmer Rouge mounted violent raids against Vietnamese villages, murdering innocent civilians on that side of the border. By Pol Pot's own admission, the Khmer Rouge had begun the process of reclaiming Cambodian territory and punishing those illegally occupying it.

By December 1978, Hanoi had had enough. On Christmas Day, it launched a full-scale invasion of Cambodia, rebranded Democratic Kampuchea by the Khmer Rouge. In less than two weeks, PAVN troops drove Pol Pot's regime out of power, ending its reign of terror and compelling its remaining forces to seek refuge in remote areas along the Thai border and inside Thailand itself. At once, the Vietnamese established a new, friendly government in Phnom Penh under Heng Samrin (b. 1934). To the consternation of the international community, their forces did not withdraw. According to Hanoi, PAVN troops stayed to protect the new government and the Cambodian people from the still-threatening Khmer Rouge. A more cynical view is that the occupation gave purpose to thousands of soldiers who would otherwise be demobilized and out of work. Whatever Hanoi's actual reasoning, the Khmer Rouge did not desist. From bases in Western Cambodia and Thailand, it waged guerrilla warfare against the occupiers and the regime they had created. In a strange twist of events, vengeful American leaders conspired with their unforgiving Chinese counterparts through a compliant Thai government to "bleed" Vietnamese forces in Cambodia by proffering military and other assistance to the Khmer Rouge. The plan worked: some 55,000 Vietnamese troops lost their lives serving in Cambodia between 1978 and 1989, nearly equating the number of Americans killed in the Vietnam War. Cambodia proved to be Vietnam's own, well, Vietnam.

Washington also sought to isolate Hanoi diplomatically by denouncing its occupation of a sovereign state, much as Hanoi had done to Washington during their war. The anti-occupation campaign was immensely successful: Vietnam, the former darling of progressive governments and movements everywhere, became an international pariah. No country but the Soviet Union, itself subject to international condemnation for its war in Afghanistan and dismal human rights record at home, cooperated closely with it. International seclusion compounded the economic and other hardships endured by the people.

THIRD INDOCHINA WAR

Vietnam's occupation of Cambodia, coming as it did in the immediate aftermath of the signing of the Soviet-Vietnamese Friendship Treaty, distressed Chinese leaders. From their vantage point, the Vietnamese were complicit in a Soviet plan to get back at China for the Sino-Soviet dispute. With Laos already under a pro-Hanoi regime, strategic encirclement of China, a longtime fear of Beijing leaders, was nearly complete. The Chinese balanced against the Soviet threat by inching closer to the United States. In early January 1979, Deng Xiaoping paid a visit to President Jimmy Carter (in office 1977–81), telling him that the Vietnamese had been acting like "naughty children" and would have to be "spanked." Implicitly, the Chinese leader sought Carter's sanction to attack Vietnam. He received it, and braced his forces for war.

The Third Indochina War, known in Vietnam at the time as the War Against Chinese Expansionism, and today as the Sino-Vietnamese Border War, began on 17 February 1979. On that day, approximately 200,000 Chinese troops swept into Vietnam's northernmost provinces from staging areas along their common border. The PAVN, which had been preparing for that contingency, resisted fiercely, its capabilities enhanced by valuable intelligence and an influx of modern weaponry airlifted from the Soviet Union. In a show of solidarity with the Vietnamese, intended to bolster their confidence while alarming the Chinese to the possibility of a two-front war, Moscow deployed a portion of its armed forces along the border with China and ordered its troops already inside Mongolia to do the same. Facing stiff Vietnamese resistance and the prospect of a wider war involving the Soviet Union, Beijing started pulling its forces back during the first week of March. Retreating Chinese units followed a "scorched-earth" policy, destroying everything in their path including power plants and other utilities, roads, bridges, even people's homes as well as crops, food stocks, and livestock. There was nothing noble about it, but China's purportedly punitive war achieved its main goal.

The war ended on 16 March, less than four weeks after it began, with both sides claiming victory. Brief as it was, the conflict exacted a heavy toll on both armies. Chinese forces suffered in excess of 20,000 casualties, including at least 7,000 killed. Vietnamese casualties were two to three times those of the Chinese, and included hundreds of civilians caught in the crossfire. Those numbers aside, by most accounts the war was a victory for Hanoi. Not for the first time, it had won a military contest despite suffering disproportionately higher casualties.

The 1979 Sino-Vietnamese confrontation had lasting repercussions. It fueled anti-Chinese sentiment in Vietnam, already running high, prompting active discrimination and repression against Vietnamese of Chinese descent. Questioning the loyalty to the SRVN of all ethnic Chinese, Vietnamese authorities confiscated their property, including stores and other businesses, and forcibly relocated thousands. Following the flight to China of Hoang Van Hoan (1905–91), a prominent member of the pro-Chinese faction inside the CPV, Le Duan ordered the purge from Party and government ranks of some 20,000 known and presumed supporters of that faction, including most ethnic Chinese. The brouhaha exacerbated economic and other afflictions confronting the nation. Through the first half of the 1980s, Vietnam ranked among the poorest countries on earth. It had also become a closed, isolated "hermit state," not unlike North Korea today. Those circumstances made it almost entirely dependent on the Soviet Union to function. In fact, at no point in their history were the two countries closer. Unfortunately for Hanoi, the relationship was a lopsided one. So much for enjoying the fruits of sovereignty! Out of fear, despair, and hopelessness, tens of thousands more people, most of them of Chinese ancestry, took to the sea, marking the high tide of the maritime exodus from Vietnam. This is what Le Duan and the CPV had to show for decades spent fighting foreign aggressors, and millions of lives sacrificed.

DOI MOI

In July 1986, Le Duan died. His tenure as Party head had lasted more than twenty-five years, one of the longest in the history of the communist camp. The impact of his passing on Vietnam was enormous. In a way, it changed everything. Most consequentially, it allowed for the rise of a new crop of leaders more attuned to the needs and wants of the masses and the expectations of the international community.

A few months after Le Duan's death, in December, the Party held its Sixth Congress. The assembled delegates endorsed a radical plan calling for expansion and acceleration of economic and social reforms only recently introduced, including revival of the private sector, and promulgation of new, even more liberal measures. "Aside from its own intrinsic importance," Le Duan's succession in Vietnam, like Stalin's in the Soviet Union, "acted as a catalyst for pressures and tendencies" that already existed but "previously had limited opportunity for expression and realization."[2] The primary aim of the plan was to boost economic productivity and overall standards of living while reducing dependency on the Soviet Union. While the death of Le Duan expedited adoption of the plan, circumstances also warranted it. By now, inflation was running at 500 percent. This had much to do with Le Duan's own lack of economic guile and, specifically, a failed reform of the currency, wages, and commodity prices he had championed. The Congress confirmed Nguyen Van Linh as new CPV Secretary responsible for leading that ambitious but necessary effort – extricating Vietnam from its rut. Linh was a former protégé of Le Duan who had succeeded him as head of COSVN following his, Le Duan's, recall to the North. The two men had a falling out in the late 1970s over economic planning in Southern Vietnam that resulted in Linh's expulsion from the Politburo. He was rehabilitated just before Le Duan's death. At seventy-one years of age, Linh was young compared to other top Party bosses, and more affable and reform-minded. In a turn of events telling of the new mood in Hanoi, Le Duc Tho, Le Duan's closest, most loyal and devoted supporter, was dropped from the Politburo and forced to retire, as were a number of other Le Duan loyalists and/or members of the "old guard," including Truong Chinh and Pham Van Dong. Possibly, it was Tho himself who insisted that a new breed of leaders be sworn in at the Congress, and the old guard be forced to retire.

These and other changes announced during the Party Congress became part of a policy called *Doi moi*, Vietnamese for "renovation," intended to reform and thus save Vietnamese communism. Its promulgation marked the end of the Le Duan-Stalinist era in Vietnam. Often characterized as a Vietnamese *Perestroika* – the reformist policy of political and economic restructuring introduced by CPSU General Secretary Mikhail Gorbachev (in office 1985–91) in the Soviet Union a few months earlier, *Doi moi* in its early stages was more akin to Khrushchev's post-Stalinist "thaw." That is, its most salient feature was the de-Le Duanization of Vietnamese political, economic, and social life. Nguyen Van Linh's legacy in Vietnam was much like Khrushchev's in the Soviet Union. Both men sought to improve the lives of their people through partial liberalization of the domestic economy and better relations with Western countries. Each also supported the return of democratic centralism in decision-making. As Khrushchev tolerated publication of writings by dissidents like Alexander Solzhenitsyn, Linh permitted Nguyen Huy Thiep (b. 1950) and others to disseminate their controversial literary works relating hardships endured by Vietnamese soldiers and civilians during and after the Vietnam War, until then strictly forbidden.

Economic and social reform in Vietnam got into high gear in 1991, the result of two circumstances. The first was the CPV's Seventh Congress in June, which confirmed a new Secretary named Do Muoi (b. 1917) and a younger, more pragmatic Politburo keenly interested in modernization, science, and technology. The second was dissolution of the Soviet Union in December, which followed the demise of communist regimes across East Europe two years earlier. The collapse of communism in Europe compromised not only the legitimacy of the communist system in Vietnam itself, but also the foreign trade, aid, and expertise upon which the government and its people had become so reliant. The fall of the Soviet Union impressed upon Hanoi's new leaders the imperative need to grow the domestic economy and make the country more self-sufficient. Meaningful, far-reaching reform ensued. Over the next few years, collectivized farming ended: farmers received their own plots of land, and agricultural prices were freed. Also, foreign investment projects across a variety of sectors, including manufacturing, hospitality, real estate, and communication, received government sanction. In fits and starts, these changes transformed Vietnam from a centrally planned economy to a socialist-oriented market economy. Through all this, access to Western-style education in Vietnam remained extremely limited.

In a quest for new friends and markets, Hanoi also reconfigured its international relations. As economic development and regime survival became strategic priorities, ideology ceased being a factor in foreign policymaking, and thus an obstacle to improved relations with most other countries.

Hanoi took the biggest step toward ending its diplomatic isolation by pulling the last of its forces from Cambodia in September 1989. Two years later, in October 1991, it entered into the Comprehensive Cambodian Peace Agreement with nineteen other states, including the United States and China. Resolution of the Cambodian conflict paved the way for normalization of diplomatic and trade relations with dozens of countries.

Among the countries courted by Hanoi was China. Tensions with Beijing had sunk to a new low in March 1988, when Chinese forces attacked and occupied a Vietnamese position in the Spratly Islands of the South China Sea that resulted in the death of sixty-four young Vietnamese sailors. Pressed by circumstances, Vietnamese leaders tried to put the past behind them, signaling their desire to renew ties with Beijing following the Tiananmen Square incident of June 1989. As the rest of the world condemned the brutal crackdown on the pro-democracy movement that left somewhere between 240 and 3,000 student protesters dead, Hanoi publicly endorsed it, stating it had been an unpleasant necessity.

Chinese leaders immediately picked up on Hanoi's signal, and the two governments got to talking again. Already, healthy, largely illicit trading had resumed between Northern Vietnamese and Southern Chinese. Goods smuggled from China actually sustained Vietnamese border communities. If these victims of the Third Indochina War could put the past behind them in the interest of their own welfare, surely their leaders could do the same. In fall 1990, a high-level SRVN delegation secretly traveled to China for consultative talks. A few weeks later, Deputy Premier General Vo Nguyen Giap, the hero of the war against France, attended the Asian Games in Beijing, becoming the first ranking Vietnamese to make an official visit to China in over a decade. Hanoi and Beijing normalized relations in November 1991, a month after the Cambodian settlement, and just as the Soviet Union breathed its last.

Before long, China became Vietnam's most valuable trade partner, so much so that Vietnamese authorities grew alarmed their people were starting to depend on their northern neighbor as they had on the Soviet Union during the 1980s – that is, too heavily. Hanoi's main challenge now became weaning its people off near-absolute dependency on China, and limit or otherwise balance against its growing influence in Vietnam.

US-VIETNAM NORMALIZATION

As previously explained, during the war against the United States, Vietnamese communist leaders had proved to be expert at balancing between the Soviet Union and China. Skillful exploitation of their dispute, and manipulation of each, had enabled Hanoi to secure maximal assistance from both while retaining total autonomy in policymaking. As Hanoi leaders had been shrewd and resourceful in wartime, they remained so in peacetime. To lessen and offset its growing dependence on China in the early 1990s, Hanoi turned to none other than the United States.

Washington and Hanoi had come close to normalizing their diplomatic relations during the presidency of Jimmy Carter, but the process collapsed in 1978 over the question of US reconstruction aid to Vietnam, pledged by the Nixon administration in the 1973 Paris agreement but never delivered. Relations between the two governments remained frigid for the next thirteen years. It was not until late 1991 that they took the first concrete step toward finally putting the past behind them. Following lengthy negotiations between American and Vietnamese officials, the Joint POW–MIA Accounting Command, whose mandate is to recover the remains of unaccounted-for US personnel from Vietnam and other war theaters, set up a permanent task force in Hanoi. The task force became the first American government agency on Vietnamese soil since the end of the war. Three years later, in a gesture intended to augur the dawn of a new era in US–Vietnam relations, and promote enhanced cooperation between the two governments, US Pacific Command Chief Admiral Charles Larson (1936–2014) visited Vietnam. By the time of his visit, Americans were already starting to appreciate the merits of that country as a tourist destination. Following in the footsteps of late 1980s pioneers, increasing numbers of students, doctoral candidates for the most part, also came to learn Vietnamese and conduct archival or field research. A community of expatriates, looking for business opportunities and seeking to be the first to capitalize on Vietnam's transition to a market economy, was budding.

In February 1994, US President Bill Clinton (in office 1993–2001) announced the lifting of the trade embargo imposed on Vietnam years before. A little over a year later, in June 1995, the SRVN and the United States normalized diplomatic relations with a view to expanding bilateral trade. The following month, Vietnam became the seventh member of the Association of Southeast Asian Nations (ASEAN) promoting inter-regional trade, investment, peace, and stability, but originally created (in 1967) to fight the spread of communism in the region. In November 1995, Robert McNamara (1916–2009), Secretary of Defense in the Kennedy and Johnson administrations, visited Hanoi and met with some of his former enemies, including Nguyen Thi Binh and Vo Nguyen Giap. He took the opportunity to reiterate an admission made in a recent memoir that the United States had been "terribly wrong" to increase its commitment to South Vietnam in the aftermath of Diem's overthrow in late 1963. Many Vietnamese appreciated McNamara's candor and recognition that the United States had committed a grave error by becoming militarily involved in their country. In conjunction with the other important developments that year, the visit by the former Defense Secretary did a lot to heal the wounds of the American War in Vietnam. History, it seemed, had come full circle for the Vietnamese.

REINTEGRATION INTO INTERNATIONAL SOCIETY

Hanoi's reconciliation with its former enemy and, eventually, the rest of the international community paid big dividends for Vietnam, particularly in the areas of trade, development, and tourism. Foreign direct investment increased dramatically during the second half of the 1990s, as tourism boomed. In 2000, the SRVN government legalized private business, established a stock market, and unilaterally lowered trade barriers. The next year, it entered into a comprehensive bilateral trade agreement (BTA) with the United States. The net effect of these policies was to not just increase the living standards of Vietnamese, especially those in cities, but also lessen the country's dependence on China, which had been one of Hanoi's purposes all along. Since then, Vietnam has enjoyed the world's second-fastest growth rate per person: nearly six percent a year, behind only China. Its efforts to reintegrate the global community reached a new milestone in 2007, when it gained membership of the World Trade Organization (WTO).

The pace of development and economic growth has only accelerated since. Today, Vietnam boasts middle-income status, even though seven out of ten of its people still live in the countryside. The population is young – the median age was thirty-one in 2016 – and extremely well educated. For the first time, Vietnamese academics and the institutions of higher learning that employ them are making concerted efforts to expose their students to more rigorous "international standards" in fields including the Humanities and Social Sciences. Rote learning is giving way to an education stressing the merits of critical and analytical thinking, albeit very slowly, and with some pushback from the authorities. Vietnam's membership of the Trans-Pacific Partnership (TPP), a trade pact that was to include the United States and other Asia-Pacific countries, promised to boost development and economic growth even further. Unfortunately, the administration of President Donald Trump (in office 2017–present) killed the TPP. At present, key exports include highly coveted commodities, such as oil, rice, marine products, coffee, rubber, garments, and shoes.

Neither a transformed and thriving economy nor the warming of relations with the United States and other Western countries has translated into political change, however. Vietnam remains for the time being a one-party state firmly under the thumb of the CPV. Its people enjoy no political freedoms whatsoever. Open criticism of leaders and calls for reform of the political system are not tolerated and, in fact, severely punished. The Party clearly has no intent to lose its stranglehold over power. Despite its marked impact elsewhere, social media has had no meaningful bearing on the political life of the state, and bloggers and other political and social activists are frequently jailed for allegedly threatening national security. As long as the Party keeps their bellies full and *Honda* motorbikes running, the majority of Vietnamese seems ready to tolerate it. Signs of revolution against one-party rule remain absent, for now.

Today, relations with China are tense, again, owing to resurgence of the dispute over rock formations in the South China Sea. As that dispute demonstrates, Hanoi leaders remain obsessive about their country's sovereignty and territorial integrity; and it still takes nothing, literally, to make them butt heads with their neighbors to the North. On the flip side, the row with Beijing has resulted in closer ties with the United States. During a visit to Hanoi in May 2016, US President Barack Obama (in office 2009–17) announced the lifting of a longstanding arms embargo on Vietnam. That, plus Obama's friendly demeanor, impressed upon the Vietnamese the merits of friendship with his country. Taking to social media, some deplored the fact that that could not have happened sooner. Yet others went as far as commenting that Vietnam would have been better off if the United States had won the Vietnam War. Ho Chi Minh and Le Duan must have been turning in their graves, though no one reported movement from Ho's body exposed at the mausoleum bearing his name in Hanoi.

* * *

How should we remember the American military intervention in Vietnam? How should we account for Hanoi's final victory despite repeated military failures, staggering human and material losses, and the near-destruction of the country? What should we make of the war's impact on the Vietnamese? What did it all mean?

FIGURE E.1 PAVN soldiers on their way to Saigon, 1975. Courtesy of National Archives Center 3, Hanoi.

For all the bloodshed, destruction, havoc, and pain it caused, the American War merely delayed the inevitable. Because of it, the collapse of the regime in Saigon and the victory of communist armies happened in 1975 instead of a decade earlier. As long as Le Duan remained at the helm, Hanoi was never going to give up on its goal of reunifying the country under the authority of the Communist Party. No price was too great and no sacrifice too small for his regime to achieve that outcome and meet other core objectives. Vietnamese communist forces and North Vietnamese civilians manifested astounding resolve and resilience throughout the war. However, they persevered and triumphed because their leaders gave them no choice. Much as historians of the war and others have praised the merits of the brave men and women who sacrificed so much to secure their country's complete independence and reunification – and they certainly were brave – those men and women ultimately acted on orders from authorities in Hanoi. Nationalism and patriotism admittedly were powerful motive forces for them, but they did not dictate the course of the anti-American war effort; Hanoi, and Le Duan in particular, did that.

The outcome of the Vietnam War was determined not by the patriotism of its people or the sum of its battles, but by the grit, resourcefulness, and remarkable organizational skills of Le Duan and other Vietnamese communist leaders. These men carefully and meticulously managed their struggle and the human and material resources necessary to sustain it for as long as necessary. They were obsessed with discipline and internal cohesion, and adhered to their basic positions with unshakable tenacity. Despite daunting logistical challenges and tragic miscalculations of their own doing, they maintained close and effective control of their party and armed forces, including the LAF, at most times. Admittedly, those forces lost many if not most battles, but successes on the political and diplomatic fronts offset all setbacks on the military front, including dismal failures in the Tet and Spring Offensives, allowing Hanoi to win the war. Tuong Vu is absolutely correct when he writes that "[w]ithout Hanoi's determination to unify the country under its rule, Vietnam would likely remain divided today, as China and Korea still are."[3]

Still other, related factors contributed to the final triumph of Vietnamese communist leaders. The most notable were their fixation with defending the sovereignty and territorial integrity of Vietnam; their dogged commitment to reunification and independence on their terms; their centralization of political authority and supremacy in policymaking; their intolerance and swift repression of dissent; their adeptness to bounce back after devastating defeats; their unmatched capacity to control information as well as to rouse, rally, and mobilize civilians on both sides of the 17th parallel; their superior skills at manipulating and harnessing world opinion through ingenuous use of diplomatic tools, contacts, and channels; their ability to take advantage of the Sino-Soviet dispute to exact maximal material support from both Moscow and Beijing; and, finally, their callous disregard for the death and suffering of their own compatriots. All things being equal, Hanoi's victory in the Vietnam War demonstrated that the formula for success in a struggle against a powerful enemy is not resolute armed struggle exclusively, but the careful calibration of military, political, and diplomatic activities under the direction of a single-minded, puritanical, and unwavering leadership.

In retrospect, the failure of both North Vietnamese and American decision-makers to correctly appraise the extent of the others' commitment to their strategic goals may well have been the greatest tragedy of the Vietnam War. Each leadership proved incapable of understanding the other's intentions, and the degree of its motivation to realize them. Just as Washington had no clear sense of who Le Duan was, of his steely resolve to win, or even that he called the shots in Hanoi, Le Duan and the VWP Politburo never grasped, or else refused to acknowledge, the depth of Johnson's desire to avoid a humiliating defeat in Vietnam, on the one hand, and of Nixon's dedication to peace with honor, to dignified exit from the war, on the other. There was a profound failure by both Hanoi and Washington during the Vietnam War to correctly assess the identities, personalities, and general proclivities of each other's decision-makers. And that was largely the reason the war lasted as long as it did, and proved so costly and devastating in the end.

By this rationale, the American failure in Vietnam stemmed in large part from Washington's inability, or refusal, to understand, not Vietnamese culture and history generally, as so many Western scholars have maintained, but the North's political culture and the identity, worldview, resoluteness, and ruthlessness of decision-makers there specifically. Conversely, Hanoi's triumph over the United States had to do less with historical determinism than manipulation of contemporary circumstances and shrewd, astute policymaking by Le Duan and his comrades.

The Vietnam War claimed the lives of approximately 1.3 million Vietnamese, according to conservative estimates. Of those, more than a third were North Vietnamese and Viet Cong soldiers; some 600,000 were civilians, the rest consisting of ARVN combat deaths. By official Vietnamese account, 981,000 PAVN and LAF troops died in the war. The bodies of more than 300,000 of them were never recovered. The number of their South Vietnamese counterparts unaccounted for remains unknown, but is presumably in the tens of thousands. Beyond its human cost, the war tore families apart, shattered individual lives and dreams, squandered human potential, and effectively wasted an entire generation of young men and women. In the end, Hanoi secured the total victory it had sought since Le Duan took over the reins of power from Ho Chi Minh in 1963–4.

Ho will forever remain an iconic figure, the most extraordinary Vietnamese political leader of the twentieth century. After all, he provided the vision that guided the Vietnamese Revolution and inspired his people throughout the American War. However, it was not Ho but the hardnosed Le Duan who realized that vision. The Vietnamese themselves had to pay a terrible price, but after more than a century their country was finally reunified under a single, fully sovereign government. Vietnam has come a long way since the "Great Spring Victory" of communist armies in 1975. Its future is bright, but it will take some time before the wounds of war heal completely. In this rendition, set against the backdrop of the Cold War, David did not come out unscathed from his contest with Goliath.

Notes

1   Tuong Vu, *Vietnam's Communist Revolution: The Power and Limits of Ideology* (New York: Cambridge University Press, 2017), 238.
2   Seweryn Bialer, *Stalin's Successors: Leadership, Stability and Change in the Soviet Union* (Cambridge: Cambridge University Press, 1980), 66; Carlyle A. Thayer, "National Leadership in Vietnam: Continuity and Change in the Party's Central Committee, 1960–1985," paper presented at *"Postwar Vietnam: Ideology and Action" Conference*, Brighton, England, September 1985, 17–9.
3   Tuong Vu, *Vietnam's Communist Revolution*, 291.

Annotated Bibliography

As indicated in the Introduction, a vast number of books have been written about the Vietnam War. Their quality fluctuates greatly. Featured below are some of the better titles, arranged by topic.

Vietnamese Communist Experience in the Vietnam War (1954–75)

Surprisingly, few works have focused on the subject of this study: that is, the Vietnamese communist experience in the war. Ang Cheng Guan has produced first-rate works recounting that experience, and communist decision-making in particular, including *The Vietnam War from the Other Side: The Vietnamese Communists' Perspective* (New York: Routledge, 2002); *Ending the Vietnam War: The Vietnamese Communists' Perspective* (New York: Routledge, 2004); and *Vietnamese Communists' Relations with China and the Second Indochina Conflict, 1956–1962* (Jefferson: McFarland & Company, 1997). Equally prolific in relating the communist perspective, and a pioneer in that realm, has been William Duiker, whose *The Communist Road to Power in Vietnam* [2nd ed.] (Boulder: Westview Press, 1996) is the richest history of Vietnamese communism. Duiker's biography of Ho Chi Minh, *Ho Chi Minh: A Life* (New York: Theia, 2000), offers fascinating insights on its most famous adherent, as does Sophie Quinn-Judge's *Ho Chi Minh: The Missing Years, 1919–1941* (Berkeley: University of California Press, 2003). Huynh Kim Khanh's *Vietnamese Communism, 1925–1945* (Ithaca: Cornell University Press, 1982) remains the best study of the origins of the communist movement in Vietnam.

Pierre Asselin's *Hanoi's Road to the Vietnam War, 1954–1965* (Berkeley: University of California Press, 2013) and Lien-Hang Nguyen's *Hanoi's War: An International History of the War for Peace in Vietnam* (Chapel Hill: University of North Carolina Press, 2012) complement each other nicely, and together constitute the most comprehensive assessment of Vietnam's American War based on Vietnamese archival sources. Tuong Vu's *Vietnam's Communist Revolution: The Power and Limits of Ideology* (New York: Cambridge University

Press, 2017) is an excellent recent study of the Vietnamese communist world-view. Ken Post's five-volume *Revolution, Socialism and Nationalism in Viet Nam* (Brookfield: Dartmouth Publishing Co., 1989–94) is a little more dated, but represents the most comprehensive study of the Vietnamese communist struggle for independence and national reunification written from a Marxist perspective. A more personal experience is related in Bui Tin, *From Enemy to Friend: A North Vietnamese Perspective on the War* (Annapolis: Naval Institute Press, 2002).

The history of North Vietnam's armed forces, the People's Army of Vietnam (PAVN), is addressed in Douglas Pike, *PAVN: People's Army of Vietnam* (New York: Da Capo Press, 1991) and Greg Lockhart, *Nation in Arms: The Origins of the People's Army of Vietnam* (Sydney: Allen & Unwin, 1989). An indispensable, official military history of the American War is Military Institute of Vietnam (translated by Merle Pribbenow), *Victory in Vietnam: The Official History of the People's Army of Vietnam, 1954–1975* (Lawrence: University of Kansas Press, 2002). Another insightful Vietnamese history of the conflict is Le Kinh Lich (ed.), *The 30-Year War, 1945–1975 – Volume II: 1954–1975* (Hanoi: The Gioi Publishers, 2002). A richly detailed and engaging history of the Ho Chi Minh Trail is provided in John Prados, *Blood Road: The Ho Chi Minh Trail and the Vietnam War* (New York: Wiley & Sons, 1999).

On Vietnamese communist diplomacy, the "diplomatic struggle," see Luu Van Loi, *Fifty Years of Vietnamese Diplomacy, 1945–1995 – Volume 1: 1945–1975* (Hanoi: The Gioi Publishers, 2000); Nguyen Dy Nien, *Ho Chi Minh Thought on Diplomacy* (Hanoi: The Gioi Publishers, 2004); and Ton That Thien, *The Foreign Politics of the Communist Party of Vietnam: A Study in Communist Tactics* (New York: Crane Russak, 1989). Luu Van Loi and Nguyen The Anh, *The Le Duc Tho-Kissinger Negotiations in Paris* (Hanoi: The Gioi Publishers, 1995) offers riveting and invaluable insights on Hanoi and the secret Paris talks.

The Viet Cong – that is, Southern Vietnamese communist – experience is considered in David Hunt, *Vietnam's Southern Revolution: From Peasant Insurrection to Total War* (Amherst: University of Massachusetts Press, 2008). Revolutionary strategies and tactics in the South are expertly related in David Elliott, *The Vietnamese War: Revolution and Social Change in the Mekong Delta, 1930–1975* [concise ed.] (Armonk: M.E. Sharpe, 2007); Jeffrey Race, *War Comes to Long An: Revolutionary Conflict in a Vietnamese Province* (Berkeley: University of California Press, 1972); George Tanham, *Communist Revolutionary Warfare: From the Vietminh to the Viet Cong* (Westport: Praeger, 2006); William Andres, *The Village War: Vietnamese Communist Revolutionary Activity in Dinh Truong Province, 1960–64* (Columbia: University of Missouri Press, 1973); Carlyle Thayer, *War by Other Means: National Liberation and Revolution in Viet-Nam, 1954–60* (Cambridge: Unwin Hyman Publishers, 1989); and Douglas Pike, *Viet Cong: The Organization and Techniques of the National Liberation Front of South Vietnam* (Cambridge: MIT Press, 1966). Robert Brigham considers Viet Cong foreign relations in *Guerrilla Diplomacy: The NLF's Foreign Relations and the Viet Nam War* (Ithaca: Cornell University Press, 1998). Truong Nhu Tang, *A Viet Cong Memoir* (New York: Vintage Books, 1985) and Nguyen Thi Dinh, *No Other Road to Take: Memoirs of Mrs. Nguyen Thi Dinh* (Ithaca: Cornell Southeast Asia Program Data Paper no. 102, 1976) are both absorbing first-hand accounts.

Other useful studies of the Vietnamese communist experience include Adam Fforbe and Susan Paine, *The Limits of National Liberation: Problems of Economic Management in the Democratic Republic of Vietnam* (London: Croom Helm, 1987); Melvin Gurtov, *Hanoi on War and Peace* (Santa Monica: Rand Corporation, 1967); Hoang Van Chi, *From Colonialism to Communism: A Case History of North Vietnam* (New York: Pall Mall Press, 1964); P. J. Honey, *Communism in North Vietnam: Its Role in the Sino-Soviet Dispute* (Westport: Greenwood Press, 1973); Ho Khang, *The Tet Mau Than 1968 Event in South Vietnam* (Hanoi: The Gioi Publishers, 2001); Hy Van Luong, *Revolution in the Village: Tradition and Transformation in North Vietnam, 1925–1988* (Honolulu: University of Hawaii Press, 1992); Benedict Kerkvliet, *The Power of Everyday Politics: How Vietnamese Peasants Transformed National Policy* (Ithaca: Cornell University Press, 2005); Edwin Moïse, *Land Reform in China and North Vietnam: Consolidating the Revolution at the Village Level* (Chapel Hill: University of North Carolina Press, 1983); Kim Ninh, *A World Transformed: The Politics of Culture in Revolutionary Vietnam, 1945–1965* (Ann Arbor: University of Michigan Press, 2002); Patricia Pelley, *Postcolonial Vietnam: New Histories of the National Past* (Durham: Duke University Press, 2002); W. R. Smyser, *The Independent Vietnamese: Vietnamese Communism between Russia and China, 1956–1969* (Athens: Ohio University Center for International Studies, Southeast Asia Series no. 55, 1980); and Jon Van Dyke, *North Vietnam's Strategy for Survival* (Palo Alto: Pacific Books, 1972), which addresses how the DRVN and its people coped with US bombings.

History of Vietnam (Origins–Present)

An outstanding, must-read general history of Vietnam is Christopher Goscha's *Vietnam: A New History* (New York: Basic Books, 2016). Early Vietnamese history is the focus of Keith Taylor, *The Birth of Vietnam* (Berkeley: University of California Press, 1983). Taylor recently produced the more comprehensive *A History of the Vietnamese* (New York: Cambridge University Press, 2013), which is quite detailed but not reader-friendly. D. R. SarDesai's *Vietnam: Past and Present* [4th ed.] (Boulder: Westview Press, 2009) is respectable. Ben Kiernan's *Viet Nam: A History from Earliest Times to the Present* (New York: Oxford University Press, 2017) is more meticulous and recent. Other interesting but more dated works are Joseph Buttinger, *Vietnam: A Political History* (Westport: Praeger, 1968); Neil Jamieson, *Understanding Vietnam* (Berkeley: University of California Press, 1993); and Nguyen Khac Vien, *Vietnam: A Long History* (Hanoi: Foreign Languages Publishing House, 1987), which presents the official, Vietnamese communist interpretation of Vietnam's own past. Alexander Woodside, *Vietnam and the Chinese Model: A Comparative Study of Nguyen and Ch'ing Civil Government in the First Half of the Nineteenth Century* (Cambridge: Harvard University Press, 1971), offers intriguing glimpses into Vietnam's last dynasty.

General History of the Vietnam/American War (1954–75)

The best, most readily accessible history of the Vietnam War, that expertly addresses both sides, is William Turley's *The Second Indochina War: A Concise Political and Military History* [2nd ed.] (Lanham: Rowman & Littlefield, 2009).

The most widely used text on the war is George Herring's *America's Longest War: The United States and Vietnam, 1950–1975* [5th ed.] (New York: McGraw-Hill, 2013). Other excellent and reader-friendly studies are Stanley Karnow, *Vietnam: A History* [2nd ed.] (New York: Penguin, 1997); Mark Atwood Lawrence, *The Vietnam War: A Concise International History* (New York: Oxford University Press, 2008); and John Prados, *Vietnam: The History of an Unwinnable War, 1945–1975* (Lawrence: University Press of Kansas, 2009).

Dated but classic works include Robert Buzzanco, *Masters of War: Military Dissent and Politics in the Vietnam Era* (New York: Cambridge University Press, 1996); Phillip Davidson, *Vietnam at War: The History 1946–1975* (Novato: Presidio Press, 1988); Frances Fitzgerald, *Fire in the Lake: The Vietnamese and the Americans in Vietnam* (New York: Random House, 1972); James Harrison, *The Endless War: Vietnam's Struggle for Independence* (New York: McGraw-Hill, 1983); George Kahin and John Lewis, *The United States in Vietnam* (New York: Dial, 1967); Gabriel Kolko, *Anatomy of a War: Vietnam, the United States, and the Modern Historical Experience* (New York: Pantheon Books, 1985), which presents a strong Marxist viewpoint; Guenter Lewy, *America in Vietnam* (New York: Oxford University Press, 1978); Timothy Lomperis, *The War Everyone Lost – and Won: America's Intervention in Viet Nam's Twin Struggles* (Baton Rouge: Louisiana State University Press, 1984); Michael Maclear, *The Ten Thousand Day War – Vietnam: 1945–1975* (New York: St. Martin's Press, 1981); Neil Sheehan, *A Bright Shining Lie: John Paul Vann and America in Vietnam* (New York: Random House, 1988); Ralph Smith's three-volume history entitled *An International History of the Vietnam War* (London: Macmillan Press, 1983–1991); Harry Summers, *On Strategy: The Vietnam War in Context* (Novato: Presidio Press, 1982); Thomas Thayer, *War Without Fronts: The American Experience in Vietnam* (Boulder: Westview Press, 1985); Jayne Werner and David Hunt (eds.), *The American War in Vietnam* (Ithaca: Cornell Southeast Asia Program, 1993); and Jayne Werner and Luu Doan Huynh (eds.), *The Vietnam War: Vietnamese and American Perspectives* (Armonk: M.E. Sharpe, 1993).

More recent and better-referenced general histories of the Vietnam War include David Anderson, *The Vietnam War* (New York: Palgrave Macmillan, 2005); Mark Philip Bradley, *Vietnam at War* (New York: Oxford University Press, 2009); Marc Philip Bradley and Marilyn Young (eds.), *Making Sense of the Vietnam Wars: Local, National, and Transnational Perspectives* (New York: Oxford University Press, 2008); Arthur Dommen, *The Indochinese Experience of the French and the Americans: Nationalism and Communism in Cambodia, Laos, and Vietnam* (Bloomington: Indiana University Press, 2001), an astoundingly detailed account of the war across the Indochinese Peninsula; William Duiker, *Sacred War: Nationalism and Revolution in a Divided Vietnam* (New York: McGraw-Hill, 1995), which does great justice to the communist side; Marc Jason Gilbert (ed.), *Why the North Won the Vietnam War* (New York: Palgrave Macmillan, 2002); Gary Hess, *Vietnam and the United States: Origins and Legacy of War* (Boston: Twayne Publishers, 1990); Michael Lind, *Vietnam – The Necessary War: A Reinterpretation of America's Most Disastrous Military Conflict* (New York: The Free Press, 1999); Sophie Quinn-Judge, *The Third Force in the*

Vietnam Wars: The Elusive Search for Peace, 1954–75 (Chicago: I. B. Tauris, 2017); Robert Schulzinger, *A Time for War: The United States and Vietnam, 1941–1975* (New York: Oxford University Press, 1997); Andrew Wiest, *The Vietnam War, 1956–1975* (Oxford: Osprey Publishing, 2002); and Marilyn Young, *The Vietnam Wars, 1945–1990* (New York: Harper Collins, 1991), which remains a seminal work after all this time. Robert McNamara, James Blight and Robert Brigham, *Argument without End: In Search of Answers to the Vietnam Tragedy* (New York: Public Affairs, 1999) is an interesting read.

Colonial Era (1858–1945)

The literature on the French colonial period is much richer in French than it is in English. One of the best histories is Pierre Brocheux and Daniel Hémery's work, translated from the French, *Indochina: An Ambiguous Colonization, 1858–1954* (Berkeley: University of California Press, 2010). Other important studies are Eric Jennings, *Vichy in the Tropics: Pétain's National Revolution in Madagascar, Guadeloupe, and Indochina, 1940–1944* (Stanford: Stanford University Press, 2001); Martin Murray, *The Development of Capitalism in Colonial Indochina (1870–1940)* (Berkeley: University of California Press, 1980); Ngo Vinh Long, *Before the Revolution: The Vietnamese Peasants under the French* (New York: Columbia University Press, 1991); and Milton Osborne, *The French Presence in Cochinchina and Cambodia: Rule and Response (1859–1905)* (Bangkok: White Lotus Press, 1997). One of the West's most enduring legacies in Vietnam, Catholicism, is the object of Charles Keith's *Catholic Vietnam: A Church from Empire to Nation* (Berkeley: University of California Press, 2012). A famous book relating the impact of colonialism on the Vietnamese peasantry is James Scott, *The Moral Economy of the Peasant: Rebellion and Subsistence in Southeast Asia* (New Haven: Yale University Press, 1976). The United States and colonial Indochina is the focus of Mark Philip Bradley's superb *Imagining Vietnam and America: The Making of Postcolonial Vietnam, 1919–1950* (Chapel Hill: University of North Carolina Press, 2000).

The Vietnamese response to the French, and the emergence of Vietnamese nationalism and anti-colonialism, has been addressed in a number of excellent studies. The most notable are William Duiker, *The Rise of Nationalism in Vietnam, 1900–1941* (Ithaca: Cornell University Press, 1976); Hue-Tam Ho Tai, *Radicalism and the Origins of the Vietnamese Revolution* (Cambridge: Harvard University Press, 1992); David Marr's terrific two-volume study comprising *Vietnamese Anticolonialism, 1885–1925* (Berkeley: University of California Press, 1971) and *Vietnamese Tradition on Trial, 1920–1945* (Berkeley: University of California Press, 1981); and Shawn McHale, *Print and Power: Confucianism, Communism, and Buddhism in the Making of Modern Vietnam, 1920–1945* (Honolulu: University of Hawaii Press, 2008). Truong Buu Lam's *Patterns of Vietnamese Response to Foreign Intervention: 1858–1900* (New Haven: Yale University Southeast Asia Studies, 1967) and his edited *Colonialism Experienced: Vietnamese Writings on Colonialism, 1900–1931* (Ann Arbor: University of Michigan Press, 2000) provide an assortment of Vietnamese primary sources in English translation. Peter Zinoman's award-winning *The Colonial Bastille: A History of Imprisonment in*

Vietnam, 1862–1940 (Berkeley: University of California Press, 2001) provides spellbinding insights on the role French prisons played in the radicalization of Vietnamese nationalists, and communists in particular.

World War II in Indochina, and the so-called August Revolution of 1945, are comprehensively explored in David Marr, *Vietnam 1945: The Quest for Power* (Berkeley: University of California Press, 1995) and Stein Tønnesson, *The Vietnamese Revolution of 1945: Roosevelt, Ho Chi Minh, and de Gaulle in a World at War* (Newbury Park: Sage, 1991). See also Geoffrey Gunn, *Rice Wars in Colonial Vietnam: The Great Famine and the Viet Minh Road to Power* (Lanham: Rowman & Littlefield, 2014). On America's wartime collaboration with the Vietminh see the first-person narrative by Archimedes Patti, *Why Vietnam?: Prelude to America's Albatross* (Berkeley: University of California Press, 1980) and Dixee Bartholomew-Feis, *The OSS and Ho Chi Minh: Unexpected Allies in the War against Japan* (Lawrence: University Press of Kansas, 2006).

Indochina War (1945–54)

Again, the literature in English is not as exhaustive as that in French when it comes to the Indochina or Franco-Vietminh War of 1946–54, but there are some very good studies available. The lead-up to the war is skillfully addressed by David Marr in *Vietnam: State, War, and Revolution (1945–1946)* (Berkeley: University of California Press, 2013) and Stein Tønnesson in *Vietnam 1946: How the War Began* (Berkeley: University of California Press, 2009).

Good studies of the war's various dimensions include Mark Atwood Lawrence and Fredrik Logevall (eds.), *The First Vietnam War: Colonial Conflict and Cold War Crisis* (Cambridge: Harvard University Press, 2007); Kathryn Edwards, *Contesting Indochina: French Remembrance between Decolonization and Cold War* (Berkeley: University of California Press, 2016); Bernard Fall, *Street Without Joy: Indochina at War, 1946–54* (Harrisburg: Stackpole, 1961); and Ellen Hammer, *The Struggle for Indochina, 1940–1955* (Stanford: Stanford University Press, 1966). The Battle of Dien Bien Phu is covered in Bernard Fall, *Hell in a Very Small Place* (Philadelphia: Lippincott, 1966); Jules Roy, *The Battle of Dien Bien Phu* (New York: Harper & Row, 1965); and Martin Windrow, *The Last Valley: Dien Bien Phu and the French Defeat in Vietnam* (Cambridge: Da Capo Press, 2004). The Geneva Conference that ended the Indochina War and split Vietnam into two halves is addressed in James Cable, *The Geneva Conference of 1954 on Indochina* (New York: St. Martin's Press, 1986); Robert Randle, *Geneva 1954: The Settlement of the Indochinese War* (Princeton: Princeton University Press, 1969); and James Waite, *The End of the First Indochina War: A Global History* (New York: Routledge, 2012).

On the US role in the Indochina War see James Arnold, *The First Domino: Eisenhower, the Military, and America's Intervention in Vietnam* (New York: William Morrow & Co., 1991); Melanie Billings-Yun, *Decision Against War: Eisenhower and Dien Bien Phu, 1954* (New York: Columbia University Press, 1988); Lloyd Gardner, *Approaching Vietnam: From World War II through Dienbienphu* (New York: W. W. Norton & Company, 1988); Gary Hess, *The United States' Emergence as a Southeast Asian Power, 1940–1950*

(New York: Columbia University Press, 1987); Lawrence Kaplan, Denise Artaud, and Mark Rubin (eds.), *Dien Bien Phu and the Crisis of Franco-American Relations, 1954–1955* (Lanham: Rowman & Littlefield, 1997); Ted Morgan, *Valley of Death: The Tragedy at Dien Bien Phu that Led America into the Vietnam War* (New York: Random House, 2010); John Prados, *The Sky Would Fall – Operation Vulture: The U.S. Bombing Mission in Indochina, 1954* (New York: Dial Books, 1983); Andrew Rotter, *The Path to Vietnam: Origins of the American Commitment to Southeast Asia* (Ithaca: Cornell University Press, 1987); Ronald Spector, *Advice and Support: The Early Years of the U.S. Army in Vietnam, 1941–1960* (New York: The Free Press, 1985); and Kathryn Statler, *Replacing France: The Origins of American Intervention in Vietnam* (Lexington: University Press of Kentucky, 2007). Fredrik Logevall's *Embers of War: The Fall of an Empire and the Making of America's Vietnam* (New York: Random House, 2012), is a brilliant, Pulitzer Prize-winning account that engagingly considers the Indochina War and the origins of the American commitment in Vietnam. Mark Atwood Lawrence's *Assuming the Burden: Europe and the American Commitment to War in Vietnam* (Berkeley: University of California Press, 2005) is also excellent in explaining the roots of US involvement.

Interwar Era (1954–65)

Bernard Fall's *The Two Viet-Nams* (Westport: Praeger, 1963) and *Viet-Nam Witness, 1953–66* (Westport: Praeger, 1966) as well as Jean Lacouture's *Vietnam: Between Two Truces* (New York: Vintage Books, 1966) are dated but quite decent. Fredrik Logevall's *The Origins of the Vietnam War* (New York: Longman, 2001) is a nice introductory text addressing the 1954–65 era. Mark Moyar, *Triumph Forsaken: The Vietnam War, 1954–1965* (New York: Cambridge University Press, 2006) is a solid yet controversial history of the interwar period.

Recently, renewed interest in the presidency of Ngo Dinh Diem in Saigon has spawned a slew of studies. Those that stand out are Philip Catton, *Diem's Final Failure: Prelude to America's War in Vietnam* (Lawrence: University Press of Kansas, 2002); Jessica Chapman, *Cauldron of Resistance: Ngo Dinh Diem, the United States, and 1950s Southern Vietnam* (Ithaca: Cornell University Press, 2013); Seth Jacobs, *America's Miracle Man in Vietnam: Ngo Dinh Diem, Religion, Race, and U.S. Intervention in Southeast Asia* (Durham: Duke University Press, 2004) and *Cold War Mandarin: Ngo Dinh Diem and the Origins of America's War in Vietnam, 1950–1963* (Lanham: Rowman & Littlefield, 2006); Edward Miller, *Misalliance: Ngo Dinh Diem, the United States, and the Fate of South Vietnam* (Cambridge: Harvard University Press, 2013), arguably the best book on Diem; Geoffrey Shar, *The Lost Mandate of Heaven: The American Betrayal of Ngo Dinh Diem, President of Vietnam* (San Francisco: Ignatius Press, 2015); and Geoffrey Stewart, *Vietnam's Lost Revolution: Ngo Dinh Diem's Failure to Build and Independent Nation, 1955–1963* (New York: Cambridge University Press, 2017), which is almost as good as Miller's book. Monique Demery's *Finding the Dragon Lady: The Mystery of Vietnam's Madame Nhu* (New York: Public Affairs Books, 2013) is a mesmerizing account of Diem's sister-in-law and South Vietnam's First Lady. More dated but nonetheless valuable studies are Ellen

Hammer, *A Death in November: America in Vietnam, 1963* (New York: E.P. Dutton, 1987) and Robert Scigliano, *South Vietnam: Nation Under Stress* (Boston: Houghton Mifflin, 1963).

On the US role in that period see David Anderson, *Trapped by Success: The Eisenhower Administration and Vietnam, 1953–1961* (New York: Columbia University Press, 1991); James Carter, *Inventing Vietnam: The United States and State Building, 1954–1968* (New York: Cambridge University Press, 2008); Jessica Elkind, *Aid Under Fire: Nation Building and the Vietnam War* (Lexington: University Press of Kentucky, 2016); Neil Jamieson, *Inventing Vietnam: The United States and State Building, 1954–1968* (Berkeley: University of California Press, 2008); Howard Jones, *Death of a Generation: How the Assassinations of Diem and JFK Prolonged the Vietnam War* (New York: Oxford University Press, 2003); George Kahin, *Intervention: How America Became Involved in Vietnam* (New York: Knopf, 1986); David Kaiser, *American Tragedy: Kennedy, Johnson, and the Origins of the Vietnam War* (Cambridge: Harvard University Press, 2000); Edwin Moïse, *Tonkin Gulf and the Escalation of the Vietnam War* (Chapel Hill: University of North Carolina Press, 1996); John Newman, *JFK and Vietnam: Deception, Intrigue, and the Struggle for Power* (New York: Warner Books, 1992); Gareth Porter, *Perils of Dominance: Imbalance of Power and the Road to War in Vietnam* (Berkeley: University of California Press, 2005); and William Rust, *Kennedy in Vietnam* (New York: Scribner, 1985). Two books by David Halberstam, *The Making of a Quagmire: America and Vietnam during the Kennedy Era* (New York: Knopf, 1988) and *The Best and the Brightest* (New York: Random House, 1972), are dated but important.

American War (1965–73)

The American War in Vietnam has been the object of several respectable studies. On the Johnson administration and the war, see Larry Berman, *Planning A Tragedy: The Americanization of the War in Vietnam* (New York: W. W. Norton & Company, 1983) and *Lyndon Johnson's War: The Road to Stalemate in Vietnam* (New York: W. W. Norton & Company, 1991); Lloyd Gardner, *Pay Any Price: Lyndon Johnson and the Wars for Vietnam* (Chicago: Ivan R. Dee, 1995); George Herring, *LBJ and Vietnam: A Different Kind of War* (Austin: University of Texas Press, 1994); Michael Hunt, *Lyndon Johnson's War: America's Cold War Crusade in Vietnam, 1945–1968* (New York: Hill & Wang, 1996); Fredrik Logevall, *Choosing War: The Lost Chance for Peace and the Escalation of War in Vietnam* (Berkeley: University of California Press, 2001); and H. R. McMaster, *Dereliction of Duty: Lyndon Johnson, Robert McNamara, the Joints Chief of Staff and the Lies that Led to Vietnam* (New York: Harper Collins, 1997). On the Nixon period, consult William Bundy, *A Tangled Web: The Making of Foreign Policy in the Nixon Presidency* (New York: Hill & Wang, 1998); Jeffrey Kimball, *Nixon's Vietnam War* (Lawrence: University Press of Kansas, 1998); and David Schmitz, *Richard Nixon and the Vietnam War* (Lanham: Rowman & Littlefield, 2014).

The military dimensions of the US war are the focus of two excellent studies by Gregory Daddis, *No Sure Victory: Measuring U.S. Army Effectiveness and Progress in the Vietnam War* (New York: Oxford University Press, 2011) and

Westmoreland's War: Reassessing American Strategy in Vietnam (New York: Oxford University Press, 2014). See also Larry Cable, *Conflict of Myths: The Development of Counter-Insurgency Doctrine and the Vietnam War* (New York: New York University Press, 1988); James Gibson, *The Perfect War: Technowar in Vietnam* (Boston: Atlantic Monthly Press, 1986); Bruce Palmer, *The 25-Year War: America's Military Role in the Vietnam War* (Lexington: University Press of Kentucky, 1984); U.S. Grant Sharp, *Strategy for Defeat: Vietnam in Retrospect* (Novato: Presidio Press, 1982); Lewis Sorley, *A Better War: The Unexamined Victories and the Final Tragedy of America's Last Years in Vietnam* (New York: Mariner Books, 2007); and Shelby Stanton, *The Rise and Fall of an American Army: U.S. Ground Forces in Vietnam, 1965–1973* (Novato: Presidio Press, 1985). On the US bombing of North Vietnam see the topnotch study by Mark Clodfelter, *The Limits of Air Power: The American Bombing of North Vietnam* (New York: The Free Press, 1989).

On the Tet Offensive and its aftermath, see William Allison, *The Tet Offensive: A Brief History with Documents* (New York: Routledge, 2008); James Arnold, *Tet Offensive 1968: Turning Point in Vietnam* (Westport: Praeger, 2004); Marc Jason Gilbert and William Head (eds.), *The Tet Offensive* (Westport: Praeger, 1996); Don Oberdorfer, *Tet!: The Turning Point in the Vietnam War* (Baltimore: Johns Hopkins University Press, 2001); David Schmitz, *The Tet Offensive: Politics, War, and Public Opinion* (Lanham: Rowman & Littlefield, 2005); Ronald Spector, *After Tet: The Bloodiest Year in Vietnam* (New York: The Free Press, 1993); James Willbanks, *The Tet Offensive: A Concise History* (New York: Columbia University Press, 2006); and James Wirtz, *The Tet Offensive: Intelligence Failure in War* (Ithaca: Cornell University Press, 1994). On the war's other great campaign, the Spring Offensive, refer to Dale Andradé, *Trial by Fire: The 1972 Easter Offensive, America's Last Vietnam Battle* (New York: Hippocrene Books, 1995) and Stephen Randolph's masterful study, *Powerful and Brutal Weapons: Nixon, Kissinger, and the Easter Offensive* (Cambridge: Harvard University Press, 2007).

The antiwar movement in the United States and elsewhere is the subject of Charles Chatfield, *The American Peace Movement: Ideals and Activism* (New York: Twayne Publishers, 1992); Charles DeBenedetti and Charles Chatfield, *An American Ordeal: The Antiwar Movement of the Vietnam Era* (Syracuse: Syracuse University Press, 1990); James Dickerson, *North to Canada: Men and Women against the Vietnam War* (Westport: Praeger, 1999); Michael Foley, *Confronting the War Machine: Draft Resistance during the Vietnam War* (Chapel Hill: University of North Carolina Press, 2003); Marc Jason Gilbert (ed.), *The Vietnam War on Campus: Other Voices, More Distant Drums* (Westport: Praeger, 2001); Todd Gitlin, *The Whole World is Watching: Mass Media in the Making and Unmaking of the New Left* (Berkeley: University of California Press, 2003); Simon Hall, *Peace and Freedom: The Civil Rights and Antiwar Movements in the 1960s* (Philadelphia: University of Pennsylvania Press, 2004) and *Rethinking the American Anti-War Movement* (New York: Routledge, 2010); Mary Hershberger, *Traveling to Vietnam: American Peace Activists and the War* (Syracuse: Syracuse University Press, 1998); Andrew Hunt, *The Turning: A History of Vietnam Veterans Against the War* (New York: New York University Press, 1999); Penny Lewis, *Hardhats, Hippies, and Hawks: The*

Vietnam Antiwar Movement as Myth and Memory (Ithaca: Cornell University Press, 2013); Melvin Small, *Covering Dissent: The Media and the Anti-Vietnam War Movement* (New Brunswick: Rutgers University Press, 1994); Melvin Small and William Hoover (eds.), *Give Peace a Chance: Exploring the Vietnam Antiwar Movement* (Syracuse: Syracuse University Press, 1992); and Judy Tzu-Chun Wu, *Radicals on the Road: Internationalism, Orientalism, and Feminism during the Vietnam Era* (Ithaca: Cornell University Press, 2013), which provides an enthralling take on the American antiwar movement.

For details about the peace process and the talks in Paris, refer to Pierre Asselin, *A Bitter Peace: Washington, Hanoi, and the Making of the Paris Agreement* (Chapel Hill: University of North Carolina Press, 2002) and Larry Berman, *No Peace, No Honor: Nixon, Kissinger, and Betrayal in Vietnam* (New York: The Free Press, 2001). Allan Goodman's *The Lost Peace: America's Search for a Negotiated Settlement of the Vietnam War* (Stanford: Hoover Institution Press, 1978) is also useful but dated, as are David Kraslow and Stuart Loory, *The Secret Search for Peace in Vietnam* (New York: Random House, 1968) and Wallace Thies, *When Governments Collide: Coercion and Diplomacy in the Vietnam Conflict, 1964–1968* (Berkeley: University of California Press, 1980). George Herring (ed.), *Secret Diplomacy of the Vietnam War: The Negotiating Volumes of the Pentagon Papers* (Austin: University of Texas Press, 1983) includes worthwhile documentary evidence, plus sound insights from Herring himself. The memoir by Henry Kissinger, *White House Years* (Boston: Little, Brown and Company, 1979) and his more recent *Ending the Vietnam War: A History of America's Involvement in and Extrication from the Vietnam War* (New York: Simon & Schuster, 2003) are valuable, albeit somewhat polemical and self-serving. Lloyd Gardner and Ted Gittinger (eds.), *The Search for Peace in Vietnam, 1964–1968* (College Station: Texas A&M University Press, 2004) has much merit, as does James Hershberg's painstakingly-researched and entrancing *Marigold: The Lost Chance for Peace in Vietnam* (Stanford: Stanford University Press, 2012).

The South Vietnamese experience in the war remains poorly documented. Bui Diem, *In the Jaws of History* (Boston: Houghton Mifflin, 1987) is written by a former South Vietnamese ambassador to the United States. Nguyen Tien Hung and Jerrold Schecter, *The Palace File* (New York: Harper & Row, 1986) similarly presents an official interpretation of events. Keith Taylor (ed.), *Voices from the Second Republic of South Vietnam (1967–1975)* (Ithaca: Southeast Asia Program Publications, 2015) is quite decent. On the armed forces of the Saigon regime, see Robert Brigham, *ARVN: Life and Death in the South Vietnamese Army* (Lawrence: University Press of Kansas, 2006) and Andy Wiest, *Vietnam's Forgotten Army: Heroism and Betrayal in the ARVN* (New York: New York University Press, 2009).

A few outstanding works exist on the role of Hanoi's allies during the war, and should be read by all serious students. They include Chen Jian, *Mao's China and the Cold War* (Chapel Hill: University of North Carolina Press, 2001); Mari Olsen, *Soviet-Vietnam Relations and the Role of China, 1949–64: Changing Alliances* (New York: Routledge, 2006); Qiang Zhai, *China and the Vietnam Wars* (Chapel Hill: University of North Carolina Press, 2000); and the two studies based on Russian archives by Ilya Gaiduk, *Confronting Vietnam: Soviet Policy Toward the*

Indochina Conflict, 1954–1963 (Stanford: Stanford University Press, 2003) and *The Soviet Union and the Vietnam War* (Chicago: Ivan R. Dee, 1996). The best works on the Sino-Soviet dispute, and its implications for the war in Vietnam, are Nicholas Khoo, *Collateral Damage: Sino-Soviet Rivalry and the Termination of the Sino-Vietnamese Alliance* (New York: Columbia University Press, 2011); Lorenz Lüthi, *The Sino-Soviet Split, 1956–1966* (Princeton: Princeton University Press, 2008); and Sergei Radchenko, *Two Suns in the Heavens: The Sino-Soviet Struggle for Supremacy, 1962–1967* (Stanford: Stanford University Press, 2009).

Civil War (1973–75)

Few works have been published in English specifically addressing the last two years of the war, after the United States withdrew the last of its combat forces. Two riveting accounts are Frank Snepp, *Decent Interval: An Insider's Account of Saigon's Indecent End Told by the CIA's Chief Strategy Analyst in Vietnam* (Lawrence: University Press of Kansas, 2002) and George Veith, *Black April: The Fall of South Vietnam, 1973–75* (New York: Encounter Books, 2012). Other valuable works are Alan Dawson, *55 Days: The Fall of South Vietnam* (Englewood Cliffs: Prentice Hall, 1977); Edward Haley, *Congress and the Fall of South Vietnam and Cambodia* (Rutherford: Associated University Presses, 1982); Stuart Herrington, *Peace with Honor? An American Reports on Vietnam, 1973–75* (Novato: Presidio Press, 1983); Arnold Isaacs, *Without Honor: Defeat in Vietnam and Cambodia* (Baltimore: Johns Hopkins University Press, 1983); Gareth Porter, *A Peace Denied: The U.S., Vietnam, and the Paris Agreements* (Bloomington: Indiana University Press, 1975); and James Willbanks, *Abandoning Vietnam: How America Left and South Vietnam Lost Its War* (Lawrence: University Press of Kansas, 2004).

Postwar Era (1975–Present)

Comprehensive studies of Vietnam in the postwar era include William Duiker, *Vietnam: Revolution in Transition* (Boulder: Westview Press, 1995); David Elliott, *Changing Worlds: Vietnam's Transition from Cold War to Globalization* (New York: Oxford University Press, 2012); and Eero Palmujoki, *Vietnam and the World: Marxist-Leninist Doctrine and the Changes in International Relations, 1975–93* (New York: St. Martin's Press, 1997).

On the 1979 Sino-Vietnamese Border War specifically see Stephen Morris, *Why Vietnam Invaded Cambodia: Political Culture and the Causes of War* (Stanford: Stanford University Press, 1999); Odd Arne Westad and Sophie Quinn-Judge (eds.), *The Third Indochina War: Conflict between China, Vietnam and Cambodia, 1972–79* (New York: Routledge, 2006); and Xiaoming Zhang, *Deng Xiaoping's Long War: The Military Conflict between China and Vietnam, 1979–1991* (Chapel Hill: University of North Carolina Press, 2015). The ongoing Sino-Vietnamese dispute in the South China Sea is placed in its proper historical context in Bill Hayton's terrific *The South China Sea: The Struggle for Power in Asia* (New Haven: Yale University Press, 2014).

Index